Advanced Financial Reporting

Advanced Financial Reporting
A Complete Guide to IFRS

Derry Cotter

B. Comm., FCA, MA (Econ.) (Manch.)
University College Cork

Financial Times
Prentice Hall
is an imprint of

Harlow, England • London • New York • Boston • San Francisco • Toronto • Sydney • Singapore • Hong Kong
Tokyo • Seoul • Taipei • New Delhi • Cape Town • Madrid • Mexico City • Amsterdam • Munich • Paris • Milan

Pearson Education Limited
Edinburgh Gate
Harlow
Essex CM20 2JE
England

and Associated Companies throughout the world

Visit us on the World Wide Web at:
www.pearson.com/uk

First edition 2012

ISBN: 978-0-273-73235-8

British Library Cataloguing-in-Publication Data
A catalogue record for this book is available from the British Library

Library of Congress Cataloging-in-Publication Data
Cotter, Derry.
  Advanced financial reporting : a complete guide to IFRS / Derry Cotter. – 1st ed.
    p. cm.
  ISBN 978-0-273-73235-8 (pbk.)
  1. Financial statements–Standards. 2. International business enterprises–Accounting–Standards. 3. International financial reporting standards. I. Title.
  HF5681.B2C598 2012
  657'.30218–dc23
                                                              2011026819

10 9 8 7 6 5 4 3 2 1
14 13 12 11

Typeset in 9/12pt Stone Serif by 35
Printed by Ashford Colour Press Ltd., Gosport

Brief contents

Supporting resources

Visit **www.pearsoned.co.uk/cotter** to find valuable online resources:

For instructors
- Complete, downloadable Instructor's Manual
- PowerPoint slides that can be downloaded and used for presentations

For more information please contact your local Pearson Education sales representative or visit **www.pearsoned.co.uk/cotter**

Contents

About this book

Advanced Financial Reporting provides a comprehensive guide to all international accounting standards. Each IFRS and IAS is explained in a user-friendly way, and all important points are illustrated in almost 300 worked examples.

International accounting standards comprise over 3,000 pages of material which is extremely technical and difficult to understand. By interpreting and applying these standards, this book should prove to be of significant benefit to users. The focus on double-entry principles throughout will enable readers to finely hone their financial accounting skills, and to apply these skills in the particular context of international accounting standards.

This book is intended for third-level students who have previously done an introductory course in financial reporting, and for those who are undertaking the examinations of the professional accountancy bodies. By focusing on the practical application of international accounting standards, it should also prove useful to accountants in practice.

A separate section is devoted to each major area of financial reporting. Part 1 examines the history of accounting. Parts 2 and 3 outline the IASB's conceptual framework and the regulatory environment. These provide the theoretical underpinning for the later sections, which examine areas such as accounting for assets, consolidated financial statements, accounting for liabilities and equity, and financial instruments. There are also individual sections that focus on the presentation of financial statements, the rules for small and medium-sized entities, and the transition to IFRS for first-time adopters. Specialist areas, such as agriculture and the extractive industries, are grouped together, and the use of financial statements for financial analysis purposes is also examined in detail.

Throughout the book the application of international accounting standards is illustrated in almost 300 worked examples. End of chapter questions provide users with an opportunity to test their knowledge, with answers provided as an online resource.

■ Key terminology

Equity is defined in the IASB *Framework* as the residual interest in the assets of the entity after deducting all of its liabilities. Increases and decreases in equity can arise from a number of sources.

(i) Items recorded in *profit or loss*

These are items of income and expense that are recognised in an entity's income statement. Examples include revenue, cost of sales, administrative expenses, profit or loss on disposal of a long-term asset, and income tax expense. Throughout this book, references to I/S should be interpreted as relating to the income statement.

The net result is *profit for the year*. This forms part of an entity's statement of comprehensive income.

(ii) Items recorded in *other comprehensive income*

These are items that are recognised in an entity's statement of comprehensive income, but outside of profit or loss. Examples include a revaluation surplus on property and an actuarial gain/loss on a defined-benefit pension scheme. Throughout this book, references to OCI should be interpreted as relating to other comprehensive income.

Other comprehensive income forms part of an entity's statement of comprehensive Income.

(iii) Items recorded *directly* in equity

Transactions with owners are recorded directly in equity without being routed through the statement of comprehensive income. Examples include the issue of shares and the payment of a dividend.

A number of acronyms are used throughout the book, and a full list of these is provided on page xviii.

■ How this book links with the financial statements of business entities

The primary focus of this book is on the impact of the IASB's accounting standards on the financial statements of business entities. A sample set of financial statements is set out below, and chapter-number references are provided.

ABC Group plc
Consolidated statement of financial position at 31 December 2010

	€M	Chapter reference
Assets		
Non-current assets		
Property, plant and equipment	6,460	13
Intangible assets	500	14
Investment property	200	15
Investment in associates	600	27
Investment in joint ventures	400	28
Financial asset	700	38 and 39
	8,860	
Current assets		
Construction contracts	1,200	12
Inventories	1,300	11
Asset held for sale	300	17
Trade and other receivables	2,700	39
Cash and cash equivalents	1,200	39
	6,700	
Total assets		
	15,560	
Liabilities		
Current liabilities		
Trade and other payables	3,850	39
Pension costs accrual	500	20
Current tax payable	50	19
	4,400	
Non-current liabilities		
Term loan	400	38
Deferred tax	100	19
Lease obligations	200	31
Long-term provisions	500	21
	1,200	
Total liabilities	5,600	

	€M	Chapter reference
Net assets	9,960	
Equity capital		
Share capital	3,000	38
Revaluation surplus	1,500	13
Deferred income	300	33
Retained earnings	4,140	
	8,940	
Non-controlling interests	1,020	23
Total equity	9,960	

ABC Group plc
Consolidated statement of comprehensive income for the year ended
31 December 2010

	€M	Chapter reference
Revenue	9,100	32
Cost of sales	(7,230)	
Gross profit	1,870	
Distribution costs	(700)	
Administrative expenses	(250)	
Other expenses	(150)	
Finance costs	(600)	35
Profit before tax	170	
Income tax expense	(50)	19
Profit for the year from continuing operations	120	
Other comprehensive income		
Revaluation surplus	400	13
Total comprehensive income for the year	520	

	€'000	
Profit attributable to:		
Owners of the parent	100	
Non-controlling interests	20	24
	120	

Notes

Events after the reporting period (see Chapter 30)
On 2 January 2011, ABC Group made a 1 for 4 rights issue at €1.50 per share. The rights issue was fully subscribed for.

On 8 February 2011, the headquarters of ABC Group was damaged in a fire. Due to an administrative error, the building was not insured, and consequently there is an estimated impairment loss of €3.8M in respect of the building. As this loss occurred after the reporting period it is a non-adjusting event (see Chapter 16).

Contingent liability (see Chapter 21)
On 30 November 2010, a director of ABC Group instigated legal proceedings against the group. On the basis of legal advice, the board of directors is confident that this claim will not be successful.

Share options (see Chapter 18)

The employees and directors of ABC Group plc have options to purchase shares in the group. Details of the directors' share option agreement are provided in the Directors' Report.

Related party disclosures (see Chapter 36)

In June 2010, the ABC Group extended a loan of €200,000 to Mr D. Donegan, who is a director of the parent company, ABC Holdings. The loan was repaid in full in November 2010, including interest at the current market rate.

Support materials

■ Solutions to end-of-chapter questions

Solutions to the end-of-chapter questions are provided as an online resource.

■ Double entry

This book requires students to have a knowledge of double-entry bookkeeping. Most introductory textbooks provide good coverage of this area. For students wishing to obtain other reference material, the following additional resources are available:

- *Double Entry Book-Keeping* by T. S. Grewal, published by Sultan Chand.
- *Double Entry Book-Keeping Toolkit*, published by Chartered Accountants Ireland.
- *Crack the Books* by June Menton, published by Chartered Accountants Ireland.

■ Glossary of terms

A glossary of commonly used terms is provided at the back of the book.

■ Useful website addresses

The IASB website provides extensive material on IASB standards, exposure drafts, discussion papers, as well as outlining the up-to-date position on current IASB projects. Some material is available on a subscription-only basis. The IASB website address is *http://www.ifrs.org/Home.htm*.

Deloitte's IAS Plus website provides excellent summaries of the IASB's international accounting standards. The IAS Plus website address is *http://www.iasplus.com/index.htm*.

The other big four accounting firms also provide a range of useful information relating to international accounting standards. Their website addresses are as follows:

- Ernst & Young: *http://www.ey.com/BE/en/Issues/IFRS*
- KPMG: *http://www.kpmg.com/Global/en/WhatWeDo/Special-Interests/Global-IFRS-institute/Pages/default.aspx*
- PricewaterhouseCoopers: *http://www.pwc.com/gx/en/ifrs-reporting/ifrs-publications.jhtml*

The FASB website also has information on international accounting standards, with an emphasis on US/IASB convergence. See *http://www.fasb.org/home*.

The major **accountancy bodies** also provide educational resources in the area of international accounting standards:

- Association of Chartered Certified Accountants: *http://www.accaglobal.com/*
- CPA Ireland: *http://www.cpaireland.ie/*
- Chartered Accountants Ireland: *http://www.charteredaccountants.ie/*
- Institute of Chartered Accountants of Scotland: *http://www.charteredaccountants.ie/*

List of acronyms

AICPA	American Institute of Certified Public Accountants
APB	Accounting Principles Board
ASB	Accounting Standards Board
ASC	Accounting Standards Committee
ASSC	Accounting Standards Steering Committee
B/S	Balance sheet
CGU	Cash-generating unit
CGT	Capital gains tax
CPP	Constant purchasing power
DPS	Dividend per share
EPS	Earnings per share
FASB	Financial Accounting Standards Board
FIFO	First-in-first-out
FRS	Financial reporting standard
FV	Fair value
FVNA	Fair value of net assets
FVTPL	Fair value through profit or loss
GAAP	Generally accepted accounting practice
IAS	International accounting standard
IASB	International Accounting Standards Board
IFRIC	International Financial Reporting Interpretations Committee
IFRS	International financial reporting standard
I/S	Income statement
LIFO	Last-in-first-out
NASA	National Aeronautics and Space Administration
NCA	Non-current assets
NBV	Net book value
NRV	Net realisable value
OCI	Other comprehensive income
PAT	Positive accounting theory
PBIT	Profit before interest and tax
PP&E	Property, plant and equipment
PV	Present value
ROCE	Return on capital employed
SAR	Share appreciation right
SFAS	Statement of financial accounting standards
SIC	Standing Interpretations Committee
SOFP	Statement of financial position (i.e. balance sheet)
TC	Total costs
WDV	Written-down value

Acknowledgements

I wish to thank the following accountancy bodies for giving me permission to use their past examination questions:

- Association of Chartered Certified Accountants
- Chartered Accountants Ireland
- Institute of Certified Public Accountants in Ireland

I would like to acknowledge the professionalism and dedication of Pearson's editorial team, in particular Katie Rowland, Philippa Fiszzon, Gemma Papageorgiou, Summa Verbeek and Philip Tye.

The advice of my friends and colleagues has also been invaluable, and I am indebted to David Ahern, Liz Ahern, Sandra Brosnan, Paula Cotter, Andrew Crosbie, Eamon Fagan, Maire Kavanagh, Niall MacLochlainn, Orla McCarthy, Liz O'Donoghue, Patrick O'Driscoll and Claire O'Sullivan-Rochford, whose assistance is greatly appreciated.

The constructive suggestions and guidance provided by four anonymous reviewers were of great benefit, and I am extremely grateful to them.

I wish also to record my appreciation of University College Cork, who granted me sabbatical leave to undertake the writing of this book. I would especially like to acknowledge the assistance of Ciaran Murphy, whose support and encouragement made the writing of this book possible.

Finally, I owe a huge debt of gratitude to my wife Carmel, and my sister Mary, who have helped in so many ways throughout this journey.

■ Publisher's acknowledgements

We are grateful to the following for permission to reproduce copyright material:

Figures

Figure 5.1 from Extract from 2009 Annual Report of HJ Heinz (p1).

Tables

Table on page 422 from Ryannair Holdings plc.

Text

Extract on page 44 from Debenhams' Annual Report 2010; Extract on page 60 from Baxter 2009 Sustainability Report sustainability.baxter.com/sustainability_at_baxter/priorities_goals/green_supply_chain.html; Extract on page 142 from Independent News and Media 2007.

Exam questions

Chartered Accountants Ireland extracts from the FAE Financial Reporting papers in the post 2002 period and material from CAP2 papers from Summer 2006, Autumn 2007, Summer 2008, Autumn 2008, Summer 2009 and Autumn 2009.

We are grateful to the Association of Chartered Certified Accountants (ACCA) for permission to reproduce past examination questions. The suggested solutions in the exam answer bank have been prepared by us, unless otherwise stated.

CPA Ireland: Q3.3 based on question 2 April 2010 Advanced Corporate Reporting examination of The Institute of Certified Public Accountants in Ireland; Q6.1 from question 3 August 2008 Advanced Financial Accounting examination of The Institute of Certified Public Accountants in Ireland (CPA); Q48.1 from question 5 April 2007 Advanced Financial Accounting examination of The Institute of Certified Public Accountants in Ireland.

In some instances we have been unable to trace the owners of copyright material and we would appreciate any information that would enable us to do so.

Part 1

A BRIEF HISTORY OF ACCOUNTING

1 The rise of accounting

Chapter 1

The rise of accounting

Accountants are generally recognised as making a valuable contribution to society, by providing the information that allows entrepreneurship to flourish, business to operate efficiently, stakeholders' interests to be protected, shares to be fairly priced, and taxation and audit requirements to be satisfied. Accounting, however, has not always enjoyed such an established position, and today there is often a tendency to take our profession's status for granted. It is interesting, therefore, to examine the factors that have brought accounting to the pre-eminent place that it occupies in today's business world.

How it all began

Our story begins in primitive times, when cave dwellers collected enough food to satisfy their daily requirements. Before long, the more enterprising among them would set aside some for future use. In effect that was surplus capital, and it represented the first step towards the accumulation of wealth. Soon, they were exchanging their surplus for commodities owned by different cave dwellers. This exchange, which constituted a form of barter, was the first step in the development of a system of commerce.[1]

Record keeping is thought to have begun around 4000 BC, in Babylonia and Assyria. Chatfield[2] describes the Babylonians as obsessive bookkeepers, with records being kept by scribes, who are regarded as the predecessors of today's accountants. The governments of Babylonia recruited hundreds of scribes to record the collection of taxes, which were paid in the form of cereals, cattle and other farm commodities.

Although barter remained popular as a method of exchange, its limitations soon became apparent. For a trade to take place the parties needed to want what each other had, and the items needed to be of similar value. Chatfield describes the dilemma vividly:

> One is reminded of the Andaman Islander, carrying his surplus possession to the marketplace and waiting there, sometimes for days, in the hope of finding another trader who wanted his goods and had something of equal value which he in turn wished to have.

Traders therefore began to seek a unit of value, or currency, in which the worth of all commodities could be measured. Woolf[1] observes how the Lydians are credited with the invention of coinage around 900 BC, and how gradually this became the common unit of currency. Paper money was invented in China at the end of the eighth century AD.

A system of numeration was then required. Woolf recalls Sir Francis Galton's travels of Africa where

> . . . he found men from whom he was required to buy one sheep at a time, because they could not understand that for two sheep, at two plugs of tobacco each, he must give them a lump sum of four plugs of tobacco.

It was common at that time to represent numbers with pebbles arranged in sets of ten, a practice which was to lead to the invention of the abacus. Although these pebbles provided the stepping stones for the advancement of accounting, Chatfield describes how the backwardness of accounting systems used by the Greeks and Romans can be attributed to their methods of numerical notation. These methods were inferior partly due to the large variety of symbols used for numbers (the Greeks used 28). A second problem was that the Greeks and Romans failed to represent the value of a number by reference to its position in relation to other numbers. Thus, as numbers could not be added like Arabic numbers, there was little point in arranging amounts in columns. As Chatfield points out, without a columnar separation of receipts and payments, giving rise to the concept of debit and credit, **double-entry bookkeeping** was not possible.

Evolution of double-entry bookkeeping

This problem was overcome by the development of Arabic numerals in India by the Hindus around AD 600. The most important event in the history of accounting, however, occurred in 1494, with the publication by Italian friar, Luca Pacioli, of *Summa de Arithmetica, Geometria, Proportioni et Proportionalita* (everything about Arithmetic, Geometry and Proportion). The *Summa* contained the first printed description of double-entry bookkeeping, and facilitated by improved literacy levels, and the invention of paper two centuries earlier, the *Summa* was translated into five languages as the Italian method spread throughout Europe.

Although double-entry bookkeeping facilitated the move from a feudal to a commercial society, its use was limited mainly to summarising accounting records, and bringing order to the venture accounts of business merchants. No effort was made, however, to match income with the expenditure incurred in creating it, and consequently there was no clear concept of profit, nor any means of evaluating the performance of a business over time. Given the lack of outside investment in firms, there was little external accountability and the production of financial statements was not considered important. Nonetheless, a knowledge of double-entry bookkeeping was seen as promoting economic expansion at the beginning of the sixteenth century.[3]

Accounting was to come centre stage with the arrival of the Industrial Revolution in the nineteenth century. The UK Joint Stock Companies Act of 1844 provided access to incorporation, which had previously been possible only by royal charter or by private act. This resulted in the widespread separation of ownership from control, and with most companies adopting double-entry bookkeeping after 1850, the preparation of financial statements for shareholders bolstered an emerging accounting profession. The importance of double-entry bookkeeping at that time cannot be overstated, some even controversially viewing its existence as a prerequisite for the spread of capitalism.[4]

The accounting profession continued to expand during the following decades, establishing itself as a conservative discipline, its primary function seen as the recording of business transactions and events, and the provision of reliable information on firms' performance and financial position.

Throughout much of the twentieth century, accounting maintained its traditional role as an impartial and neutral observer of the business world. Indeed, during that time, the entire corporate world was benignly regarded as the primary driver of wealth creation. Employees and other stakeholders offered unconditional loyalty to the corporate ethos, and accountability was rarely an issue. Such a neutral role provided accounting with little scope to effect change, or to be regarded as a discipline with the potential to have economic consequences.

Zeff,[5] however, explains how in the 1970s, society began to hold its institutions responsible for the consequences of their actions. An example was the link between asbestos and lung disease which, although established as far back as 1924, did not result in the first successful litigation against an asbestos manufacturer until 1971. The late 1970s also saw an explosion of lawsuits in the United States, and huge awards were made against companies, resulting in an insurance crisis, as insurers refused to provide companies with an adequate level of product liability cover.

Consequently, as society demanded increased accountability of its institutions, regulatory bodies, such as the FASB in the US and the ASSC in the UK, were increasingly judged on the economic consequences of their rules. It became apparent that financial statements could have a significant economic impact, and the perception of accounting as an impartial observer of the business world began to change.

Economic consequences of financial statements

Today, it is widely accepted that **financial statements** affect overall wealth levels, and can lead to the redistribution of wealth between interest groups. There are several documented examples of the economic consequences of accounting standards, and some examples are outlined below:

- In 1975, the ASSC's proposal in ED 14 to write off all R&D expenditure to expense provoked an angry response from the UK aerospace industry, on the grounds that government funding was based on balance sheet asset levels.[6] Under intense pressure to withdraw its proposal, the ASSC issued ED 17, and later SSAP 13, which permitted the inclusion of certain R&D expenditure as an asset.

- In 2000, the ASB was held partly culpable for the decision by employers to replace defined-benefit pension plans with defined-contribution plans. Defined-benefit plans provide a guaranteed amount of pension to employees, whereas no guarantee is provided by employers in the case of defined-contribution plans.

  The allegation against the ASB related to the publication of FRS 17, *Retirement Benefits*, which required that pension scheme deficits should be recognised immediately as a liability, rather than continue to be amortised over the expected service lives of employees in the scheme.

- During the 2008 US presidential election, the Republican candidate, John McCain, blamed accounting's fair value rules for contributing to the global financial crisis. Those concerns were echoed by Nicolas Sarkozy, who held the presidency of the European Union at that time. Amid falling stock prices, investment banking firms such as Lehman Brothers were forced to write down the value of their assets, spreading panic among investors, and triggering further falls in stock prices which led to a deepening of the crisis.

- When the IASB issues a revised *leasing standard*, it is expected that lessees will be required to include all leased assets and the associated liability in their balance sheet. This will result in higher gearing ratios and in a lower return on investment ratio for lessee firms. The effect will be significant, for example in the airline industry, where some carriers own few of the aircraft in their fleet. In terms of economic consequences, the inclusion of all leases as a liability may result in investors adjusting their share portfolios, leasing becoming less attractive as a means of financing, and providers of goods and services reassessing the credit limits of customers that make extensive use of operating leases.

Summary

Since the first known records were kept in 4000 BC, accounting has provided the means for business transactions to be recorded. The development of Arabic numerals around AD 660 provided the foundation for double-entry bookkeeping, which was first documented in Luca Pacioli's *Summa* in 1494. The Industrial Revolution of the nineteenth century brought about the separation of owners and managers, greatly increasing the demand for external accountability, and leading to the development of today's accounting profession.

The perception of accounting as an unbiased recorder of business transactions continued throughout most of the twentieth century. Since the 1970s, however, there has been a realisation that accounting information also has the power to affect wealth levels in our society. This impact is called economic consequences, and it emphasises the fact that accounting is a living science that shapes and changes the world in which we live.

Throughout its history, accounting has adapted to myriad changes, not least of which have occurred during the last century. Although economic influences have shifted and changed over time, as a discipline accounting has continued to increase in importance. Bruce[7] maintains that the technological revolution has, in fact, given financial accounting a new-found standing:

> Once upon a time financial reporting was little more than just the figures . . . And then there was an evolution of information technology. As soon as screens appeared on everyone's desks everyone was involved in all of the business. Finance was no longer a back-room function. Everyone had been given the ability to participate.

■ References

1. Woolf, A. H. (1912). *A Short History of Accountants and Accountancy.* London: Gee.

2. Chatfield, M. A. (1974). *History of Accounting Thought.* New York: Krieger Publishing Co. Inc.

3. Eucken, W. (1951). *The Foundations of Economics: History and Theory in the Analysis of Economic Reality.* Chicago: University of Chicago Press.

4. Sombart, W. (1916). *Der moderne Kapitalismus.* Munich Leipzig: Duncker and Humblot.

5. Zeff, S. A. (1978). The rise of economic consequences. *Journal of Accountancy,* 146 (6), pp. 56–63.

6. Hope, A. J. B. and Gray, R. (1982). Power and Policy Making: The development of an R&D Standard. *Journal of Business Finance and Accounting,* 9 (4), pp. 531–58.

7. Bruce, R. (2005). *Accountancy,* 136 (1344), p. 25.

Part 2

A CONCEPTUAL FRAMEWORK FOR FINANCIAL REPORTING

Chapter 2

A conceptual framework for financial reporting

Imagine you are a skilled surgeon about to perform a complex and intricate procedure on which the life of a patient depends. You will ensure that the appropriate team personnel are present in the operating theatre, and that your instruments have been carefully sterilised. From the time that you make the first incision, you will rely on your expert knowledge, as other members of the team assist by monitoring the patient's heart and blood pressure levels. Afterwards, post-operation check procedures will be strictly followed, such as ensuring that all instruments used have been recovered, before the patient is transferred to the intensive care unit for monitoring.

The objective of the procedures described above is to ensure that all appropriate surgical guidelines are adhered to. These guidelines, based on well-established medical principles, aim to eliminate the need for ad hoc decision-making by the surgeon and his team. A similar body of theory exists in other respected disciplines, such as economics, engineering and law, thus ensuring that practitioners in those fields are also equipped with expert sources of guidance.

The challenge in **financial reporting** is to have a similar body of theory that will underpin the preparation of accounting standards. This body of theory, known as a **conceptual framework**, would produce accounting standards that are:

- based on agreed fundamental accounting principles; and
- internally consistent.

Definition

A conceptual framework for financial reporting can be defined as

> . . . a constitution, a coherent system of interrelated objectives and fundamentals that can lead to consistent standards and that prescribes the nature, function and limits of financial accounting and financial statements.[1]

An overview of a conceptual framework for financial reporting is provided in Figure 2.1. One must first identify the objectives of financial reporting. The reporting entity is then defined, based on the form (e.g. a group) that can best provide the information required by users of financial information. One then identifies the qualitative characteristics that information should have to satisfy the objectives of financial reporting. The elements of financial statements (e.g. **assets**, **liabilities** and equity) are defined, along with the criteria for their recognition and how they should be measured. Finally, there is the matter of how the elements are presented in the financial statements and what disclosures should be provided.

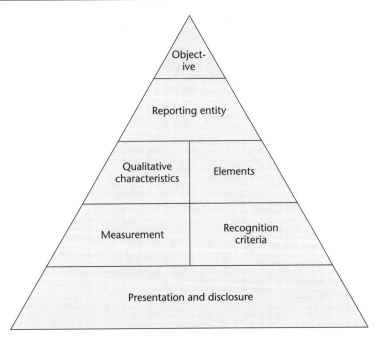

Figure 2.1 **Conceptual framework for financial reporting**

Development of a conceptual framework for financial reporting

There have been several efforts over the years to develop an agreed conceptual framework for financial reporting. However, no one approach has, to date, achieved sufficient consensus, and the search continues. Details of previous efforts are outlined in Appendix 2.1.

In October 2004, the International Accounting Standards Board (IASB) and the US standard-setting body, the Financial Accounting Standards Board (FASB), agreed to collaborate to develop a single framework. It is intended that this will replace the previous framework, which was published in 1989 by the IASC (predecessor of the IASB), and the FASB Concept Statements of the 1970s and 1980s.

It was agreed that the project would be divided into phases, with each phase being published separately on its completion. Details are as follows:

- Phase A: Objectives and qualitative characteristics (completed September 2010)
- Phase B: Elements
- Phase C: Measurement
- Phase D: Reporting entity (exposure draft published March 2010)
- Phase E: Presentation and disclosure
- Phase F: Purpose and status
- Phase G: Application to not-for-profit entities
- Phase H: Remaining issues

Phase A of the conceptual framework project has been completed and it was published by the IASB in September 2010. Details are outlined below. For those sections of the conceptual framework that are still under construction, details of the IASC's previous Framework are included as Appendix 2.2.

IASB conceptual framework 2010 (Phase A)

■ Purpose and status

The conceptual framework sets out the concepts that underlie the preparation and presentation of financial statements for external users. Its primary purpose is to underpin the issue of principle-based standards by the IASB. The conceptual framework is not an IFRS, and nothing in the conceptual framework overrides any specific IFRS. Should there be a conflict between the conceptual framework and an IFRS, the requirements of the IFRS will take precedence.

■ Chapter 1: The objective of general purpose financial reporting

Decision usefulness

The IASB framework states that the objective of general purpose financial reporting is to provide financial information that is useful to:

- existing and potential investors, and
- lenders and other **creditors**

in making decisions about providing resources to an entity. Those decisions involve buying, selling or holding an entity's **shares** or debt capital, and providing loans and other forms of credit.

Decision-making involves having to make judgements about future events. The fact that the framework focuses on providing financial information for this purpose, is consistent with the IASB's commitment to fair value as a measurement basis for assets, equity and liabilities.

Many investors, lenders and other creditors cannot require reporting entities to provide information directly to them, and they are therefore dependent on the information in general purpose financial reports. Consequently, they are the primary users to whom those reports are directed.

Other parties, such as employees, analysts, government and the general public may also find general purpose financial reports useful. However, those reports are not primarily directed to these other groups.

The conceptual framework recommends that a reporting entity's economic resources and claims on those resources are reported on as follows:

- *details* **of economic resources and claims on those resources** are contained in the **statement of financial position;**
- *changes* **in those economic resources and claims** that relate to an entity's financial performance during a period are included in the **statement of comprehensive income;**
- changes in an entity's **cash flows** are reflected in its statement of cash flows;
- changes in an entity's economic resources, not relating to its economic performance (e.g. the issue of shares), are shown in the statement of changes in equity.

As noted above, the IASB views the objective of financial reporting as the provision of information for decision-making. This may not be a straightforward matter, however. Demski[2] maintains that the criteria for evaluating what information will be the most useful are situation-specific, and will depend on factors such as the decision-making model and the information-processing capabilities of the user.

A country's political, economic and social systems are also important in determining what objectives accounting information is expected to satisfy. For example, Burgraaf[3] refers to the way in which Western accounting is geared towards providing information about profit and the financial position. In a socialist society, however, the focus of accounting is on providing information for the planning process. It may not be feasible, therefore, to get agreement on a single objective of financial reporting information on a global basis.

Stewardship

Stewardship can be defined as

the careful and responsible management of something entrusted to one's care.[4]

Throughout history, stewardship has been regarded as an important objective of financial reporting, and there has been criticism of its omission from the IASB's conceptual framework. Instead, as outlined above, the IASB has identified decision usefulness as the sole objective of financial reporting, and one which can meet the needs of stewardship.

Lennard[5] reports that two IASB members set out an 'alternative view' when the IASB published its preliminary views relating to the first chapters of their conceptual framework. The dissenting members described the role of stewardship as follows:

Stewardship is concerned with the accountability of the directors, or management board, of a business entity to its proprietors or owners. This is at the heart of the financial reporting process in many jurisdictions.

The dissenting IASB members view stewardship and decision usefulness as being complementary, and expressed a preference that both be identified as separate objectives of financial reporting.

Lennard[5] argues that stewardship should not be viewed solely as providing a check on the integrity and efficiency of management. It gives management the opportunity, he maintains, to enter into dialogue with shareholders regarding the challenges and opportunities that their company faces. Thus, he sees stewardship extending beyond its accountability role, to become a fundamental building block of **corporate governance.**

Whittington[6] views the explicit omission of stewardship from the IASB's framework as having a significant effect on continental Europe. He cites Germany as a country in which there is a strong link between corporate reporting and the law, making stewardship a key objective of financial reporting. In some European countries Whittington sees stewardship going beyond accountability to shareholders, to encompass tax authorities, employees and others in the wider community.

By contrast, Whittington points out that, in the United States, most disciplining of managers takes place primarily in the stock market. For example, a manager whose performance disappoints may find that his stock options have lost value because of a fall in the company's share price. In the US, the requirement to file accounts only applies to company's whose shares are publicly traded. A natural consequence of this, according to Whittington, is that financial statements are viewed as serving the decision-making needs of market participants (e.g. potential investors) rather than the stewardship needs of existing shareholders.

Accruals basis

With the exception of the statement of cash flows, the IASB's conceptual framework requires that financial statements are prepared on the accruals basis of accounting. This means that transactions and events are recognised and reported in the financial statements when they occur, and not as cash is received or paid.

Example 1 Mandrigo Limited, which has an accounting year end of 31 December, sold goods for €40,000 on 20 December 2010. The customer was allowed 60 days' credit.

In preparing its financial statements for the year ended 31 December 2010, Mandrigo will record revenue of €40,000 in its statement of comprehensive income. A **trade receivable** of €40,000 will also be included in the statement of financial position at 31 December 2010.

■ Chapter 2: The reporting entity

This chapter, which is Phase D of the framework, is currently under development by the IASB and the FASB.

■ Chapter 3: Qualitative characteristics of useful financial information

The qualitative characteristics are the attributes that make the information in financial statements useful to users. Two fundamental qualitative characteristics are identified by the IASB. These are relevance and faithful representation.

(i) Relevance

Information is relevant when it is capable of making a difference in the decisions made by users. Financial information can make a difference if it has predictive value, confirmatory value or both.

Information has predictive value if it can be used to predict future outcomes.

Example 2 Anne Smith is considering an investment in the equity shares of Mandrigo Limited, on the basis that she will receive a dividend twice a year. On 1 January 2011, Mandrigo Limited has retained earnings from previous years of €600,000. This is relevant information, as it can help Ms Smith to predict that Mandrigo will be able to pay a **dividend** on her investment.

Mandrigo Limited makes a profit of €300,000 for the year ending 31 December 2011. This information is also relevant, as it confirms Ms Smith's prediction that she will receive a dividend on her investment.

The relevance of information is also affected by its *materiality*. Information is material if its omission or misstatement could influence decisions that users make about a specific reporting entity. As illustrated in Examples 3 and 4 below, the materiality of information depends on its nature and magnitude.

Example 3 Mandrigo Limited has extended loans of €500,000 to directors at 31 December 2011.

Loans to directors may affect a user's decision to invest in an entity, irrespective of the monetary amount of the loans. Therefore, the directors' loans of €500,000 would be considered as information that is relevant to users.

Example 4 Mandrigo Limited disposed of machinery on 31 October 2011 for €20,000, incurring a loss of €5,000 on the sale.

The disposal of the machinery, and the related loss, are relevant information as far as users of the financial statements of Mandrigo Limited are concerned. The amount involved is not material, however, and therefore separate disclosure of the transaction is not required.

Materiality provides a threshold or cut-off point rather than being a primary qualitative characteristic that information must have to be useful.

(ii) Faithful representation

This means that the financial information which is presented is reliable. Faithful representation requires information that is:

- complete
- neutral
- free from error

Example 5 Mandrigo Limited purchased a machine on 1 January 2012 for €600,000.

Outline how information about this machine should be presented in the financial statements of Mandrigo Limited.

Solution Faithful representation requires that information relating to the machine purchased by Mandrigo Limited should be complete, neutral and free from error.

Completeness requires that the machine be included with other machinery in Mandrigo's statement of financial position, and that there is a clear statement of the way in which this group of assets is valued. The machinery is likely to be valued at cost less accumulated depreciation.

Neutrality requires that information is presented without bias. Thus, information relating to Mandrigo's machinery should not be manipulated to increase the probability that it will be received favourably or unfavourably by users.

Freedom from error does not mean that information is accurate in all respects. For example, Mandrigo Limited must make an estimate of the machine's useful life for the purposes of charging depreciation. This estimate is based on professional judgement and it cannot be guaranteed to be perfectly accurate.

Applying the fundamental qualitative characteristics

Information must be both relevant and faithfully represented if it is to be useful. Information is not useful if it is:

- faithfully represented but not relevant; or
- relevant but not faithfully represented.

The application of these characteristics is illustrated in Example 6 below.

Example 6 On 31 December 2010, Mandrigo Limited was the subject of litigation proceedings involving a customer claiming that she had been injured when using one of the company's products. Mandrigo is disputing the claim, maintaining that any injury was due solely to negligence on the customer's part. At 31 December 2010, it was unclear whether the customer had a bona fide case against Mandrigo, or what amount of damages was likely to be awarded.

The litigation proceedings constitute *relevant* information as far as the users of Mandrigo's financial statements are concerned. However, the information is not reliable, as the existence of a valid claim is uncertain, as is the possible amount of damages that may be involved. Therefore, no provision should be made in Mandrigo's financial statements for any loss, but it may be appropriate to disclose details of the claim.

Enhancing qualitative characteristics

Comparability, verifiability, timeliness and understandability enhance the usefulness of information that is relevant and faithfully represented. These enhancing characteristics should be maximised to the extent possible. However, they cannot make information useful if that information is irrelevant or not faithfully represented.

Comparability

Comparability enables users to understand similarities and differences in items. Similar things should look alike, and different things must look different. For example, the income from inventory sold by Mandrigo Limited should be recorded as revenue. The sale of a non-current asset (e.g. buildings) should *not* be recorded as revenue. This allows users to compare Mandrigo's revenue over time, as it is presented on a consistent basis, and only includes the sales of inventory.

The comparison of an entity's financial statements over time allows users to identify trends in its financial position and performance. Users must also be able to compare the financial statements of different entities.

This requires that users be informed of the accounting policies employed in the preparation of financial statements, of any changes in these policies and the effects of such changes.

Example 7 Mandrigo Limited has used the FIFO method for measuring the cost of inventory in previous years. A change to the weighted average cost basis is being considered in the year ended 31 December 2010.

Should Mandrigo change its method of measuring inventory, details of this change and the effect of the change should be disclosed in its financial statements for the year ended 31 December 2010.

Verifiability

Verifiability means that different knowledgeable and independent observers could reach consensus that the way in which an item is recorded is a faithful representation.

For example, it should be possible to verify the carrying amount of inventory in the financial statements by checking the quantities and costs, using a method such as first-in-first-out.

Timeliness

Timeliness means having information available to decision-makers in time to be capable of influencing their decisions.

So as to provide information on a timely basis, it may be necessary to report before all aspects of a transaction or other event are completely known. Alternatively, if reporting is delayed until all aspects are known, the information may be highly reliable but of little use to users. This problem is illustrated in Example 8 below.

Example 8 Mandrigo Limited acquired 100% of the share capital of Swan Limited on 1 December 2010 at a cost of €2M in cash. The fair value of the identifiable net assets of Swan Limited at that date was estimated at €1.6M. However, this amount was subject to change, as the tax liability of Swan Limited was under review at the acquisition date.

Outline how the acquisition of Swan should be accounted for in the consolidated financial statements of Mandrigo Limited for the year ended 31 December 2010.

Solution In preparing its financial statements, Mandrigo should use provisional values for the identifiable net assets of Swan. These values can be amended up to 12 months from the date of acquisition (i.e. until 30 November 2011).

Although the provisional values are not completely reliable, they are used so that the acquisition of Swan can be reflected in Mandrigo's financial statements on a timely basis.

Thus, at 1 December 2010, the acquisition of Swan will be recorded by Mandrigo as follows:

	Dr	Cr
	€'000	€'000
Net assets	1,600	
Goodwill	400	
Bank		2,000

Understandability

Users are assumed to have a reasonable knowledge of business, economic activities and accounting. However, relevant information should not be excluded on the grounds that it is too complex for some users to understand.

The cost constraint on useful financial reporting

Providers of financial information (i.e. businesses) incur costs in collecting, processing, verifying and publishing financial information. Users (e.g. investors) ultimately bear these costs, however, in the form of reduced returns. Users also incur costs in analysing and interpreting the information provided.

Thus, the reporting of financial information involves costs, and it is important that those costs are justified by the benefits of reporting that information. It is not possible, therefore, for general purpose financial statements to provide all the information that every user finds relevant.

Summary

A conceptual framework is a body of theory that underpins the practical application of a discipline. In financial reporting, a conceptual framework would facilitate the production of accounting standards that are:

- based on agreed fundamental accounting principles; and
- internally consistent.

The contents of a conceptual framework are summarised in Figure 2.1 towards the beginning of this chapter.

The IASB and the FASB are engaged in a collaborative project to produce a revised conceptual framework for financial reporting. This framework is being published on a phased basis, and to date two chapters have been completed.

Chapter 1 states that the **objective** of general purpose financial reporting is to provide financial information about an entity that is useful to existing and potential investors, and to lenders and other creditors. These users are regarded as the primary groups for whom general purpose financial statements are prepared. The omission of stewardship as a separate objective of financial reporting has been a controversial issue.

Chapter 3 states that the information entities provide in their financial statements should have certain **qualitative characteristics**. The key characteristics are identified as relevance and faithful representation. The framework additionally outlines how comparability, verifiability, timeliness and understandability enhance the usefulness of information that is relevant and faithfully represented.

The remaining chapters of the conceptual framework have yet to be published.

■ References

1. Financial Accounting Standards Board (1976). *Conceptual Framework for Financial Accounting and Reporting: Elements of Financial Statements and their Measurement.* Scope and Implications of the Conceptual Framework Project section, p. 1.

2. Demski, J. S. (1980). *Information Analysis,* 2nd edn. Reading, Mass.: Addison-Wesley.

3. Burgraaf, J. A. (1983). The political dimensions of accounting standards setting in Europe. In *Accounting Standards Setting: an International Perspective.* London: Pitman Books Limited.

4. *Merriam-Webster Dictionary.*

5. Lennard, A. (2007). Stewardship and the objectives of financial statements: a comment on IASB's preliminary views on an improved conceptual framework for financial reporting. *Accounting in Europe,* 4 (1), pp. 51–66.

6. Whittington, G. (2008). Harmonisation or discord? The critical role of the IASB conceptual framework review. *Journal of Accounting and Public Policy,* 27, pp. 495–502.

7. Sprouse, R. T. (1983). Standard Setting: the American Experience. In *Accounting Standards Setting: an International Perspective.* London: Pitman Books.

8. Accounting Principles Board (1970). Statement No. 4, *Basic Concepts and Accounting Principles Underlying Financial Statements of Business Enterprises.*

9. Hope, A. and Gray, R. (1982). Power and policy making: the development of an R&D standard. *Journal of Business Finance and Accounting,* 9 (4), Winter, pp. 531–58.

10. ASC – this body came about as a result of a shortening of the name of the ASSC.

11. Hicks, J. R. (1948). *Value and Capital.* Oxford: Oxford University Press, p. 172.

Appendix 2.1

Previous efforts to develop a conceptual framework for financial reporting

A number of efforts have been made at national level to develop a conceptual framework for financial reporting. Most have been concentrated in the US and the UK, and a chronological summary of developments in these countries is outlined below.

■ The United States

In 1958 the American Institute of Certified Public Accountants recommended the establishment of the Accounting Principles Board (APB) and the preparation of Accounting Research Studies (ARS). This led to the publication in 1961 of ARS No. 1 and ARS No. 3 in 1962. Both studies were promptly rejected by the APB in APB Statement No. 1 in 1962. Sprouse[7] refers to the following quotation from that statement: '. . . they are too radically different from present generally accepted accounting principles for acceptance at this time'.

In 1970 the APB[8] published Statement No. 4. Sprouse[7] maintained that this statement described the *way things are* rather than the way they *ought to be*. The demise of the APB could be attributed, at least in part, to its failure to develop a theoretical framework for accounting. It was replaced in 1973 by the Financial Accounting Standards Board.

The development of a conceptual framework was one of the seven projects on the FASB's initial agenda. The report of the AICPA Study Group on the Objectives of Financial Statements (The Trueblood Report) was published in October 1973, and provided the basis on which the FASB was to launch its conceptual framework project.

Between 1978 and 2000, the FASB published the following Statements of Financial Accounting Concepts (SFACs):

- SFAC No. 1 Objectives of Financial Reporting by Business Enterprises (1978);
- SFAC No. 2 Qualitative Characteristics of Accounting Information (1980);
- SFAC No. 5 Recognition and Measurement in Financial Statements of Business Enterprises (1984);
- SFAC No. 6 Elements of Financial Statements (1985);
- SFAC No. 7 Using Cash Flow Information and Present Value in Accounting Measurements (2000).

In 1994 The AICPA published a report entitled *Improving Business Reporting – a Customer Focus: Meeting the Information Needs of Investors and Creditors*. The report emphasised the importance of the following information for users of financial statements:

- **Trends** – for example, five-year summaries of key statistics such as earnings per share;
- **Substance of transactions** – for example, the inclusion of leased assets in the statement of financial position of a lessee;
- **Significant risks** – relating to the valuation of assets and liabilities.

■ The United Kingdom

In 1971 the Accounting Standards Steering Committee (ASSC) published Statement of Standard Accounting Practice No. 2 (SSAP2), *Disclosure of Accounting Policies*. This statement outlined four fundamental accounting concepts, which were to underlie the periodic financial statements of business entities:

- going concern
- accruals
- consistency
- prudence

Unfortunately these concepts did not ensure that subsequent SSAPs would be based on a theoretical framework of accounting. Evidence is provided by Hope and Gray,[9] for example, that SSAP 2 provided little protection from vested interest groups seeking to influence the development of subsequent accounting standards.

In 1975 the ASSC issued a discussion paper, *The Corporate Report*. This report considered, among other things, what should be the objective of corporate reports, who are the users of accounting information, and what are their needs. *The Corporate Report* was regarded by many as breaking the mould, in that it envisaged the scope of financial reporting as being much broader than was the case with previous ASSC publications. *The Corporate Report* failed to receive the attention that it merited at that time, principally because the government-commissioned *Sandilands Report* on inflation accounting, published later in the same year, necessitated an urgent response from the ASSC.

In 1978 the Accounting Standards Committee (ASC[10]) issued *Setting Accounting Standards; a Consultative Document*. This document identified the absence of a single agreed definition for *income* and *value*.

In 1981, the ASC published a report which had been commissioned from Professor Richard Macve. The report, entitled *A Conceptual Framework for Financial Reporting*, concluded that it is '. . . unlikely that searching for an agreed conceptual framework, in abstraction from individual problems of disclosure and method, will be successful' (p. 21).

Macve reached this conclusion principally because of the fact that there was no universally accepted definition of *income* and *value*, and also due to a lack of agreement as to the objectives of accounting. Macve, therefore, concluded that 'A conceptual framework for accounting should be regarded rather as a common basis for identifying issues, for asking questions and for carrying out research than as a packet of solutions' (p. 14).

In 1988 the Institute of Chartered Accountants in Scotland published a report entitled *Making Corporate Reports Valuable*. A key objective of the report was that corporate reports would become more understandable and contain less technical jargon. The report was also critical of historical cost, and recommended that financial statements be prepared on a current value basis. The importance of portraying economic reality was emphasised, with the adoption of substance over form being highlighted.

In 1999 the Accounting Standards Board (ASB), having replaced the ASC nine years earlier, issued its *Statement of Principles*. It contained the following chapters:

- Chapter 1: The objective of financial statements
- Chapter 2: The reporting entity
- Chapter 3: The qualitative characteristics of financial information
- Chapter 4: The elements of financial statements
- Chapter 5: Recognition in financial statements
- Chapter 6: Measurement in financial statements
- Chapter 7: Presentation of financial information
- Chapter 8: Accounting for interests in other entities

Appendix 2.2

Extract from the IASC's 1989 conceptual framework (adopted by the IASB in April 2001)

This extract covers the following sections of the 1989 framework that have not been updated in the IASB's 2010 conceptual framework;

- Elements of financial statements
- Recognition of the elements of financial statements
- Measurement of the elements of financial statements
- Capital and capital maintenance

■ Elements of financial statements

(i) Elements relating to financial position

Assets
An asset is a resource controlled by an entity as a result of past events and from which future economic benefits are expected to flow to the entity.

Example 1 On 1 January 2010, Mandrigo Limited leased a machine for seven years from Leaso Limited. The estimated useful life of the machine is seven years.

Mandrigo controls the machine for substantially all of its useful life, and it will receive the future economic benefits that flow from the asset. The machine should therefore be included as an asset in Mandrigo's financial statements, notwithstanding the fact that Leaso Limited may retain legal ownership.

Liabilities
A liability is a present obligation arising from past events, the settlement of which is expected to result in an outflow of economic benefits.

Example 2 Mandrigo Limited purchased goods on 1 November 2010 for €200,000, and received 3 months' credit from the supplier.

Mandrigo has an obligation to pay for goods which were purchased on 1 November 2010. Therefore, Mandrigo should recognise a liability in its financial statements at 31 December 2010 as follows:

	Dr €'000	Cr €'000
Purchases	200	
Trade payables		200

Equity
Equity is the residual interest in the assets of an entity after deducting all its liabilities.

Example 3 Tarbert Limited was incorporated on 1 January 2010. At that date, the company had €100,000 in cash, in respect of shares purchased by investors at par. During 2010, Tarbert purchased goods for €40,000 and sold the same goods for €90,000. Tarbert also incurred distribution expenses of €15,000. All transactions were in cash.

Prepare an excerpt from the statement of financial position of Tarbert Limited at 31 December 2010.

Statement of Financial Position of Tarbert Limited at 31 December 2010

	€'000
Assets	
Bank	135
Equity	
Share capital	100
Retained earnings	35
Total equity	135

Tarbert's equity at 31 December 2010 amounts to €135,000.

(ii) Elements relating to financial performance

Income

Income is increases in economic benefits during an accounting period that result in an increase in equity, other than those that arise from contributions from equity holders.
  Income encompasses both revenue and gains:

■ *revenue* arises in the course of the ordinary activities of an entity, and includes sales, fees, interest, dividends, royalties and rent;
■ *gains* are income that may not arise in the ordinary activities of an entity. They include, for example, the profit on disposal of an asset, and the revaluation surplus on a long-term asset.

In Example 3 above, Tarbert's income for 2010 is €90,000.

Expenses

Expenses are decreases in economic benefits during an accounting period, other than those relating to distributions to equity holders. They encompass:

■ expenses that arise in the course of the ordinary activities of an entity, such as cost of sales and depreciation;
■ losses that may or may not arise in the course of the ordinary activities of an entity. They include losses from disasters such as fire, and a loss arising on the disposal of a long-term asset.

In Example 3 above, Tarbert's expenses for 2010 are €55,000.

■ Recognition of the elements of financial statements

Recognition is the inclusion of an element (i.e. asset, liability, equity, income or expense) in an entity's income statement or statement of financial position.
  The IASB framework stipulates that an item meeting the definition of an element should be recognised if:

■ it is probable that any future economic benefits will flow to or from the entity; and
■ the item has a cost or value that can be measured reliably.

Example 4 Mandrigo Limited sold goods on credit for €100,000 on 1 December 2010.

This transaction gives rise to both income and an asset. It is probable that the future economic benefit (i.e. a cash inflow) will be received by Mandrigo, and this benefit can be measured reliably. As the recognition criteria are satisfied, both the income and asset should be recognised in the financial statements of Mandrigo:

	Dr €'000	Cr €'000
Trade receivables	100	
Revenue		100

Example 5 The Mandrigo brand name is considered to be quite exclusive and to be of significant value. Management is anxious to include the brand as an asset in the financial statements at 31 December 2010.

The brand name must be assessed under the recognition criteria of the IASB framework:

- it is probable that any future economic benefits associated with the brand will flow to Mandrigo;
- the value of the brand cannot however be measured reliably.

Therefore, Mandrigo's brand name should *not* be recognised in the financial statements. Disclosure of the estimated value of the brand can however be *disclosed* in the notes that accompany the financial statements.

◼ Measurement of the elements of financial statements

While the IASB indicates that historical cost is the measurement basis that is most frequently used in preparing financial statements, it does not express a preference for one basis over another. In practice, historical cost is usually combined with other measurement bases, and the principal alternatives are identified as follows.

(i) Historical cost

- Assets are recorded at the amount paid at the time that they were acquired.
- Liabilities are recorded at the amount of proceeds received in return for taking on the obligation, or in some cases (e.g. income taxes) at the amount expected to be paid to clear the liability.

Example 6 On 1 January Mandrigo Limited raised a loan of €200,000 to fund the purchase of a machine. Mandrigo uses historical cost as the measurement basis for machinery.

The machine should be recorded at its cost price of €200,000, and it should be depreciated over its useful economic life. Mandrigo has received €200,000 from the lender in return for taking on the obligation to repay the amount borrowed. Therefore, the loan should be recorded as a liability of €200,000. The following journal entries will be required:

	Dr €'000	Cr €'000
Bank	200	
Loan		200
(Being loan of €200,000 raised on 1 January)		
Machine	200	
Bank		200
(Being purchase of machine)		

(ii) Current cost

- Assets are carried at the amount that would have to be paid to acquire an equivalent asset currently.
- Liabilities are carried at the undiscounted amount that would be required to settle the obligation currently.

Example 7 Mandrigo Limited purchased a new head office building on 1 January 2010 for €1.5 million in cash. Mandrigo uses the revaluation model to value its property assets, and the fair value of the head office on 31 December 2010 was €1.7M.

The head office building should be recorded initially at its cost of €1.5M. This value is increased to €1.7M on 31 December 2010:

	Dr €'000	Cr €'000
Building	1,500	
Bank		1,500
(Being purchase of building on 1 January 2010)		
Building	200	
Revaluation surplus – OCI		200
(Being revaluation of building on 31 December 2010)		

(iii) Realisable (settlement) value

- Assets are carried at the amount that could currently be obtained by selling them in an orderly disposal.
- Liabilities are carried at their settlement values.

Example 8 Mandrigo Limited was carrying a significant inventory of 12-inch plastic piping at 31 December 2010. The plastic piping had cost €250,000 to manufacture, but was sold in January 2011 for €180,000.

The inventory of plastic piping should be included as an asset at 31 December 2010 at the lower of its cost and net realisable value. The inventory should therefore be valued at €180,000.

(iv) Present value

- Assets are carried at the discounted value of the future net cash inflows they are expected to generate in the normal course of business.
- Liabilities are carried at the discounted value of the future net cash flows that are expected to be required to settle the liabilities in the normal course of business.

Example 9 On 1 January 2010, Mandrigo Limited signed an agreement to lease a factory building for a five-year period. At 31 December 2010, the building remained unoccupied, as Mandrigo had shelved its scheduled production plans. It is not envisaged that the building will have an alternative viable use, and there is little likelihood that it will be sub-leased to a third party.

At 31 December 2010, the discounted value of the remaining lease payments amounted to €306,000.

Outline how this lease agreement should be accounted for by Mandrigo Limited in its financial statements for the year ended 31 December 2010.

Solution	The lease agreement is an onerous contract for Mandrigo at 31 December 2010. An onerous contract is one in which the cost of meeting the obligations exceeds the related benefits. Therefore, at 31 December 2010, a liability should be recorded for the discounted value of the future net cash outflows associated with the lease. The following journal entry will be required:

	Dr €'000	Cr €'000
Lease costs – I/S	306	
Lease liability – SOFP		306

■ Capital and capital maintenance

Profit can be regarded as the increase in capital during a period, excluding amounts contributed or withdrawn by owners. Therefore, profit is the residual after the amount of capital at the beginning of a period has been maintained.

The government-appointed Sandilands Committee, in 1975, defined profit by modifying the definition of economic profit provided by Hicks:[11]

> A company's profit for the year is the maximum value which the company can distribute during the year and still expect to be as well off at the end of the year as it was at the beginning.

Two concepts of capital maintenance are outlined in the IASC framework.

(i) Financial capital maintenance

Under this concept, a profit is earned only if the financial (or money) amount of the net assets at the end of the period exceeds the amount of net assets at the beginning of the period (after excluding any distributions to, and contributions from, owners during the period).

Financial capital maintenance can be measured either in:

■ nominal monetary units (i.e. historical cost, where inflation is ignored), or
■ units of constant purchasing power.

(ii) Physical capital maintenance

Under this concept, a profit is earned only if the physical productive capacity of an entity at the end of a period exceeds the physical productive capacity at the beginning of the period (after excluding any distributions to, and contributions from, owners during the period).

The issue of capital maintenance is discussed in further detail in Chapter 3 below.

QUESTIONS

2.1 An important requirement of the IASB's *Conceptual Framework for Financial Reporting* is that an entity's financial statements should faithfully represent the transactions and events that it has undertaken.

Required:
Explain what is meant by faithful representation.

2.2 PORTO

During the year ended 31 March 2011, PORTO experienced the following transactions or events:

(i) Entered into a finance lease to rent an asset for substantially the whole of its useful economic life.

(ii) The company's income statement prepared using historical costs showed a loss from operating its hotels, but the company is aware that the increase in the value of its properties during the period far outweighed the operating loss.

Required:
Explain how you could treat items (i)–(ii) above in PORTO's financial statements and indicate on which of the qualitative characteristics of the IASB Framework that your treatment is based.   (ACCA)

2.3 Since its formation in 2001, the International Accounting Standards Board has endeavoured to issue accounting standards that are principles-based. Discuss the importance of a conceptual framework for the development of principles-based standards.

2.4 In 2004, the IASB and FASB began collaborating on the development of an agreed conceptual framework for accounting. Outline the reasons why these two regulatory bodies have embarked on this joint initiative.

Chapter 3

Alternative income models

Let us assume that you deposit €10,000 cash in a safe in 2011. Ten years later, in 2021, you will be able to buy less for your money, as its purchasing power is likely to have fallen due to inflation. Inflation can therefore be described as an increase in prices that results in a fall in the purchasing power of money.

Inflation has been at a low single-digit level for many years, and consequently it has received little attention in modern-day financial reporting. Mumford,[1] however, maintains that during times of high inflation, there is controversy within the accounting profession, as the impact of alternative inflation-accounting techniques is examined. At these times, the threat of government intervention also increases, as all policy options are considered in an effort to bring inflation under control.

The kernel of the inflation-accounting problem relates to the definition of *income*. This is the term that economists use to describe the equivalent, in personal terms, of the profit earned by a business. The following definition of profit, developed by the Sandilands Committee,[2] is based on the definition of income provided by the eminent economist Sir John Hicks:[3]

> *A company's profit for the year is the maximum value which the company can distribute during the year and still be as well off at the end of the year as it was at the beginning.*

Hicks' approach is regarded as being arguably the most realistic way in which the profit of a business can be measured. Three alternative methods of accounting for inflation are now compared to establish which best satisfies the profit measure that Hicks has outlined.

Historical cost accounting

Financial statements have traditionally been prepared using **historical cost accounting** rules. Under these rules, inflation is ignored. Profit is computed as the difference between the selling price of an asset and its original cost (or in the case of assets like machinery and buildings as the difference between selling price and depreciated original cost).

Example 1 Scamp Limited bought goods for €1,000 and sold them one year later for €1,600 cash. The cost of replacing the goods was €1,200. The general economy-wide rate of inflation was 9% per annum.

Historical cost profit is computed as follows:

	€
Revenue	1,600
Cost of sales	(1,000)
Profit	600

€1,000 is held back out of revenue to replace the goods that have been sold. This results in Scamp's *nominal* capital (i.e. the original cost of the goods sold) being maintained by the business. Profit of €600, which is available to pay dividends, includes €200 that is needed (in addition to the original cost of €1,000) to replace the goods sold. Thus, during a period of inflation, historical cost accounting overstates a firm's true profit.

When prices are rising, historical cost accounting also overstates profit by charging depreciation on the original cost of an asset, rather than on its (higher) replacement cost. Once again, the amount of profit that can be paid out as a dividend is overstated.

Another feature of historical cost is that a firm's assets are not included at their fair value in the statement of financial position. Assets such as land and buildings may be worth more than what they cost, but this increase in value is not recorded under historical cost.

Despite its drawbacks, however, historical cost continues to be the primary valuation method used in practice. Because historical cost values are based on actual transactions (e.g. the purchase cost of an asset), the information is regarded as being objective and reliable.

Historical cost accounting is normally used when evaluating management's stewardship of a business. Financial statements are required to be prepared under historical cost when computing a firm's taxation charge, and because it involves less subjectivity than other valuation methods, historical cost also helps to simplify the audit function. Finally, historical cost accounting has stood the test of time, being the principal accounting method used over several centuries.[4]

Current purchasing power

As outlined above, inflation results in a reduction in the amount of goods and services that a fixed amount of money can buy. The objective of the **current purchasing power** (CPP) method is to ensure that a business can purchase the same amount of *general* goods and services, despite the fact that inflation has resulted in price increases.

The outcome of the CPP method can be seen by revisiting Example 1 above.

Profit is computed as follows:

	€
Revenue	1,600
Cost of sales*	(1,090)
Profit	510

*Cost of sales = €1,000 × 109% (i.e. including a general price increase of 9%).

€1,090 is held back out of revenue, thus enabling Scamp to replace the goods sold with new goods which, if their price increased in line with general inflation, would cost 10% more. The actual cost of the goods that Scamp must replace, however, has increased by 20%. Consequently, the current purchasing power method fails to maintain a firm's capital, when the rate of price increase of goods sold by the business exceeds the general inflation rate.

Thus, profit of €510, which is available to pay dividends, includes €110 that is needed (in addition to the original cost of €1,000) to replace the goods sold.

CPP is appealing as a method of accounting for inflation primarily because of its simplicity. It fails to maintain the *physical* capital of a business, however, as it does not protect against individual price increases in the specific assets of a business.

In 1973 CPP was proposed as a method of accounting for inflation in the UK and Republic of Ireland. In that year the ASSC issued ED 8, which recommended that companies be required to produce supplementary financial statements (in addition to their main financial statements) based on CPP principles. In 1974 the ASSC issued Provisional SSAP 7, which contained proposals similar to those of ED 8. Fearful that CPP might actually cause inflation rates in the UK to increase, in 1974 the UK government set up its own committee of inquiry into inflation accounting. In its report in 1975, the Sandilands Committee recommended the adoption of current cost accounting.

It should be noted, however, that the IASB requires a CPP approach to be employed when preparing the financial statements of an entity that is based in a hyperinflationary economy. This is further discussed in Chapter 37.

Current cost accounting

The objective of current cost accounting (CCA) is to ensure that a business can purchase the same goods and services (or maintain its existing operating capability, say by replacing petrol engines with electric engines) despite the fact that inflation has resulted in price increases.

The outcome of the CCA method can be seen by revisiting Example 1 above.

Profit is computed as follows:

	€
Revenue	1,600
Cost of sales*	(1,200)
Profit	400

*Cost of sales = the cost of replacing the goods that have been sold, with identical goods.

€1,200 is held back out of revenue, thus enabling Scamp to replace the goods that have been sold with identical goods. Consequently, the CCA method enables a business to maintain its *physical* capital, and it is the method that best satisfies Hicks' definition of profit.

As mentioned above, a version of CCA was proposed in 1975 by the government-appointed Sandilands Committee. The ASC (the new name for the ASSC in 1976) issued ED 18 *Current Cost Accounting* in 1976. This was replaced by ED 24 in 1979, which was followed by the publication of SSAP 16 *Current Cost Accounting* in 1980. Many companies, however, failed to adopt SSAP 16, and having been made non-mandatory in 1985, it was withdrawn in 1986.

A number of factors can explain why SSAP 16 did not achieve more widespread support:

- CCA requires that a separate price index be applied to each asset, and it is therefore considered to be a time-consuming and costly method to implement;
- CCA figures are considered more subjective than historical cost figures, and are therefore less reliable for stewardship and audit purposes;
- The tax authorities refused to accept inflation-adjusted financial statements for the purposes of computing a firm's tax charge. This greatly reduced the attractiveness of CCA from a commercial perspective.

Which method is used in practice?

Businesses often use more than one method of valuation in a single set of financial statements. For example, a firm may record its inventory at historical cost, while at the same time valuing its land and buildings at replacement cost. Thus, no one method dominates, and the statement of financial position can comprise a mix of historical cost and current cost asset valuations. As a consequence, a firm's profit figure is unlikely to be based fully on historical cost or indeed on CCA.

Summary

Accounting for price level changes has received little attention in recent years, as inflation has been running at low single-digit levels. However, should the inflation rate increase significantly, there will once again be concerns about how best to account for price changes.

The most realistic measure of profit is based on the definition of income provided by Sir John Hicks. This definition states that:

A company's profit for the year is the maximum value which the company can distribute during the year and still be as well off at the end of the year as it was at the beginning.

Three alternative valuation methods are examined in this chapter, so as to determine which of them computes profit in a manner that is most consistent with Hicks. Neither historical cost nor current purchasing power succeeds in maintaining the physical capital of the business. Current cost accounting performs best, ensuring that sufficient profits are retained by a business to maintain its operating capability.

Historical cost accounting has for several centuries been the dominant method in practice. It is common, however, for the statement of financial position of a business to also include assets valued at replacement cost. This is particularly likely in the case of assets such as land and buildings and investment property.

■ References

1. Mumford, M. (1979). The end of a familiar inflation accounting cycle. *Accounting and Business Research*, 9 (34), pp. 98–104.

2. *Report of the Inflation Accounting Committee* (1975). London.

3. Hicks, J. R. (1948). *Value and Capital*, 2nd edn. Oxford: Oxford University Press, p. 172.

4. Ijiri, Y. (1970). A defense for historical cost accounting. In *Asset Valuation*, edited by Robert R. Sterling. Houston, Tex.: Scholars Book Co.

QUESTIONS

3.1 You are the financial director of a private manufacturing company and your managing director has recently queried you on the reasons why historical cost profits are distorted by inflation.

Required:
You are required to write a brief memorandum explaining the major causes of such distortion, with particular reference to your company.

3.2 Non-current assets are seldom replaced by identical assets. It would be unrealistic to base current costs and depreciation on the current cost of a similar asset, when an equivalent modern asset, incorporating technological change, could do the same work and perhaps cost only half as much.

Required:
(a) Identify those situations where the use of price indices is inappropriate in determining the gross current replacement cost of non-current assets; and

(b) Explain how the value of a modern equivalent asset is derived in situations of major technological change.

3.3 GREENVILLE Limited

The board of GREENVILLE Limited is aware that certain items are included at valuation in GREENVILLE's financial statements, and has heard a number of business commentators make reference to fair values when discussing the global economic crisis of 2008.

Required:
Prepare a report addressed to the board of GREENVILLE Limited, which considers:

(a) The arguments for and against fair value accounting; and

(b) The issue of fair value and the role of accounting standards in the global economic crisis.
(Adapted from CPA Ireland)

3.4 SPRUCE Limited

SPRUCE Limited was incorporated on 1 January 2010, with €300,000 of equity capital, a machine which cost €200,000 and inventory of €100,000. Sales for the year ended 31 December 2010 were €500,000 and expenses (not including depreciation) amounted to €180,000. All transactions were in cash.

The following additional information is available:

- The machine has an estimated useful life of 5 years;
- At 31 December 2010, the cost of replacing the opening inventory was €125,000;
- The replacement cost of the machine at 31 December 2010 was €250,000;
- The general rate of inflation for the year ended 31 December 2010 was 10%.

Required:
Calculate the profit earned by SPRUCE Limited for 2010, under three alternative concepts of capital maintenance.

Part 3

FINANCIAL REPORTING REGULATION

Chapter 4

The regulatory environment

In financial reporting, the primary objective of regulation is to ensure that business entities comply with a code of behaviour in respect of information included in financial statements. The need for financial regulation was originally motivated by the desire to protect banks and creditors which supplied businesses with capital or goods and services. The spread of joint stock companies in the nineteenth century, however, brought about a separation of ownership and control, resulting in demands for increased protection of the shareholder/investor group. The requirement for an audit was shortly to follow, with financial statements having to be certified before being presented to shareholders.

Not surprisingly, the primary purpose of financial regulation is *fraud prevention*. The establishment of the US Securities and Exchange Commission in 1934 was the direct result of widespread corporate fraud preceding the Wall Street Crash of 1929. In more recent times, the collapse of US power giant Enron, amid startling revelations of dubious business practices, has resulted in a spate of new regulations. These include the Sarbanes–Oxley Act in the United States, and similar **corporate governance** rules have been issued in many other countries.

Beaver[1] identifies three additional reasons for financial reporting regulation:

- management has an incentive to suppress unfavourable information;
- free-riders (e.g. competitors) benefit from, but do not contribute to, the publication of accounting information. Thus, in the absence of regulation, accounting information would be under-produced;
- inequality of information: in the absence of regulation, some stakeholders (e.g. pension funds) would possess superior information compared with other less influential stakeholders.

Sources of regulation

The three principal sources of financial reporting regulation are identified in Figure 4.1, where financial statements include:

- a statement of financial position (i.e. a balance sheet)
- a statement of comprehensive income
- a statement of cash flows

Figure 4.1 **Sources of financial reporting regulation**

■ Legislation

Legislation is law which has been enacted by a legislature (e.g. a parliament). Corporate legislation is usually published in the form of Companies Acts, which contain laws relating to limited liability companies. For EU member states, legislation is also developed by means of EU Directives.

Company legislation typically establishes a set of broadly based rules for corporate entities, and these are supplemented by other sources of regulation.

■ Stock Exchange rules

Each stock exchange (e.g. London, New York, Tokyo) has its own individual regulations, which must be complied with by companies whose securities are quoted on that exchange. For example, the London Stock Exchange requires companies to publish half-yearly interim financial statements, while the New York Exchange requires that companies report on a quarterly basis.

■ Accounting standards

Many countries have their own standard-setting bodies that publish standards containing detailed regulations for business entities in that jurisdiction. For example, the **Accounting Standards Board** (ASB) issues accounting standards in the UK, while the same function is performed by the **Financial Accounting Standards Board** (FASB) in the US.

International accounting standards are issued by the International Accounting Standards Board (IASB), and Figure 4.1 identifies the IASB as a key regulatory influence in determining how financial statements are prepared and presented. The IASB was formed in 2001, succeeding the International Accounting Standards Committee (IASC) which had been established in 1973. Accounting standards issued by the IASC were known as International Accounting Standards (IASs), and these were inherited by the IASB in 2001. Many IASs are still in existence, albeit in revised form in most instances. Standards issued by the IASB are known as International Financial Reporting Standards (IFRSs).

The development of an IFRS follows a due process procedure, which usually begins with the issue of a discussion paper by the IASB. An exposure draft follows, and after considering submissions and comments from interested third parties, the IASB may proceed with the publication of an IFRS.

The regulatory structure within which the IASB operates is outlined in Figure 4.2.

- The IASB reports to the *IFRS Foundation*, which appoints the members of the IASB and raises funding for the standard-setting process.
- *The IFRS Advisory Council* liaises with organisations and individuals who have an interest in financial reporting. The IFRS Advisory Council also provides advice to the IASB regarding its agenda and priorities.
- The IASB is also supported by the *IFRS Interpretations Committee*, which provides practical guidance on the application of IFRSs. This committee was previously known as the International Financial Reporting Interpretations Committee (IFRIC), whose interpretations, known as IFRICs, are still in force. IFRIC was established in 2002, replacing the Standing Interpretations Committee (SIC), some of whose guidance statements (SICs) still apply today.
- A comprehensive list of current Accounting Standards is attached in Appendix 4.1.

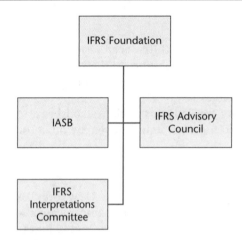

Figure 4.2 IASB's regulatory structure

The key influences on the IASB are identified in Figure 4.3 below:

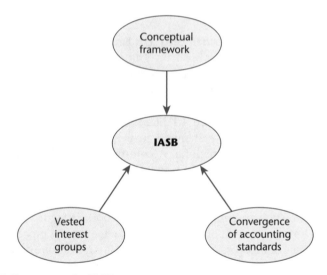

Figure 4.3 Key influences on the IASB

(i) *Conceptual framework.* This comprises an integrated set of theoretical principles on which accounting standards are based. A conceptual framework ensures that IFRSs are internally consistent and therefore less reliant on ad hoc conventions and rules. The IASB's **conceptual framework** is discussed in detail in Chapter 2.

(ii) *Vested interest groups.* As outlined above, the IASB follows due process in developing an IFRS, and the issue of a discussion paper and exposure draft affords outside interest groups the opportunity to influence the IASB's deliberations. There have been several instances of attempts by outside parties to achieve an outcome appropriate to their interests. For example, the aerospace industry successfully lobbied against a proposal by the UK regulatory body, the Accounting Standards Committee, to write off all development costs as an expense in the 1970s.[2]

Governments have also made infrequent, but important, interventions in the regulatory process. Most recently, the IASB's requirement for financial assets to be stated at **fair value** was widely perceived as contributing to the global financial crisis. This requirement was relaxed after the IASB came under intense pressure from international governments.

(iii) *Convergence of accounting standards.* Global convergence of international accounting standards is one of the stated objectives of the IASB. Huge strides have been made in recent years towards the achievement of this goal. Approximately 90 countries now require publicly quoted companies to comply with international accounting standards in their group accounts. This includes EU member countries, where compliance with IFRS has been mandatory since 1 January 2005.

Work continues towards the convergence of US accounting practice with IFRS, and in February 2010 the Securities and Exchange Commission voted unanimously to support the continued move towards adopting IFRS for US public companies. A definitive decision on adoption is expected in 2011, with 2015 being the earliest date that compliance with IFRS would be required.

A constraint on the spread of international accounting standards has been that IFRSs have only been mandatory for the group financial statements of companies whose securities are quoted on a recognised stock market. In 2009, however, the IASB issued an IFRS for SMEs, which provides a stand-alone set of rules for **small and medium-sized entities**. This IFRS is likely to extend the IASB's influence to an unprecedented number of entities on a worldwide basis. The IFRS for SMEs is discussed in detail in Chapter 49.

Management

Management is responsible for the preparation of financial statements and therefore plays a key role in the financial reporting regulatory environment. This is reflected in Figure 4.4.

One could view management's role as being simply to report objectively in accordance with the various regulatory requirements. In doing so, management may nonetheless exercise accounting policy choice in a manner that is in its own interests or that of the entity. For example, in a time of rising property prices, profit could be increased by using the fair value model to account for investment property.

Watts and Zimmerman[3] have used **positive accounting theory** (PAT) to explain management's choice of accounting policies. PAT contains three hypotheses:

- *Bonus plan hypothesis.* Management whose bonuses are based on accounting profits, are likely to use accounting policies that increase profit.
- *Debt : equity hypothesis.* Firms with a high level of borrowing are likely to use accounting policies that increase profit. This will assist highly geared firms to meet lending conditions such as the time interest covered ratio (i.e. profit before interest/interest), and thereby avoid penalties.

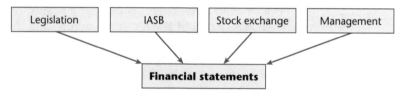

Figure 4.4 **Factors determining the content of financial statements**

- *Size hypothesis.* Large firms are more likely to use accounting policies that reduce profit, so as to avoid any unfavourable attention that high profits might attract (e.g. oil companies may want to avoid government controls on petrol prices).

Management may also decide to employ *creative accounting techniques* for any of the following reasons:

- to reduce taxation;
- to control dividends;
- pressure from analysts and big institutional investors to meet profit targets; and
- big bath theory, which maintains that new management will maximise losses and blame them on their predecessors. This should result in the new management taking credit for improved results going forward.

It is essential, when accounting standards are being developed, that regulatory bodies such as the IASB are fully cognisant of management's part in the process. As outlined above, when preparing financial statements, management will seek to achieve objectives that are in their own interests and that of their firm. Through their interpretation and application of accounting standards, and their choice of accounting policies, management plays a critical role in the preparation and presentation of financial statements. By being aware of the factors that influence and motivate management, the IASB can be more effective in fulfilling their regulatory function.

Impact of financial statements

The foregoing discussion has focused on the issues that determine the content and presentation of an entity's **financial statements**. So as to fully appreciate the role of the regulatory process, it is also important to understand the impact which financial statements have on the various user groups and on society in general. This impact is outlined in Figure 4.5.

Economic consequences

Throughout most of the twentieth century, business corporations were benignly regarded as the primary drivers of wealth creation. Accountability was rarely an issue, as employees and other stakeholders offered unconditional loyalty to the corporate ethos. An example was the US tobacco industry which, though raising serious health concerns since the 1950s, did not succumb to the first successful legal action until 1996.[4] The industry's primary defence during that time was to blame smokers for choosing to use their products despite the known risks.

Zeff,[5] however, explains how in the 1970s, society began to hold its institutions '. . . responsible for the social, environmental and economic consequences of their actions . . .' A prime example was the *Challenger* space shuttle disaster in 1986, which resulted in the deaths of all seven crew members. The Rogers Commission which investigated the accident was critical of NASA's safety culture, and the US House Committee on Science and Technology concluded that the fundamental problem was poor technical decision-making by top NASA and contractor personnel.

A similar culture of accountability has evolved in the area of financial regulation. For example, in 2000, the UK standard-setting body, the ASB, was held partially responsible

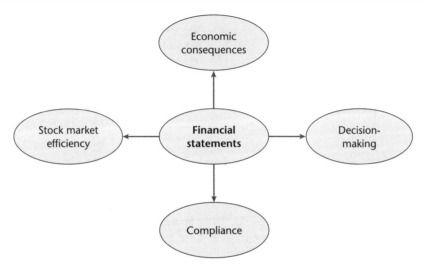

Figure 4.5 Impact of financial statements

when employers began to replace defined-benefit pension plans with defined-contribution plans. The change resulted in a transfer of risks to employees, as employee pensions under defined-contribution plans depend on the future performance of fund assets, rather than being guaranteed by employers. The allegation against the ASB arose from the publication of FRS 17, *Retirement Benefits*, which required that pension scheme deficits should be recognised immediately as a liability, rather than being amortised over the expected service lives of employees in the scheme. This requirement meant that pension deficits crystallised immediately in the financial statements, making defined-contribution plans less attractive from an employer's perspective.

As noted previously, the IASB's requirement for financial assets to be stated at fair value was widely perceived as contributing to the recent global financial crisis. This requirement was relaxed after the IASB came under intense pressure from international governments.

Thus, it is generally accepted that financial statements have significant economic consequences.

■ Stock market efficiency

Stock market efficiency is assessed by the speed and accuracy that share prices reflect new information. Many studies have shown that share prices react to new accounting information, which confirms that published financial statements contribute to stock market efficiency. Thus, financial statements have an important role in ensuring that quoted share prices reflect the fair value of an entity's securities.

■ Compliance

Financial statements play a crucial role in enabling businesses to fulfil their statutory obligations. This includes the submission of tax information to the revenue authorities, the furnishing of annual financial statements to shareholders, the fulfilment of a company's audit requirement, and the filing of an annual return with the Companies Registration Office or similar authority.

■ Decision-making

Financial statements serve as a valuable tool for decision-making purposes, such as the purchase and sale of shares. They are also used by lending institutions when assessing credit applications, by creditors when evaluating orders for goods or services, by governments when allocating grants and subsidies, and by trade unions as part of the wage-negotiation process.

Summary

This chapter has presented the regulatory environment within which financial statements are prepared.

The International Accounting Standards Board is a key contributor to the regulatory process. Motivated by its desire to achieve global convergence of financial reporting practices, the IASB accepts submissions from various interested parties as part of the process of developing international financial reporting standards. The IASB's conceptual framework is an important component in ensuring that its IFRSs are based on a set of internally consistent principles.

Legislation and stock exchange rules are other key sources of financial reporting regulation.

Management also has a crucial role to play in determining the content of financial statements. Positive accounting theory proposes three hypotheses to explain how management may exercise its choice of accounting policies. Reasons are also offered as to why management may elect to employ creative accounting techniques when preparing financial statements.

In discussing the impact of financial statements, it is explained how they contribute to an efficient stock market, assist with an entity's compliance obligations and facilitate decision-making. Finally, it is argued that financial statements can have significant economic consequences.

The overall regulatory environment is now presented in Figure 4.6.

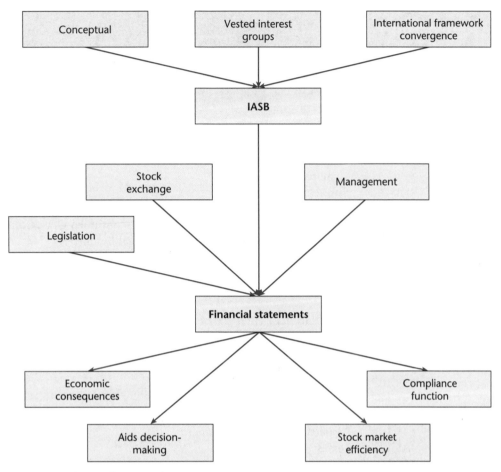

Figure 4.6 **The regulatory environment**

■ References

1. Beaver, W. (1981). *Financial Reporting: an Accounting Revolution*. Englewood Cliffs, NJ: Prentice-Hall.

2. Hope, A. and Gray, R. (1982). Power and policy making: the development of an R&D standard. *Journal of Business Finance and Accounting*, Vol. 9, No. 4, Winter, pp. 531–58.

3. Watts, R. and Zimmerman, J. (1978). Towards a positive theory of the determination of accounting standards. *The Accounting Review*, January, pp. 112–34.

4. Daynard, R. A., Bates, C. and Francey, N. (2000). Tobacco litigation worldwide. *British Medical Journal*, 8 January, pp. 111–13.

5. Zeff, S. (1978). The rise of economic consequences. *The Journal of Accountancy*, December, pp. 56–63.

Appendix 4.1

Extant accounting standards

IFRS 1	First-time Adoption of International Financial Reporting Standards
IFRS 2	Share-based Payment
IFRS 3	Business Combinations
IFRS 4	Insurance Contracts
IFRS 5	Non-current Assets Held for Sale and Discontinued Operations
IFRS 6	Exploration for and Evaluation of Mineral Resources
IFRS 7	Financial Instruments: Disclosures
IFRS 8	Operating Segments
IFRS 9	Financial Instruments
IAS 1	Presentation of Financial Statements
IAS 2	Inventories
IAS 7	Statement of Cash Flows
IAS 8	Accounting Policies, Changes in Accounting Estimates and Errors
IAS 10	Events after the Reporting Period
IAS 11	Construction Contracts
IAS 12	Income Taxes
IAS 16	Property, Plant and Equipment
IAS 17	Leases
IAS 18	Revenue
IAS 19	Employee Benefits
IAS 20	Accounting for Government Grants and Disclosure of Government Assistance
IAS 21	The Effects of Changes in Foreign Exchange Rates
IAS 23	Borrowing Costs
IAS 24	Related Party Disclosures
IAS 26	Accounting and Reporting by Retirement Benefit Plans
IAS 27	Consolidated and Separate Financial Statements
IAS 28	Investments in Associates
IAS 29	Financial Reporting in Hyperinflationary Economies
IAS 31	Interests in Joint Ventures
IAS 32	Financial Instruments: Presentation
IAS 33	Earnings per Share
IAS 34	Interim Financial Reporting
IAS 36	Impairment of Assets
IAS 37	Provisions, Contingent Liabilities and Contingent Assets
IAS 38	Intangible Assets
IAS 39	Financial Instruments: Recognition and Measurement
IAS 40	Investment Property
IAS 41	Agriculture

QUESTIONS

4.1 Briefly outline what you consider to be the role of the International Accounting Standards Board.

4.2 A significant number of entities and countries around the world have adopted International Financial Reporting Standards (IFRS) as their basis for financial reporting, often regarding these as a means to improve the quality of information or corporate performance. However, while the advantages of a common set of global reporting standards are recognised, there are a number of implementation challenges at the international and national levels, if the objective of an improved and harmonised reporting system is to be achieved.

Required:
Discuss the implementation challenges faced by the International Accounting Standards Board (IASB) if there is to be a successful move to International Financial Reporting Standards.　　　　　(ACCA)

4.3 Whilst acknowledging the importance of high-quality corporate reporting, the recommendations to improve it are sometimes questioned on the basis that the marketplace for capital can determine the nature and quality of corporate reporting. It could be argued that additional accounting and disclosure standards would only distort a market mechanism that already works well and would add costs to the reporting mechanism, with no apparent benefit. It could be said that accounting standards create costly, inefficient and unnecessary regulation. It could be argued that increased disclosure reduces risks and offers a degree of protection to users. However, increased disclosure has several costs to the preparer of financial statements.

Required:
(a) Explain why accounting standards are needed to help the market mechanism work effectively for the benefit of preparers and users of corporate reports.

(b) Discuss the relative costs to the preparer and benefits to the users of financial statements, of increased disclosure of information in financial statements.　　　　　(ACCA)

4.4 It is extremely important that financial reporting be subject to rules and regulations. The rules and regulations which apply to financial reporting may be collectively referred to as the 'regulatory framework'.

(a) Explain the need for regulation in the context of financial reporting.

(b) Describe briefly the main sources of accounting regulations.　　　　　(Chartered Accountants Ireland)

Chapter 5

The annual report

Most large cities need an integrated transport system to cope with the volume of traffic that passes through on a daily basis. This is especially the case in capital cities, which have a big local population, but must also act as a hub for those visiting from abroad or travelling to and from regional areas. Take Victoria Station in Westminster, which is a London Underground station. It services national rail routes, and also provides train access to Gatwick Airport. There is a local bus station in the forecourt, and a nearby terminal for long-distance coach travel. Taxis are available to transport passengers throughout the Greater London area.

Companies whose shares are publicly traded are required by law to prepare an **annual report**. In a regulatory context, an annual report resembles an information hub, offering a financial service which is comparable to the integrated transport network provided at London's Victoria Station. Chapter 4 identified the key sources of regulation as legislation, accounting standards and stock exchange rules. The information required by each of these sources is channelled into the annual report, along with additional voluntary information provided by management. Thus, an integrated set of financial information is provided annually to shareholders in a single document. The annual report can also be accessed by other users such as creditors, employees, analysts and the general public.

Contents of the annual report

Typically, an annual report includes the following information, in roughly the following sequence:

- Financial highlights
- Chairman's report
- Report of the Chief Executive Officer
- Information about the company's products and personnel
- Directors' report
- Statement of directors' responsibilities
- Statement of corporate governance
- Environmental report*
- Report on corporate and social responsibility*
- Auditor's report
- Financial statements

* Some companies publish an additional report, separate from the annual report, to address these issues.

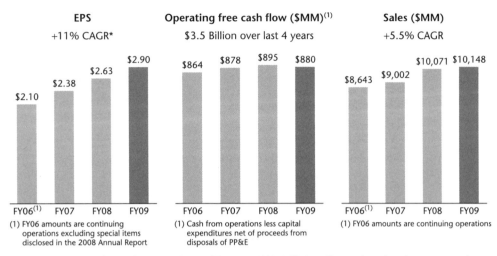

Figure 5.1 **Extract from the 2009 Annual Report of H. J. Heinz.** (Reproduced with permission).

Financial highlights

Key measures, such as revenue, profit and earnings per share are highlighted, with five years of figures being provided in line with stock exchange requirements. This information is often presented in the form of a bar chart, which facilitates easy comparison of figures for different years. Figure 5.1 is an extract from the 2009 Annual Report of the H. J. Heinz Company, showing the company's financial highlights.

Chairman's report

The chairman is the head of the board of directors, and the chairman's report contains an overview of the company's performance and future prospects. This is often presented in a favourable light.

Report of the Chief Executive Officer (CEO)

The CEO is responsible for giving a company leadership, and for ensuring that a company's operations are run efficiently. The report of the CEO provides a detailed analysis of a company's operations, with particular emphasis on the past year.

Information about a company's products and personnel

This section of the annual report provides an opportunity to impress the reader with the strength of the company's brands and personnel, and it is often presented in eye-catching colour.

Directors' report

This report provides the names of a company's directors, a summary of the company's activities, details of the dividend that is proposed in respect of the reporting year, and any events after the reporting period that may materially affect the company's finances.

Statement of directors' responsibilities

This section of the annual report outlines the principal responsibilities of the directors, which include:

- preparation of the annual report in accordance with legislation, generally accepted accounting practice, and the rules of the stock exchange on which the company's securities are listed;
- preparation of financial statements that give a true and fair view;
- confirmation that the directors have complied with the above requirements.

Statement of corporate governance

This statement includes information about a company's corporate governance structures, with particular reference to the independence of a company's non-executive directors. It also provides details of internal committees, such as the audit and remuneration committees.

Environmental report

This considers the company's performance in respect of sustainability issues, such as the use of renewable energy sources and details on emission levels. The following is an excerpt from the annual report of Debenhams for 2010:

> A cross-functional steering committee meets regularly and as a measure of the importance of sustainability issues to Debenhams, it has now become a committee of the board . . . due to our increased purchasing of green electricity from renewable sources, we have reduced our net carbon footprint by 29 per cent and 26,563 tonnes CO_2 since 2009.

Environmental reporting is discussed in more detail in Chapter 6.

Report on corporate and social responsibility

This report focuses on issues such as work practices, learning and development, health and safety, customer engagement, charitable initiatives and involvement with the community. Corporate social reporting is discussed in more detail in Chapter 6.

Auditor's report

The auditor expresses an opinion as to whether the company's financial statements are in accordance with its records, and whether they provide a true and fair view of the company's performance and financial position. The auditor also confirms whether the financial statements have been prepared in accordance with accounting standards and legislation.

Financial statements

A company's financial statements should comprise statements on its financial position, its comprehensive income, cash flows and changes in equity. Notes to the financial statements should also be included.

Evolution of the annual report

Based on the findings of a study by Lee of 25 of the largest British industrial companies, in 1965 the average length of the annual report was 26 pages. This had increased to 36 pages in 1978 and to 54 pages in 1988.[1] By 2006 the average length had reached 129 pages.[2] Thus, the passage of time has seen the annual report evolve from a document of modest size to one that contains, on average, well over 100 pages. The remainder of this chapter explores the reasons why the length of the annual report has changed so dramatically. The *content* of the annual report is also examined, to ascertain if changes in its composition have taken place over time.

■ Increase in voluntary content, 1965–88

The most significant finding in Lee's study was the percentage increase in the voluntary page count between 1965 and 1988. On average, annual reports devoted 15 pages to satisfying regulatory requirements in 1965, and 25 pages in 1988 – an increase of 67%. The page count relating to voluntary disclosures, however, went from 11 in 1965 to 29 in 1988 – an increase of 164%. An analysis of Lee's findings is shown in Table 5.1.

Table 5.1 Content of annual reports of UK companies, 1965–88

	1965	1988
Total page count	26	54
Regulatory page count	15	25
Voluntary page count	11	29
Narrative page count	8	19
Pictorial page count	3	10
Operational page count	8	16
Product page count	1	12

Advances in technology are an important factor in explaining the increased page count in respect of pictorial and product-based information in particular. None of the annual reports featured high-resolution colour in 1965, whereas all did in 1988. The fusion of pictures and narrative was used by 20% of companies in 1965, and 96% in 1988.

Lee offers an additional explanation for the increase in the voluntary content of annual reports in the period 1965–88. He quotes Sikes,[3] who maintains that companies use the annual report for the purpose of creating their own corporate personality:

> The audience for annual reports extends beyond stock-holders and employees. Executives use them as calling cards, salesmen as credentials, personnel departments as recruiting tools and financial analysts as a means of evaluating a company's performance.
>
> The opening pages can be visual corporate propaganda in its purest form. The reality you see is the reality the firm wants you to see . . . Chief executive officers are primped for portraits as lovingly as pet poodles, and oil rigs are lit as theatrically as the set of Miami Vice. The real story lies in the back pages' financial figures, a territory frequently neglected by designers – perhaps in the hope that shareholders will do the same.

Lee also refers to Ewen,[4] who describes how, in the politics of style, the perception of goods and services dominates over their substance. This results in value being based on aesthetic appeal rather than on intrinsic worth. Style becomes critical to survival, because in a world of *dynamic obsolescence*, a company's products or services can quickly become outdated. Ewen goes on to describe annual reports as the domain of designers who slip fantasy between facts and figures.

The results of Lee's study are consistent with the views advanced by Ewen and Sikes. Further support is provided by Lee's finding that, while only 12% of the companies in his sample employed design consultants in 1965, this had increased to 80% in 1988. It seems clear, therefore, that during the period covered by Lee's study, companies began to use the annual report as a marketing and public relations tool.

■ Increase in regulatory content, 1988–2006

In the post-1988 period, there has been an increased focus on narrative reporting in corporate annual reports. There has been a shift away from historical information to the provision of management's views about future opportunities and risks. This has seen major organisations suggest the reporting of information that is forward-looking, non-financial and soft.[5] In particular there has been an enhanced awareness of the importance of qualitative, non-financial information about a company's employees, its environment and customers, and its involvement in social and community issues.[6]

An example of the above change was the Operating and Financial Review (OFR), which was introduced in the UK by the Accounting Standards Board in July 1993. It required a company to identify the main factors that influenced its development, performance and financial position in the past, and those that were likely to do so in the future. The OFR, as proposed by the ASB, was non-mandatory, and was a voluntary statement of best practice for companies to include in the narrative sections of their annual report.

The preparation of an OFR became a legal requirement for UK-listed companies in March 2005, for periods commencing on or after 1 April 2005. In November 2005, the UK government revised that decision, and the OFR was made non-mandatory from 12 January 2006. A requirement to prepare a Business Review, which had been introduced in March 2005, remained however. The Business Review is similar to the OFR and it includes the following requirements:

■ a balanced and comprehensive analysis of the development and performance of the company during the year, and its position at the year end;
■ a description of the principal risks and uncertainties facing the company;
■ analysis, using financial and non-financial information, of environmental matters, the company's employees and social and community issues.

The information required by the Business Review is provided in various sections, throughout the annual report (e.g. in the Directors' Report, Report of the CEO, Chairman's Statement etc.). Prior to 2005, many companies were already disclosing the information required by the Business Review in their annual reports. The disclosure of that information is now a mandatory requirement.

The collapse of Enron in 2001, amidst allegations of serious accounting abuses, has also led to increased disclosures in corporate annual reports. For example, the Sarbanes–Oxley Act, which was enacted in the United States in 2002, requires additional disclosures relating to matters such as off-balance sheet items and the adequacy of a company's internal controls.

Disclosure requirements have also increased for those companies preparing their financial statements in accordance with the rules of the International Accounting Standards Board. The adoption of IASB standards became mandatory for EU-listed companies in respect of their group accounts for periods beginning on or after 1 January 2005.

It is not surprising, therefore, that there has been an increase in the regulatory content of corporate annual reports. As outlined, above, this has occurred partly due to increased disclosures resulting from post-Enron legislation, and partly from the adoption of the IASB's accounting standards. The mandatory inclusion of narrative style information has also resulted in a reclassification of information that was previously provided on a voluntary basis. These changes are reflected in Table 5.2.

Table 5.2 illustrates the dramatic increase in the regulatory content of annual reports since Lee's analysis in 1988. This has resulted in an increase of 139% in the average total page count during the period 1988–2006.

Table 5.2 **Annual reports of UK companies, 1988-2006**

	1988	2006
Average page count	54	129
Regulatory page count	25	112
Voluntary page count	29	17

One might imagine that, given the environmental implications of paper usage, companies would restrict the length of their annual reports. This is not proving to be the case, however, as companies are increasingly relying on information published on their websites, with shareholders being provided with a hard copy of the annual report only on request.

Summary

- The annual report is the information hub of a company whose shares are publicly traded.
- The annual report contains the information required by the three primary regulatory sources (legislation, accounting standards and stock exchange rules), along with voluntary information provided by management.
- There is evidence that companies use their annual report to increase their power and to create a corporate image.
- The voluntary content of the annual report increased significantly between 1965 and 1988.
- More recently, disclosures that were voluntary have been made mandatory, there has been an increased focus on disclosures of narrative information, and the adoption of IFRS has also resulted in additional disclosures.
- Consequently, there has been a dramatic increase in the regulatory content of annual reports in the period 1988-2006.

References

1. Lee, T. (1994). The changing form of the corporate annual report. *The Accounting Historians Journal*, 21 (1).
2. Walsh, D. and Cotter, D. (2011). The changing form of the corporate report 1988-2006. Paper presented at the annual conference of the Irish Accounting and Finance Association.
3. Sikes, G. (1986). *Art and Allegory*. Metropolis.
4. Ewen, S. (1988). *All Consuming Images: the Politics of Style in Contemporary Culture*. New York: Basic Books.
5. Beattie, V. (2000). The future of business reporting: a review article. *Irish Accounting Review*, 7 (1), pp. 1-36.
6. Solomon, J. F. and Edgley, C. R. P. (2008). The abandoned mandatory OFR: a lost opportunity for SER? *Social Responsibility Journal*, 4 (3), pp. 324-48.

Chapter 6

Accountability

In a perfect world every business would discharge its responsibilities honestly, and there would be no suspicion of wrongdoing. In such a world it would not be necessary to monitor activities or to have penalties to punish fraudulent behaviour. There would still be a need for rules, of course, but only to ensure that business transactions were recorded consistently across firms.

The world in which we live falls some way short of the one outlined above. Griffiths,[1] in fact, paints an entirely different picture:

> Every company in the country is fiddling its profits. Every set of published accounts is based on books which have been gently cooked or completely roasted. The figures which are fed twice a year to the investing public have all been changed in order to protect the guilty. It is the biggest con trick since the Trojan horse.

The behaviour to which Griffiths refers is commonly known as *creative accounting*. Left unchecked, creative accounting has the potential to undermine an entire economic system. Investors, being unable to distinguish between good firms and bad firms, would be unwilling to purchase shares in what Akerlof[2] calls a *market for lemons*. Consequently, companies would be cut off from a key source of capital to fund investment and expansion.

This chapter considers the reasons why firms engage in creative accounting, and the structures and controls that can be put in place to help eliminate such practices.

Creative accounting

Creative accounting can be defined as the presentation of information in a manner that is inconsistent with the underlying facts. It has been a problem throughout the twentieth century and continues to challenge regulators into the new millennium.

Madbid.com provides a good example of how numbers can be presented in a creative way. On the Madbid website, the BBC is quoted as saying that 'Goods can be won for a fraction of their retail price.' *The Times* is quoted as saying that 'The average saving on high street prices is 98%.' A closer examination of the Madbid website reveals a somewhat different story. Bids, which have a face value of 1 cent, cost up to 33 cents each to purchase from Madbid. During an auction, the price of an item increases by 1 cent every time that someone places a higher bid. However, the cost of placing a bid that is 1 cent higher varies between 25 and 33 cents.

For example, the Madbid website features an Audi 1.2 Sportback which was auctioned for €2,529 in January 2011. The total amount paid by bidders (only one of whom could win) was between €63,225 (i.e. 25 × €2,529) and €83,457 (i.e. 33 × €2,529). Based on a listed recommended retail price of €16,320, Madbid earned a profit of at least €46,905, and possibly as much as €67,137, from the auction of the Audi.

Figure 6.1 **Creative presentation**

Figure 6.1 provides a good visual example of creative presentation. Although the two figures in the picture are the same size, the figure at the rear appears in fact to be larger.

Creative accounting can have significant economic consequences. For example, if it is used to reduce a firm's tax charge, there is a transfer of resources from society to the firm. If creative accounting is used to overstate a firm's share price, there will be a transfer of resources from investors to the firm when new shares are issued. Share price overstatement will also result in investors who are selling the company's shares benefiting at the expense of buyers. If management uses creative accounting techniques to maximise their level of remuneration, there is a transfer of resources from shareholders to management.

Reasons for creative accounting

There are many reasons that provide an incentive for management to engage in creative accounting. Watts and Zimmerman's[3] **positive accounting theory** maintains that management is influenced by:

- the size hypothesis
- the debt/equity hypothesis
- the bonus plan hypothesis

The size hypothesis argues that large firms may want lower profits so as to avoid unfavourable political costs, such as government-imposed price restrictions on their products or services. Firms with high debt/equity ratios may wish to increase their profits in order to comply with loan agreements, which typically require profits to be a certain multiple of the interest charge for the period. Thirdly, management may be motivated to increase their firm's profit where managerial bonuses are based on accounting earnings. Positive accounting theory was outlined in greater detail in Chapter 4, and it is also discussed in Chapter 9.

The 'big bath' theory provides another rationale for the use of creative accounting practices by management. This involves new management maximising a firm's losses immediately following their appointment. The objective is to hold their predecessors responsible, while allowing the new management to take the credit for enhanced future profits.

In his book *Creative Financial Accounting*, Naser[4] reports on the reasons given by auditing practitioners and management for the use of creative accounting practices. These are summarised as follows:

- to meet limits on borrowing and gearing
- desire to reduce taxation
- desire to control dividends
- pressure from big institutional investors

■ Examples of creative accounting

There are many examples of creative accounting practices. Some of these are discussed below.

(i) Obfuscation hypothesis

This involves communicating good news with clarity and the use of short words. Bad news, on the other hand, is communicated in a manner that is more difficult to comprehend. The use of obfuscation is most commonly found in those parts of the annual report that involve a significant amount of narrative, such as the Chairman's Statement.

(ii) Earnings management

The earnings management literature outlines how management may engage in income smoothing practices so as to reduce the risk perceptions of their firm:

- *Smoothing through allocation over time.* Management can manipulate the periods in which expenses are recognised. For example, the useful life of assets can be adjusted, thereby affecting the amount of depreciation charged as an expense.
- *Use of discretionary accruals.* Income can also be smoothed by the use of discretionary accruals. For example, management can determine the amount to be provided as a provision for bad debts, or the amount of a provision in respect of a warranty on a company's products or services.

(iii) Off-balance-sheet financing

This involves a firm's debt being omitted from its statement of financial position. This was the main creative accounting technique employed by Enron, prior to its bankruptcy in 2001. Using other companies, called special purpose vehicles (SPVs), Enron raised enormous amounts of debt funding. Although Enron exercised control over these SPVs, the loans raised by them were not included in the statement of financial position of the Enron Group. This had the effect of significantly understating the amount of loans outstanding.

(iv) Revenue recognition

There are many ways in which companies can use creative accounting techniques to recognise revenue before it is earned. One such practice, known as 'channel stuffing', involves a distributor supplying more goods to retail outlets than can be sold to customers. The distributor records these goods as revenue, thereby inflating profits, but the goods are later returned by the retailers as they cannot be sold.

Another technique to distort revenue has been employed by the pharmaceutical company Elan. This practice, which involved the sale of product lines, was uncovered by the *Wall Street Journal*[5] in 2002. For example, when Elan was selling the rights to a drug called Permax for $47.5M, it recorded the sale as part of product revenue. This gave the impression that Elan's drug sales for the period had increased by $47.5M, whereas in fact this increase related to the disposal of an asset. The correct treatment would have been to record the proceeds of $47.5M separately as 'Profit on disposal of a product line', and to ensure that this amount was excluded from revenue in the income statement.

(v) Overstating assets

This involves the failure by a firm to record impairments relating to the value of assets such as machinery, property, inventory, investments and receivables.

(vi) Aggressive capitalisation of costs

Some firms may decide to capitalise costs (e.g. research & development) which others write off routinely.

Another example of creative presentation is outlined in Figure 6.2. Clearly, the face in Figure 6.2 cannot be trusted, confirmation of which is obtained by rotating it 90 degrees in an anticlockwise direction.

Figure 6.2 Is this the face of an honest man?

■ How effective is creative accounting?

The jury is still out on this question. An increase in a company's earnings might be achieved by using longer asset lives, resulting in a lower depreciation charge. As this can be easily observed, however, the users of the firm's financial statements are unlikely to be misled. Some creative accounting techniques are not easy to spot however. For example, Enron's use of off-balance-sheet financing was difficult to detect, even for the company's auditors.

It has also been found that financial analysts, who have expertise in interpreting companies' financial statements, may not always be able to detect a firm's use of creative accounting (see Breton and Taffler[6]). Likewise, Naser[4] documents the case of the UK conglomerate, Polly Peck, whose impending demise was camouflaged by the use of creative accounting techniques.

Figure 6.3 provides a good example of how effective presentation can make an enclosed vertical line appear to be shorter than a line of the same length that is not enclosed.

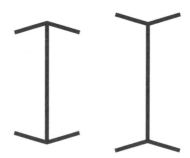

Figure 6.3 Line length

■ How can creative accounting be prevented?

It is unlikely that creative accounting can ever be eliminated entirely. A number of approaches can, however, be effective in reducing its incidence.

Financial regulation

Legislation provides the basic weaponry in the war against creative accounting. In prescribing the statutory regulations that must be complied with, the Companies' Acts establish a solid platform for the prevention of creative accounting.

Legislative requirements have also become more onerous since the collapse of Enron in 2001. For example, the Sarbanes–Oxley Act, enacted in the United States in 2002, requires compliance with a rigorous set of new rules.

Financial reporting standards also have a crucial role to play. Regulatory bodies, such as the IASB, are constantly revamping their accounting standards in order to combat creative accounting. There is, for example, a continuing effort to make accounting rules more uniform, so as to reduce the flexibility for firms to engage in creative accounting practices. **The IASB's accounting standards are the primary focus of this book.**

Monitoring, enforcement and penalties

An external audit of a company's financial statements plays a crucial role in the prevention of creative accounting. This involves an independent assessment to determine whether the financial statements give a true and fair view of a company's performance and financial position.

In the post-Enron world, a large number of additional policing bodies have been established worldwide, to monitor and enforce companies' accounting and legal requirements. These include oversight bodies which monitor the conduct of the accounting and auditing professions.

Harsher penalties can act as a deterrent against breaches of regulatory rules. A prime example is the 25-year prison sentence passed down to Bernie Ebbers, former CEO of WorldCom. Ebbers was convicted of fraud and conspiracy in 2005, as a result of WorldCom's false financial reporting, which resulted in a loss of $100 billion to investors.

Corporate governance

Adherence to a Corporate Governance Code can enable a company to establish appropriate structures to prevent the use of creative accounting practices. For example, the appointment of a majority of non-executive directors on a company's board acts as a control against abuses by management. Corporate governance is discussed in further detail below.

Focus on ethics

An emphasis on ethics in education can also play a significant role in helping to reduce the use of creative accounting practices by management. This is discussed in greater detail below.

Creating a culture of whistle-blowing in organisations

Insiders are often aware of creative accounting practices long before they become known to those outside an organisation. Management can help to eradicate creative accounting practices by providing support for a culture of whistle-blowing in their organisation. This can assist in bringing accounting irregularities to light at an early stage. Whistle-blowing is discussed in greater detail below.

Corporate social reporting

Creating a culture of good citizenship in an organisation helps to extend management's focus beyond the needs of the shareholder/investor group. Thus, a commitment to corporate social reporting makes management reportable to a broader range of stakeholders, thus reducing the motivation to engage in creative accounting. This is discussed in greater detail below.

Corporate governance

Corporate governance is defined by the Australian Stock Exchange as

. . . the system by which companies are directed and managed. It influences how the objectives of the company are set and achieved, how risk is monitored and assessed, and how performance is optimised.

The introduction to this book explains how company formations during the Industrial Revolution in the nineteenth century led to the separation of ownership and management. Munzig[7] outlines how the need for corporate governance is directly linked to that separation. Essentially, it involves a manager (i.e. the agent) raising capital from shareholders (i.e. the principal) for the purpose of investing in a company. The shareholders need the manager to generate a return on the funds invested, but have no guarantee that their funds will not be expropriated or used for projects that involve an excessive level of risk. This dilemma is described as the agency problem, which has previously been explained by Coase[8] and Jensen and Meckling.[9]

The agency problem involves what is known as moral hazard, which exists when one party is responsible for the interests of another but has an incentive to put his or her own interests first.[10] For example, a manager may have an incentive to invest in high-risk projects knowing that, should the investment fail, it is the shareholders who will suffer a loss of capital.

Contracts are therefore drawn up between the agent and principal, with a view to ensuring that the agent's actions are in the best interests of the principal. For example, management remuneration levels might be based on corporate earnings, or significant investments of capital in individual projects might require prior shareholder approval.

A key objective of corporate governance is therefore to ensure that contracts between management and shareholders are implemented effectively. The role of corporate governance, however, extends beyond that of establishing and monitoring contracts between managers and shareholders. The modern corporation is seen to have broader societal responsibilities, which include a commitment to a code of ethical behaviour and good citizenship. The role of corporate governance therefore extends to ensuring that corporations also fulfil their commitments to stakeholders such as employees, suppliers of goods and services, conservationists and other interest groups who have a valid claim on an entity's resources.

The following statement from Johnson & Johnson illustrates the group's commitment to corporate governance:

> The values embodied in Our Credo guide the actions of the people of the Johnson & Johnson Family of Companies at all levels and in all parts of the world. They have done so for more than 60 years. These Credo values extend to our accounting and financial reporting responsibilities. Our management is responsible for timely, accurate, reliable and objective financial statements and related information. As such:
>
> - We maintain a well-designed system of internal accounting controls.
> - We encourage strong and effective corporate governance from our Board of Directors.
> - We continuously review our business results and strategic choices.
> - We focus on financial stewardship.

■ Corporate governance failures

The most infamous case of corporate governance failure involved the US power giant Enron, which filed for bankruptcy in 2001. Enron was the seventh largest company in the United States, and its collapse, which also took down its auditors Arthur Andersen, sent shock waves through the entire community. Munzig[7] identifies the following corporate governance failures in Enron:

- Management was not acting in the best interests of shareholders, which in effect was a manifestation of the principal–agent problem.
- Management used sophisticated techniques to produce misleading financial results.
- Due to the lack of board independence (Enron management had a major board presence), management was able to extract excessive remuneration at the shareholders' expense.

An additional problem was that Enron insisted on investing its employees' pension funds in the company's own equity shares. This failed to provide the employees with an acceptable level of risk diversification, resulting in widespread hardship when the stock price collapsed.

■ Policy response to corporate governance failures

There was a widespread regulatory response to the failure of Enron and the subsequent demise of other companies such as WorldCom (the largest bankruptcy filing in US history, prior to Lehman Brothers in 2008). The most important policy response has arguably been in the US, where the Sarbanes–Oxley Act was passed in the summer of 2002. Provisions of the Act include the prohibition of insider lending to a firm's executives and directors, penalties for accounting restatements reflecting misconduct, and a requirement that members of audit committees be independent. The Act also strengthens auditor independence by limiting the scope of non-audit and consulting services for audit clients.[11]

Other jurisdictions also have corporate governance codes. For example, the UK Corporate Governance Code, which is based on principles rather than rules, sets out best practice guidelines. Companies listed on a stock exchange must explain if they do not comply with the provisions of the UK Corporate Governance Code.

A sample corporate governance code is attached in Appendix 6.1. This is the Code of Governance Principles for South Africa, which was fully updated in September 2009.

■ Does corporate governance increase shareholder value?

One rationale for the increased focus on corporate governance in recent years is that improved monitoring leads to an increase in a company's share price. Another is that it reduces excessive risk-taking. There is little empirical support, however, for the above hypotheses, and several studies have found no significant linkage between corporate governance and the level of shareholder wealth.[12]

In the absence of an established benefit to shareholders, Miller[13] poses the question as to why firms are willing to commit resources to improve corporate governance. Perhaps, Miller suggests, it is because benefits from enhanced corporate governance may actually accrue to a wider set of stakeholders than shareholders. It is also likely that the increased focus on corporate governance is not voluntary, as regulatory changes may have left firms with no option but to take corporate governance issues more seriously than heretofore.

Ethics

An increased focus on ethics in education can also act as a barrier against creative accounting. One view is that ethics is best taught as a separate course module, thus providing the attention that the subject merits. An advantage of this approach is that ethics receives guaranteed coverage. A risk, however, is that it may be considered to be of theoretical importance only, while having little relevance to actual decisions in practice. Another limitation is that if the ethics module is optional, only some students will choose it.

An alternative approach is to include the coverage of ethics across individual course modules. For example, if taught as part of financial reporting, ethics would be viewed as an integral part of decisions in financial reporting. A drawback of not having a separate ethics module, however, is that its coverage may be regarded as discretionary, and due to time constraints it may not receive the attention that it merits.

■ Traditional view

The conventional view is that ethics involves having to make a choice between right and wrong. For example, it would be difficult to justify the theft of another firm's intellectual property rights, or the acceptance of a bribe in return for not reporting an illegal activity of one's employer. In practice, however, ethics can involve more than exercising a simple choice between right and wrong.

■ Right versus right

Sophocles' Greek tragedy, *Antigone*, provides a vivid illustration of the difficulties that ethical dilemmas can pose. When her brother, Polyneices, is declared a traitor, Antigone is forced to make a tragic choice. Creon, the king of Thebes, ordains that Polyneices' body must be left unburied, and that anyone not obeying his command will themselves be put to death. Faced with such a choice, Antigone cites the 'laws of the heavens' and her family honour, and decides to provide her brother with a proper burial. Her execution by entombment follows, as does the death of her fiancée, Haemon, who is also the king's son. Unable to bear her son's death, Creon's wife also takes her own life, leaving the king a broken man.

In his book *Defining Moments*, Badaracco[14] outlines how traditional models are of little use in resolving dilemmas such as that faced by Antigone. For example, sleep test ethics maintains that the best alternative is the one that doesn't keep one awake at night. Clearly, sleep test ethics was of little use to Antigone, for whom neither option is palatable. John Stuart Mill's utilitarian ethics would recommend doing whatever brings about the greatest good for the greatest number of people. Kant suggests that people do their moral duty, which means that the innocent should be protected. Neither Kant nor John Stuart Mill offer Antigone a way of resolving her dilemma.

Badaracco outlines the case of Steve Lewis, a black lawyer, who was recruited by a US law firm during the 1960s when racial tensions were at a peak in the United States. Lewis is requested to accompany a group to Missouri, with the objective of securing a contract from the state treasurer, who is also black. The request presents Lewis with an ethical dilemma. If he goes as a token black member of the team, he believes that he is being disloyal to his cultural roots. If he does not go, he will be letting his firm down, which will adversely affect his career prospects.

In analysing Steve Lewis's dilemma, Badaracco quotes Aristotle and Nietzche (a nineteenth-century Prussian arts scholar), who view personal decisions as the most recent link in the long chain of a person's past decisions, actions and experiences. Badaracco also draws on Machiavelli, who advises that one must be pragmatic and not become a martyr for one's beliefs.

Steve Lewis needed a plan of action which would preserve the values that he cared about, without making him a noble, young unnoticed martyr. His decision was to join the presentation team, but on the basis that he wanted to earn his place, he requested and received a part in the presentation.

■ Ethics and creative accounting

Managers who use creative accounting practices are acting unethically and in a way that may be illegal. Managers who behave in this way are sometimes motivated, however, by a complex set of factors. Dan Vassela,[15] CEO of Novartis, describes the pressures of producing results on a quarterly basis. He explains how analysts set short-term targets which Wall Street expects to be achieved. Vassela describes the pressure exerted by investors and the press, and the personal pressure of delivering on promises that he has made. He also outlines the weight of expectation involved in having to match the profit announcements of his competitors, and of trying to ensure the survival of his company into the future.

Vasella explains that the tyranny of quarterly results is one that is imposed from within. He maintains that

> It is wrong to worry about whether you will be the hero next month . . . An individual can be corrupted by what's going on around him, and . . . if you want to cheat, you will always find a way. You might get caught, but many don't. And every time they don't, the tyranny of self-deception gets stronger.

Vasella's experience makes it clear that managers who wish to behave ethically often have to withstand significant pressures from a variety of sources. Resisting the temptation to engage in creative accounting requires the strength of character not to be compromised by having to meet short-term targets and expectations.

Whistle-blowing

Whistle-blowing has been defined by Nadler and Schulman[16] as '. . . calling attention to wrongdoing that is occurring within an organisation'. Management can aid the early detection of creative accounting in their organisation by encouraging a culture that encourages and supports whistle-blowing.

Whistle-blowing has, however, had a difficult evolution. Boatright[17] describes how in a 1971 speech, James M. Roche, then chairman of the General Motors Corporation, attacked the process of whistle-blowing:

> Some of the enemies of business now encourage an employee to be disloyal to the enterprise. They want to create suspicion and disharmony, and pry into the proprietary interests of the business. However this is labelled – industrial espionage, whistle-blowing or professional responsibility – it is another tactic for spreading disunity and creating conflict.

Glazer[18] identified 10 cases of whistle-blowing and examined the personal consequences for each of the whistle-blowers. The cases include that of Justin Rose who was hired as an in-house attorney in 1973 by Associated Milk Producers Incorporated, where he quickly became aware of illegal payments being made to politicians. When Rose attempted to highlight these payments, he was faced with severe retaliation from his employers:

> My attempt (to talk to the board) happened on a weekend during their convention in Minneapolis. Labour Day followed, and then Tuesday I went into work. I found a guard posted at my door; locks had been changed. The general manager demanded to see me. My services had become very, very unsatisfactory. When I was fired, I felt virtually a sense of relief. (p. 34)

Parmarlee and others[19] surveyed 72 women who had filed complaints of unfair discrimination with Wisconsin's Equal Rights Division. Following their complaint, the women reported being excluded from staff meetings, suffering a loss of perquisites, receiving less desirable work assignments, obtaining a heavier workload, having their work more stringently criticised and being pressured to drop their action. Similarly, in a survey of other whistle-blowers, Jos and others[20] found that 69% of those in the private sector and 59% of those in the public sector lost their jobs. Others, in the same survey, experienced a reduction in responsibilities or salary, or suffered harassment or work transfer.

These cases demonstrate that, traditionally, whistle-blowers have frequently met with severe retaliation by their own organisations. This is likely to be a response to the uncertainty that whistle-blowers create, and retaliation may be intended to silence the perpetrator, or prevent the complaint from being made public. It may also be intended to discredit the whistle-blower, or to deter others from complaining in the future.

■ Changing attitude towards whistle-blowing

Zeff[21] explains how in the 1970s, the traditional view of organisations began to change. Hitherto seen as providers of employment and creators of wealth, in the 1970s organisations began to be held responsible for the social, economic and environmental consequences of their transactions. The late 1970s saw an explosion of lawsuits in the United States, and huge awards were made against companies, resulting in an insurance crisis as insurers refused to provide an adequate level of product liability cover.

Referring to the ill-fated *Challenger* space shuttle flight in 1986, Near[22] outlines how Morton Thiokol, manufacturers of the defective O-rings in the booster rockets, had ignored the pre-flight protests of one of their engineers. As a result of the crash, Morton Thiokol faced lawsuits from the families of the seven astronauts who died, and were forced to withdraw from future bids for NASA contracts.

As companies were made more accountable for their actions, the attitude towards whistle-blowers also began to change. Gradually, whistle-blowing became more acceptable, and various authors began to expound its virtues.

Boyle[23] explains how the actions of whistle-blowers can benefit society:

> The potential negatives of organizational power are generally kept in check by a combination of market forces and government regulation. However, situations occur that the market and government are not able to correct before society is adversely impacted. In these situations it is incumbent upon the individual to intercede (i.e. blow the whistle) on behalf of the common good.

Paul and Townsend[24] advise employers to create an atmosphere of trust in an organisation, thereby encouraging employees to report wrongdoing without fear of reprisal. Slovin[25] justifies the installation of a whistle-blowers' hotline within organisations on the basis that US businesses are defrauded of more than $600 billion each year. Allard[26] maintains that organisations without reporting mechanisms, such as whistle-blower hotlines, suffer fraud-related losses that are more than twice as high as those which employ such mechanisms.

Arguably the most famous whistle-blower is Sherron Watkins who, as Vice President of Corporate Development, is credited by many as having exposed the Enron scandal in 2001. Her actions, which uncovered numerous unacceptable practices, have been an influential factor in elevating the whistle-blower to a figure who is not merely socially responsible, but who can also add value to a company.

■ Legislative support

As the perception of the whistle-blower's role has continued to improve, legislative changes have also offered support. The Sarbanes–Oxley Act, enacted in the United States in 2002, contained measures designed to protect whistle-blowers against retaliation by employers. The Whistleblower Protection Act was enacted in the United States in 2007, and was further amended in 2009. There have, however, also been setbacks in the regulatory area, with the US Supreme Court in the case of *Garcetti* v. *Ceballos* (2006) ruling that government employees did not have protection from retaliation by their employers under the First Amendment of the Constitution.

■ Results of empirical studies

Applebaum and Mosseau[27] report that 44% of non-management employees do not report misconduct that they observe. Similarly, Gurchiek[28] maintains that only 47% of individuals are likely to report unethical activities that occur in the workplace. Buckley and others[29] reported a generally positive attitude to whistle-blowing among the employees of an Irish financial services company. They also found that employees cited a sense of responsibility to their organisation as a significant reason for not whistle-blowing. This suggests that organisations need to be more active in espousing the advantages of whistle-blowing if their employees are to be convinced of its benefits.

A further finding of the same study was that female employees are more willing to whistle-blow than their male counterparts.

Corporate social reporting

Corporate social reporting (CSR) can be defined as

a concept whereby companies integrate social and environmental concerns in their business operations and in their interaction with their stakeholders on a voluntary basis. (European Commission)

CSR can help to protect the environment, conserve natural resources and encourage companies to address and resolve societal issues. It can, however, also contribute to profitability by boosting a firm's competiveness. The 2008 European Competiveness Report found that CSR can have a positive impact on six different components of competiveness: cost structure, human resources, customer perspective, innovation capacity, management of risk and reputation, and financial perfomance.[30]

In her book *Just Good Business*, Kellie McElhaney describes how Darrell Meyers, a Wal-Mart employee, suggested that light bulbs should be removed from the company's vending machines. His idea was adopted, resulting in savings of more than $1 million dollars a year.

CSR can also help to establish a reputation for good citizenship, which can be a valuable asset should a company come under critical scrutiny. An example is Starbucks which has been a target of anti-globalisation activists. Starbucks' active involvement in CSR, however, has helped to provide a defence against its detractors. This includes paying a premium for coffee beans grown on environmentally and socially responsible farms. Starbucks also makes donations to local literacy organisations, regional AIDS walks and other worthwhile causes.

The development of a CSR strategy highlights the need for companies to account to stakeholders beyond the traditional shareholder/investor grouping. These additional stakeholders are employees, suppliers, customers, the environment and society in general. As outlined above, the principal drivers of creative accounting include a desire to reduce taxation and to control dividends, both of which are designed to enhance the wealth of a firm's shareholders. As CSR results in a broadening of corporate accountability, the interests of shareholders are less likely to be pursued at the expense of other stakeholders. Consequently, as companies increase their focus on CSR this may lead to a reduction in the use of creative accounting practices.

Environmental accounting

In recent years there has been an increasing awareness of the impact of business on the world's natural resources. The destruction of the rain forests and the onset of global warming have contributed to extreme weather conditions and left several species of animals facing extinction. The widespread flooding in Australia in January 2011 is indicative of the fact that the world is facing serious climate change issues that will have to be addressed urgently.

The potential for business to seriously damage our ecosystem has been made starkly evident by the magnitude of BP's oil spill in the Gulf of Mexico in April 2010. It is feared that oil from what is America's second largest oil spill (the Exxon Valdez 1989 spill is the largest) may have serious long-term consequences for the entire Gulf region. It is believed that the undersea oil has posed a direct threat to large marine wildlife such as sharks, and also to tiny life forms such as shrimps, crabs and worms. By endangering the latter populations, which are the foundation of the marine food chain, the oil could potentially have a chronic long-term effect on the wider Gulf ecosystem.[31]

■ Disclosure of environmental information in companies' annual reports

It has become increasingly common for companies to disclose environmental information in their annual reports. This has been motivated largely by investors' concerns about the risks posed by environmental issues, such as emission levels and toxic waste management. Improved disclosure has also resulted from a realisation that a company's commitment to using renewable energy sources, rather than fossil fuels, enhances its corporate image and its long-term business prospects.

Baxter International Inc., a global healthcare company, puts environmental issues at the front of its agenda by issuing a separate Sustainability Report. In respect of its operations and products, Baxter states its priorities as follows:

1. Baxter will drive a green supply chain.
2. Baxter will drive reductions in its carbon footprint.
3. Baxter will drive reductions in its natural resource use.
4. Enhanced product stewardship.

In its 2009 Report, Baxter committed itself to the following environmental goals by the year 2015:

- Reduce the carbon footprint of Baxter's US car fleet by 20% from 2007 baseline
- Incorporate green principles into Baxter's purchasing programme with its top 100 suppliers
- Reduce greenhouse gas emissions by 45%, indexed to revenue, from 2007 baseline
- Increase energy usage of renewable power to 20% (of total)
- Reduce total waste generation by 30%, indexed to revenue, from 2005 baseline
- Reduce energy usage by 30%, indexed to revenue, from 2005 baseline
- Eliminate 5,000 tonnes of packaging material from products sent to customers
- Reduce water usage by 35%, indexed to revenue, from 2005 baseline
- Implement two projects to help protect vulnerable watersheds or provide communities with enhanced access to clean water
- Identify new opportunities to replace, reduce and refine (3Rs) the use of animal testing

Baxter's commitment to environmental sustainability is to be lauded, and the disclosures in its Sustainability Report are extremely informative. There is, however, a lack of authoritative guidance among standard setters such as the IASB regarding the disclosures that should be provided in respect of environmental issues. This leaves investors unable to adequately assess a company's exposure to environmental risks, or to carry out a reliable comparison of companies in this respect.

■ Accounting for environmental costs

To date, the IASB has dealt with environmental accounting issues in its mainstream standards. For example, IAS 36 *Impairment of Assets* and IAS 37 *Provisions, Contingent*

Liabilities and Contingent Assets refer to environmental issues. Other standards, such as IAS 16 *Property, Plant and Equipment* can also be employed to deal with issues of an environmental nature. It is likely, however, that the IASB will issue more specific reporting requirements for environmental matters in the future. This is likely to result from increased legislative requirements relating to environmental issues. For example, in the future, a company may have to obtain a certificate to verify its use of renewable energy sources.

Example 1   BP incurred a pre-tax loss of $32.2 billion relating to the Gulf of Mexico oil spill in April 2010. This included $2.9 billion in respect of costs incurred up to 30 June 2010. The balance relates to a provision for clean-up and legal settlement costs, which have been estimated on a fair value basis.

BP is of the view that it is entitled to recover $1.43 billion of the above costs from its joint venture partners. However, its joint venture partners are withholding payment of these costs pending the outcome of investigations surrounding the incident.

Outline how the above amounts should be accounted for by BP in its quarterly financial statements for the three months ended 30 June 2010.

Solution   The $2.9 billion of costs incurred up to 30 June 2010 should be recognised as an expense in the income statement of BP, and also as a liability in its statement of financial position to the extent that amounts owed are unpaid at that date.

The balance of $29.3 billion should be charged as an expense in BP's income statement, and recognised as a provision (i.e. a liability of uncertain timing or amount) in its statement of financial position. This treatment is required by IAS 37.

The total loss incurred of $32.2 billion should be separately disclosed in BP's statement of comprehensive income for the three months ended 30 June 2010.

The following journal entry will be required:

	$B	$B
Environmental costs related to Gulf of Mexico oil spill – I/S	32.2	
Bank/other creditors – SOFP		2.9
Provision for environmental costs – SOFP		29.3

There is also an amount of $1.43 billion that BP believes it is entitled to recover from its joint venture partners. However, as outlined in BP's interim financial statements for the three months ended 30 June 2010:

> Under IFRS, recovery must be virtually certain for receivables to be recognised. While BP believes that it has a contractual right to recover the partners' shares of the costs incurred, no amounts have been recognised in the financial statements.

BP's treatment concurs with the requirements of IAS 37. Although the $1.43 billion should not be recognised as income or as an asset, it may be disclosed as a contingent asset in BP's financial statements.

Example 2   Let us assume that BP paid $600 million in setting up a new oil rig in 2011. In addition it was estimated that the costs of dismantling the oil rig, on completion of drilling, would amount to $30 million on a fair value basis.

Outline how the above amounts should be accounted for by BP in its 2011 financial statements.

Solution   The oil rig should initially be recognised as a non-current asset at its cost of $600 million. However, in accordance with IAS 37, a provision should be set up for the dismantling costs, with non-current assets being increased by an equivalent amount. The following journal entry is required:

	$M	$M
Oil rig: non-current asset – SOFP	630	
Bank		600
Provision for dismantling costs – SOFP		30

Summary

The use of creative accounting practices in the corporate sector can have negative economic consequences for society. Left unchecked, creative accounting has the potential to undermine an entire economic system. This chapter outlines the reasons why companies engage in creative accounting, and provides examples of techniques that have been used in practice. It is argued that a range of measures, when used together, present the best means of preventing the practice and spread of creative accounting.

Financial reporting regulation, which is a key defence, includes both legislation and the accounting standards of bodies such as the IASB. To discourage creative accounting, regulatory requirements must also be enforced and monitored, with appropriate penalties being imposed for non-compliance. Commitment to a corporate governance code can also help, by establishing solid organisational structures, designed to discourage the use of creative accounting.

If creative accounting is to be eradicated, however, it will also be necessary to reshape corporate culture. An increased focus on ethics in education has a role to play, in emphasising the importance of integrity when making business decisions. A commitment to corporate social responsibility and to an environmentally friendly company culture can also contribute, by creating a culture of good citizenship, and a realisation that firms are accountable to a broad range of stakeholders. Finally, providing a supportive environment for whistle-blowers will ensure that when creative accounting abuses do occur, they will be exposed as early as possible.

■ References

1. Griffiths, I. (1986). *Creative Accounting*. London: Unwin Hyman Limited.

2. Akerlof, G. A. (1970). The market for lemons: quality uncertainty and the market mechanism. *Quarterly Journal of Economics*, 84, pp. 488–500.

3. Watts, R. L. and Zimmerman, J. L. (1978). Towards a positive theory of the determination of accounting standards. *The Accounting Review*, LIII (1), pp. 112–34.

4. Naser, K. H. M. (1993). *Creative Financial Accounting: Its Nature and Use*. Prentice Hall International (UK) Limited.

5. *Wall Street Journal* (2002). Elan's revenue gets a quick lift from its complicated accounting. 29 January.

6. Breton, G. and Taffler, R. (1995). Creative accounting and investment analyst response. *Accounting and Business Research*, 25 (98), pp. 81–92.

7. Munzig, P. G. (2003). Enron and the economics of corporate governance. Department of Economics, Stanford University. [Online] Available at: http://www.econ.stanford.edu

8. Coase, Ronald (1937). The nature of the firm. *Economica*, 4, 386–405.

9. Jensen, Michael and Meckling, William (1976). Theory of the firm: managerial behavior, agency costs and ownership structure, *Journal of Financial Economics*, 3, pp. 305–60.

10. Dowd, K. (2009). Moral hazard and the financial crisis. *Cato Journal*, 29 (1).

11. Cornford, A. (2004). Enron and internationally agreed principles for corporate governance and the financial sector. G-24 Discussion Paper Series, No. 30, June.

12. Johnson, S. A., Moorman, T. C. and Sorescu, S. M. (2009). A reexamination of corporate governance and equity prices with updated and supplemental results. *The Review of Financial Studies*, 22 (11), pp. 4753–786.

13. Miller, A. D. (2010). Book review. *The British Accounting Review*, 42, pp. 132–33.

14. Badaracco, J. L. (1997). *Defining Moments*. Harvard Business School Press.

15. Vassela, D. (2002). Temptation is all around us. *Fortune*, 18 November, pp. 67–71.

16. Nadler, J. and Schulman, M. (2006). www.scu.edu/ethics

17. Boatright, J. (2003). *Ethics and the Conduct of Business*. New Jersey: Prentice Hall.

18. Glazer, M. (1983). *Ten whistleblowers and how they fared. The Hastings Center Report*, 13 (6), pp. 33–41.

19. Parmerlee, M. A., Near, J. P. and Jensen, T. C. (1982). Correlates of whistleblowers' perceptions of organizational retaliation. *The Administrative Science Quarterly*, 27 (1), pp. 17–34.

20. Jos, P. H., Tompkins, M. E. and Hays, S. W. (1989). In praise of difficult people: a portrait of a committed whistleblower. *Public Administration Review*, 49 (6), pp. 552–61.

21. Zeff, S. (1978). The rise of economic consequences. *The Journal of Accountancy*, December, pp. 56–63.

22. Near, J. P. (1989). Whistleblowing: encourage it! *Business Horizons*, 32 (1), pp. 2–7.

23. Boyle, R. D. (1990). A review of whistleblower protections and suggestions for change. *Labour Law Journal*, 41 (12), pp. 821–30.

24. Paul, R. J. and Townsend, J. B. (1996). Don't kill the messenger! Whistleblowing in America – a review with recommendations. *Employee Responsibilities and Rights Journal*, 9 (2), pp. 149–60.

25. Slovin, D. (2006). Blowing the whistle. *Internal Auditor*, 63 (3), pp. 45–9.

26. Allard, J. (2006). Ethics at work. *CA Magazine*, 139 (6), pp. 30–5.

27. Applebaum, S. H. and Mousseau, H. (2006). Whistleblowing: international implications and critical cases. *The Journal of the American Academy of Business, Cambridge*, 10 (1), pp. 7–13.

28. Gurchiek, K. (2006). US workers unlikely to report office misconduct. *HR Magazine*, 51 (5), pp. 38–9.

29. Buckley, C., Cotter, D., Hutchinson, M. and O'Leary, C. (2010). Empirical evidence of lack of significant support for whistleblowing. *Corporate Ownership & Control*, 7 (3), Spring, pp. 275–83.

30. Responsible industry. *Enterprise and Energy* online magazine (29 July 2010).

31. Gauging the long-term impacts of the BP oil spill. The Editors of E/The Environmental Magazine. http://www.thedailygreen.com/environmental-news/latest/gulf-oil-spill-impacts-460610.

Appendix 6.1

An integrated framework of corporate governance principles

The Code of Governance Principles for South Africa (known as King III), which was published in September 2009, sets out an integrated framework of corporate governance. It contains the following sections:

(i) Ethical leadership and corporate citizenship
(ii) Boards and directors
(iii) Audit committees
(iv) The governance of risk
(v) The governance of information technology
(vi) Compliance with laws, codes, rules and standards
(vii) Internal audit
(viii) Governing stakeholder relationships
(ix) Integrated reporting and disclosure

(i) Ethical leadership and corporate citizenship

The board of directors should ensure that the company is a responsible corporate citizen, and that management cultivates a culture of ethical conduct. Ethics should be integrated into all company practices, procedures, policies and conduct. The company's ethics performance should be assessed, monitored and reported on.

(ii) Boards and directors

Boards should comprise a majority of non-executive directors (i.e. someone not involved in the management of the company), including an independent non-executive chairman. The board should appoint the CEO, who should be separate from the chairman. Meetings should be held at least four times per annum, and the board should ensure that there is transparent and effective communication with stakeholders on all aspects, including negative aspects, of the business. The board should appoint an audit, risk and remuneration committee.

(iii) Audit committees

The audit committee should be chaired by an independent non-executive director who is not the chairman of the board. The audit committee is responsible for ensuring that there is integrated reporting and an effective internal and external audit function. The committee should also determine annually whether the expertise, resources and experience of the finance function is appropriate. The audit committee is responsible for the appointment of the external auditor, and for developing a policy under which the external auditor may perform non-audit services.

The following is an extract from the corporate governance statement of Johnson & Johnson:

> The Audit Committee is composed solely of independent directors with the financial knowledge and experience to provide appropriate oversight. They meet regularly to review internal control matters as well as key accounting and financial reporting issues.

(iv) Governance of risk

The board is responsible for the governance of risk, and is required to approve the company's risk management policy and plan. Risk tolerance limits should be set and monitored by the board.

(v) Governance of information technology

The board should ensure that the company's IT strategy is integrated with its overall business strategy. The CEO should appoint the Chief Information Officer, who will be responsible for the management of IT. The board should monitor and evaluate material investments in IT, and ensure that significant IT projects deliver value and an appropriate return on investment. In respect of risk management, the board should be satisfied that adequate arrangements are in place for disaster recovery. The board is responsible for ensuring that information security and privacy are properly managed.

(vi) Compliance with laws, codes, rules and standards

Compliance is a board responsibility and it should be a standing agenda item. Compliance should be part of the company's risk management process. It should also be part of the culture of the company.

(vii) Internal audit

A company should establish and maintain an effective internal audit function. The evaluation of a company's corporate governance processes should be included as part of its internal audit. Internal audit should contribute to the company's goal to achieve strategic objectives, and should identify the risks that may prevent or delay the realisation of strategic goals.

The following is an extract from the corporate governance statement of Johnson & Johnson:

> Our professionally trained internal auditors travel worldwide to monitor our system of internal accounting controls. This system is designed to provide reasonable assurance that assets are safeguarded and that transactions and events are recorded properly. Our internal controls include self-assessments and internal and external audit reviews of our operation companies, which concludes with our 'Management's Report on Internal Control Over Financial Reporting', printed in our Annual Report.

(viii) Governing stakeholder relationships

Communication with stakeholders should be transparent and expressed in language that is simple and easy to understand. The board should ensure that disputes, both internal and external, are resolved effectively. Arbitration, mediation and conciliation should be considered as alternatives to legal proceedings when seeking resolution of disputes.

(ix) Integrated reporting and disclosure

In their annual report, companies should report on the operations of the company, the sustainability issues affecting the business, the financial results, and the results of its operations and cash flows. The annual report should be complete, timely, relevant, accurate, honest and accessible. It should be comparable with the company's past performance and should cover both positive and negative aspects of impacts on stakeholders.

QUESTIONS

6.1 (a) What is enviromental accounting?

(b) Why might businesses consider adopting environmental accounting as part of their accounting systems? (CPA Ireland)

6.2 Discuss the ethical responsibility of the company accountant in ensuring that manipulation of the financial statements does not occur. Your answer should focus in particular on the statement of cash flows. (Adapted from ACCA)

6.3 RIBBY Limited

RIBBY is considering selling its subsidary, Hall. Just prior to the year end, Hall sold inventory to Ribby at a price of $6 million. The carrying value of the inventory in the financial records of Hall was $2 million. The cash was received before the year end, and as a result the bank overdraft of Hall was virtually eliminiated at the year end. After the year end the transaction was reversed and it was agreed that this type of transaction would be carried out again when the interim financial statements were produced for Hall, if the company had not been sold by that date.

Required:

Discuss how the manipulation of financial statements by company accountants is inconsistent with their responsbilities as members of the accounting profession, setting out the distinguishing features of a profession and the privileges that society gives to a profession. (ACCA)

6.4 BETH Limited

BETH is currently suffering a degree of stagnation in its business development. Its domestic and international markets are being maintained, but it is not attracting new customers. Its share price has not increased, whilst that of its competitors has seen a rise of between 10 and 20%. Additionally, it has recently received a significant amount of adverse publicity because of its poor environmental record, and it is to be investigated by regulators in several countries.

Although BETH is a leading supplier of oil products, it has never felt the need to promote socially responsible policies and practices or make positive contributions to society because it has always maintained its market share. It is renowned for poor customer support, having little regard for the customs and cultures in the communities where it does business. It has recently made a decision not to pay the amounts owing to certain small and medium entities (SMEs), as the directors feel that SMEs do not have sufficient resources to challenge the non-payment in a court of law. The management of the company is quite authoritarian and tends not to value employees' ideas and contributions.

Required:

(a) Describe to the BETH Group the possible advantages of producing a separate environmental report.

(b) Discuss the corporate social responsibilities of the BETH Group and whether a change in the ethical and social attitudes of the management could improve business performance. (Adapted from ACCA)

6.5 At a recent international meeting of business leaders, Seamus O'Brien said that multi-jurisdictional attempts to regulate corporate governance were futile because of differences in national cultures. He drew particular attention to the Organisation for Economic Cooperation and Development (OECD) and the International Corporate Governance Network (IGGN) codes, saying that they were 'silly attempts to harmonise practice'. He said that in some countries, for example, there were 'family reasons' for making the chairman and chief executive the same person. In other countries, he said, the separation of these roles seemed to work. Another delegate, Alliya Yongvanich, said that the roles of chief executive and chairman should always be separated because of what she called 'accountability to shareholders'.

One delegate, Vincent Viola, said that the right approach was to allow each country to set up its own corporate governance provisions. He said it was suitable for some countries to produce and abide by their own 'very structured' corporate governance provisions, but in some other parts of the world the local culture was to allow what he called 'local interpretation of the rules'. He said that some cultures valued highly structured governance systems while others do not care as much.

Required:

(a) Explain the role of the chairman in corporate governance.

(b) Assess the benefits of the separation of the roles of chief executive and chairman that Alliya Yongvanich argued for, and explain her belief that 'accountability to shareholders' is increased by the separation of these roles.

(c) Critically evaluate Vincent Viola's view that corporate governance provisions should vary by country. (ACCA)

6.6 COUNTRYWIDE PUBLISHING Limited

COUNTRYWIDE PUBLISHING Ltd ('COUNTRYWIDE') is a family-owned newspaper publisher which has been in existence for over a century. The chairman holds a controlling stake in the company. He does not get involved in the day-to-day running of the business, and his role is confined to occasional attendance at board meetings and becoming involved in strategic matters as directed to do so by the editor.

The editor is responsible for all aspects of day-to-day management of the newspaper, including the editorial content of each issue, and she has overall responsibility for the production and distribution process. The following quote was taken from an interview with the editor:

> We need to look at our editorial content. I want to see more aggressive styles of journalism. For example, we are about to launch a new section which seeks to run exposés of the private lives of the local rich and famous.

A market intelligence report was carried out for COUNTRYWIDE, and a key finding was that the overall market position of the *Daily News* is deteriorating, with this trend accelerating on an annual basis. Of particular concern is the reduction in advertising revenue and this may be linked to the profile of the newspaper's readership. The *Daily News* reader is typically in the 45–60 age group and lives in rural Ireland. Increasingly, this is a demographic group which advertisers are less interested in targeting.

The company has entered into discussions with MEDIA KING Inc. ('MEDIA KING'), a multinational media company which is interested in expanding into the Irish market. MEDIA KING would provide funding for projects which are mutually profitable, and would acquire a percentage of COUNTRYWIDE's equity. The editor is very keen to work with MEDIA KING, and has emphasised the importance of presenting the results of the company in the best possible light in advance of any deal.

Required:

Describe *two* potential ethical issues, and set out what improvements the company should make to its corporate governance arrangements to enable it to better deal with these issues.

(Adapted from Chartered Accountants Ireland)

6.7 COMPCOM Limited

COMPCOM Ltd ('COMPCOM') is an Irish-based manufacturer of specialist computer components. The company was founded three years ago by Michael Peters and John Williams, who are both PhD graduates in electronics from a local university. The founders are fascinated by computer technology and have a strong belief in the importance of innovation and leading-edge product development. The founders are the only shareholders and the only directors of the company. No board meetings are held, and the AGM is seen as a legal formality.

Since its foundation, the company has specialised in components which are designed to enhance the performance and reliability of personal computers. Much of the technology employed was invented by the founders and was patented by them when they were at university. These patents are due to expire in two years' time.

In order to maintain their position at the leading edge of technology, the proprietors have always placed a considerable emphasis on research and development. The company currently employs 30 full-time research scientists who work closely with local universities, in converting theoretical research into working prototypes ready for the production line. Some of their more recent product designs have been sourced through close liaison with graduate students in universities.

The company sells its products to the major PC manufacturers. These companies are becoming increasingly demanding in terms of their requirements for components that are both high quality and low price. The production process requires the use of highly specialist machinery and also requires very skilled labour, since it involves very careful manual handling of materials and instant judgements regarding pressure and heat employed in the manufacturing process.

In many cases those components, which require significant manual assembly operations, are manufactured under subcontract in Third World countries. The production manager has said that he does not ask any questions about how these suppliers can deliver the product at such a low unit price. The production process generates toxic waste, which can be very expensive to dispose of. Given the increasing pressure on margins, the production manager has been using unlicensed waste disposal companies to dispose of this material.

The company founders have indicated a degree of scepticism about the value of having regular management information. They believe they get an excellent feel for the business through their hands-on involvement in day-to-day activities. At the insistence of the bank, quarterly management accounts are prepared by the auditors. The company employs a small firm of auditors, which has expressed concern about some aspects of the accounting treatment in the areas of stock valuation and accounting for research and development. However, the auditors have issued an unqualified audit opinion in each of the last three financial years.

Required:

1. What corporate governance arrangements should this company put in place?

2. Describe TWO potential ethical issues, and recommend how they should be dealt with.

(Adapted from Chartered Accountants Ireland)

6.8 BUSINESS INFORMATION SYSTEMS Ltd

BUSINESS INFORMATION SYSTEMS Ltd ('BISTEL') is an Irish registered company and a wholly owned subsidiary of CLASP Inc. ('CLASP'), which is a privately owned, US-based corporation.

Toby Jones is the owner and CEO of CLASP. He established the company 25 years ago. Over that time they have developed the market-leading financial information system 'Strategic Financial Systems' (SFS). BISTEL is the sole distributor of SFS across Ireland, and along with selling the product licences, offers clients implementation consultancy and after-sales support. They had been looking to expand the market for SFS outside of the US and so set up BISTEL a little over 3 years ago as a wholly owned subsidiary of CLASP after James Doyle (a local entrepreneur in Ireland) visited CLASP in the US during a trade mission when they agreed he would be the man to take SFS to the local market in Ireland.

James was a great help in getting the company set up, doing all the legwork. He made sure all the legal work was carried out, found the company suitable offices in a great location, and he started the promotion of the company. However, something appears to have gone seriously wrong, because over the past few years CLASP has pumped €3 million into BISTEL and have had no return on that investment.

Board members have been following James' guidance on responsibilities and duties, but are beginning to feel that they have not been doing things right. There have been no board meetings since the company was set up. Also, the board have received no financial information whatsoever from James.

BISTEL have 45 staff in total but only 11 clients. James has always insisted that the more staff they have the more impressed the guys at CLASP will be. James can be quite aggressive and domineering and does not like anyone pushing him on sales; his response is that he is well on top of it, that the sales pipeline is full and it is just a waiting game before it is all converted into contracts. The client services manager says that sales look very promising for the future; there are a lot of good quality companies that they are currently making sales proposals to. However, a lot of the staff are quite disillusioned as they see James entertaining all the time, playing golf and jetting off to international sporting events (obviously first class the whole way!) but the company seems to be getting very little in return in the way of solid work.

The company is always running new advertisements and marketing campaigns, which are being developed all the time. Staff sometimes question whether the company is sending a mixed message to the market, as it always seems to be reinventing itself. Again, this is something that James looks after personally, and he gets very touchy if pushed on it. James's wife is the owner of the advertising agency that BISTEL uses.

The company's auditor has some very serious concerns over BISTEL. They were appointed auditors in 2006 and have yet to finalise any audited accounts for the company. Consequently, they can only assume that very little of the regulatory compliance for the company has been completed – tax returns, filing of accounts, etc. They feel there is a serious lack of corporate governance and responsibility within the company.

The financial information they have received to date has been sketchy at best. They have been unable to get any payroll details whatsoever, and they suspect that the payroll taxes and social security deductions may be seriously in arrears. This is an area that James looks after himself. Another concern of the auditors is the 'trophy' building which BISTEL occupies, and the rent the company would appear to be paying. The building is state of the art and very prominent in the city. The company is currently only occupying half of the building but is paying rent for the full building. The annual rental of the building is extortionate, given other properties available in the area, and it has also come to their attention that James is an investor in the property company that owns the building that BISTEL is occupying.

Required:

1. Identify and explain any ethical issues you feel should be drawn to the attention of CLASP.

2. Detail the corporate governance arrangements that BISTEL should put in place and explain how these will counteract the ethical issues identified.

(Adapted from Chartered Accountants Ireland)

Part 4

PRESENTATION OF FINANCIAL STATEMENTS

Chapter 7

Presentation of financial statements

The purpose of financial statements is to provide information about the financial position, financial performance and cash flows of an entity that is useful for **making economic decisions**. The financial statements should also show the results of management's **stewardship** of the resources entrusted to it.

These objectives are addressed by IAS 1 *Presentation of Financial Statements*, which seeks to ensure that an entity's financial statements are comparable with previous periods and with the financial statements of other entities. IAS 1 sets out the overall framework and responsibilities for the presentation of financial statements, guidelines for their structure and minimum requirements for the content of the financial statements.

Overall considerations of IAS 1

- *Fair presentation* (i.e. financial statements are free from factual error and undue bias) and compliance with IFRS
- **Going concern** basis assumed unless otherwise stated
- **Accrual** basis of accounting
- *Materiality and aggregation* (each material class of similar items to be presented separately. Dissimilar items to be presented separately unless immaterial)
- *Comparatives* (in the financial statements and notes)
- *Offsetting* (assets and liabilities, and income and expenses not to be offset unless permitted or required by a Standard or Interpretation)
- *Frequency of reporting* (a complete set of financial statements to be presented at least annually)
- *Consistency of presentation and classification* is required from one period to the next, unless there is a change in accounting policy, or an IFRS requires a change in presentation

Components of financial statements

A complete set of financial statements should include:

- a statement of financial position at end of period
- a statement of comprehensive income for the period
- a statement of changes in equity for the period
- a statement of cash flows
- notes, comprising a summary of significant accounting policies and other explanatory information, and

- a statement of financial position as at the beginning of the earliest comparative period,* when an entity:
  - applies an accounting policy retrospectively, or
  - makes a retrospective restatement of items in its financial statements, or
  - when it reclassifies items in its financial statements

* For example, an entity preparing its financial statements, for the year ending 30 April 2010, may apply an accounting policy retrospectively. The entity will be required to prepare three statements of financial position, at the following year ends: 30 April 2010, 2009 and 2008.

Statement of financial position

An entity must present a classified **statement of financial position**, separating current and non-current assets and liabilities. Only if a presentation based on liquidity provides information that is reliable and more relevant may the current/non-current split be omitted.

Minimum items to be presented in the statement of financial position:

(a) property, plant and equipment;
(b) investment property;
(c) intangible assets;
(d) financial assets (excluding amounts shown under (e), (h) and (i));
(e) investments accounted for using the equity method;
(f) biological assets;
(g) inventories;
(h) trade and other receivables;
(i) cash and cash equivalents;
(j) total of assets classified as held for sale, and assets included in disposal groups classified as held for sale in accordance with IFRS 5.
(k) trade and other payables;
(l) provisions;
(m) financial liabilities (excluding amounts shown under (k) and (l));
(n) liabilities and assets for current tax, as defined in IAS 12;
(o) deferred tax liabilities and deferred tax assets, as defined in IAS 12;
(p) liabilities included in disposal groups, classified as held for sale;
(q) non-controlling interests, presented within equity; and
(r) issued capital and reserves attributable to equity holders of the parent.

Additional line items may be needed to fairly present the entity's financial position.

IAS 1 does not prescribe the format of the statement of financial position. For example, assets can be presented as current then non-current, or vice versa, and liabilities and equity can be presented as current then non-current, and then equity, or vice versa. A sample statement of financial position is set out below.

ABC plc

Statement of financial position at 31 December 2010

	2010	2009
	€'000	€'000
Assets		
Non-current assets		
Property, plant and equipment	7,460	5,490
Intangible assets	500	400
Investments	900	1,450
	8,860	7,340
Current assets		
Inventories	2,500	1,500
Trade and other receivables	3,000	2,500
Cash and cash equivalents	1,200	1,100
	6,700	5,100
Total assets	15,560	12,440
Liabilities		
Current liabilities		
Trade and other payables	4,350	3,460
Current tax payable	50	140
	4,400	3,600
Non-current liabilities		
Term loan	400	600
Deferred tax	100	150
Long-term provisions	700	550
	1,200	1,300
Total liabilities	5,600	4,900
Net assets	9,960	7,540
Equity capital		
Share capital	4,020	2,100
Revaluation surplus	1,800	1,400
Retained earnings	4,140	4,040
Total equity	9,960	7,540

◼ Statement of comprehensive income

An entity must present all items of income and expense recognised in a period:

(i) in a single statement of comprehensive income, or

(ii) in two statements: a separate income statement, and a second statement, beginning with profit or loss and displaying components of other comprehensive income.

Information to be presented in the statement of comprehensive income

(a) revenue;

(b) finance costs;

(c) share of the profit or loss of associates and joint ventures accounted for using the equity method;

(d) tax expense;

(e) a single amount comprising the total of:

(i) the post-tax profit or loss of discontinued operations and

(ii) the post-tax gain or loss recognised on the disposal of the assets or disposal group(s) constituting the discontinued operation;

(f) profit or loss;

(g) each component of other comprehensive income classified by nature (excluding amounts in (h));

(h) share of the other comprehensive income of associates and joint ventures accounted for using the equity method; and

(i) total comprehensive income.

Profit or loss (i.e. (f) above) and **total comprehensive income** (i.e. (i) above) should each be analysed as follows in the statement of comprehensive income:

▪ Non-controlling interests, and
▪ Owners of the parent

No items may be presented as **extraordinary items**.

When items of income or expense are material, an entity shall disclose their nature and amount separately. Circumstances that would give rise to the separate disclosure of items of income and expense include:

(a) write-downs of inventories to net realisable value, or of property, plant and equipment to their recoverable amount, as well as reversals of such write-downs;

(b) restructurings of the activities of an entity and reversals of any provisions for the costs of restructuring;

(c) disposals of items of property, plant and equipment;

(d) disposals of investments;

(e) discontinuing operations;

(f) litigation settlements; and

(g) other reversals of provisions.

Expenses should be analysed either by nature (depreciation, purchases of materials, etc.) or by function (cost of sales, selling, administrative, etc.).

IAS 1 does not prescribe an exact format for the statement of comprehensive income. A sample statement is set out below, containing a single statement of comprehensive income.

ABC plc
Statement of comprehensive income for the year ended 31 December 2010

	2010 €'000	2009 €'000
Revenue	9,100	7,800
Cost of sales	(7,230)	(5,790)
Gross profit	1,870	2,010
Distribution costs	(700)	(600)
Administrative expenses	(250)	(200)
Other expenses	(150)	(140)
Finance costs	(600)	(560)
Profit before tax	170	510
Income tax expense	(50)	(140)
Profit for the year from continuing operations	120	370
Other comprehensive income		
Revaluation surplus	400	300
Total comprehensive income for the year	520	670

All profit and total comprehensive income is attributable to the owners of the parent.

■ Statement of changes in equity

A **statement of changes in equity** (SOCIE) shows how the amount of an entity's equity has changed during the period. The SOCIE should contain the following information:

(i)   Total comprehensive income for the period.

(ii) For each component of equity, the effects of any retrospective application or retrospective restatement recognised in accordance with IAS 8.

(iii) For each component of equity, a reconciliation between the carrying amount at the beginning and the end of the period, separately disclosing changes resulting from:

   ■ profit or loss;
   ■ other comprehensive income; and
   ■ transactions with owners, showing separately distributions (e.g. dividends) and contributions by owners (e.g. shares issued).

An entity shall present, either in the SOCIE or in the notes, the amount of dividends recognised as distributions to owners during the period and the related amount of dividends per share.

A sample SOCIE is outlined below.

ABC plc
Statement of changes in equity for the year ended 31 December 2010

	Share capital €'000	Retained earnings €'000	Revaluation surplus €'000	Total equity €'000
Balance at 1 January 2009	2,100	2,700	1,100	5,900
Changes in accounting policy	–	1,000	–	1,000
Restated balance	2,100	3,700	1,100	6,900
Changes in equity for 2009				
Dividends	–	(30)	–	(30)
Total comprehensive income for the year	–	370	300	670
Balance at 31 December 2009	2,100	4,040	1,400	7,540
Changes in equity for 2010				
Issue of share capital	1,920	–	–	1,920
Dividends	–	(20)		(20)
Total comprehensive income for the year	–	120	400	520
Balance at 31 December 2010	4,020	4,140	1,800	9,960

■ Notes to the financial statements

The notes must:

■ present information about the basis of preparation of the financial statements and the specific accounting policies used;

■ disclose the information required by IFRSs, or that is necessary to understand the financial statements, which is not presented elsewhere.

IAS 1 states that the notes are normally presented in the following order:

- statement of compliance with IFRSs;
- summary of significant accounting policies;
- supporting information for items presented in the SOFP, the statement of comprehensive income, the separate income statement (if presented), the SOCIE and the statement of cash flows;
- other disclosures, including:
  - contingent liabilities (see IAS 37) and unrecognised contractual commitments; and
  - non-financial disclosures (e.g. the entity's financial risk management objectives and policies – see IFRS 7).

■ Sources of estimation uncertainty

An entity must disclose information regarding its assumptions about the future, and other major sources of estimation uncertainty at the end of the reporting period. This does not involve the disclosure of budget information or forecasts.

■ Capital

An entity must disclose information that enables users of its financial statements to evaluate the entity's objectives, policies and processes for managing capital.

■ Dividends

An entity must disclose the amount of **dividends** proposed or declared before the financial statements were authorised for issue but not recognised as a distribution to owners during the period, and the related amount per share.

■ Other disclosures

An entity should disclose the following, if not disclosed elsewhere in the financial statements:

- domicile and legal form of the entity;
- country of incorporation;
- address of registered office;
- description of the nature of the entity's operations and principal activities;
- name of the parent and ultimate parent if the entity is part of a group; and
- if it is a limited life entity, information regarding the length of its life.

Summary

IAS 1 prescribes the basis for the presentation of general purpose financial statements. The overall objective of the Standard is to ensure that an entity's financial statements are comparable with previous periods and with the financial statements of other entities. IAS 1 specifies the components of a complete set of financial statements and outlines their required presentation and contents.

QUESTIONS

7.1 WHITE plc

The trial balance of WHITE plc at 31 December 2010 was as follows:

	Dr €	Cr €
Purchases	321,700	
Revenue		552,600
Inventory at 1 January 2010	22,300	
Office expenses	5,630	
Returns outwards		4,670
Returns inwards	2,450	
Distribution expenses	32,870	
Admin expenses	61,230	
Wages and salaries	74,000	
Buildings (cost)	150,000	
Equipment (cost)	70,000	
Motor vehicles (cost)	85,000	
Accumulated depreciation of buildings		11,600
Accumulated depreciation equipment		27,500
Accumulated depreciation motor vehicles		29,250
Trade receivables	46,800	
Trade payables		34,200
Retained earnings 1 January 2010		9,870
6% Debentures		50,000
Share capital (150,000 €1 ordinary shares)		150,000
Bank		2,290
	871,980	871,980

The following information is available, none of which has been taken into account in the preparation of the trial balance above:

(a) Inventory at 31 December 2010 was purchased for €30,000. Included in this amount is inventory which cost €10,000 and has a net realisable value of €2,000.

(b) Vehicles are used for distribution. Buildings usage is divided equally between distribution and administration. Equipment is used for administration purposes.

(c) Buildings are to be depreciated annually at 1% straight line, equipment at 20% straight line, and vehicles at 25% reducing balance.

(d) Equipment was sold on 31 December 2010 for €15,000. This has been credited to revenue. The original cost was €20,000 and it had been purchased on 31 December 2008. Except for cash and revenue, no further entries have been made in the books.

(e) Bad debts of €2,600 are to be written off, and a provision for bad debts at the rate of 5% is to be introduced.

(f) Taxation for the year is estimated at €9,860.

(g) Accruals of €3,500 for administration expenses are required, and prepayments of €5,600 have been identified within distribution expenses.

(h) The interest on the debentures has not yet been paid.

Required:

(a) Show the necessary entries which are required based on the information in (a) to (h) above.

(b) Prepare a statement of comprehensive income and a statement of financial position for WHITE plc for the year ended 31 December 2010, in accordance with IAS 1.

Chapter 8

Statement of cash flows

Profit is a measure of the long-term success of a business. Over time, profit provides funds to repay loans, invest in an entity's asset infrastructure, and to provide a return to shareholders in the form of a dividend.

In the short term, however, a firm's survival is far more dependent on having adequate **cash resources** than on its ability to generate profits. The fact that a business is profitable in fact is no guarantee that it will remain solvent.

Example 1   Bramble Limited had an opening cash balance of €20,000 on 1 December 2010. Sales for December amounted to €200,000, all of which were on credit. Goods costing €100,000 were purchased in December, half of which were paid for during the month. Bramble incurred expenses of €50,000 for December, of which €15,000 was unpaid at 31 December. There was no opening or closing inventory.

Calculate Bramble Limited's profit for December 2010 and its cash balance at the end of the month.

Solution   Bramble's **profit** for December can be calculated as follows:

	€'000
Revenue	200
Cost of sales	(100)
Gross profit	100
Expenses	(50)
Profit before tax	50

Bramble's **cash surplus/deficit** for December is computed as follows:

	€'000
Receipts	–
Payments:	
Cash purchases	(50)
Expenses	(35)
Cash deficit for the month	(85)

Bramble has earned a profit of €50,000 for December, yet its cash balance has fallen by €85,000. Having begun the month with a cash balance of €20,000, at 31 December Bramble is overdrawn by €65,000.

The reason why Bramble's profit for December was €135,000 greater than its net cash flow relates to the fact that the income statement is prepared on an accrual basis. Thus, revenue is recorded when sales are invoiced, rather than when cash is received from customers.

79

Other business transactions also affect cash flow and profits in different ways:

- the full cost of **non-current** assets purchased (e.g. machinery) has an immediate impact on cash flow, but is deducted from profit as depreciation over the life of the asset;
- an increase in inventories results in a negative cash flow for a business, but has no impact on profit;
- payments to stakeholders (e.g. dividends and the capital element of loan repayments) reduce a firm's cash balance but do not affect profit.

IAS 7 *Statement of Cash Flows* requires entities to provide information about the historical changes in cash and cash equivalents in a statement of cash flows.

Definitions

The following terms are defined by IAS 7:

- *Cash* comprises cash on hand and demand deposits;
- *Cash equivalents* are short-term, highly liquid investments, that are readily convertible to known amounts of cash, and which are subject to an insignificant risk of changes in value.

An investment normally qualifies as a cash equivalent only when it has a short maturity of, say, three months or less from the date of acquisition.

Presentation of a statement of cash flows

IAS 7 requires that the statement of cash flows should report cash flows during the period, classified into the following activities:

- operating
- investing
- financing

Operating activities

Operating activities are the principal revenue-producing activities of an entity, and other activities that are not investing or financing activities. Examples of cash flows relating to operating activities are receipts from customers and payments to suppliers.

Investing activities

Investing activities are the acquisition and disposal of long-term assets and other investments not included in cash equivalents. Examples of cash flows from investing activities are:

- cash payments to acquire property, plant and equipment and intangibles;
- cash receipts from the sale of property, plant and equipment and intangibles;
- cash payments to acquire equity or debt instruments of other entities, and joint ventures;
- cash advances and loans made to other parties.

■ Financing activities

Financing activities are activities that result in changes in the size and composition of the equity and borrowings of an entity. Examples of cash flows arising from financing activities are:

- cash proceeds from the issue of shares or other equity instruments;
- cash payments to owners to acquire or redeem the entity's shares;
- cash proceeds from issuing **debentures**, loans and other short or long-term borrowings;
- cash repayment of amounts borrowed.

Reporting cash flows

In a statement of cash flows, cash flows are reported separately as follows.

■ Reporting cash flows from operating activities

IAS 7 requires an entity to report cash flows from operating activities, using either:

(i) the **direct method**, whereby major classes of gross cash receipts and gross cash payments are disclosed; or

(ii) the **indirect method**, whereby profit or loss is adjusted for the effects of transactions of a non-cash nature, any deferrals or accruals of past or future operating cash receipts or payments, and items of income or expense associated with investing or financing cash flows.

Entities are encouraged by IAS 7 to report cash flows from operating activities using the direct method.

■ Reporting cash flows from investing and financing activities

IAS 7 requires that an entity should report separately most major classes of gross cash receipts and gross cash payments arising from investing and financing activities.

Statement of cash flows – an example

The statement of comprehensive income of Bramble Limited for the year ended 31 December 2010 is presented below. The statement of financial position of Bramble at 31 December 2010 is also shown.

Prepare a statement of cash flows for the year ended 31 December 2010, using:

(a) the direct method, and
(b) the indirect method.

Statement of comprehensive income of Bramble Ltd
for the year ended 31 December 2010

	2010 €'000
Revenue	1,800
Cost of sales	(950)
Gross profit	850
Distribution costs	(120)
Administrative expenses	(80)
Other expenses	(100)
Finance costs	(20)
Profit before tax	530
Income tax expense	(148)
Profit for the year from continuing operations	382

Statement of financial position of Bramble Ltd at 31 December 2010

	2010 €'000	2009 €'000
Assets		
Non-current assets		
Property, plant and equipment	1,693	555
Intangible assets	250	250
	1,943	805
Current assets		
Inventories	269	240
Trade receivables	395	322
Cash and cash equivalents	155	130
	819	692
Liabilities		
Current liabilities		
Trade payables	212	182
Accrued interest	5	3
Current tax payable	148	130
	365	315
Non-current liabilities		
Term loan	120	135
Net assets	2,277	1,047
Equity		
Share capital	270	100
Share premium	1,150	402
Revaluation reserve	80	80
Retained earnings	777	465
Total equity	2,277	1,047

The following information is available:

(i) Cost of sales includes depreciation of €60,000.

(ii) There were no disposals of non-current assets during 2010.

(iii) Expenses in the statement of comprehensive income include the following payments to employees:

- cost of sales €250,000
- distribution €25,000
- administration €20,000

(iv) A dividend of €70,000 was paid in March 2010.

Solution

(a) **Statement of cash flows for the year ended 31 December 2010 (*direct* method)**

	€'000	€'000
Cash flows from operating activities		
Cash receipts from customers (i)	1,727	
Cash paid to suppliers (iii)	(894)	
Cash paid to employees	(295)	
Cash generated from operations	538	
Interest paid (iv)	(18)	
Income tax paid (v)	(130)	
Net cash flow from operating activities		390
Cash flows from investing activities		
Purchase of property, plant and equipment (vi)		(1,198)
Cash flows from financing activities		
Proceeds from issue of share capital (vi)	918	
Repayment of long-term loan	(15)	
Dividends paid	(70)	
Net cash flow from financing activities		833
Net increase in cash and cash equivalents		25
Cash and cash equivalents at 1 January 2010		130
Cash and cash equivalents at 31 December 2010		155

Workings

(i) *Cash receipts from customers* are computed as revenue + opening trade receivables – closing trade receivables (i.e. 1.8M + 322,000 – 395,000).

(ii) *Purchases* are equal to cost of sales (excluding depreciation) + closing inventory – opening inventory – amounts paid to employees included in cost of sales (i.e. 890,000 + 269,000 – 240,000 – 250,000).

(iii) *Cash paid to suppliers of goods and services* equals purchases + distribution, administrative and other expenses (excluding wages and salaries) + opening trade payables – closing trade payables (i.e. 669,000 + 255,000 + 182,000 – 212,000).

(iv) *Interest paid* is the amount of interest payable for the year, less accrued interest at the year end + opening accrued interest (i.e. 20,000 – 5,000 + 3,000).

(v) *Income tax paid* is the tax charged for the year + opening tax liability – closing tax liability (i.e. 148,000 + 130,000 – 148,000).

(vi) *Property, plant and equipment purchased* equals closing PPE – opening PPE + depreciation charge for year (i.e. 1.693M – 555,000 + 60,000).

(vii) *Proceeds from issue of share capital* equals closing share capital – opening share capital + increase in share premium (i.e. 270,000 – 100,000 + 748,000).

(b) Statement of cash flows for the year ended 31 December 2010 (*indirect* method)

	€'000	€'000
Cash flows from operating activities		
Profit before taxation	530	
Adjustments for:		
Depreciation	60	
Interest expense	20	
	610	
Increase in trade receivables	(73)	
Increase in inventories	(29)	
Increase in trade payables	30	
Cash generated from operations	538	
Interest paid	(18)	
Income tax paid	(130)	
Net cash from operating activities		390
Cash flows from investing activities		
Purchase of property, plant and equipment		(1,198)
Cash flows from financing activities		
Proceeds from issue of share capital	918	
Repayment of long-term loan	(15)	
Dividends paid	(70)	
Net cash flow from financing activities		833
Net increase in cash and cash equivalents	25	
Cash and cash equivalents at 1 January 2010	130	
Cash and cash equivalents at 31 December 2010	155	

Disclosures

IAS 7 requires an entity to disclose:

- the components of cash and cash equivalents;
- a reconciliation of the amounts in its statement of cash flows with the equivalent items reported in the statement of financial position;
- the amount of significant cash and cash equivalent balances held by an entity that is not available for use by the group.

Summary

IAS 7 requires that entities prepare a statement of cash flows to provide information about changes in cash and cash equivalents. The Standard requires cash flows to be classified into the following activities:

- operating
- investing
- financing

IAS 7 permits an entity to report cash flows from operating activities using either the direct method or the indirect method.

QUESTIONS

8.1 SMITH Limited
The following information has been extracted from the financial statements of SMITH Limited:

Statement of financial position at:

	31/12/2010		31/12/2009	
	€'000	€'000	€'000	€'000
Non-current assets				
Buildings	750		750	
Vehicles	1,200		925	
Accumulated depreciation – vehicles	(565)		(535)	
		1,385		1,140
Current assets				
Inventory	32		25	
Trade receivables	90		65	
Cash	15		35	
Investments	25		12	
Interest receivable	39		25	
	201		162	
Current liabilities				
Trade payables	180		145	
Bank overdraft	25		50	
Interest payable	21		14	
	226		209	
Net current liabilities		(25)		(47)
		1,360		1,093
Non-current liabilities				
Debentures		(500)		(400)
12% Preference Shares		(75)		(75)
Net assets		785		618
Share capital and reserves				
Ordinary share capital		670		620
Share premium account		100		75
Retained profit/(loss)		15		(77)
		785		618

Statement of comprehensive income for the year ended 31/12/2010

	€'000	€'000
Revenue		750
Cost of sales		(480)
Gross profit		270
Operating expenses		(150)
Operating profit		120
Interest payable	(18)	
Interest receivable	30	12
Profit for the year		132

Additional information:

1. The investment represents a 30-day government bond.
2. The additional debentures were acquired by the firm on 1/1/2010.
3. Motor vehicles were disposed of during the year for €290,000. These vehicles had a net book value of €320,000 at the disposal date.
4. Dividends of €40,000 were paid during 2010.
5. Depreciation charged for the year amounted to €30,000.

Required:

(a) Prepare a statement of cash flows for SMITH Ltd for the year ended 31/12/2010, using the indirect method.

(b) Based upon the information provided in the question, and your answer to part (a) above, critically assess SMITH Ltd's cash-flow position *and* overall performance for 2010. What advice would you offer to the firm's management?

8.2 ROMA Limited

ROMA Limited's statement of comprehensive income for the year ended 31 December 2010 and the statements of financial position at 31 December 2009 and 2010 are as follows:

Statement of comprehensive income for the year ended 31 December 2010

	€'000
Revenue	1,878
Less: cost of sales	−1,224
Gross profit	654
Other operating income	66
Operating expenses	−276
Operating profit	444
Investment income	54
Profit before interest and tax	498
Less: interest payable	−72
Profit before tax	426
Taxation	−138
Profit for year	288
Retained earnings brought forward from last year	78
Retained earnings carried forward	366

Statement of financial position at 31 December

	2010 €'000	2009 €'000
Non-current assets		
Land and buildings	720	720
Plant and equipment	978	930
	1,698	1,650
Current assets		
Inventories	126	132
Trade receivables	420	360
	546	492
Total assets	2,244	2,142

	2010 €'000	2009 €'000
Equity		
Ordinary shares	726	444
Retained earnings	366	78
	1,092	522
Non-current liabilities		
Debentures	750	1,200
Current liabilities		
Bank overdraft (repayable on demand)	168	204
Trade payables	162	168
Corporation tax	72	48
	402	420
Total equity and liabilities	**2,244**	**2,142**

Note: During 2010, the business spent €120,000 on additional plant and machinery. There were no other acquisitions or disposals of non-current assets.

Required:
Prepare a cash flow statement for Roma Limited for the year ended 31 December 2010 in accordance with IAS 7.

8.3 ALEXI Limited

The financial statements of ALEXI Limited for the year ended 31 December 2010 are set out below:

Statement of financial position at:

	31.12.2010		31.12.2009	
Non-current assets (NBV)				
Buildings	1,249,000		648,200	
Other	204,600		152,900	
Investments	284,000	1,737,600	72,000	873,100
Current assets				
Inventory	166,800		144,800	
Trade receivables	97,500		128,600	
Bank	–		200	
	264,300		273,600	
Current liabilities				
Trade payables	70,960		84,940	
Taxation	25,000		37,000	
Dividends	76,000		50,000	
Bank overdraft	33,000		–	
	204,960		171,940	
Net current assets		59,340		101,660
Total assets less current liabilities		1,796,940		974,760
Non-current liabilities				
5% Debentures		300,000		90,000
Net assets		1,496,940		884,760
Equity and reserves				
€1 Ordinary shares		1,240,000		700,000
Share premium		68,000		–
Revaluation surplus		140,000		100,000
Retained earnings		48,940		84,760
		1,496,940		884,760

Statement of comprehensive income for the year ended 31 December (Extract)

	2010	2009
Profit before tax	65,180	167,200
Taxation	(25,000)	(37,000)
Profit after tax	40,180	130,200

Additional information:

(i) A market issue of shares was made on 1 January 2010.

(ii) Dividends received amount to €17,000 and interest received €24,000 during 2010, both of which had been credited to the income statement.

(iii) The debentures were issued on 1 January 2010 and all interest due had been paid.

(iv) Buildings costing €800,000 had been purchased during 2010 and the depreciation charged for 2010 on other assets was €50,000. The only assets revalued during the year were the buildings.

(v) During 2010 equipment originally purchased at €110,400 was sold for €43,800, accumulated depreciation being €55,400. The difference on disposal had been taken to the income statement.

(vi) Dividends of €76,000 were proposed and ratified during the period.

Required:

Prepare a statement of cash flows for ALEXI Limited in accordance with IAS 7.

Chapter 9

Accounting policies, changes in accounting estimates and errors

If financial statements are to be useful for decision-making purposes, and for evaluating management's stewardship of an entity's resources, they must be prepared on a consistent basis from one period to the next. Should an entity change its method of inventory valuation from FIFO to weighted average cost in the current period, for example, it may also be necessary to adjust the inventory of previous periods for comparability purposes.

Similarly, a material error relating to a prior period may need to be amended retrospectively, as it could otherwise distort the comparison of **financial statements** over time.

IAS 8 addresses all of the above issues.

Overview

IAS 8 prescribes the criteria for selecting and changing accounting policies. It also deals with changes in accounting estimates and corrections of errors. A key objective of IAS 8 is to increase the comparability of an entity's financial statements over time and with the financial statements of other entities.

Accounting policies

Accounting policies are those principles, bases, conventions, rules and practices applied by an entity in preparing and presenting financial statements.

When an IFRS specifically applies to a transaction, the accounting policy or policies applied to that item are determined by applying that IFRS.

In essence, accounting policies involve:

- recognising
- selecting measurement bases for, and
- presenting

assets, liabilities, gains, losses and changes to equity.

Example 1 Cherry Limited commenced the construction of a new head office building on 1 January 2010. The building was completed on 30 November 2010. Cherry Limited incurred interest costs of €75,000 on funds raised to finance the construction. These interest costs related to the period 1 January 2010–30 November 2010.

Outline how Cherry Limited should account for the interest costs incurred in relation to its new head office building.

Solution   IAS 23 *Borrowing Costs* requires that an entity shall capitalise borrowing costs that are directly attributable to the construction of a qualifying asset as part of the cost of the asset. Therefore, the required *accounting policy* is to **recognise** the interest as an asset. Consequently, interest costs of €75,000 should be capitalised as part of the cost of the new head office building as follows:

	Dr €'000	Cr €'000
Buildings	75	
Bank		75

In the absence of an IFRS that specifically applies to a transaction, management should use its judgement to develop an accounting policy which results in information that is relevant and reliable. In making such judgements, management should refer to:

- the requirements in IFRSs dealing with similar and related issues; and
- the definitions, recognition criteria and measurement concepts for assets, liabilities, income and expenses in the IASB framework.

Management may also consider the most recent pronouncements of other standard-setting bodies that use a similar conceptual framework, to the extent that these do not conflict with IASB sources.

■ Consistency of accounting policies

IAS 8 requires that an entity should apply its accounting policies consistently, unless different policies are permitted or required for a category of items.

Example 2   Cherry Limited valued its inventory on a first-in-first-out (FIFO) basis in its financial statements for 2009 and in previous years. Therefore, Cherry Limited should continue to value its inventory on a FIFO basis in its 2010 financial statements, as this has been the **measurement basis** used in previous periods.

Example 3   Cherry Limited has acquired a majority 75% stake in a number of subsidiary companies during 2010. Explain how the non-controlling interest in these subsidiaries should be measured in the consolidated financial statements of the Cherry Group.

Solution   IFRS 3 *Business Combinations* gives an acquirer a choice of measuring any non-controlling interest in an acquiree at acquisition date:

- at fair value; or
- at the non-controlling interest's proportionate share of the acquiree's identifiable net assets.

This choice is available for each business combination separately. Thus, Cherry can choose between two accounting policies when **measuring** non-controlling interest in each of its subsidiaries.

■ Changes in accounting policy

An entity is permitted to change an accounting policy only if the change:

- is required by an IFRS; or
- results in the financial statements providing reliable and more relevant information.

Example 4   Cherry Limited has previously shown certain overheads within cost of sales. It now proposes to show those overheads within administrative expenses, on the basis that the information provided in the financial statements will be more relevant.

Does this involve a change in:

Recognition	No – the overheads are still being recognised as expenses
Presentation	Yes – the overheads are now being presented within administrative expenses
Measurement basis	No – measurement is still on a historical cost basis

Although there is no change to the recognition and measurement basis of costs, they are being **presented** differently in the income statement. As a positive answer to any of the above three questions will suffice, this is therefore a change in accounting policy.

The following are **not** changes in accounting policy:

- The application of an accounting policy for transactions, other events or conditions that differ in substance from those previously occurring. See Example 5 below.
- Applying an accounting policy to a transaction or event that did not exist in the past.
- A change in the method of depreciation.

Additionally, the initial application of a new accounting policy to revalue assets in accordance with IAS 16 *Property, Plant and Equipment* or IAS 38 *Intangible Assets* should be dealt with under the rules of those standards.

Example 5   Cherry Limited purchased a building in 2008 for €2.5M. The building, which was used by company personnel, was included in the financial statements at cost. In December 2010, the building was vacated and was let to an unrelated party at a market rental. The building is included in the financial statements at 31 December 2010 at its fair value of €4M.

Outline how the building should be accounted for by Cherry Limited in its financial statements.

Solution   The building should be reclassified as investment property at 31 December 2010, and as Cherry Limited is employing the revaluation model it should be stated at fair value in accordance with IAS 40 *Investment Property*.

The question arises as to whether the revised treatment constitutes a change in accounting policy. IAS 40 states that owner-occupied property does not qualify as investment property. Therefore, in its 2008 and 2009 financial statements, Cherry Limited was precluded from classifying the building as investment property. In December 2010, however, following its rental to a third party, the building for the first time satisfies the qualifying conditions of IAS 40.

Thus, in reclassifying the building as investment property at 31 December 2010, Cherry Limited is merely responding to the fact that the building is now different in substance. Therefore, its reclassification as investment property is *not* a change in accounting policy.

■ Applying changes in accounting policies

An entity shall account for a change in accounting policy resulting from the initial application of an IFRS in accordance with the specific **transitional provisions**, if any, in that IFRS. Otherwise, an entity should apply the change **retrospectively**. Thus, retrospective application will apply when there are no specific transitional provisions, or where an entity changes an accounting policy voluntarily.

*Retrospective application means adjusting the following on the basis of the new accounting policy:**

- the opening balance of each affected component of equity for the earliest prior period presented; and
- the other comparative amounts disclosed for each period presented;
- providing an additional statement of financial position at the beginning of the earliest comparative period presented (required by IAS 1 *Presentation of Financial Statements*).

* If full retrospective application is not practicable, the entity should apply the new policy at the beginning of the earliest period for which retrospective application is practicable.

Example 6 Ripe Limited has traditionally valued its inventory on a weighted average cost basis. However, on 31 December 2010 it has decided to instead adopt a FIFO basis of valuation. Ripe Limited's inventory was included in its financial statements, on a weighted average cost basis, in previous years as follows:

31 December 2009	€8M
31 December 2008	€5M

It was estimated that the use of FIFO leads to an increase of 20% in the valuation of closing inventory of Ripe Limited in 2008 and 2009. No difference arises in respect of earlier periods.

Required:

(i) Outline the accounting treatment which should be applied by Ripe Limited in respect of its change in inventory valuation. Ignore tax.

(ii) Provide an extract from the statement of changes in equity of Ripe Limited for the year ended 31 December 2010.

(iii) Show the journal entry required at 31 December 2009 to give effect to your recommendation.

Solution As the use of FIFO represents a change in the **measurement basis** employed for inventory valuation, it constitutes a change in accounting policy. In accordance with IAS 8, the retrospective application of FIFO is therefore required. This will have the following effect:

	2008	2009
Opening inventory ↑	–	€1M
Purchases ↑	–	–
Closing inventory ↑	€1M*	€1.6M†
Thus, cost of sales ↓, and retained earnings ↑	€1M	€.6M

* €5M × 20%
† €8M × 20%

Retrospective application is effected as follows.

(a) Adjust the opening balance of each affected component of equity:

This will be reflected in Ripe Limited's statement of changes in equity as follows:

Extract from statement of changes in equity for the year ended 31 December 2010

	Share capital	Retained earnings	Total equity
Balance at 1 January 2009	X	Y	X + Y
Change in accounting policy		€1M	€1M
Restated balance	X	Y + €1M	X + Y + €1M
Changes in equity for 2009			
Dividends			
Total comprehensive income for the year		Z‡	
Balance at 31 December 2009			
Changes in equity for 2010			
Dividends			
Total comprehensive income for the year			
Balance at 31 December 2010			

‡ Includes adjustment of + €.6M in respect of change to FIFO

(b) Comparative amounts for 2009.

(i) *Statement of comprehensive income for year ended 31 December 2009*
- Cost of sales will be decreased by €.6M, with a consequent increase in profit of €.6M

(ii) *Statement of financial position as at 31 December 2009*
- Inventory will be increased by €1.6M
- Retained earnings will be increased by €1.6M

(c) An additional statement of financial position should be presented as at 1 January 2009 in accordance with IAS 1 *Presentation of Financial Statements.*

(d) Journal entry at 31 December 2009.

	Dr €'000	Cr €'000
Inventory	1,600	
Retained earnings		1,600
(Being effect of change in accounting policy at 31 December 2009)		

■ How does management decide what accounting policies to use?

If a particular accounting treatment is required by the IASB, there is no policy choice to be exercised by management. For example, IAS 2 requires that inventory be valued at the lower of cost and net realisable value. This is the required treatment, and no other alternative is permitted.

Sometimes, however, management does have to exercise a choice. For example, IAS 40 permits investment property to be valued either at cost or **fair value**. Investment property is property that is held to earn rental income or capital appreciation or both (see Chapter 15 for a full discussion of investment property).

Example 7   Seed Limited purchased investment property 'A' on 1 January 2011 for €1.5M. The fair value of property 'A' on 31 December 2011 is €2M. Seed Limited does not own other investment property.

If Seed Limited records investment property at fair value, its profit for 2011 will increase by €.5M, due to the rise in value of property 'A'. However, if property 'A' is valued at cost, no increase in profit will be recorded during 2011.

The impact of alternative accounting treatments on a firm's profit may be the key to understanding how management chooses its accounting policies. In Example 7 above, if Seed Limited wants to report higher profits, it will record property 'A' at fair value. If Seed Limited wishes profits to be lower, property 'A' will be recorded at cost.

Why, we might ask, would the management of a firm want profit to be higher, or indeed to be lower? **Positive accounting theory (PAT)** puts forward three hypotheses in an effort to answer that question:

(i)   *Bonus plan hypothesis*: Management are likely choose accounting policies that increase profit, when their bonus is at least partially based on the profit figure. This hypothesis is presented in Figure 9.1.

(ii)   *Size hypothesis*: Very large firms will use accounting policies that reduce profit, when excessive profits might attract government price controls, taxation levies, etc.

(iii)   *Debt/equity hypothesis*: Firms with a high level of debt will use accounting policies that increase profit. This increases the likelihood that profits will be sufficient to cover interest charges, thereby avoiding penalties that would otherwise be imposed by the firm's bank.

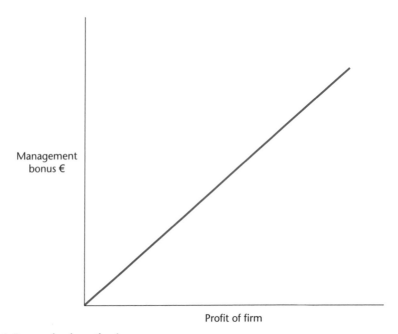

Figure 9.1 **Bonus plan hypothesis**

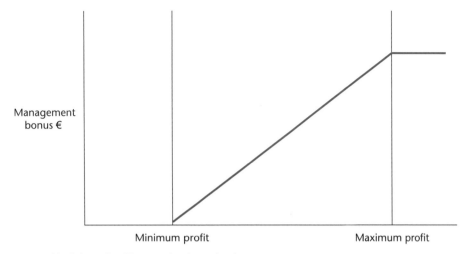

Figure 9.2 **Healy's revised bonus plan hypothesis**

■ Does PAT provide a valid explanation of how firms choose their accounting policies?

Tests of the theory have been supportive, but the results have not proved conclusive. PAT has also been refined since it was first put forward by Watts and Zimmerman[1] in 1978. For example, in 1985 Healy[2] published a research paper which showed that management bonuses may not always be maximised by increasing a firm's profit figure. Healy explains how in some remuneration schemes:

■ a bonus is only paid when a minimum profit figure is achieved; and
■ no additional bonus is paid after a firm's profit reaches a specified maximum level.

Healy's revised explanation of the bonus plan hypothesis is outlined in Figure 9.2.

Figure 9.2 illustrates how management bonuses remain at zero until the firm's profit exceeds a specified minimum level. Once profit reaches a maximum level, no *additional* bonuses are paid.

Thus, there is **no** incentive for management to use accounting policies to increase profit when:

■ a firm's profit is less than the minimum, and management is unable to raise it above that level; or
■ when a firm's profit is already in excess of the maximum level.

Although positive accounting theory does not appear to always work in practice, it nonetheless provides us with an insight into the decision criteria used by management in choosing a firm's accounting policies. The theory requires further refinement, however, before it can be relied on to accurately predict accounting policy choice.

Changes in accounting estimates

Many items in financial statements cannot be measured with precision, and must therefore be estimated. For example, estimates may be required of:

- bad debts;
- inventory obsolescence;
- the fair value of financial assets or financial liabilities;
- the future lives of, or expected pattern of consumption of, the future economic benefits embodied in depreciable assets.

A change in accounting estimate involves an adjustment of:

- the carrying amount of an asset or a liability; or
- the amount of the periodic consumption of an asset.

Changes in accounting estimate result from *new information or new developments*, and they are *not* therefore corrections of errors.

■ Accounting treatment

The effect of a change in an accounting estimate should be recognised prospectively by including it in profit or loss in:

- the period of the change, if the change affects that period only; or
- the period of the change and future periods, if the change affects both

Additionally, where a change in an accounting estimate gives rise to changes in assets and liabilities, or relates to an item of equity, it is recognised by adjusting the relevant statement of financial position item in the period of the change.

Example 8   Cherry Limited purchased a machine on 1 January 2008 for €300,000. The machine was depreciated at 10% per annum on a straight-line basis. During 2010, developments in the marketplace meant that the product manufactured by the machine would become obsolete after the end of 2012.

Outline how the depreciation of the machine should be adjusted by Cherry Limited in its financial statements for the year ended 31 December 2010.

Solution   The machine was depreciated by €30,000 in 2008 and 2009, resulting in a net book value of €240,000 at 31 December 2009. New information, however, has resulted in the machine having a further useful life of only three years from 1 January 2010.

This is a change in an accounting estimate, as it relates to a change in the amount of periodic consumption of an asset. The net book value of the machine at 1 January 2010 should be depreciated over its remaining useful life of three years. Therefore, the annual depreciation charge should be adjusted to €80,000 for 2010–2012. In the SOFP, there will be a consequent adjustment of the amount of equity and the net book value of the machine.

Errors

All *material* prior period errors must be corrected retrospectively in the first set of financial statements authorised for issue after their discovery. An error is material if, due to its nature or size, its omission could influence the economic decisions of users of financial statements.

Example 9   Cherry Limited has invested a substantial amount of resources in promoting its brand names over the last five years. These amounts were capitalised as an intangible asset in the year in which the expenditure was incurred. At 31 December 2009, expenditure totalling €20M was included in Cherry's SOFP. A further €3M was invested in Cherry's brands during 2010.

Outline how Cherry Limited's expenditure on its brands should be accounted for in its financial statements for the year ended 31 December 2010.

Solution   IAS 38 *Intangible Assets* states that internally generated brands should not be recognised as an intangible asset. Cherry Limited's capitalisation of amounts invested in its brand names is therefore an error. On the assumption that the error is material, it should be corrected retrospectively in the financial statements for the year ended 31 December 2010. The procedure for effecting this amendment is similar to that outlined in Example 6 above.

Example 10   In July 2010, Cherry Limited discovered that a purchase invoice from a supplier for €21,000 was incorrectly recorded as €12,000.

Outline how this transaction should be accounted for in Cherry Limited's financial statements.

Solution   The understatement of the purchase invoice does not constitute a material error. Therefore, retrospective amendment is not required, and the error should be corrected in the 2010 financial statements as follows:

	Dr €	Cr €
Cost of sales	9,000	
Trade payables		9,000

Disclosures

(a) **Prior period errors:**
- the nature of the prior period error;
- for each prior period presented, to the extent practicable, the amount of the correction:
  - for each financial statement line item affected; and
  - for basic and diluted EPS, if IAS 33 applies to the entity;
- the amount of the correction at the beginning of the earliest prior period presented; and
- if retrospective restatement is impracticable, a description of how the error has been corrected.

(b) **Changes in accounting estimates:**
- the nature and amount of a change in an accounting estimate;
- if the amount of the effect in future periods is not disclosed because estimating it is impracticable, that fact should be disclosed.

Summary

IAS 8 prescribes the criteria for selecting and changing accounting policies. It also deals with changes in accounting estimates and corrections of errors.

Accounting policies

Accounting policies involve:

- recognising
- selecting measurement bases for, and
- presenting assets, liabilities, income, expenses and changes to equity.

When an IFRS specifically applies to a transaction, the accounting policy or policies applied to that item are determined by applying that IFRS. An entity should apply its accounting policies consistently. An entity is permitted to change an accounting policy only if the change

- is required by an IFRS; or
- results in the financial statements providing reliable and more relevant information.

An entity shall account for a change in accounting policy resulting from the initial application of an IFRS, in accordance with the specific **transitional provisions**, if any, in that IFRS. Otherwise, an entity should apply the change **retrospectively**.

Changes in accounting estimates

A change in accounting estimate involves an adjustment of:

- the carrying amount of an asset or a liability; or
- the amount of the periodic consumption of an asset.

The effect of a change in an accounting estimate should be recognised prospectively.

Errors

Material prior period errors should be corrected retrospectively.

References

1. Watts, R. L. and Zimmerman, J. L. (1978). Towards a positive theory of the determination of accounting standards. *The Accounting Review*, LIII (1), pp. 112–34.
2. Healy, P. (1985). The effect of bonus schemes on accounting decisions. *Journal of Accounting and Economics*, 7 (1), pp. 85–107.

QUESTIONS

9.1 BLUE Limited

Previously BLUE Ltd ('BLUE') depreciated its computer equipment using the reducing balance method at 25% per annum. The directors of BLUE are proposing to depreciate the computer equipment using the straight-line method over three years. This decision involves a change in:

(a) accounting policy
(b) estimate
(c) accounting policy and estimate
(d) none of the above.   (Chartered Accountants Ireland)

9.2 PARTWAY

PARTWAY's main activity is in the travel industry, selling package holidays (flights and accommodation) to the general public. The terms under which PARTWAY sells its holidays are that a 10% deposit is required on booking and the balance of the holiday must be paid six weeks before the travel date. In previous years PARTWAY has recognised revenue (and profit) from the sale of its holidays at the date the holiday is actually taken. From the beginning of November 2009, PARTWAY has made it a condition of booking that all customers must have holiday cancellation insurance and as a result it is unlikely that the outstanding balance of any holidays will be unpaid due to cancellation. In preparing its financial statements to 31 October 2010, the directors are proposing to change to recognising revenue (and related estimated cost) at the date when a booking is made. The directors also feel that this change will help to negate the adverse effect of comparison with last year's results (year ended 31 October 2009) which were better than the current year's.

Required:
Comment on whether PARTWAY's proposal to change the timing of its recognition of its revenue is acceptable and whether this would be a change of accounting policy.   (ACCA)

9.3 TRAM Limited – correction of material error

When preparing its financial statements for the year to 30 June 2011, TRAM Limited discovers that the sales figure for the year to 30 June 2010 had been understated by €100,000. Trade receivables at 30 June 2010 had been understated by the same amount. The error is regarded as material.

TRAM Limited's draft income statement for the year to 30 June 2011, before correcting this error is as follows:

	2011 €'000	2010 €'000
Revenue	1,660	1,740
Cost of sales	(670)	(730)
Gross profit	990	1,010
Expenses	(590)	(560)
Profit before taxation	400	450
Income tax expense	(80)	(90)
Profit for the year	320	360

Retained earnings at 1 July 2009 were €860,000. No dividends were paid during the two years to 30 June 2011. It should be assumed that TRAM Limited's tax expense is always 20% of its profit before tax.

(a) Prepare a statement of comprehensive income for the year ended 30 June 2011 showing the restated comparative figures for the year ended 30 June 2010.

(b) Compute TRAM Limited's restated retained earnings at 30 June 2011 after correcting the above error.

9.4 DONNELLY

During the year ended 31 December 2010, DONNELLY Limited discovered that amortisation of €250,000 of an intangible asset for the previous year had not been charged. An extract from the statement of comprehensive income for the current and prior year before correction of this error is shown below:

	2010 €	2009 €
Gross profit	500,000	650,000
Expenses including amortisation	(410,000)	(181,000)
Profit before tax	90,000	469,000
Income tax expense	(27,000)	(140,700)
Profit for the year	63,000	328,300
Retained earnings before correction of the error:		
At 1 January	1,200,000	871,700
At 31 December	1,263,000	1,200,000

Required:

Redraft the extract of the statement of comprehensive income, after correction of the error, together with the statement of changes in equity (retained earnings only) and the appropriate disclosure note. Assume a tax rate of 30%, with amortisation being fully deductible for tax purposes.

(Chartered Accountants Ireland)

Chapter 10

Interim financial reporting

Interim financial statements are commonly published by companies across the globe. The frequency varies across jurisdictions, with quarterly reporting being the norm in the United States, while interim statements are usually prepared on a half-yearly basis in the UK and the Republic of Ireland.

IAS 34 *Interim Financial Reporting* does not require entities to publish interim financial reports. However, their publication is commonly a stock exchange requirement for entities whose shares are publicly traded.

Should an entity wish to publish interim financial reports that are in accordance with international accounting standards, it must comply with the requirements of IAS 34.

IAS 34 specifically encourages publicly traded entities to:

- provide interim financial reports at least as of the end of the first half of their financial year; and
- make their interim financial reports available not later than 60 days after the end of the interim period.

Entities have the option of publishing a complete set of financial statements in their interim financial report. Alternatively, they may provide a condensed set of financial statements consisting, at a minimum, of the following components:

- a condensed statement of financial position
- a condensed statement of comprehensive income
- a condensed statement of changes in equity
- a condensed statement of cash flows; and
- selected explanatory notes

The principal selected explanatory notes that should be provided (if the information is material and not provided elsewhere in the report) are as follows:

- a statement that the same accounting policies and methods of computation are used in the interim financial statements, as compared with the most recent annual financial statements, or a description of the nature and effect of any changes;
- explanatory comments about the seasonality or cyclicality of interim operations;
- the nature and amount of changes to estimates reported in prior financial years;
- issues, repurchases and repayments of debt and equity;
- dividends paid;
- certain segment information, if required by IFRS 8;
- events after the interim period that have not been reflected in the financial statements for the interim period;
- the effect of changes in the composition of the group during the interim period (e.g. business combinations).

Part 5

ACCOUNTING FOR ASSETS

Chapter 11

Inventories

If you walk along the high street you will find yourself drawn to the window displays flaunting the latest in fashion and style. Inside, every available space is packed with the stores' offerings as they bid for a share of your custom. Out of town, a carpet manufacturer loads rolls of brightly coloured carpets onto a lorry, while inside the factory, wool is readied to be spun into myriad patterns as the production staff work to complete a row of partly finished carpets.

Inventory, which incorporates raw materials, work in progress and goods for sale, can be a very significant asset in a business. As a component of an entity's cost of sales, any variation in the value of inventory also has a direct effect on profit or loss for the period.

The rules for valuing inventories are contained in IAS 2 *Inventories*, which defines inventories as assets:

- held for sale in the ordinary course of business;
- in the process of production for such sale; or
- in the form of materials or supplies to be consumed in the production process or in the rendering of services.

The above definition highlights the fact that inventory must be held for sale in the ordinary course of business. Thus, an entity's stationery supplies for own use would not constitute inventory as they are not held for sale. Property held for sale would not normally be classed as inventory, as it is not held for sale in the *ordinary course of business*. An exception would be a property development company, for whom land and houses held for sale would clearly be part of inventory.

Objective of IAS 2

The objective of IAS 2 is to prescribe the accounting treatment for inventories. The Standard provides guidance for computing the cost of inventories and for subsequently recognising an expense, including any write-down to net realisable value. IAS 2 also provides guidance on the cost formulas used to allocate costs to inventories.

Scope

IAS 2 applies to all inventories, except:

- work in progress arising under construction contracts (see IAS 11);
- financial instruments (see IAS 32, IAS 39 and IFRS 9);
- biological assets related to agricultural activity (see IAS 41).

Valuation of inventory

IAS 2 requires that inventories be valued at the lower of cost and **net realisable value**.

Cost

Cost is defined as being that expenditure which has been incurred in bringing the inventories to their present location and condition. Cost includes:

Costs of purchase:

■ purchase price including import duties, transport and handling costs, and any other directly attributable costs, less trade discounts, rebates and subsidies (see Appendix 11.1).

Costs of conversion:

■ costs directly related to production (e.g. direct labour):
■ fixed production overheads (e.g. rent of factory) and variable production overheads (e.g. depreciation of machinery) (see Appendix 11.2).

Other costs:

■ Other costs are included only to the extent that they are incurred in bringing the inventories to their present location and condition. For example, it may be appropriate to include certain non-production overheads or product design costs for specific customers.
■ Interest costs should also be included if they relate to inventories that meet the definition of a qualifying asset (see IAS 23 *Borrowing Costs*).

Costs *not* to be included in inventory:

■ abnormal waste
■ storage costs
■ administrative overheads not related to production
■ selling costs
■ foreign exchange differences on inventories purchased
■ interest costs when inventories are purchased on deferred settlement terms

■ Techniques for measuring cost

The standard cost or the retail method may be used for convenience if the results approximate cost. Standard costs should be regularly reviewed and revised if necessary.

The retail method is often used in the retail industry for measuring inventories of large numbers of rapidly changing items with similar margins. The cost of the inventory is determined by reducing its sales value by the appropriate percentage gross margin.

Example 1 Multiple plc, which runs a chain of supermarkets, uses the retail method for computing the cost of its inventories. The total sales value of its inventories at 31 December 2010 was €10M and the typical gross profit margin is 15%.

The cost of Multiple plc's inventory will be computed as €8.5M (i.e. €10M × 85%) using the retail method.

■ Cost formulas

If a number of interchangeable items have been purchased or manufactured at different times, IAS 2 requires that the cost of such inventory items be computed on either the **first-in-first-out (FIFO)** or **weighted average cost** formula.

The same cost formula should be used for all inventories having a similar nature and use to an entity. See Appendix 11.3.

■ By-products

If the production process results in minor by-products, the costs of the main products are calculated after deducting the net realisable value of the by-products.

Example 2 Tracer Limited is a manufacturer of carpets. A small amount of surplus material is generated as part of Tracer's manufacturing process, and this is used for the production of rugs. The inventory of rugs on hand at 31 December 2010 had a net realisable value of €40,000.

Rugs are a by-product of Tracer Limited's primary production process, which involves the manufacture of carpets. The net realisable value of the rugs at 31 December 2010 should be deducted from the costs of producing Tracer Limited's main product.

	Dr €'000	Cr €'000
Inventory – SOFP	40	
Cost of sales – I/S		40

Net realisable value (NRV)

IAS 2 defines NRV as the estimated selling price in the ordinary course of business, less the estimated costs of completion and the estimated selling costs.

IAS 2 requires that inventory be valued at the lower of cost and NRV.

- this test should be performed for each item of inventory, or groups of similar items;
- if the NRV of raw materials is less than cost, however, no reduction is necessary provided that the goods into which the materials are to be incorporated can still be sold at a profit.

Example 3 Tracer Limited, which manufactures carpets, is carrying an inventory of wool at 31 December 2010. The purchase cost of the wool inventory was €200,000 and its net realisable value is €60,000.

The wool is the main raw material which Tracer uses for its manufacturing process. As long as it can be incorporated into the finished carpets at a profit, the inventory of wool can be valued at its cost of €200,000, and it is not necessary to use NRV in this case.

When a previous write-down to NRV is no longer justifiable, the write-down should be reversed. The reversal is limited to the amount of the original write-down. See Appendix 11.4.

Disclosure

- Accounting policy for measuring inventories, including the cost formula.
- The total carrying amount of inventories, and the carrying amount in classifications appropriate to the entity (e.g. raw materials, WIP and finished goods).
- Carrying amount of inventories carried at fair value less costs to sell.
- Amount of inventories recognised as an expense during the period.
- Amount of any write-down of inventories recognised as an expense in the period.
- Amount of any reversal of a write-down to NRV, and the circumstances that led to such a reversal.

Summary

- Inventory is a very significant asset in the financial statements of many business entities.
- IAS 2 requires inventories to be valued at the lower of cost and net realisable value.
- Cost comprises costs of purchase, costs of conversion and any other costs incurred in bringing the inventories to their present location and condition.
- Net realisable value is the estimated selling price in the ordinary course of business, less estimated costs of completion and selling costs.

Appendix 11.1

Costs of purchase

Costs of purchase should be exclusive of recoverable VAT, trade discounts, rebates, etc. but inclusive of import duties, transport and handling costs and any other directly attributable costs.

Example Y Ltd (which is registered for VAT) purchased 1,000 units of raw materials X on credit on 1 November 2010. The purchase invoice details were as follows:

	€
1,000 units of product X	10,000
Less trade discount @ 5%	(500)
	9,500
Transport and handling costs	400
	9,900
VAT @ 21%	2,079
Total invoice price	11,979

Y Ltd should record the purchase of raw material X in its nominal ledger as follows:

	Dr	Cr
	€	€
Raw materials purchases	9,900	
VAT – SOFP	2,079	
Trade payables		11,979

When Y Ltd prepared its financial statements on 31 December 2010, 200 units of raw material X were still in inventory.

The following journal entry is therefore required at that date:

	Dr	Cr
	€	€
Closing inventory – SOFP	1,980	
Cost of sales – I/S		1,980

This results in the income statement being charged only with those units consumed during the period (i.e. €9,900 – €1,980).

Appendix 11.2

Costs of conversion

Costs of conversion comprise:

- costs directly related to production (e.g. direct labour);
- fixed and variable production overheads (e.g. rent of factory, depreciation of machinery).

Fixed production overheads are allocated to the costs of conversion based on the normal capacity of the production facilities. Normal capacity is the production expected to be achieved on average over a number of periods under normal circumstances.

Costs of conversion will be incurred in respect of work in progress and finished goods, both of which are added to as part of the production process. This contrasts with inventories of raw materials and goods for resale, which only include the costs of purchase.

Example Tracer Limited purchased 10,000 units of raw material Z at €8 per unit (exclusive of VAT and trade discounts) during the year ended 31 December 2010.

In producing 5,000 units of finished product 'O' the 10,000 units of raw materials were utilised. In addition, 20,000 direct labour hours were required for conversion at a rate of €5 per hour.

Fixed production overheads for the year of €90,000 (including depreciation of machinery €5,000) were incurred and paid in full.

Variable production overheads of €7 per unit of finished product 'O' were also incurred and paid in full.

The level of production of 5,000 units was less than Tracer Limited's normal level of activity of 6,000 units.

During 2010, 4,000 units of finished product 'O' were sold.

Outline how Tracer Limited should account for its inventory of product 'O' at 31 December 2010.

Solution Tracer Limited will record its costs as follows:

	Dr €	Cr €
Raw material purchases – I/S	80,000	
Trade payables		80,000
Direct wages – I/S	100,000	
Bank		100,000
Fixed production overheads – I/S	90,000	
Bank		85,000
Accumulated depreciation machinery		5,000
Variable production overheads – I/S	35,000	
Bank		35,000

All the costs incurred during 2010 have been charged to the income statement as expenses. This fails to take account, however, of the fact that 1,000 units of finished goods inventory 'O' are on hand at the year end.

The inventory of finished goods 'O' is therefore valued as follows at 31 December 2010:

	€
Raw materials: 2,000 units at €8 per unit	16,000
Direct wages: 4,000 hours at €5 per hour	20,000
Fixed production overheads (see note 1)	15,000
Variable production overheads: 1,000 units at €7 per unit	7,000
	58,000

The following nominal ledger entry is therefore required at 31 December 2010:

	Dr	Cr
	€	€
Finished goods inventory – SOFP	58,000	
Cost of sales – I/S		58,000

This journal entry achieves two objectives:

(i) Inventory of product 'O' is included as an asset in the SOFP at 31 December 2010.

(ii) Only the cost of goods sold is now charged as an expense in the income statement.

Note 1

Production overheads should be allocated for inventory valuation purposes based on the *normal* level of activity (i.e. 6,000 units).

Thus, the correct computation of fixed production overhead for inclusion in closing inventory is as follows:

$$€90,000 \times 1,000/6,000 = €15,000$$

If *actual* production of finished product 'O' were used, the amount of fixed production overhead attributed to closing inventory would be €18,000 (i.e. €90,000 × 1,000/5,000). This would incorrectly result in expenses charged to the income statement being €3,000 lower (i.e. €18,000 – €15,000), resulting from Tracer Limited not achieving its normal production targets.

Appendix 11.3

Cost formulas

Example Y Ltd was incorporated on 1 January 2010 and purchased raw material inventory as follows during the period ended 30 June 2010:

1/1/2010	100 units at €10 per unit excluding VAT
1/2/2010	100 units at €12 per unit excluding VAT
1/3/2010	300 units at €13 per unit excluding VAT
1/4/2010	300 units at €14 per unit excluding VAT
1/5/2010	100 units at €15 per unit excluding VAT
1/6/2010	100 units at €16 per unit excluding VAT

Y Ltd had 200 units of raw material on hand at 30 June 2010.

Compute the value of the closing inventory of raw material on the following bases:
- *first-in-first-out*
- *weighted average cost*

Solution The nominal ledger record of purchases for the period will be as follows:

	Dr	Cr
	€	€
Raw material purchases – I/S	13,400	
Trade payables		13,400

The valuation of the 200 units of inventory on hand at 30 June 2010 will depend on the costing formula used:

(a) First-in-first-out (FIFO)
In this case the most recent units purchased are deemed to be those still held. Thus, the closing inventory will be valued as follows: (100 at €15) + (100 at €16) = €3,100

(b) Weighted average cost
The use of this method would result in the following closing inventory valuation:

(i)   Total cost of units purchased €13,400
(ii) Number of units purchased 1,000
(iii) Average purchase price per unit €13.4 (i.e. €13,400/1,000)
(iv) Closing inventory valuation: 200 × €13.4 = €2,680

Appendix 11.4

Net realisable value

IAS 2 requires that inventory should be valued at the lower of cost and net realisable value (NRV). NRV is defined by IAS 2 as the selling price less:

- all further costs to completion; and
- the estimated costs necessary to make the sale.

Example 1   At 31 December 2010, P Ltd had 100 units of product Y in inventory, which had been partially completed. All 100 units were to be sold to B Ltd. The list price per unit was expected to be €10, but B Ltd normally receives a trade discount of 5%.
    Completion cost of the 100 units was estimated as follows:

- wages €400
- production overheads €200

Selling and distribution expenses were forecast at €100. The production cost of bringing 100 units to their present location and condition was €600.

Outline how the inventory of product Y should be valued in the financial statements of P Limited at 31 December 2010.

Solution   NRV is calculated as follows:

	€
Estimated selling price net of trade discounts	950
Less costs to complete	(600)
Less selling and distribution expenses	(100)
Net realisable value	€250
Costs incurred to date	€600

Lower of cost and NRV equals €250. Thus, the inventory should be valued at €250, and the following journal will be required at 31 December 2010:

	Dr	Cr
	€	€
Inventory – SOFP	250	
Cost of sales – I/S		250

IAS 2 also requires that the comparison of cost and NRV be performed on an item-by-item basis, or for groups of similar items.

Example 2 The following are details of cost and NRV of finished goods held in inventory by A Limited.

Product	Cost	NRV	Lower of cost and NRV
	€	€	€
J	1,000	800	800
K	800	500	500
L	400	700	400
M	500	200	200
N	600	200	200
O	300	300	300
P	900	600	600
Q	2,000	2,500	2,000
	6,500	5,800	5,000

A Ltd should value its finished goods inventory at €5,000. If cost and NRV had been compared on a total level, finished goods inventory would have been valued at €5,800.

It is essential therefore that cost and NRV be compared on an item-by-item basis, or for groups of similar items.

QUESTIONS

11.1 BACH Limited

BACH Ltd ('BACH') sells four products direct to the public: Concerto, Minuet, Sonata and Symphony. The following information is available with respect to these products as at 31 December 2010:

Product	Units held in inventory	Original purchase cost per unit	Selling and distribution costs per unit	Selling price per unit
		€	€	€
Concerto	400	90	9	104
Minuet	500	102	12	110
Sonata	600	111	15	130
Symphony	700	120	18	135

The value of inventory to be included in BACH's financial statements at 31 December 2010 in accordance with IAS 2 *Inventories* is:

(a) €233,500
(b) €237,600
(c) €268,800
(d) €273,000

(Chartered Accountants Ireland)

11.2 Reversal of NRV write-down

Inventories included in the draft financial statements of BENNETT for the year ended 31 December 2010 at a value of €130,000, could currently be sold for €280,000 as the product has become very popular with consumers. These inventories originally cost €190,000, but had been written down to €130,000 at 31 December 2009.

Required:
Outline the correct accounting treatment of the company's inventories in the financial statements of BENNETT for the year ended 31 December 2010. Set out any relevant journals. Disclosure notes are *not* required.

(Chartered Accountants Ireland)

11.3 IMPART Limited

IMPART Limited is engaged in the manufacture of machine parts. The company's limited production capacity results in most parts being sold immediately on completion. Thus, at 31 December 2010, only raw materials and work in progress were in inventory.

(i) Raw materials

One type of raw material was used in the production process. Purchases of this raw material were made during the year as follows:

20 January	10,000 units at €5 per unit
30 June	5,000 units at €6 per unit
21 December	3,000 units at €7 per unit

The price per unit given above includes VAT at 21%.

Management uses the FIFO basis for valuing inventory, and 5,000 units of raw material are on hand at 31 December 2010.

(ii) Work in progress

Two types of machine part are in inventory at 31 December 2010. Details of both were as follows:

	Part Y	Part Z
	€	€
Raw material cost	2,000	1,000
Direct labour	1,000	500
Fixed production overheads*	400	200
Administrative overheads	200	100
	3,600	1,800
Estimated cost to complete	1,400	1,200
Estimated selling costs	200	200
Estimated selling price	3,000	4,000

* Production overhead costs were allocated on the basis of actual direct labour hours worked during the year. Due to a strike in November, however, the hours worked during 2010 amounted to only 90% of those normally worked.

(iii) In November 2010, a consignment of completed machine parts was sold at cost of €100,000 to A. Smith, a director of IMPART Limited. The company's normal mark-up on cost is 50%.

Required:

(a) You are required to state how the raw material inventory and work in progress should be valued in the financial statements of IMPART Limited at 31 December 2010.

(b) Outline (using journal entries where appropriate) how the machine parts in (iii) above should be dealt with in IMPART Limited's financial statements.

Chapter 12

Construction contracts

Imagine that your business has won the contract to construct a tunnel to connect two parts of a city separated by water. Your immediate concern will be with planning, ensuring that all technical and environmental provisions of the project are complied with. Over time, the construction will be rolled out and the project will take perhaps three years to complete.

Although you may be affected by tunnel vision, you will still have to consider how you should account for the contract at the end of each reporting period. You will not want to wait until completion to recognise all of the profit, so you will have to consider how much contract revenue and costs should be recognised in each period. In the unfortunate event of the tunnel becoming loss making, you will have to decide how to account for that as well.

IAS 11 *Construction Contracts*

IAS 11 defines a construction contract as a contract specifically negotiated for the construction of an **asset**, or a group of assets that are closely interrelated or interdependent. Typically, a construction contract takes a number of accounting periods to complete, and a critical outcome of IAS 11 is that revenue and costs are spread over the term of the contract, resulting in the overall profit, if any, also being recognised over a number of periods.

If a contract covers more than one asset, the construction of each asset should be treated as a separate construction contract when:

- separate proposals have been submitted for each asset;
- each asset has been subject to separate negotiation; and
- the costs and revenues of each asset can be identified.

Example 1   Sound Construction Limited has been appointed to construct a medical centre, which will provide complementary services such as physiotherapy, health screening, pharmacy, general practitioner care and X-ray. The centre is held in shared ownership by the various medical personnel who will provide services at the centre, and the pricing and fit-out of each unit will be separately agreed with each owner occupier.

Outline how the construction of the medical centre should be accounted for by Sound Construction Limited.

Solution   Sound Construction Limited should treat the construction of each unit as a separate contract on the following basis:

- separate proposals will be submitted for each unit;
- each unit will be subject to separate negotiation; and
- the costs and revenues of each unit can be identified.

A group of contracts should be treated as a single construction contract when:

- the group of contracts is negotiated as a single package;
- the contracts are so interrelated that they are, in effect, part of a single project; and
- the contracts are performed concurrently or in a continuous sequence.

Example 2   Buildwell Limited is currently preparing a tender for the construction of a suburban shopping centre. The centre will contain one anchor tenant and several smaller tenants offering a range of goods and services. The submission requires a separate contract proposal for each unit to be submitted to the shopping centre developer, Scope Properties Limited. However, one construction firm will be appointed to undertake the entire project.

Outline how the construction of the shopping centre should be accounted for by Buildwell Limited, should the company's tender be successful.

Solution   Buildwell Limited should account for the construction of the shopping centre as a single contract. This conclusion is reached on the following basis:

- the centre will contain a number of tenants, but its construction is being negotiated as a single package;
- the contracts are in effect part of a single project; and
- the shopping centre units will be constructed in a continuous sequence.

Identifying contract costs and revenue

■ Contract costs should include:

- costs that relate directly to the specific contract;
- costs that are attributable to contract activity in general and can be allocated to the contract; and
- such other costs that can be specifically charged to the customer under the terms of the contract.

Contract revenue comprises:

- the initial amount of revenue agreed in the contract; and
- variations in contract work, claims and incentive payments, which are
  - probable to result in revenue, and
  - capable of being reliably measured.

Example 3   Assume that Buildwell Limited's tender was successful and that construction of the shopping centre commenced on 1 January 2010. The following costs and revenues were incurred up to 31 December 2010:

Costs

Materials	€2,250,000
Labour	€1,200,000
Allocated company overhead	€200,000

Revenues
The value of work done up to 31 December 2010 was €4M.

The total contract price is €10M and total costs are estimated at €7.5M.

Invoices totalling €3M had been sent to Scope Properties Limited during 2010, relating to work done up to 31 December 2010. Amounts received from Scope Properties amounted to €2.2M.

Outline the amount of contract costs and revenue that arise in respect of Buildwell Limited's shopping centre project.

Solution   Contract costs comprise a total of €3.45M (i.e. labour + materials). Allocated company overhead cannot be attributed to the shopping centre contract.

Contract revenue, approved by the client's architect, amounts to €4M at 31 December 2010.

Accounting for construction contracts

When the outcome of a construction contract can be estimated reliably, revenue and costs should be recognised in proportion to the stage of completion of contract activity. This results in profit on a construction contract being recognised gradually over the term of the contract.

Example 3 revisited   In accounting for construction contracts, costs and revenue are recorded in the contract account. The entries relating to Buildwell Limited's shopping centre contract are outlined below:

Contract a/c

	€'000		€'000
(1) Bank/trade payables	3,450	(2) Cost of sales	3,450
(3) Revenue	4,000	(4) Trade receivables	3,000
		Balance c/f at 31/12/2010	1,000
	7,450		7,450

Revenue

	€'000		€'000
T/F to income statement	4,000	(3) Contract a/c	4,000

Cost of sales

	€'000		€'000
(2) Contract a/c	3,450	T/F to income statement	3,450

Presentation in financial statements

■ Income statement

Revenue and contract costs should be included in the income statement.

■ Statement of financial position

An entity should present the following amounts in its statement of financial position:

(i) the gross amount due from customers for contract work as an **asset** (see note 1); and

(ii) the gross amount due to customers for contract work as a **liability** (see note 2).

Note 1: A contract in progress will give rise to an *asset* when costs incurred + recognised profits (less recognised losses) are > progress billings. The following amounts are netted off in arriving at the amount of the asset in (i) above:

- costs incurred plus recognised profits, less
- the sum of recognised losses and progress billings.

Note 2: A contract in progress will give rise to a *liability* when costs incurred + recognised profits (less recognised losses) are < progress billings. The following amounts are netted off in arriving at the amount of the liability in (ii) above:

- costs incurred plus recognised profits, less
- the sum of recognised losses and progress billings.

Example 3 revisited	An extract from the financial statements of Buildwell Limited is shown below:

Income statement (extract) for the year ending 31 December 2010

	€'000
Revenue	4,000
Less cost of sales	(3,450)
Operating profit	550

Statement of financial position (extract) at 31 December 2010

	€'000
Current assets	
Amounts due from customers for contract work*	1,000
Trade receivables†	800

* Costs incurred + recognised profits – amounts invoiced (i.e. balance on contract a/c), i.e. €3.45M + €550,000 – €3M.
† Trade receivables = amounts invoiced less amounts received (i.e. €3M – €2.2M).

Alternative contract outcomes

If a contract is expected to be *profitable*, revenue and costs should be recognised on a percentage-of-completion basis, as outlined in Example 3 above.

An expected *loss* on a contract should, however, be recognised immediately.

If the outcome of a contract *cannot be estimated reliably*:

- no profit should be recognised
- contract costs should be expensed as incurred
- contract revenue should be recognised only to the extent that contract costs incurred are expected to be recoverable

These potential outcomes are summarised in Table 12.1.

Table 12.1 **Alternative contract outcomes**

Contract outcome	Revenue measurement	Cost measurement
Profitable	On % of completion basis	On (%) of completion basis
Expected loss	On % of completion basis	Balancing figure to give loss
Uncertain	Equal to cost as long as costs are recoverable	Costs incurred in period

Procedure for dealing with construction contracts

(a) *Ascertain if contract is at a sufficiently advanced stage to determine if an overall profit or loss will accrue*:
  - If expected outcome can be ascertained, proceed to (b) below.
  - If not, charge costs incurred in period as an expense, and let revenue equal costs to the extent that costs incurred are recoverable.

(b) *Overall outcome of contract can be reliably estimated*:
  (i) *Expected profit* – record costs and revenue on a percentage completion basis.
  (ii) *Expected loss* – provide in full. Record revenue on a percentage of completion basis. Costs are the balancing figure to produce the required loss.

(c) *Record entries as in Builders Limited question below.*

(d) *Present information in income statement and statement of financial position* – see Builders Limited question in Appendix 12.1.

Disclosure

- Amount of contract revenue
- Methods used to determine contract revenue
- Methods used to determine stage of completion
- For contracts in progress at end of the reporting period:
  - aggregate costs incurred and recognised profits;
  - amount of advances received;
  - amount of retentions.

New standard dealing with construction contracts

The IASB is due to publish a new standard, called *Revenue from Contracts with Customers*, during 2011. This standard will replace IAS 11. The new standard is likely to withdraw the method of recognising revenue on a percentage of completion basis. Instead, revenue will be recognised when the customer obtains control of the promised goods or services.

Summary

- IAS 11 requires that revenues and costs on profitable contracts should be recognised on a stage of completion basis. Therefore, profit is recognised gradually over the term of the construction contracts.
- The expected loss should be recognised immediately on any loss-making contracts.

Appendix 12.1

Builders Limited – an example

Example   Builders Limited commenced business on 1 June 2010 as building contractors. The following details relate to the three uncompleted contracts in the company's books on 31 May 2011.

	Contract name		
	Apple €	Pear €	Plum €
Cost of work to 31 May 2011	31,000	28,000	10,300
Cost of work to 31 May 2011, as certified	30,470	27,280	9,640
Value of work to 31 May 2011 as certified by client's architects	38,500	22,000	14,300
Progress payments invoiced to 31 May 2011	33,000	17,600	11,000
Progress payments received by 31 May 2011	27,500	17,600	11,000
Estimate of:			
Final costing including future costs of rectification and guarantee work	33,000	38,500	66,000
Final contract price	41,800	30,800	88,000

Required:

(a) a statement showing calculations for each contract;

(b) to show, as an extract, the information which should appear in the statement of comprehensive income for the year ending 31 May 2011, and the statement of financial position at 31 May 2011.

Solution   **Apple:** As this contract is almost complete and the outcome can be calculated with a reasonable degree of certainty, profit can be recognised on a stage of completion basis.

Pear: The loss to date of €5,280 is the net figure after deducting cost of sales of €27,280 from the turnover of €22,000. The total loss on this contract is likely to be €7,700 (€38,500 − €30,800). A further provision of €2,420 for foreseeable losses is therefore required in the financial statements.

Plum: As this contract is in its early stages, it is difficult to foresee whether an overall profit will ultimately accrue. For this reason, it may not be prudent to recognise any profit.

Assessment of eventual outcome of contracts

	Apple	Pear	Plum
Final contract price	41,800	30,800	88,000
Estimate of total cost	33,000	38,500	66,000
Estimated profit (loss)	8,800	(7,700)	22,000

Builders Ltd
Income statement (extract) for the year ending 31 May 2011

	€
Revenue	70,140
Less cost of sales	(69,810)
Operating profit	330

Builders Ltd
Statement of financial position (extract) at 31 May 2011

	€
Current assets	
Amounts due from customers for contract work	8,730 (see note 1 below)
Trade receivables	5,500 (Apple contract)
Current liabilities	
Amounts due to customers for contract work	700 (see note 2 below)

Note I: Contracts where there is a gross amount due *from* customers (i.e. an asset in SOFP)

Item	Apple contract	Pear contract	Total
	€	€	€
Costs to date	31,000	28,000	59,000
Add recognised profits	8,030*		8,030
Less recognised losses		(7,700)	(7,700)
Less amounts billed	(33,000)	(17,600)	(50,600)
Net amount	6,030	2,700	8,730

* Value of work certified – cost of work certified.

Note 2: Contracts where there is a gross amount due *to* customers (i.e. a liability in SOFP)

Item	Plum contract
	€
Costs to date	10,300
Add recognised profits	–
Less recognised losses	–
Less amounts billed	(11,000)
Net amount	(700)

Solution to Builders Limited – T a/c Approach

Contract a/c

	Apple	Pear	Plum		Apple	Pear	Plum
(1) Bank	31,000	28,000	10,300	(2) Cost of sales	30,470	27,280	9,640
(3) Revenue	38,500	22,000	9,640	(4) Trade receivables	33,000	17,600	11,000
Bal. c/f			700	Bal. c/f	6,030	5,120	–
	69,500	50,000	20,640		69,500	50,000	20,640

Revenue

	Apple	Pear	Plum		Apple	Pear	Plum
Income statement	38,500	22,000	9,640	(3) Contract a/c	38,500	22,000	9,640

Cost of sales

	Apple	Pear	Plum		Apple	Pear	Plum
(2) Contract a/c	30,470	27,280	9,640	Income statement	30,470	29,700	9,640
(6) Provision for loss		2,420					
	30,470	29,700	9,640		30,470	29,700	9,640

Provision for losses

	Apple	Pear	Plum		Apple	Pear	Plum
Balance c/f	–	2,420	–	(6) Cost of sales		2,420	

Bank

	Apple	Pear	Plum		Apple	Pear	Plum
(5) Trade receivables	27,500	17,600	11,000	(1) Contract a/c	31,000	28,000	10,300

Trade receivables

	Apple	Pear	Plum		Apple	Pear	Plum
(4) Contract a/c	33,000	17,600	11,000	(5) Bank	27,500	17,600	11,000
				Balance c/f	5,500		
	33,000	17,600	11,000		33,000	17,600	11,000

The amounts for inclusion in the **income statement** are derived as follows:

Revenue: €70,140 (i.e. €38,500 + €22,000 + €9,640)
Cost of sales: €69,810 (i.e. €30,470 + €29,700 + €9,640)

The amounts for inclusion in the SOFP are derived as follows:

(1) Contracts where there is a gross amount due *from* customers (i.e. asset in SOFP)

Item	Apple contract €	Pear contract €	Total €
Balance on contract a/c at 31 May 2011	6,030	5,120	10,950
Less provision for losses	–	(2,420)	(2,420)
Current asset in SOFP	6,030	2,700	8,730

(2) Contracts where there is a gross amount due *to* customers (i.e. liability in SOFP)

Item	Plum contract €
Liability in SOFP (i.e. balance on contract a/c at 31 May 2011)	(700)

QUESTIONS

12.1 FITZWILLIAM CONSTRUCTION

On 1 January 2010 FITZWILLIAM CONSTRUCTION entered into a contract to develop a building for a third party. The contract sum was €1.7M and the building work is well under way, with costs incurred to date of €920,000. The project has now run into difficulties and the project manager estimates that the costs to completion will be a further €850,000.

Required:

Advise the company as to the correct accounting treatment and disclosure for the contract under consideration with reference to relevant international accounting standards, together with supporting journals. (Chartered Accountants Ireland)

12.2 PINBALL

PINBALL began work on a long-term construction contract during the year ended 31 December 2009 to construct a bypass around two towns. Details of the contract at 31 December 2009 are as follows:

	€'000
Contract price	16,000
Costs incurred	5,800
Estimated costs to completion	10,400
Value of work certified	6,000
Cash received from client	6,800

An underground stream has been discovered under part of the proposed route of the bypass and the costs of dealing with this have been included in the estimated costs to completion shown above. PINBALL is confident that the contractee will bear the additional costs and the contract price will be increased to €20,000,000. PINBALL recognises revenue and profit on long-term contracts on the basis of work certified to date.

Required:

Calculate the figures to be included in PINBALL's statement of comprehensive income for the year ended 31 December 2009 and statement of financial position at that date.

(Chartered Accountants Ireland)

12.3 ZEPPELIN plc

ZEPPELIN plc ('ZEPPELIN') is an Irish company involved in the manufacture of airplanes for both private and commercial use. For internal reporting purposes, the company is divided into two cash-generating units (CGUs): Private and Commercial. During the year ended 31 December 2010, the Private CGU negotiated three separate fixed price contracts to build a private jet for three wealthy football club owners.

	Contract 1 €'000	Contract 2 €'000	Contract 3 €'000
Contract price	10,000	12,000	14,000
Costs incurred to 31 December 2010	5,600	6,000	5,040
Estimated costs to complete contract	5,600	4,000	7,560
Progress billings to 31 December 2010	4,800	6,500	5,000
Estimated percentage of contract complete at 31 December 2010	50%	60%	40%

Required:

Illustrate how each of the contracts negotiated by the Private CGU should be reflected in ZEPPELIN's statement of comprehensive income for the year ended 31 December 2010 and statement of financial position at that date. (Chartered Accountants Ireland)

12.4 BRANDA CONSTRUCTION

(a) BRANDA CONSTRUCTION has two construction contracts outstanding at the end of its financial year 31 December 2010. Details are as follows:

	Contract A	Contract B
	€	€
Total contract price	50,000	40,000
Costs incurred to date	28,000	30,000
Expected future costs	12,000	18,000
Progress billings	24,000	20,000
Advance payments	8,000	nil
% complete 31 December 2010	60%	50%
% complete 31 December 2009	30%	uncertain

In relation to Contract A, revenue recognised in the year to 31 December 2009 was €14,000 and costs of €11,000 were charged.

Contract B was at an early stage of completion at the 31 December 2009 but there was no indication at that date that it was likely to make a loss. Total costs incurred on Contract B at the 31 December 2009 amounted to €4,000.

You are required to show the relevant income statement and statement of financial position entries for Contract A and Contract B for the year ended 31 December 2010 in accordance with IAS 11 *Construction Contracts*.

(b) The question of allocation of total profit over the various accounting periods during which a construction contract takes place is an important and difficult issue. Two alternative approaches have emerged over the years, the completed contract method and the percentage of completion method.

Explain these approaches to recognising profit and state clearly which method is adopted in IAS 11.

Chapter 13

Property, plant and equipment

Property, plant and equipment are tangible items that:

- are held for use in the production or supply of goods or services, for rental to others or for administrative purposes; and
- are expected to be used during more than one period.

This definition excludes assets such as goodwill, patents and trademarks, which lack physical substance and are therefore not tangible. Assets held for sale are also excluded, as such assets are not expected to be used for more than a single period.

This area is regulated by IAS 16 *Property, Plant and Equipment* which sets out the rules for the accounting treatment of this type of asset. The principal areas covered are as follows:

- the recognition of assets
- determination of their carrying amounts
- depreciation charges and impairment losses to be recognised

Recognition

■ General

Items of property, plant and equipment should be recognised as assets when it is probable that:

- the future economic benefits associated with the asset will flow to the enterprise; and
- the cost of the asset can be measured reliably.

■ Items of property, plant and equipment acquired for safety or environmental reasons

Although some items may not directly increase future economic benefits, they may be necessary for an entity to obtain the future economic benefits from its other assets. An example of such an item is fire safety equipment, which should be recognised as an addition to property, plant and equipment, in accordance with IAS 16.

■ Subsequent costs

(i) Day-to-day servicing costs

An entity should ***not*** recognise the costs of day-to-day servicing of an item as being property, plant and equipment. These costs should be recognised in profit or loss as they are incurred. An example would be the regular servicing of a furnace. Costs of day-to-day servicing are primarily the costs of labour and consumables, and may include the cost of small parts.

(ii) Replacement of parts of property, plant and equipment

Parts of some items of property, plant and equipment may require replacement at regular intervals (e.g. the seats in an aircraft). Such parts will be included in property, plant and equipment when the cost is incurred, if the recognition criteria (i.e. future benefits and measurement reliability) are met.

The carrying amount of those parts that are replaced is derecognised in accordance with the derecognition provisions of IAS 16.

Example 1 On 1 July 2010 Tracer Limited replaced a lift in one of its factory buildings. The cost of the new lift was €250,000, and the carrying amount of the old lift was €56,000. The old lift had a zero disposal value, and the present value of the cost of decommissioning the new lift was estimated to be €20,000.

In accordance with IAS 16 the costs of the replacement lift are included in property, plant and equipment. The estimate of the costs of decommissioning the new lift should also be included in the asset's cost.

The gain or loss arising from the derecognition of the old lift is included in the income statement, and is not included in revenue.

	Dr €'000	Cr €'000
Buildings	250	
Bank		250
(Being cost of new lift)		
Buildings	20	
Provision for dismantling – SOFP		20
(Being estimated decommissioning costs of new lift)		
Loss on derecognition of old lift – I/S	56	
Buildings		56
(Being loss on disposal of old lift – disclose separately, in accordance with IAS 1, subject to materiality)		

(iii) Major inspections

A condition of continuing to operate an item of property, plant and equipment (e.g. an aircraft) may be the performance of regular major inspections for faults. When each major inspection is carried out, its cost is recognised in the carrying amount of property, plant and equipment if the recognition criteria (i.e. future economic benefits and measurement reliability) are satisfied.

Any remaining carrying amount of the cost of the previous inspection (as distinct from physical parts) is derecognised.

Measurement at recognition

Property, plant and equipment should initially be measured at cost.

Elements of cost

Cost comprises an asset's purchase price, including import duties and non-refundable purchase taxes (after deducting trade discounts and rebates), together with any costs directly attributable to bringing the asset into working condition for its intended use, and the initial estimate of dismantling and removal costs.

Directly attributable costs include the following:

- costs of employee benefits
- acquisition costs such as stamp duty and import duties
- costs of site preparation and clearance
- initial delivery and handling costs
- costs of testing whether the asset is functioning properly
- installation and assembly costs
- professional fees.

The overriding requirement in capitalising directly attributable costs is that they must be *incremental,* and would therefore have been avoided if the asset had not been constructed or acquired.

The following are examples of costs that are *not* capitalised as part of property, plant and equipment:

- opening a new facility
- introducing a new product or service (including advertising and promotion)
- conducting business in a new location or with a new class of customer
- administration and other general overhead costs.

Recognition of costs in the carrying amount of property, plant and equipment **ceases** when the item is in the location and condition necessary for it to be capable of operating in the manner intended by management. Thus, costs incurred in using or redeploying an item are *not* included in the carrying amount of that item. Examples include:

- costs incurred while an item has yet to be brought into use, or is operated at less than full capacity;
- initial operating losses, such as while waiting for demand to build up;
- costs of relocating or reorganising part or all of an entity's operations.

The cost of a self-constructed item (e.g. a new factory built by an enterprise) is computed using the same principles as outlined above. The cost of abnormal amounts of materials, labour, or other resources incurred is *not* included in the cost of the asset.

Example 2   During 2010, Tracer Limited decided to construct a portable sales kiosk for the promotion and marketing of the company's products. The following costs were incurred:

	€
Purchase of materials (before deducting trade discount of 5%)	30,000
Labour costs	25,000
Correction of design error	2,000
Marketing costs associated with promotion of products:	
incurred during construction	1,200
incurred after completion of construction	1,500
Safety checks	1,300
Interest costs incurred during construction	3,000
Present value cost at 31 December 2010 of dismantling sales kiosk	1,000
	65,000

Outline how the above costs should be accounted for in the financial statements of Tracer Limited.

Solution   The following should be capitalised as part of the construction cost of the sales kiosk:

	€
Materials (net of trade discount)	28,500
Labour costs	25,000
Safety checks	1,300
Financing costs	3,000
Estimated dismantling costs	1,000
	58,800

- The cost of correcting *design errors* is not capitalised as this is considered an abnormal cost.
- *Marketing costs* are not capitalised as they are not necessary to bring the sales kiosk into working condition.
- Financing costs are capitalised, as required by IAS 23 *Borrowing Costs*.

Thus, the following journal entry will be required:

	Dr	Cr
	€	€
Expenses – I/S	4,700	
Buildings	58,800	
Bank		63,500
Trade payables	1,500	
Discount received – I/S		1,500

▇ Measurement of cost

General

Cost is the cash price equivalent at the recognition date.

Deferred payment

If payment is deferred beyond normal credit terms, the difference between the total payment and the cash price equivalent must be recognised as interest over the credit period, unless such interest is capitalised in accordance with IAS 23.

Example 3   Bright Limited purchased machinery on 1 January 2010. The purchase cost was €20,000, and this was payable on 1 January 2011. Normal credit terms are three months, and the normal cash price is €18,000.

	Dr	Cr
	€	€
Machinery	18,000	
Trade payables		18,000
(Being cost of machinery at cash price equivalent)		
Interest costs – I/S	2,000	
Trade payables		2,000
(Being interest costs for year ending 31 December 2010)		
Trade payables	20,000	
Bank		20,000
(Being payment for the machinery on 1 January 2011)		

An asset exchanged for another asset

If an asset is acquired in exchange for another asset (whether similar or dissimilar in nature) the cost of the asset acquired will be measured at fair value unless:

- the transaction lacks commercial substance; or
- the fair value of neither the asset received nor the asset given up is reliably measurable.

Example 4   Superior Limited has agreed to exchange a land site, which it owns, for a building which has a fair value of €340,000. The carrying value of the land site in the financial statements of Superior Limited is €300,000.

	Dr €'000	Cr €'000
Building	340	
Land		300
Profit on disposal of land site – I/S		40

If the acquired item cannot be measured at **fair value**, its cost is measured at the carrying amount of the asset given up.

Measurement after recognition

General

IAS 16 permits two accounting models.

(i) *Cost model* – the asset is carried at cost less accumulated **depreciation** and **impairment**.
(ii) *Revaluation model* – the asset is carried at a revalued amount, being:
   - its fair value at the date of revaluation; less
   - subsequent depreciation and impairment.

Revaluation model

Critics of IAS 16 have argued that the revaluation of assets is subjective and open to abuse by the management of companies that wish to manipulate their accounting numbers. By contrast, the upward revaluation of tangible assets is not permitted in the United States.

IAS 16 sets out the following requirements in respect of the revaluation model.

(i) Frequency of revaluations

Revaluations should be carried out regularly, to ensure that the carrying amount of an asset does not differ materially from its fair value at the end of the reporting period.

(ii) Treatment of accumulated depreciation at time of revaluation

When an item of property, plant and equipment is revalued, any accumulated depreciation at the revaluation date is treated in one of the following ways:

(a) *Eliminated against the gross carrying amount of the asset, and the net amount restated to the revalued amount.*

Example 5 A building was previously revalued to €2.4M, and accumulated depreciation stands at €192,000. The building is now being revalued to €3.6M.

	Dr €'000	Cr €'000
Accumulated depreciation	192	
Buildings		192
(Being elimination of accumulated depreciation against carrying value of the building)		
Buildings	1,392	
Revaluation surplus – OCI		1,392
(Being revaluation of building to €3.6M)		

Or

(b) *Restated proportionately with the change in the gross carrying amount of the asset, so that the carrying amount of the asset after revaluation equals its revalued amount.*

Applying this approach to the amounts in Example 5:

Accumulated depreciation of €192,000 equals 8% of the value of the asset of €2.4M.
Let X equal the new gross revalued amount:

$$X - 0.08X = €3.6M$$
$$X(1 - 0.08) = €3.6M$$
$$X = €3.6M/0.92$$
$$X = €3.913M$$

	Dr €'000	Cr €'000
Asset (€3.913M – €2.4M)	1,513	
Accumulated depreciation (€3.913M × 8%) – €192,000		121
Revaluation surplus – OCI		1,392

(iii) Revaluation by asset class

If an item of property, plant and equipment is revalued, the entire class of assets to which that asset belongs should be revalued.

(iv) Revaluation which results in an increase in value

The increase should be credited to equity as a revaluation surplus, unless it represents the reversal of a revaluation decrease of the same asset previously recognised as an expense, in which case it should be recognised as income.

Example 6 Trumps Limited purchased land in 2005 for €1M. The land was revalued to €800,000 on 31 December 2007, the deficit being charged as an expense. At 31 December 2010, the land is being revalued to €2.2M.

	Dr €'000	Cr €'000
Land	1,400	
Revaluation surplus – OCI		1,200
Reversal of previous impairment – I/S		200

(v) Revaluation which results in a decrease in value

A decrease arising as a result of a revaluation should be recognised as an expense to the extent that it exceeds any amount previously credited to the revaluation surplus in respect of the same asset.

Example 7 Sensor Limited purchased freehold land in 2006 for €700,000. In 2008 the land was revalued to €1.3M. At 31 December 2010, the land was revalued to €500,000.

	Dr €'000	Cr €'000
Land	700	
Bank		700
(Being purchase of land in 2006)		
Land	600	
Revaluation surplus – OCI		600
(Being revaluation of land in 2008)		
Revaluation surplus – OCI	600	
Impairment write-down – I/S	200	
Land		800
(Being revaluation of land in 2010)		

(vi) Disposal of a revalued asset

Any revaluation surplus may be transferred directly to retained earnings when an asset is derecognised. The transfer to retained earnings is recorded in the statement of changes in equity (SOCIE) and is *not* made through profit or loss.

Example 8 Mentor Limited purchased freehold land in 2006 for €700,000. In 2008 the land was revalued to €1.3M. The land was disposed of during 2010 for €1.6M.

	Dr €'000	Cr €'000
Land	700	
Bank		700
(Being land purchased in 2006)		
Land	600	
Revaluation surplus – OCI		600
(Being revaluation of land in 2008)		
Bank	1,600	
Land		1,300
Profit on disposal – I/S		300
(Being disposal of land in 2010)		
Revaluation surplus – SOCIE	600	
Retained earnings – SOCIE		600

(Being transfer of revaluation surplus to
  retained earnings on disposal of the land.
This transfer is shown in the statement of changes
  in equity, and is *not* recorded in profit or loss)		

(vii) Impact of revaluation model on an entity's profit

The use of the revaluation model is likely to reduce an entity's profit and its earnings per share figure.

Under the revaluation model:

- a revaluation surplus is not recorded in profit or loss, and on disposal the revaluation surplus may be transferred to retained earnings through the statement of changes in equity;
- the annual depreciation charge is likely to be higher for depreciable assets.

| **Example 8 revisited** | If the asset in Example 8 had been measured under the **cost** model, the journal entries would be as follows: |

Land	700	
Bank		700
(Being land purchased in 2006)		
Bank	1,600	
Land		700
Profit on disposal – I/S		900
(Being disposal of land in 2010)		

Thus, the profit on disposal is €600,000 higher than under the revaluation model. There is no depreciation effect, as land is not normally a depreciable asset.

Depreciation (cost and revaluation models)

Each significant part of an item of property, plant and equipment should be depreciated separately

For example, it may be appropriate to depreciate the airframe and engines of an aircraft separately.

| **Example 9** | Sail Limited purchased a new ship on 1 January 2010 for €10M. The ship was expected to have a useful life of 50 years, and a residual value of €2M. However, lifeboats, which were purchased on the same date for €1M, are expected to have a useful life of 10 years, and a zero residual value. Sail Limited uses the straight-line method of depreciation. |

The ship will be depreciated over 50 years, resulting in an annual depreciation charge of €160,000 (i.e. (€10M – €2M)/50). However, the lifeboats will be depreciated over 10 years, with annual depreciation amounting to €100,000.

Thus, the following journal entry will be required in 2010 in respect of depreciation:

	Dr €'000	Cr €'000
Depreciation expense – I/S	260	
Accumulated depreciation – ship		160
Accumulated depreciation – lifeboats		100

Periodic depreciation charge

The **depreciation** charge for each period should be charged as an expense, unless it is included in the carrying amount of another asset. The latter would apply, for example, in the case of that part of depreciation of manufacturing plant which is included in the

133

costs of conversion of inventory. Likewise, depreciation of plant used for development activities may be included in the cost of an intangible asset, recognised in accordance with IAS 38.

Example 10 Plant which Mercer Limited purchased for €100,000 on 1 January 2010, is being utilised as part of a development project that qualifies as an intangible asset. The plant has a useful life of 10 years and an estimated residual value of €10,000.

	Dr	Cr
	€'000	€'000
Development costs – SOFP	9	
Accumulated depreciation – SOFP		9
(Being depreciation on plant for 2010, which		
is capitalised as part of development costs)		

■ Depreciation amount, period and method

The *depreciable amount* (gross carrying amount less residual value) should be allocated on a systematic basis over an asset's useful life.

The *residual value and the useful life* should be reviewed at least at each financial year end, and any change should be accounted for prospectively as a change in accounting estimate under IAS 8.

The *depreciation method* used should reflect the pattern in which an asset's economic benefits are consumed by the enterprise.

The depreciation method should be reviewed at least annually and, if the pattern of consumption of benefits has changed, the depreciation method should be changed prospectively as a change in accounting estimate under IAS 8.

Depreciation begins when an asset is available for use, and continues until the asset is derecognised, even if it is idle.

■ Impairment

IAS 36 *Impairment of Assets* deals with issues relating to the impairment of property, plant and equipment. Compensation from third parties for items of property, plant and equipment that were impaired, lost or given up, is included in profit when the compensation becomes receivable.

Derecognition

Property, plant and equipment should be removed from the statement of financial position:

- on disposal; or
- when no future economic benefits are expected from its use or disposal

The gain or loss on disposal is the difference between the proceeds and the carrying amount of the asset, and it should be recognised as income.

If payment for the asset is deferred, the consideration received should be recognised initially at the cash price equivalent. The balance is recognised as interest revenue in accordance with IAS 18. See Example 8 above.

Disclosure

The following information should be disclosed for each class of property, plant and equipment:

- the measurement basis used for determining the carrying amount
- depreciation methods used
- useful lives or depreciation rates
- gross carrying amount and accumulated depreciation and impairment losses at beginning and end of period
- reconciliation of the carrying amount at beginning and end of the period, showing:
  - additions
  - assets classified as held for sale
  - acquisitions through business combinations
  - revaluation increases or decreases
  - impairment losses
  - depreciation
  - net exchange differences on translation of financial statements
  - other changes

The following information should also be disclosed:

- restrictions on title
- expenditures capitalised in respect of property, plant and equipment during construction
- contractual commitments for the acquisition of property, plant and equipment
- compensation from third parties for any property, plant and equipment that was impaired, lost or given up that is included in profit or loss

For property, plant and equipment stated at revalued amount, the following disclosures are required:

- the effective date of the revaluation
- whether an independent valuer was involved
- methods and significant assumptions employed in estimating fair values
- how fair values were determined
- for each class of revalued property, plant and equipment, the carrying amount that would have been recognised had the assets been carried under the cost model
- the revaluation surplus, its change for the period and any restrictions on the distribution of the balance to shareholders

Summary

- Property, plant and equipment should be recognised as an asset when the future economic benefits will flow to the entity, and the asset's cost can be measured reliably.
- Measurement should initially be at cost, with entities opting subsequently either for a cost or revaluation model for valuation purposes.
- The depreciable amount of property, plant and equipment should be depreciated over its useful life, with each significant part being depreciated separately.
- Property, plant and equipment should be derecognised on disposal, or when no further economic benefits are expected from its use or disposal.

QUESTIONS

13.1 New equipment

HARRINGTON MOTORS acquired new equipment for spraying cars at a cost of €200,000 in September 2010. The equipment was tested by staff in September 2010 to ensure that it would function correctly after implementation. As a result of the testing, various adjustments were made to the equipment, without which the equipment would not function correctly. The cost associated with this period was approximately €25,000. During the last three months of 2010 the equipment was available for use but, due to a lack of marketing, it was only used intermittently. The monthly cost of running the equipment during that three-month period was €15,000.

HARRINGTON MOTORS is keen to capitalise the costs associated with this equipment, although the bookkeeper has expensed the costs to date as follows:

Dr	Plant and equipment expenses	€70,000	
Cr	Bank		€70,000

Required:
Outline your advice on the possibility of capitalising these costs and the journal entries required.

(Chartered Accountants Ireland)

13.2 Head office property

HARDING Ltd's head office is included in 'Property, plant and equipment'. In the past, HARDING has revalued the building each year and transferred any movement to the revaluation reserve.

Relevant details of the cost and fair value of the property are as follows:

	€M
Cost	20
Valuation 31 December 2009	31
Valuation 31 December 2010	29

The valuations at 31 December 2010 have not yet been incorporated into the financial statements.

Required:
Advise the Financial Director of Harding Limited as to the correct accounting treatment of the head office property. Provide relevant journals, ignoring any impact on the depreciation charge.

(Chartered Accountants Ireland)

13.3 LOADZA PRODUCTS

LOADZA PRODUCTS owns two freehold properties, one in Dublin and one in London. The company uses both as regional administrative offices. The properties had a useful life of 50 years on their date of acquisition, and the directors believe that this assumption is still appropriate at 31 December 2010. It is company policy to depreciate the properties on a straight-line basis over their estimated useful economic life.

	Date of acquisition	
	London property 1 January 2001	Dublin property 1 January 2001
Original cost	€5,000,000	€5,000,000
Net book value at 31 December 2010	€4,000,000	€4,000,000
Market value at 31 December 2010	€3,000,000	€7,000,000

In the financial statements for the year ended 31 December 2010, the directors of LOADZA PRODUCTS are proposing to show the Dublin property at market value and the London property at its depreciated historic cost. The directors believe the fall in the market value of the London property is only temporary and property values in the London area will rise in the next 1–2 years.

Required:

(a) Is the policy put forward by the directors of LOADZA PRODUCTS acceptable?

(b) Assuming that LOADZA PRODUCTS wishes to move to market value, show the relevant entries that would need to be made in LOADZA PRODUCTS' books of account.

13.4 OSCAR Limited

On 1 December 2009, OSCAR entered into a 25-year €48,000,000 lease on new premises in a prime commercial location. In the 2009 financial statements, the lease was capitalised and depreciated pro rata on a straight-line basis over its life. By December 2010, because of a scarcity of commercial space, similar leases were being exchanged for €75,000,000. Consequently, OSCAR's directors wish to revalue the lease to €75,000,000 with effect from 31 December 2010 and cease depreciating it.

Required:

(a) Explain whether the directors are permitted to revalue and cease depreciating the leased premises.

(b) Illustrate the impact of the permitted accounting treatments on OSCAR's financial statements in 2009 and 2010. (Chartered Accountants Ireland)

13.5 YELLOW

YELLOW revalues its plant and equipment every two years. It is company policy to charge a full year's depreciation in the year of acquisition and none in the year of disposal. Before the change on 31 December 2007 (see below), plant and equipment is depreciated at 20% per annum using the reducing balance method. The following information is available with respect to the company's plant and equipment:

1 January 2006	Plant and equipment purchased at a cost of €780,000
31 December 2007	Plant and equipment revalued to €550,000, with the remaining useful economic life revised to 4 years and the depreciation method being changed to straight line
31 December 2009	Plant and equipment revalued to €225,000, with the decline believed to be permanent
30 September 2010	Plant and equipment sold for €250,000

Required:

Show how the plant and equipment would be reflected in the financial statements of YELLOW for each of the years ending 31 December 2006 to 2010. (Chartered Accountants Ireland)

Chapter 14

Intangible assets

The market capitalisation* of a company is usually greater than the carrying amount of the net assets in its statement of financial position. This can relate partly to the fact that some assets (e.g. property accounted for under the cost model) are not carried at their fair value. It can also be due, however, to the fact that other items, such as the level of staff morale, managerial expertise, customer loyalty and brand value, have tended not to be recognised as assets.

A common characteristic shared by the latter category of items is that they lack physical substance – i.e. they cannot be touched in the same way as assets like inventories or property. Another is the fact that they often exist without a financial transaction, such as a payment having taken place. The rules for the recognition and measurement of this type of asset are outlined in IAS 38 *Intangible Assets*.

Scope of IAS 38

IAS 38 applies to all intangible assets except:

- intangible assets covered by another standard (e.g. intangibles held for sale, deferred tax assets, **goodwill**, and employee benefits)
- financial assets
- intangible assets arising from insurance contracts issued by insurance companies

Definitions

An intangible asset is an identifiable non-monetary asset, without physical substance.

Identifiable means that the asset arises from contractual or other legal rights, and is capable of being separated from the entity and sold or licensed.

Examples of intangible assets include:

- brand names
- mastheads
- computer software
- licences and franchises
- copyrights and patents
- customer/client lists
- quotas

* Market capitalisation is the total value of a company's shares, computed as the share price × the number of shares.

- customer and supplier relationships
- websites

Recognition

Recognition criteria

An intangible asset should be recognised if, and only if:

- it is probable that the asset's expected *future economic benefits* will flow to the entity; and
- its cost can be *measured reliably*.

If an intangible item does not meet the **definition** of an intangible asset, or does not comply with the **recognition criteria**, it should not be capitalised as an intangible asset.

IAS 38 prohibits the reinstatement of an intangible asset that was initially charged to expense.

Recognition categories of intangible assets

(i) Intangible assets acquired separately

The *probability* criterion, outlined above under recognition criteria, is always considered to have been satisfied for this category of intangible. Thus, as long as the item meets the definition of an intangible, and its cost can be reliably measured, it should be recognised as an intangible asset.

Example 1 On 1 May 2010, Rightboro Limited purchased a licence for the importation of restricted materials. The cost of the licence was €10,000.

This is an intangible asset that has been purchased separately. Its cost can be reliably measured and it satisfies the definition criteria of IAS 38. The licence should be recognised as an intangible asset as follows:

	Dr €'000	Cr €'000
Licence – SOFP	10	
Bank		10

(ii) Intangible assets acquired as part of a business combination

As regards the recognition criteria outlined above:

- the *probability* criterion is always considered to be met;
- the *reliable measurement* criterion is always considered to be met.

Expenditure (included in the acquisition cost) that does *not* meet both the definition and recognition criteria of IAS 38, should form part of the amount that is attributed to goodwill recognised at acquisition date.

Example 2 Tramp Limited acquired 100% of the equity share capital of Lady Limited on 1 January 2010, at a cost of €2.4M. The fair value of the identifiable net assets of Lady Limited at that date amounted to €1.9M, which included €250,000 in respect of product patents.

The acquisition of Lady Limited should be recorded as follows in Tramp Limited's consolidated financial statements:

	Dr €'000	Cr €'000
Net tangible assets	1,650	
Patents	250	
Goodwill (balancing figure)	500	
Bank		2,400

(iii) Research and development costs

All research costs should be charged to expense when incurred.

Development costs should be capitalised if an entity can demonstrate all of the following:

- technical feasibility
- intention to complete the intangible asset and use or sell it
- its ability to use or sell the intangible asset
- how the intangible asset will generate future economic benefits
- the availability of adequate resources to complete and use or sell the intangible asset
- its ability to measure reliably the expenditure attributable to the intangible asset during its development.

Example 3 During 2010 Brenda Limited spent €400,000 on research designed to develop a new type of waterproof footwear. Significant progress was made by 31 December 2010, but Brenda Limited has not yet committed itself to completing the project.

Brenda Limited also spent €300,000 on finalising the design of a new type of golf shoe, whose production will commence in the second quarter of 2011.

Expenditure on the waterproof footwear would be regarded as research expenditure by IAS 38, and it should be expensed as incurred.

The new golf shoe appears to be at the development phase, and on condition that it satisfies the recognition criteria of IAS 38, the expenditure should be capitalised.

	Dr €'000	Cr €'000
Research costs – I/S	400	
Development costs – SOFP	300	
Bank		700
(Being research and development costs incurred during 2010)		

If a research and development project acquired in a business combination meets the following criteria, it should be recognised as an asset at cost, even if it is partly at the research stage:

- it meets the definition of an asset; and
- it is identifiable.

Subsequent expenditure on the project is accounted for in the same way as any other research and development expenditure.

(iv) Website costs

An entity may incur internal expenditure on the development and operation of its own website. SIC Interpretation 32 outlines the accounting treatment for this type of expenditure. SIC 32 identifies the following stages of website development:

- *Planning* (e.g. feasibility studies).
- *Application and infrastructure development* (e.g. obtaining a domain name, purchasing and developing hardware and operating software).
- *Graphical design development* (e.g. designing the appearance of web pages).
- *Content development* (e.g. creating, purchasing, preparing and uploading information).

Once development is completed, the *operating* stage begins, when an entity maintains and enhances the website.

Expenditure incurred during the planning stage should be expensed as it is incurred.

The application and infrastructure development stage, the graphical design development stage and the content development stage are similar to the stages of research and development. Expenditure incurred during these stages should be recognised as an intangible asset only if:

- it is probable that the expected future economic benefits attributable to the asset will flow to the entity; and
- the cost of the asset can be reliably measured; and
- it complies with the qualifying conditions for the capitalisation of development costs under R&D.

However, expenditure incurred in the content development stage which relates to the advertising and promotion of an entity's own products and services (e.g. digital photographs of products) should be expensed as it is incurred.

Expenditure incurred during the operating stage (i.e. after the development of the website is complete) should be recognised as an expense unless:

- it is probable that the asset's expected *future economic benefits* will flow to the entity; and
- its cost can be *measured reliably*.

Example 4 New Limited paid the following costs during 2010 in relation to the development of its website:

	€'000
Feasibility studies	10
Purchase of domain name and operating software	8
Website design	5
Creation and uploading of website content	12
	35

It is expected that there will be future economic benefits and that these will flow to the entity. Management is committed to completing the website, and there are sufficient resources available to do so.

Outline how New Limited should account for the development of its website.

Solution The development of New Limited's website satisfies the recognition criteria of IAS 38 and it should be recognised as an intangible asset. However, the cost of the feasibility study should be expensed. The following journal entry is required:

	Dr €'000	Cr €'000
Expenses – I/S	10	
Website – intangible asset in SOFP	25	
Bank		35

(v) Internally generated brands, mastheads, titles, customer lists

These items, and items similar in substance, should *not* be recognised as assets.

The impact of this rule on some companies has been very significant. Independent News and Media (INM), for example, have presented an additional set of figures in their SOFP for several years, incorporating intangible assets which IAS 38 did not permit to be recognised.

The following figures are extracted from the published SOFP of INM at 31 December 2007:

	Audited – IFRS €M	Unaudited €M
Non-current assets	–	–
Intangible assets	1,805.4	3,549.3

Note 2 to the 2007 INM Financial Statements states that:

> In the opinion of the Directors, the presentation of the value of both acquired and internally generated mastheads is useful information for Shareholders, as it more accurately reflects the value of the Group's newspaper mastheads. As a result, the Group has presented an 'Alternative Balance Sheet' which includes all the Group's newspaper mastheads at their revalued amounts, including those mastheads that have been created internally . . .

The exclusion of internally generated intangible assets is regarded by some as a triumph of faithful representation over relevance. It involves the non-recognition of a *relevant* asset on the grounds that it cannot be measured *reliably*.

This issue is further explored in Examples 5 and 6 below.

Example 5 Topical Limited, which publishes newspapers, paid €1.2M during 2010 in promoting and developing its newspaper titles.

This expenditure is incurred in respect of internally developed titles, and it should be written off as an expense in the period in which it is incurred.

	Dr €'000	Cr €'000
Expenses – I/S	1,200	
Bank		1,200

Example 6 In December 2010, Topical Limited purchased a newspaper title from a rival company for €2M in cash.

This is an intangible asset that is acquired separately, and which meets the recognition criteria of IAS 38. It should be capitalised as an intangible asset as follows:

	Dr €'000	Cr €'000
Intangible asset – SOFP	2,000	
Bank		2,000

(vi) Computer software

Computer software that is an integral part of the related hardware is treated as property, plant and equipment. For example, a computer-controlled machine tool may be incapable of operating without the necessary software. In this case, the software is regarded as part of the machine and is included in property, plant and equipment. The same applies in the case of an operating system of a computer, which is also capitalised as part of property, plant and equipment.

When computer software is *not* an integral part of the related hardware, it is treated as an intangible asset.

Example 7 On 1 January 2010, Topical Limited purchased 10 computers for the company's editing offices. The total cost was €30,000, and an operating system, specific to publishing requirements, was purchased separately at a cost of €700 per system.

Outline how the computers and the operating system should be recorded by Topical Limited.

Solution The computers should be capitalised as property, plant and equipment. The dedicated operating system, without which the computers cannot function effectively, should also be capitalised as part of property, plant and equipment as follows:

	Dr €'000	Cr €'000
Property, plant and equipment	37	
Bank		37

Measurement

■ Initial measurement

Intangible assets should be measured initially at cost. Cost is the amount of cash or cash equivalents paid or the fair value of other consideration given to acquire the asset.

However, the following costs should be charged to expense when incurred:

- start-up, pre-opening and pre-operating costs
- training costs
- advertising and promotion costs
- relocation and reorganisation costs
- internally generated goodwill

■ Measurement subsequent to acquisition

An entity must choose either the cost model or the revaluation model for each class of intangible asset.

(i) Cost model

An intangible asset should be carried at its cost, less any **amortisation** and **impairment losses**.

(ii) Revaluation model

Intangible assets may be carried at a revalued amount (based on fair value) less any subsequent amortisation and impairment losses, only if fair value can be determined by reference to an active market.* Such active markets are expected to be uncommon for intangible assets. An example of where one would exist might be for product quotas or bar licences.

* Items traded in the market are homogeneous, willing buyers and sellers can normally be found at any time, and prices are available to the public.

Example 8 Cowes Limited purchased a milk quota for €200,000 in 2007. The fair value of the milk quota at 31 December 2010 was €370,000, and Cowes Limited uses the revaluation model for this class of intangible asset.

	Dr €'000	Cr €'000
Product quota – intangible asset	200	
Bank		200
Product quota – intangible asset	170	
Revaluation surplus – OCI		170

It should be noted that if an intangible asset is initially recognised as an expense, it should not be recognised as part of the cost of an intangible asset at a later date.

■ Subsequent expenditure

Subsequent expenditure on an intangible asset, after its purchase or completion, should be expensed as it is incurred, unless:

- it is probable that the expenditure will enable the asset to generate future economic benefits in excess of its originally assessed standard of performance; and
- the expenditure can be measured and attributed to the asset reliably.

Subsequent expenditure will rarely be recognised in the carrying amount of an intangible asset.

Example 9 In 2009 Bramble Limited registered a product patent in the eurozone, at a cost of €100,000. In 2010, due to the success of the product, the patent was extended to cover the United States, at an additional cost of €150,000.

The patent costs incurred by Bramble Limited in 2010 should give rise to additional future economic benefits, not attributable to the eurozone patent, and therefore the initial amount of the patent asset should be increased.

	Dr €'000	Cr €'000
Patent – intangible asset	100	
Bank		100
(Being patent registered in 2009)		
Patent – intangible asset	150	
Bank		150
(Being extension of patent in 2010)		

Subsequent expenditure on brands, mastheads, publishing titles, customer lists and items similar in substance (whether externally acquired or internally generated) is always recognised in profit or loss as incurred.

Useful lives and amortisation

Intangible assets are classified as having either a finite or indefinite life.

■ A finite life

Cost (or valuation) less residual value should be amortised over the useful life of the intangible asset.

The amortisation method should reflect the pattern in which the asset's future economic benefits are consumed by the entity. If the pattern cannot be reliably established, the straight-line method should be used.

The amortisation charge is recognised in profit or loss, unless another standard requires that it be included in the cost of another asset. The amortisation period should be reviewed at least annually.

The intangible asset should also be assessed for impairment in accordance with IAS 36.

Example 10   Briar Limited spent €20,000 on a product patent during 2009. The patent will run for 15 years, commencing from 1 January 2010. It is probable, however, that Briar Limited will only obtain economic benefits from the patent for an 11-year period. It is expected that the economic benefits of the patent will be consumed at a rate of 20% straight line per annum over the first three years, and 5% straight line over the next eight years.

The patent is an intangible asset, with a zero residual value. The depreciable amount of €20,000 should be amortised according to how its future economic benefits are consumed by Briar Limited.

	Dr €'000	Cr €'000
Amortisation of patent – I/S	4	
Patent		4
(Being amortisation of patent for year ending 31 December 2010 – i.e. €20,000 × 20%)		

■ Indefinite life

An intangible asset with an indefinite life should not be amortised.

The useful life of the asset should be reviewed annually to determine if events and circumstances continue to support an indefinite useful life for that asset. A change in the useful life from indefinite to finite should be accounted for as a change in an accounting estimate under IAS 8.

The intangible asset should also be assessed annually for impairment in accordance with IAS 36.

Derecognition

An intangible asset should be derecognised:

- on disposal; or
- when an entity does not expect future economic benefits from its use or disposal.

The gain or loss on derecognition of an intangible asset is computed as the net disposal proceeds less the carrying value. It should be recognised immediately in profit or loss.

Example 11   Scramble Limited purchased customer lists on 1 January 2010 for €90,000. The customer lists were included in intangible assets and were amortised over three years on a straight-line basis. They were sold on 1 January 2011 for €70,000, net of selling costs.

Outline how Scramble Limited should account for the customer lists in its financial statements.

Solution   The customer lists are an identifiable non-monetary asset without physical substance. Their future economic benefits are expected to flow to Scramble Limited, and their cost can be estimated reliably. Therefore, as they satisfy the definition and recognition criteria of IAS 38, the customer lists should be capitalised as an intangible asset on 1 January 2010.

Amortisation of €30,000 is expensed in 2010, and a profit of €10,000 (i.e. proceeds of €70,000 less carrying amount of €60,000) is generated on the disposal of the customer lists on 1 January 2011. This profit should be included in the profit or loss of Scramble Limited in 2011.

The following journal entries will be required:

	Dr €'000	Cr €'000
Intangible asset – SOFP	90	
Bank		90
(Being purchase of customer lists on 1 January 2010)		
Amortisation of customer lists – I/S	30	
Intangible asset – SOFP		30
(Being amortisation of customer lists for year ended 31 December 2010)		
Bank	70	
Intangible asset – SOFP		60
Gain on disposal of customer lists – I/S		10
(Being disposal of customer lists on 1 January 2011)		

Disclosure

An entity should disclose the following information for each class of intangible assets:

- whether the useful lives are indefinite or finite, and if finite the useful lives used
- amortisation methods used
- gross carrying amount
- accumulated amortisation and impairment losses
- a reconciliation of the carrying amount at the beginning and end of the period, showing:

- additions
- assets classified as held for sale
- revaluations
- impairment losses
- amortisation
- foreign exchange differences
- other changes
- carrying amount of any intangible asset assessed as having an indefinite life, and the reasons supporting the assessment of an indefinite life
- description and carrying amount of material intangible assets
- specific disclosures for intangible assets acquired by way of a government grant
- existence and carrying amounts of intangible assets with restricted title
- contractual commitments for the acquisition of intangible assets

Additional disclosures are required for:

- intangible assets accounted for at revalued amounts
- the aggregate amount of research and development expenditure recognised as an expense during the period

Summary

- An intangible asset is an identifiable non-monetary asset, without physical substance.
- An intangible asset should be recognised only if it satisfies the following criteria:
  - it is probable that the asset's future economic benefits will flow to the entity; and
  - its cost can be measured reliably.
- Intangible assets that are acquired separately, or as part of a business combination, should be recognised if they satisfy the above recognition criteria.
- All research costs are charged to profit or loss as they are incurred. Development costs that satisfy certain prerequisite conditions must be capitalised.
- Intangible assets may be measured under a cost model or a revaluation model, for each class of intangible asset.
- Revaluation gains are taken to revaluation surplus and included as other comprehensive income in the statement of comprehensive income.
- Internally generated brands, mastheads, titles, etc. should not be recognised as assets.
- Intangible assets are classified as having either a finite life or an indefinite life.

QUESTIONS

14.1 HOLLY plc – research and development

HOLLY plc is currently engaged in a research and development project to develop a new chemical. The development costs in the year ended 31 December 2009 of €5M were written off, as the management felt they were not sufficiently confident of the ultimate profitability of the project. In the year ended 31 December 2010 further development costs of €10M have been incurred, with only an estimated €200,000 of costs to be incurred in the future. Production is expected to commence in the next few months.

The total trading profits from sales of the new product are now estimated at €20M and the board has decided to complete the project. The directors have again decided to write off the costs incurred in the year ended 31 December 2010. The Group Financial Director has asked for your advice on whether this accounting treatment is in line with international accounting standards.

(Chartered Accountants Ireland)

14.2 Development projects

MAGNA MEDICAL has a research facility dedicated to developing new technology for use in specialised imaging equipment with medical applications. The company has a consistently applied accounting policy for capitalising relevant development expenditure, which is then released over the life of the associated products. During the 2010 financial year two major new projects have commenced as follows.

Project A

During 2010 MAGNA MEDICAL commenced development of a new range of portable medical scanners which use mobile phone technology to link users (nurses and doctors) located in remote areas to consultants based in regional specialist centres. The potential applications and commercial returns are believed to be exceptional and are forecast to significantly exceed development costs.

Given the strategic importance of such a product, funds are available to complete the work. According to the detailed project plans and milestones the work will take a further 12 months to complete. Costs incurred to date total €450,000, with a further €1.2M of investment required to complete the work during 2011.

Project B

During 2010 the company commenced contract development work for another medical product company, STAR MONITORS Ltd ('STAR MONITORS'), developing circuitry for use in human heart monitors. Costs incurred by MAGNA MEDICAL plus an agreed mark-up profit will be paid in full by STAR MONITORS. MAGNA MEDICAL has to date incurred €250,000 of costs in this project. STAR MONITORS made a payment on account of €100,000 in respect of this work in December 2010, although MAGNA MEDICAL has not yet invoiced any of this work to STAR MONITORS.

To date, the costs relating to both these products have been booked to deferred development expenditure in the statement of financial position of MAGNA MEDICAL. The payment from STAR MONITORS has been accounted for by:

Dr. Bank	€100,000
Cr. Capitalised development costs	€100,000

Required:
Set out how Projects A and B should be accounted for in the financial statements of MAGNA MEDICAL for the year ended 31 December 2010. *(Chartered Accountants Ireland)*

14.3 SkeTv plc

(a) RadTv Ltd has a broadcasting licence which is renewable every 10 years, once the entity provides at least an average level of service to its customers and complies with the relevant legislative requirements. The licence may be renewed indefinitely at little cost. SkeTv plc has just acquired the broadcasting licence from RadTv Ltd for €2M and the broadcasting licence has been renewed twice before the acquisition. SkeTv plc intends to renew the licence indefinitely; the evidence supports its ability to do so and the licence is expected to contribute to the entity's net cash flows indefinitely.

State clearly how you would show this intangible asset in the financial statements of SkeTv plc and the reasons for your decision.

(b) In its first year of trading to 31 December 2010, PHARMA-REP Ltd incurred the following expenditure on research and development, none of which related to the purchase of property, plant and equipment:

(i) €48,000 on successfully devising processes to convert methane into chemicals A and B.
(ii) €240,000 on developing an alcoholic drink based on chemical B.

No commercial uses have yet been discovered for chemical A. However, commercial production and sales of the alcoholic drink commenced on 1 June 2010 and is expected to produce steady profitable income during a five-year period, before being replaced. Adequate resources exist for the company to achieve this.

Required:
State clearly how you would treat the above expenditures, and determine the amount of development expenditure that PHARMA-REP Ltd should capitalise at 31 December 2010.

Chapter 15

Investment property

Identification

Investment property is defined by IAS 40 as property held to earn rentals or for capital appreciation or both, rather than for:

- use in the production or supply of goods or services or for administration purposes; or
- sale in the ordinary course of business.

■ Examples of investment property

- Land held for long-term capital appreciation
- Land held for currently undetermined future use
- Building leased out under an operating lease
- A building that is vacant but is held to be leased out under an operating lease
- Property that is being constructed or developed for future use as investment property.

■ Examples of items that are *not* investment properties

- Property intended for sale in the ordinary course of business – e.g. by a property development company (see IAS 2 *Inventories*)
- Property being constructed or developed on behalf of third parties (see IAS 11 *Construction Contracts*)
- Owner-occupied property
- Property that is leased to another entity under a **finance lease**.

■ Partial own use

Some properties are held, part for own use, and part to earn rentals or for capital appreciation. If the portions can be sold or leased out separately, they are accounted for separately. Thus, the part that is rented out would be investment property.

If the portions cannot be treated separately, the property is investment property only if the owner-occupied portion is insignificant.

Example 1 Major Limited purchased a building in January 2010 for €1.5M. Eight floors of the building are let on an operating lease to Merchant Bank Limited, with the remaining two floors being occupied by Tom Limited, which is a subsidiary of Major Limited.

Outline how the building should be accounted for by Major Limited.

Solution | **Financial statements of Major Limited**

The building is investment property, and should be accounted for as follows:

	Dr	Cr
	€'000	€'000
Investment property	1,500	
Bank		1,500

Consolidated financial statements of the Major Group

The portion that is occupied by Tom Limited is not investment property as far as the Group is concerned. On the assumption that each floor of the building has equal value, the following treatment is appropriate:

	Dr	Cr
	€'000	€'000
Investment property	1,200	
Buildings	300	
Bank		1,500
(Being separate treatment of property, as permitted by IAS 40)		

■ Ancillary services

An entity may sometimes provide ancillary services (e.g. security or maintenance) to the occupants of a building that it holds. The building should be treated as investment property if the services are insignificant to the arrangement as a whole.

If the services are significant (e.g. an owner-managed hotel), the property should be classified as owner-occupied, and therefore not as investment property.

Example 2 | Major Limited completed the development of a new shopping centre during 2010. Units are leased to tenants on operating leases, and Major Limited provides security services for the centre, each tenant paying a premium based on the square footage of their unit.

The shopping centre is a building leased out under a series of operating leases, which is an example of investment property outlined by IAS 40. The provision of the security service would appear to be insignificant to the overall arrangement, and thus does not invalidate the shopping centre from being classified as investment property.

Recognition

Investment property should be recognised as an asset when:

- it is probable that the future economic benefits associated with the property will flow to the entity; and
- the cost of the property can be reliably measured.

Measurement at recognition

Investment property should be measured initially at its cost, including transaction costs which are directly attributable, such as legal fees and property transfer taxes.

The following should *not* be included in the cost of investment property:

- *Start-up costs* (unless they are necessary to bring the property to the condition necessary for it to be capable of operating in the manner intended by management).
- *Operating losses* incurred before the investment property achieves the planned level of occupancy.
- *Abnormal waste*.

If payment for investment property is deferred, its cost is the cash price equivalent. The difference between this amount and the total payments is recognised as interest expense over the period of credit.

Measurement after recognition

Accounting policy

IAS 40 permits entities to choose either:

- a fair value model, or
- a cost model

The same model (fair value or cost) must be used for all of an entity's investment property.

Fair value model

Investment property is remeasured at **fair value**, which is the amount at which the property could be exchanged between knowledgeable, willing parties in an arm's length transaction.

Gains or losses arising from changes in the fair value of investment property should be included in profit or loss in the period in which they arise.

Example 3 Major Limited purchased investment property on 1 January 2010 for €900,000. At 31 December 2010, the fair value of the property was €1.3M.

	Dr €'000	Cr €'000
Investment property	900	
Bank		900
(Being purchase of investment property)		
Investment property	400	
Gain on revaluation of investment property – I/S		400
(Being restatement of investment property to fair value at 31 December 2010)		

The fair value of investment property should reflect market conditions at the end of the reporting period. The best evidence of fair value is given by current prices in an active market for similar property. In the absence of this information, an entity should consider using:

- current prices in an active market for different property, and adjust for the differences; or

- recent prices of similar properties on less active markets; or
- discounted cash flow projections based on reliable estimates of future cash flows.

It is normally assumed that an entity will be able to reliably determine the fair value of investment property on a continuing basis. However, when an entity first acquires an investment property:

- If the entity is unable to reliably measure the fair value of an investment property until its construction is complete, it should measure that property at cost until either its fair value becomes reliably determinable, or construction is completed (whichever is earlier);
- If the entity is unable to reliably measure the fair value of an investment property on a continuing basis, it should measure that property using the cost model. The residual value of the property should be assumed as zero, and IAS 16 rules should be applied until the investment property is sold.

If an entity has previously measured investment property at fair value, it should continue to be measured at fair value until disposal (or until the property is owner-occupied or the entity begins to develop it for subsequent sale in the ordinary course of business).

■ Cost model

After initial recognition, an entity that chooses the cost model should measure all investment property in accordance with the cost model as per IAS 16 *Property, Plant and Equipment*. Thus, investment property will be carried at cost less accumulated **depreciation** and less accumulated **impairment** losses.

Transfers to or from investment properties

Evidence of change in use	Rules for transfer
Commencement of owner occupation (transfer of investment property carried at fair value to owner-occupied property or inventories)	Fair value at the change of use date is the *cost* of the property under its new classification
Cessation of owner occupation (transfer to investment property carried at fair value)	IAS 16 should be applied up to the date of reclassification. Any difference at that date between the carrying amount under IAS 16, and the fair value, is accounted for as a revaluation under IAS 16
Transfer from inventories to investment property at fair value (e.g. commencement of an operating lease to a third party)	Any difference between the fair value at the date of transfer and the asset's previous carrying amount should be recognised in profit or loss
An investment property valued at cost during self-construction/development is valued at fair value on completion	Any difference between the fair value on completion and the previous carrying amount should be recognised in profit or loss

Example 4	On 30 December 2010, Major Limited vacated property which had been occupied by its own employees since its acquisition on 1 January 2009 for €2M. On 31 December 2010, a five-year operating lease was signed with a third party for the rental of the property. The fair value of the property at that date was €3M. The property has not been depreciated on the basis that its residual value has exceeded its carrying amount.	

Outline how the property should be treated in the 2010 financial statements, on the assumption that Major Limited uses the fair value model for investment property.

Solution	A change in use (i.e. cessation of owner occupation) occurs on 31 December 2010. The property should be reclassified as investment property at that date. The difference between fair value and the carrying amount is dealt with as a revaluation surplus under IAS 16.	

The following journal entry will be required:

	Dr €'000	Cr €'000
Investment property	3,000	
Land and buildings		2,000
Revaluation surplus – OCI		1,000
(Being reclassification of property at 31 December 2010)		

Disposals

Investment property should be derecognised (i.e. eliminated from the SOFP):

- on disposal, or
- when investment property is permanently withdrawn from use, and no future economic benefits are expected from its disposal.

The gain or loss on disposal should be calculated as the difference between

- the net disposal proceeds, and
- the carrying amount of the asset.

The gain or loss should be recognised in profit or loss in the period of disposal or retirement.

Example 5	Major Limited sold investment property on 31 December 2010 for €1.8M. The carrying amount of the property at the time of sale was €1.4M.	

	Dr €'000	Cr €'000
Bank	1,800	
Investment property		1,400
Gain on disposal of investment property – I/S		400
(Being disposal of investment property)		

If the payment for investment property is deferred, the consideration received is recognised initially at the cash price equivalent. The difference between the nominal amount of the consideration and the cash price equivalent is recognised as interest revenue in accordance with IAS 18.

			Dr	Cr
			€'000	€'000
Example 6	Assume that in Example 5 above, Major Limited gave the purchaser a deferred payment period of one year, and charged €1.9M for the investment property. At the time of sale, the cash price equivalent for this type of investment property was €1.8M.			

	Dr €'000	Cr €'000
Trade receivables (cash price equivalent)	1,800	
Investment property		1,400
Gain on disposal of investment property – I/S		400
(Being disposal of investment property in 2010)		
Trade receivables	100	
Interest revenue – I/S		100
(Being interest revenue for the year ended 31 December 2011)		
Bank	1,900	
Trade receivables		1,900
(Being receipt on 31 December 2011 of consideration for investment property)		

Disclosure

Fair value model and cost model

An entity's disclosure must include:

- Whether it uses the fair value model or the cost model
- Methods and significant assumptions used in determining the fair value of investment property
- Extent to which the fair value of investment property is based on a valuation by a qualified independent valuer. If there has been no such valuation, that fact must be disclosed
- The amounts recognised in profit or loss for:
  - rental income from investment property;
  - direct operating expenses arising from investment property during the period
- The cumulative change in fair value recognised in profit or loss on a sale from a pool of assets in which the cost model is used, into a pool in which the fair value is used.

Additional disclosures for fair value model only

- A reconciliation between the carrying amounts of investment property at the beginning and end of the reporting period.
- Any significant adjustments made to valuations obtained for investment properties.

Additional disclosures for the cost model

- Depreciation methods used
- Useful lives or depreciation rates used
- Gross carrying amounts and the accumulated depreciation at the beginning and end of the period
- A reconciliation of the carrying amount of investment property at the beginning and end of the period
- The fair value of investment property.

Summary

- Investment property is property held for rental income or capital appreciation or both.
- Investment property should be recognised as an asset when:
  - it is probable that the future economic benefits from the property will flow to the entity; and
  - the cost of the property can be reliably measured.
- Investment property should be measured initially at cost. Subsequently, either a cost or fair value model can be used for all of an entity's investment property.

QUESTIONS

15.1 FITZWILLIAM RENTAL

FITZWILLIAM RENTAL purchased a disused building in the city docklands at a cost of €1.5M on 1 January 2009. The intention at this time was to develop the property and to subsequently let the various floors to professional firms. A further €300,000 was spent over the next 11 months on renovations and improvements to the building prior to letting. The building was ready for tenant occupation on 1 December 2009. The valuation of the completed property at 31 December 2009 was €2M. Due to unforeseen difficulties in obtaining tenants, the building remained unoccupied.

In February 2010, the docklands property was valued at €2.1M and the group then decided to immediately relocate its headquarters to this building. FITZWILLIAM RENTAL managed to secure new tenants for the group's 'old' headquarters. The book value of those headquarters was €1.5M and the market value at the date of letting in February 2010 was €1.8M. The valuations of both properties were provided by independent qualified valuers.

Required:

Explain with reference to international accounting standards, the accounting treatment of the property transaction undertaken in the years ended 31 December 2009 and 31 December 2010 in the books of FITZWILLIAM RENTAL. Provide relevant disclosure details.

(Chartered Accountants Ireland)

15.2 HARDING Limited

HARDING Limited owns an investment property that is leased to a third party on a 10-year operating lease. The investment property was purchased during the year ended 31 December 2009, and was recorded in the financial statements at cost on 31 December 2009.

Relevant details of the cost and fair values of the property are as follows:

	€M
Cost	19
Valuation 31 December 2009	n/a
Valuation 31 December 2010	23

The valuation at 31 December 2010 has not yet been incorporated into the financial statements. The board would like to apply the fair value model to its investment property for the current reporting period.

(Chartered Accountants Ireland)

15.3 ASLOW plc

ASLOW plc owns a number of properties which are described below:

(i) Property A: a freehold factory and office block used entirely by ASLOW plc for its own manufacturing and administration.

(ii) Property B: a freehold office block, let at commercial rates to a large insurance company.

(iii) Property C: a leasehold factory and office block with 60 years' unexpired tenure, sublet at commercial rates to Fad Ltd, a wholly owned **subsidiary** of ASLOW.

(iv) Property D: a leasehold office block with 25 years' unexpired tenure at 1 June 2009. The property is sublet on a five-year lease at commercial rates to a shipping company in which ASLOW plc owns 35% of the ordinary share capital.

(v) Property E: a freehold cottage, originally purchased to provide assistance to employees, which is now let commercially to tenants who have no connection with the company.

The company had all the above properties valued by an independent professional valuer on 31 May 2009. The following is a summary of the valuation and original costs of the properties:

	COST		VALUATION	
	Land	Buildings	Land	Buildings
Freehold properties	€	€	€	€
(i) Property A	10,000	24,000	40,000	90,000
(ii) Property B	25,000	60,000	30,000	80,000
(iii) Property E	4,000	8,000	16,000	24,000

	Cost	Valuation
Leasehold properties	€	€
(iv) Property C	72,000	120,000
(v) Property D	60,000	90,000

All of the above properties are estimated to have a remaining useful life of 40 years from 1 June 2009. The company adopts a straight-line depreciation policy, and uses the revaluation model for all of its properties.

Required:

(a) Identify which of the above properties may be classed as investment property in the consolidated financial statements of the ASLOW Group.

(b) Prepare the necessary journal entries to incorporate the revaluations of all the properties in the consolidated financial statements of the ASLOW Group for the year ended 31 May 2010.

(c) Show the required depreciation charge for the properties, where applicable, as per IAS 16 *Property, Plant and Equipment* and IAS 40 *Investment Property*.

15.4 IRISHLINK

IRISHLINK acquired a retail complex near Dublin in July 2010 for €20M, obtaining a 10-year bank loan to fund the acquisition at a fixed rate of 5% per annum. IRISHLINK is currently renting the complex to a well-known home furnishings chain at an annual rental of €1M. The directors of IRISHLINK believe that the value of the complex at 31 December 2010 was €23M.

Required:

Explain how the following should be treated in the financial statements of IRISHLINK for the year ended 31 December 2010:

(a) retail complex

(b) bank loan and interest

(c) rental income   (Chartered Accountants Ireland)

Chapter 16

Impairment of assets

The well-known advertising slogan, 'Because I'm Worth It', has long been associated with beauty and cosmetics giant L'Oréal. In recent years, although this catchphrase has evolved into 'Because You're Worth It' and 'Because We're Worth It', the basic tenet of the statement remains the same. As assets cannot be recognised at more than what they are worth, the statement could also be applied to an entity's statement of financial position.

Consider the case of an entity that purchases a machine for €100,000, which it depreciates over five years on a straight-line basis. After two years, the machine will be included in the SOFP at its net book value of €60,000. The question that arises is whether the machine is worth €60,000 or more at that date. The entity can recover the machine's NBV in either of two ways:

- by selling the machine; or
- by continuing to use the machine

Whatever amount the entity can realise from the better of these two options is called the machine's *recoverable amount*. As long as the recoverable amount is at least €60,000, the entity can continue to include the machine in the SOFP at its NBV of €60,000. It could even attach a confirmatory sticker, proclaiming 'Because I'm Worth It!'

Thus, the primary objective of accounting for the impairment of assets is to ensure that assets are not included in the SOFP at a value that exceeds their recoverable amount. IAS 36 *Impairment of Assets* sets out the rules that must be followed in this area.

Scope of IAS 36

IAS 36 applies to all assets *except* the following:

- inventories (see IAS 2)
- assets arising from construction contracts (see IAS 11)
- deferred tax assets (see IAS 12)
- assets arising from employee benefits (see IAS 19)
- financial assets within the scope of IFRS 9
- investment property measured at **fair value** (see IAS 40)
- agricultural assets carried at fair value (see IAS 41)
- **non-current assets** (or disposal groups) held for sale (see IFRS 5).

Therefore, the assets that IAS 36 *does apply to* include the following:

- machinery
- land and buildings

- intangible assets
- **goodwill**
- investment property carried at cost, and
- investments in **subsidiaries**, associates and joint ventures carried at cost.

Definitions

- Carrying amount:

  the amount of an asset in the statement of financial position, after deducting accumulated depreciation and impairment losses.

- Fair value:

  the amount obtainable from the sale of an asset in an arm's length transaction, between knowledgeable, willing parties.

- Impairment:

  an asset is impaired when its carrying amount is greater than its recoverable amount.

- Recoverable amount:

  the higher of an asset's fair value less costs to sell, and its value in use.

- Value in use:

  the present value of the future cash flows expected to be derived from an asset (including its disposal).

Identifying an asset that may be impaired

All assets should be reviewed at the end of each reporting period for indications of impairment (see Appendix 16.1).

The recoverable amount of the following types of *intangible assets* should be computed annually, whether or not there is any indication that they may be impaired:

- an intangible asset with an indefinite useful life;
- an intangible asset not yet available for use;
- goodwill acquired in a business combination.

An indication that an asset may be impaired may indicate that the asset's expected useful life, depreciation method, or residual value may need to be reviewed and adjusted.

Impairment review procedures

Where there is evidence that an asset may be impaired, it will be necessary to establish if its carrying amount exceeds its recoverable amount. If so, an impairment write-down will be required.

The following procedure can be followed when carrying out an impairment review.

■ (a) Calculate fair value less costs to sell

If this exceeds the carrying amount of the asset in the SOFP, then no impairment write-down is necessary.

Example 1 Morgan Limited has been reviewing an item of machinery for impairment. The net book value (i.e. carrying amount) of the machine is €125,000 and its fair value less costs to sell is €140,000.

The recoverable amount of this machine is at least €140,000 (value in use could be even higher). Therefore, no impairment write-down is required.

■ (b) If fair value less costs to sell is *less than* carrying amount of asset in SOFP

It will now be necessary to compute the asset's value in use (see Appendix 16.2).

Example 2 Rugged Limited has been reviewing an item of machinery for impairment. Details are as follows:

- Net book value in SOFP = €200,000
- Fair value less costs to sell = €160,000
- Annual projected net cash inflow from asset for next five years = €40,000
- Disposal value of asset at end of useful life = €20,000
- Current borrowing cost to finance the purchase of this type of asset = 10%

Outline the procedure for an impairment review in respect of this asset.

Solution Value in use = (€40,000 × 3.79*) + (€20,000 × 0.621[†]) = €164,020

Fair value less costs to sell = €160,000

Recoverable amount (i.e. higher of fair value less costs to sell and value in use) = €164,020.

Carrying amount = €200,000

Thus, an impairment write-down of €35,980 is required.

* Annuity factor for five years at 10%.
[†] PV factor for year 5 at 10%.

The recoverable amount should be computed on an individual asset basis if possible. If this is not possible, then the recoverable amount should be computed for the asset's cash-generating unit (CGU). A CGU is the smallest identifiable group of assets that generates cash inflows which are largely independent of the cash inflows from other assets or groups of assets.

Recognising an impairment loss

An impairment loss should be recognised whenever the recoverable amount of an asset is less than its carrying amount.

The impairment loss is charged in profit or loss, unless it relates to an asset in respect of which there is a previous revaluation surplus.

Example 3 Torc Limited has been reviewing a land site which may be subject to impairment. Details are as follows:

> Cost in 2008 = €1.2M
> Carrying value in SOFP at 31 December 2010 = €1.8M
> Fair value less costs to sell at 31 December 2010 = €1M
> Value in use at 31 December 2010 = €800,000

The recoverable amount of the land at 31 December 2010 is €1M (i.e. higher of value in use and fair value less costs to sell). As this is less than the asset's carrying value of €1.8M, an impairment write-down is required.

The full entries in respect of the land, since purchase date, are outlined as follows:

	Dr €'000	Cr €'000
Land	1,200	
Bank		1,200
(Being purchase of land in 2008)		
Land	600	
Revaluation surplus – OCI		600
(Being subsequent revaluation of land)		
Revaluation surplus – OCI	600	
Impairment loss – I/S	200	
Land		800

(Being impairment loss on land in 2010. This is first offset against the revaluation surplus on the same asset, the balance of €200,000 being charged in profit or loss)

Subject to materiality considerations, the impairment loss should be separately disclosed in the income statement, in accordance with IAS 1 *Presentation of Financial Statements*.

Reversal of an impairment loss

Assets should be assessed at the end of each reporting period for evidence that an impairment loss may have decreased. If so, the asset's recoverable amount should be computed. The reversal of an impairment loss is recognised in profit or loss, unless it relates to a revalued asset.

Example 4 Let us assume that, when reviewing the land site in Example 3 above at 31 December 2011 (i.e. one year later), it is found that the recoverable amount of the land is €1.4M.

The reversal in profit or loss should not exceed the amount of the impairment loss that was originally charged in that statement. Thus the extent to which profit or loss is increased is restricted to €200,000 as follows:

	Dr €'000	Cr €'000
Land	400	
Reversal of impairment loss – I/S		200
Revaluation surplus – OCI		200
(Being reversal of impairment loss)		

The increased carrying amount of an asset due to the reversal of an impairment loss should not exceed the amount at which the asset would have been carried (net of depreciation or amortisation) had no impairment loss been recognised in prior years.

Example 5 Brook Limited purchased a machine on 1 January 2007 for €100,000. The machine was depreciated at 10% per annum on a straight-line basis for 2007 and 2008. At 31 December 2008, an impairment loss of €30,000 was recognised in respect of the machine. At 31 December 2010 this impairment loss was reversed.

The journal entries in respect of this machine will be recorded as follows:

	Dr €	Cr €
Machinery	100,000	
Bank		100,000
(Being purchase of machine on 1 January 2007)		
Depreciation expense	10,000	
Accumulated depreciation		10,000
(Being depreciation charged in each of the years 2007 and 2008)		
Impairment loss – I/S	30,000	
Machinery		30,000
(Being impairment loss at 31 December 2008)		
Depreciation expense	6,250	
Accumulated depreciation		6,250
(Being depreciation charged in each of the years 2009 and 2010, i.e. €50,000 NBV at 1 January 2009/8 years unexpired life)		
Machinery	22,500	
Reversal of impairment loss – I/S		22,500
(Being reversal of impairment loss – see note 1)		

Note 1:

Subsequent depreciation if machine had *not* suffered an impairment loss; €10,000 in 2009 and 2010	€20,000
Actual depreciation charged in 2009 and 2010	(€12,500)
Reversal of previous impairment loss of €30,000 is restricted by	€7,500

The NBV of the machine at 31 December 2010 is €60,000 (€100,000 – €10,000 – €10,000 – €30,000 – €6,250 – €6,250 + €22,500). This would have been the amount of the asset's NBV at 31 December 2010, if no impairment loss had been recognised (i.e. €100,000 less four years' depreciation at €10,000 per annum).

Impairment of goodwill

Goodwill should be tested annually for impairment.

For the purpose of impairment testing, goodwill should be allocated to each of the acquirer's cash-generating units, or groups of CGUs, that are expected to benefit from the synergies of the combination. A CGU to which goodwill has been allocated should be tested for impairment annually by comparing the carrying amount of the unit, including the goodwill, with the unit's recoverable amount.

An impairment loss is allocated to reduce the carrying amount of the assets of the CGU in the following order:

- first reduce goodwill allocated to the CGU; and
- then, reduce the other assets of the CGU on a pro rata basis.

The reversal of an impairment loss for goodwill is *not* permitted.

Example 6

In January 2008 Brook Limited set up a division within the company to examine the potential of green energy initiatives. By 2010 it was clear that the initiatives, while having the support of environmental groups, were not commercially viable. Consequently, an impairment review of the Green Energy Division was carried out at 31 December 2010. The following are details of the impairment review.

(i)

Book value of net assets of Division in SOFP	*Fair value less costs to sell of Division's net assets*
€'000	€'000
1,800*	750

* The book value of net assets comprises:

	€'000
Goodwill	450
Plant and machinery	600
Buildings	750
	1,800

(ii) Value in use

The cumulative values of future cash flows of the Green Energy Division at 31 December 2010 are estimated as follows. These figures are based on the company's approved budgets for the next five years.

	€'000
Net cash flows from operations before tax	2,145
Additional net cash flows from planned product improvement	1,000
Finance costs	800

Brook Limited's pre-tax weighted average cost of capital (WACC) is 16%.

Required:
Outline how the Green Energy Division should be accounted for by Brook Limited.

Solution

IAS 36 requires an impairment review to be carried out where indicators of impairment suggest that a company's assets may not be fully recoverable. For this purpose, the Green Energy Division is identified as a CGU, and the impairment review process requires the following procedures to be employed:

- It is necessary to establish if the carrying value of the Division's net assets is less than their recoverable amount.

- As the carrying value of the net assets (€1.8M) exceeds their fair value less costs to sell (€750,000), a value in use computation is required.

■ **Value in use computation:**

Terminal value of division's net cash flows (based on pre-tax and pre-finance cash flows as required by IAS 36)	€2.145M*
Discount factor for year 5 using a discount rate of 16%	0.4761
Present value of net cash flows of cash generating unit	€1.021M

* IAS 36 does not permit the inclusion of estimated future cash flows that are expected to arise from improving or enhancing an asset's performance. Thus, cash flows from product improvements are excluded.

■ The **recoverable amount** of the net assets of the Green Energy Division is the *higher* of:
  ■ fair value less costs to sell of €750,000: and
  ■ value in use €1,021,000.

Thus, the recoverable amount is €1,021,000. As this is less than the carrying amount of the net assets (€1.8M), the value of the Division's assets must be reduced. The required reduction of €779,000 should be accounted for as follows:

(i) Goodwill of €450,000 should be eliminated;
(ii) The balance of €329,000 should be written off against the other assets of the Division, on a pro rata basis, relative to their carrying amount in the SOFP.

Therefore, the following journal entry is required:

	Dr €'000	Cr €'000
Impairment write-off – I/S	779	
Goodwill		450
Plant and machinery (€329,000 × (€600,000/€1,350,000))		146
Buildings (€329,000 × (€750,000/€1,350,000))		183

These write-downs should be included in profit or loss for the year ended 31 December 2010, and if material they should be separately disclosed in accordance with IAS 1.

Disclosure

An entity should disclose the following for each class of asset:

■ impairment losses and reversals recognised in profit or loss for the period;
■ impairment losses on revalued assets, and reversals, recognised in other comprehensive income for the period.

For each reportable segment, disclose:

■ impairment losses and reversals recognised in profit or loss and in OCI.

For each material impairment loss recognised or reversed during the period, disclose:

■ events and circumstances that led to the recognition or reversal;
■ amount of the impairment loss;
■ for an individual asset – its nature and reporting segment;
■ for a cash generating unit – its description and amount of loss, by class of asset and segment;
■ whether recoverable amount is fair value less costs to sell or value in use;
■ if recoverable amount is fair value less costs to sell, the basis used to determine it;
■ if recoverable amount is value in use, the discount rate used.

Summary

- The recoverable amount of an asset is the higher of its fair value less costs to sell and its value in use.

- An impairment loss occurs when an asset's recoverable amount is less than the amount at which an asset is included in the financial statements.

- An impairment loss should be charged to profit or loss, unless it relates to a revalued asset, in which case the impairment loss should be offset against a revaluation surplus on the same asset.

- At the end of each reporting period, an entity should assess whether there is any indication that an asset may be impaired. Impairment testing must in any event be carried out annually for goodwill and for intangible assets with indefinite useful lives. Other assets should be tested if there is evidence of impairment.

- When testing goodwill for impairment, it should be allocated to each of the acquirer's cash-generating units (CGUs). An impairment loss for a CGU is first set off against goodwill that has been allocated to the CGU. The remaining assets of the CGU are then reduced by any remaining loss on a pro rata basis.

- Impairment losses should be reversed if the recoverable amount of an asset or CGU exceeds its carrying amount. Impairment losses relating to goodwill cannot be reversed.

Appendix 16.1

Indications of impairment

The following are identified by IAS 36 as indications that an asset may be impaired. This is not intended to be an exhaustive list.

External sources of information

- Decline in market value during the period
- Adverse changes in technological, market, economic or legal environments
- Increases in market interest rates
- Carrying amount of an entity's net assets exceeds its market capitalisation

Internal sources of information

- Evidence of obsolescence or physical damage of asset
- Adverse changes in use of asset. For example:
  - asset becoming idle;
  - plans to discontinue or restructure the operation to which the asset belongs;
  - plans to dispose of an asset before the previously planned date;
  - a reassessment of the useful life of an asset from indefinite to finite.
- Worse than expected economic performance of asset.

Appendix 16.2

Value in use

The following elements should be reflected in the calculation of an asset's value in use:

- An estimate of the future cash flows the entity expects to derive from the asset
- Expectations about possible variations in the amount or timing of those future cash flows
- The time value of money, represented by the current market risk-free rate of interest
- The price for bearing the uncertainty inherent in the asset
- Other factors, such as illiquidity, that market participants would reflect in pricing the future cash flows the entity expects to derive from the asset.

Basis for estimates of future cash flows

In measuring value in use, an entity should:

- base cash flow projections on reasonable and supportable assumptions;
- use the most recent financial budgets/forecasts approved by management. Exclude cash flows expected to arise from future restructurings, or from improving or enhancing an asset's performance;
- projections should normally cover a maximum period of five years;
- estimates of future cash flows should *not* include cash flows from financing activities, or income tax receipts or payments.

Discount rate

A **pre-tax** discount rate should be used. For an individual asset or group of assets, the discount rate is the rate the company would pay to borrow money to buy that specific asset or group of assets.

QUESTIONS

16.1 BLACK Limited

On 31 December 2010 the directors of BLACK carried out an impairment review of the company's properties and discovered that one of the properties, which had originally cost €50M, had been physically damaged. The net book value of this particular property at 31 December 2010 was €28M, while its value in use and net realisable value were €18M and €20M respectively at the same date.

Required:
What is the impairment loss to be recorded in the income statement of BLACK for the year ended 31 December 2010?

(a) nil
(b) €8M
(c) €10M
(d) €22M   (Chartered Accountants Ireland)

16.2 Portable metal detectors

Three years ago the majority of MAGNA SECURITY's turnover and profits were derived from the manufacture and sale of portable metal detectors. However, in November 2006 a rival Canadian company entered the market with cheaper and more easily portable equipment which utilised pioneering new technology capable of detecting a wider range of metals and materials even if present in smaller quantities. This 'new technology' effectively rendered MAGNA SECURITY's products uncompetitive and virtually unsaleable. As a result of an impairment review prompted by the impact on trading of the Canadian competitor, MAGNA SECURITY wrote down the value of its portable metal detector production line on the grounds of impairment and focused on other areas of its operations.

The equipment concerned comprised a production line and associated tooling, purchased and first used in operation on 1 January 2004 with a cost of €2M. The equipment was depreciated straight line over 10 years and with a full year's depreciation charged in the year of acquisition.

On 1 January 2007 MAGNA SECURITY took the decision to provide in full for the then NBV of the equipment, as the equipment was very specialised and had no value on the open market and could not be used in any other of the company's operations. The equipment was 'mothballed'.

In June 2010 the Canadian company was forced to recall and withdraw its products from sale as a result of health scares experienced by operators of the equipment. Consequently, since June 2010 MAGNA SECURITY has been inundated with enquiries and orders for its original market-leading product and production recommenced on 1 October 2010 using the previously 'mothballed' production line.

Required:
Set out the impact, if any, of the withdrawal of the Canadian competitor on the carrying value of the 'mothballed' equipment in the financial statements of MAGNA SECURITY for the year ended 31 December 2010.   (Chartered Accountants Ireland)

16.3 WILDERNESS Limited

WILDERNESS Ltd values all of its assets at their historical cost. One of its assets has a carrying amount of €100,000. The asset is depreciated on a straight-line basis with a remaining useful life of three years and a residual value of €10,000.

The asset is expected to generate net cash flows of €20,000 per year for the next three years and then be sold for €10,000. Disposal costs are expected to be negligible.

At present, the asset could be sold for €50,000 and disposal costs would be €2,000.

Required:

(a) Assuming a discount rate of 10% and that all cash flows occur at the end of each year, determine the asset's value in use.

(b) Calculate the amount of the impairment loss which has occurred and explain how this should be accounted for in accordance with IAS 36 *Impairment of Assets*.

(c) Calculate the amount of depreciation that should be charged in relation to the asset for each of the next three years assuming that the straight-line method will continue to be used.

16.4 STUDENT VILLE

STUDENT VILLE plc has provided you with the following forecast of cash flows from two of its cash-generating units, Division 1 and Division 2, for six years:

Cash flows	Division 1 €000	Division 2 €000
2011	2,400	6,000
2012	1,800	6,600
2013	2,700	5,400
2014	3,000	7,200
2015	3,300	4,500
2016	3,600	9,000

While reviewing valuations of assets at the year end, they have identified that the fair value less costs to sell of Division 1 is €15M, and the fair value less costs to sell of Division 2 is currently €21M. The appropriate discount rate for activities in Division 1 is 10% and Division 2 is 12%.

The carrying value of the assets comprising these CGUs is outlined below:

	Division 1 €000	Division 2 €000
Inventory	6,000	7,000
Goodwill	–	6,000
Tangible non-current assets	7,500	34,500

Required:

(a) Identify whether any impairment losses have taken place in Division 1 and Division 2.

(b) Allocate any impairment losses in accordance with IAS 36 *Impairment of Assets*.

Chapter 17

Non-current assets held for sale and discontinued operations

The usefulness of financial statements for decision-making purposes is dependent on the information that they contain being relevant and reliable. Should an entity decide to dispose of a building, for example, this decision should be reflected in its financial statements. Thus, by the building's reclassification from **non-current assets** to **current assets**, users of the financial statements will be informed of its imminent disposal.

Similarly, comparability over time is an essential prerequisite for **financial statements** to be useful for decision-making purposes. Should an entity discontinue one of its key product lines, for example, it would be important that this be clearly evident in its financial statements. This can be achieved by separately highlighting the results of the product line in the entity's current period income statement and that of previous periods presented.

These issues are addressed by IFRS 5 *Non-Current Assets Held for Sale and Discontinued Operations*.

Assets held for sale

Scope

The *classification* and *presentation* requirements of IFRS 5 apply to all recognised non-current assets and to all disposal groups of an entity.

The *measurement* provisions of IFRS 5 apply to all non-current assets and disposal groups, except the following:

- deferred tax assets (IAS 12)
- assets arising from employee benefits (IAS 19)
- financial assets within the scope of IAS 39
- investment properties that are accounted for under the fair value model of IAS 40
- non-current assets that are measured at fair value less costs to sell in accordance with IAS 41 *Agriculture*
- contractual rights under insurance contracts (IFRS 4).

Definition

To be classified as held for sale, a non-current asset (or *disposal group**) must meet the following conditions;

- management is committed to a plan to sell;
- asset is available for immediate sale;
- the sale is highly probable;

- an active programme to locate a buyer has been initiated;
- the sale is expected to be completed within 12 months of classification as held for sale;
- asset is being actively marketed at a sales price which is reasonable in relation to its fair value.

* A disposal group is a group of assets, with associated liabilities, which an entity intends to dispose of in a single transaction. An example would be a division within a business.

To be classified as held for sale, non-current assets (or disposal groups) need to be disposed of through **sale**. Thus, assets that are expected to be abandoned would not meet the definition. Non-current assets to be abandoned include those that are to be used to the end of their economic life, and non-current assets (or disposal groups) that are to be closed rather than sold.

■ Measurement

- *Immediately before the initial classification of an asset as held for sale.*
  The carrying amount of the asset (or the carrying amount of all the **assets** and **liabilities** in the disposal group) should be measured in accordance with applicable IFRSs/IASs.
- *After classification as held for sale:*
  - Non-current assets or disposal groups that are classified as held for sale are measured at the lower of their carrying amount and fair value less costs to sell.
  - Non-current assets or disposal groups that are classified as held for sale should not be depreciated. They should, however, be monitored for **impairment**.

■ Approach required

Step 1: Ascertain if a non-current asset (or disposal group) qualifies to be classified as being held for sale.

Step 2: Immediately before the initial classification as held for sale.
Compare the asset's carrying value with its recoverable amount. Value in use is irrelevant so:

(a) For non-current assets measured under the cost model and revalued assets suffering an impairment:
  - If fair value less costs to sell is less than carrying value, an impairment write-down is required under IAS 36 *Impairment of Assets*.
  - For non-current assets carried under the **cost model**, the write-down should be charged to profit or loss.
  - For **revalued** non-current assets, the write-down should first be offset against a revaluation surplus on the same asset, with any excess being charged to profit or loss.
(b) For revalued non-current assets *not* suffering an impairment:
  Revalue to fair value in accordance with IAS 16/IAS 38.

Step 3: Reclassify non-current asset as an asset held for sale.
Asset (or disposal group) is transferred from non-current assets to assets held for sale.

Step 4: After classification as held for sale:

- Asset held for sale should be valued at fair value less costs to sell.
- Asset is no longer depreciated, but must be monitored for impairment losses.
- An impairment loss should be charged to profit or loss, even where an asset had previously been carried at a revalued amount.

- A subsequent increase in fair value less costs to sell can be recognised in profit or loss to the extent that it does not exceed any impairment loss recognised either under IFRS 5 or previously under IAS 36.

See Examples 1–4 in Appendix 17.1.

■ Presentation in statement of financial position

Assets classified as held for sale, and assets included within a disposal group classified as held for sale, must be presented separately on the face of the SOFP, and included in current assets.

The liabilities of a disposal group classified as held for sale must be presented separately from other liabilities, and included in current liabilities.

■ Subsidiaries acquired with a view to resale and classified as held for sale

IFRS 5 applies in accounting for a **subsidiary** for which control is intended to be temporary, because the subsidiary is held exclusively with a view to disposal:

- If it is highly probable that the sale will be completed within 12 months, then the subsidiary should be accounted for, under IFRS 5, as a disposal group held for sale. The assets and the liabilities of the subsidiary should *not* be offset, and each should be presented as a separate line in the consolidated SOFP.
- The above treatment applies, even if the group will retain a non-controlling interest after its disposal of the subsidiary (e.g. the **parent** may dispose of a 60% interest in a wholly owned subsidiary). In this event, 100% of the assets and liabilities of the subsidiary should be classified as held for sale, notwithstanding the fact that a non-controlling interest will be retained.
- If the subsidiary has previously been consolidated, however, IAS 27 *Consolidated and Separate Financial Statements* requires that it must continue to be consolidated until it is disposed of. Thus, it is not classified as a disposal group held for sale.

■ Changes to a plan of sale

If the criteria to be classified as held for sale are no longer met, an entity shall cease to classify an asset (or disposal group) as held for sale.

Such an asset (or disposal group) should be measured at the *lower of*:

(i) its carrying amount before it was classified as held for sale, adjusted for any depreciation, amortisation or revaluations that would have been recognised had the asset (or disposal group) not been classified as held for sale; and

(ii) its recoverable amount (i.e. higher of fair value less costs to sell, and value in use) at the date of the decision not to sell.

Any required adjustment to the carrying value of a non-current asset that ceases to be classified as held for sale should be included in profit or loss for continuing operations. However, should a revaluation surplus exist in respect of the asset, the adjustment should be treated as a revaluation increase or decrease.

Example 1 Mist Limited had classified a property asset as held for sale in the company's SOFP at 31 March 2009. The property was included in the financial statements at €1.5M at that time, which included a revaluation surplus of €400,000.

On the 31 March 2010, it was decided not to dispose of the property, due to a scarcity of buyers in the marketplace. Mist Limited depreciates property at 2% per annum on a reducing balance basis.

It was estimated (at 31 March 2010) that the property's market value was €1M, before deducting selling costs of €30,000. Value in use was estimated at €950,000.

Outline how the property should be accounted for in the financial statements of Mist Limited for the year ended 31 March 2010.

Solution
As the property no longer satisfies the criteria to be classified as held for sale, it must be reclassified in Mist Limited's SOFP at 31 March 2010.

The property should be measured at the *lower of*:

(i) its carrying amount before it was classified as held for sale, adjusted for depreciation that would have been recognised had the asset not been classified as held for sale (i.e. €1.5M less depreciation of €30,000 = €1.47M), and

(ii) its recoverable amount which, at the date of the decision not to sell, is the higher of:
    (a) fair value less costs to sell of €970,000; and
    (b) value in use of €950,000.

Therefore, the property should be valued at €970,000 in the financial statements of Mist Limited at 31 March 2010.

The following journal entries will be required:

	Dr €'000	Cr €'000
Property	1,500	
Asset held for sale		1,500
(Being transfer of non-current asset that ceases to qualify as being held for sale)		
Revaluation surplus – OCI	400	
Impairment write-down – I/S	130	
Property		530
(Being write-down of property to its recoverable amount)		

Non-current assets or disposal groups to be abandoned

These are not classified as held for sale, as their recoverable amount will be recovered principally through continuing use. However, a disposal group should be classified as a discontinued operation on the date on which it ceases to be used, provided that on that date it satisfies the definition of discontinued operations.

Non-current assets (or disposal groups) to be abandoned include non-current assets (or disposal groups) that are to be used to the end of their economic life.

Disclosures

The following information must be disclosed in the period in which a non-current asset (or disposal group) has been either classified as held for sale or sold:

- description of the non-current asset (or disposal group);
- details of the facts and circumstances of the sale, or the expected disposal, and the expected manner and timing of that disposal;

- impairment losses and reversals of impairment losses;
- if applicable, the reportable segment in which the non-current asset (or disposal group) is presented in accordance with IFRS 8 *Operating Segments*.

Discontinued operations

■ Definition

A discontinued operation is a component* of an entity that has either been disposed of or is classified as held for sale, and:

- represents a separate major line of business or geographical area of operations;
- is part of a single coordinated plan to dispose of a separate major line of business or geographical area of operations; or
- is a subsidiary acquired exclusively with a view to resale.

* A component of an entity is any operation and cash flows that can be clearly distinguished, operationally and for financial reporting purposes.

■ Timing of classification as a discontinued operation

IFRS 5 classifies an operation as discontinued at the date:

- when an entity actually disposes of the operation; or
- when the operation satisfies the criteria to be classified as held for sale.

IFRS 5 prohibits retrospective classification as a discontinued operation, when the criteria are met after the end of the reporting period.

■ Presenting discontinued operations

The following should be presented as a single amount in the statement of comprehensive income:

- the post-tax profit or loss of discontinued operations; and
- the post-tax gain or loss recognised:
  - on the measurement at fair value less costs to sell, or
  - on the disposal
  of the assets or disposal group(s) that constitute the discontinued operation.

See Appendix 17.2.

■ Disclosure

Detailed disclosure is required of:

- revenue, expenses, pre-tax profit or loss, and related income taxes of discontinued operations;
- the gain or loss recognised on the measurement to fair value less costs to sell, or on the disposal of the assets or disposal group(s) constituting the discontinued operation, together with the related income tax expense.

The above information can be provided either in the notes, or in the statement of comprehensive income in a separate section from continuing operations. Such disclosure must cover the current and all prior periods presented in the financial statements.

Adjustments in the current period to amounts presented as a discontinued operation in prior periods must be separately disclosed. These might arise, for example, due to the resolution of uncertainties relating to the terms of the disposal, such as the selling price.

If an entity ceases to classify a component as held for sale, the results of operations of the component previously presented in discontinued operations must be reclassified and included in income from continuing operations for all periods presented.

Summary

■ Non-current assets held for sale

- IFRS 5 stipulates the requirements for non-current assets or disposal groups to be classified as *held for sale*.
- Prior to its initial classification as held for sale, the carrying amount of an asset or disposal group should be measured in accordance with applicable IFRSs/IASs.
- After classification as held for sale, non-current assets should be measured at the lower of their carrying amount and fair value less costs to sell. They should not be depreciated, but should continue to be monitored for impairment.

■ Discontinued operations

- A discontinued operation is a component of an entity that has either been disposed of or is classified as held for sale, and:
  - represents a separate major line of business or geographical area of operations;
  - is part of a single coordinated plan to dispose of a separate major line of business or geographical area of operations; or
  - is a subsidiary acquired exclusively with a view to resale.
- The following should be presented as a single amount in the statement of comprehensive income:
  - the post-tax profit or loss of discontinued operations; and
  - the post-tax gain or loss recognised, on the measurement at fair value less costs to sell, or on the disposal of the assets or disposal group(s) that constitute the discontinued operation.

Appendix 17.1

Examples of non-current assets held for sale

Example 1 **Asset carried under IAS 16 *Cost Model* (no write-down required)**

Kompany Limited has a building which has been carried under the IAS 16 *Cost Model*. At 31 March 2010, the building satisfies the conditions of IFRS 5 to be classified as *held for sale*. The following information relates to the asset at that date:

- NBV = €400,000
- fair value (i.e. market value) = €440,000
- selling costs = €20,000
- value in use = €280,000 (provided for information purposes only)

Outline how the above non-current asset should be accounted for in the financial statements of Kompany Limited.

Solution (Tax is ignored)

Step 1: The building qualifies as an asset that should be classified as held for sale.

Step 2: Immediately before the initial classification as held for sale.
IFRS 5 requires that an asset's carrying amount should be measured in accordance with applicable IFRSs/IASs.

   It is necessary therefore to examine the building for evidence of impairment under IAS 36. There is no evidence of impairment at this date, however, as the asset's recoverable amount (i.e. fair value less costs to sell, as value in use is not relevant) of €420,000 exceeds its carrying value (i.e. NBV) of €400,000.

Step 3: Reclassify non-current asset as an asset held for sale.
The asset is reclassified as follows in accordance with IFRS 5:

	Dr €'000	Cr €'000
Asset held for sale	400	
Property, plant and equipment		400
(Being reclassification of building as an asset held for sale)		

Step 4: After classification as held for sale.
No further adjustment is necessary, as the asset's carrying amount (€400,000) does not exceed its fair value less costs to sell (€420,000).

   After classification as held for sale, no further depreciation will be charged on the building, but it must continue to be monitored for impairment.

Example 2 Asset carried under IAS 16 *Cost Model* (write-down required)

Kompany Limited has a building which has been carried under the IAS 16 *Cost Model*. At 31 March 2010 the building satisfies the conditions of IFRS 5 to be classified as a non-current asset held for sale. The following information relates to the asset at that date:

- NBV = €400,000
- fair value (i.e. market value) = €360,000
- selling costs = €20,000
- value in use = €280,000 (provided for information purposes only)

Outline how the above non-current asset should be accounted for in the financial statements of Kompany Limited.

Solution   (Tax is ignored)

Step 1: The building qualifies as an asset that should be classified as held for sale.

Step 2: Immediately before the initial classification as held for sale.
IFRS 5 requires that the asset's carrying amount should be measured in accordance with applicable IFRSs/IASs.

It is necessary therefore to examine the building for evidence of impairment under IAS 36. In this case there is an impairment of the asset as its recoverable amount (i.e. fair value less costs to sell, as value in use is not relevant) of €340,000 is less than its carrying value of €400,000.

The asset is therefore written down to its recoverable amount in accordance with IAS 36:

	Dr €'000	Cr €'000
Impairment loss – I/S	60	
Property, plant and equipment		60

Step 3: Reclassify non-current asset as an asset held for sale.
The asset is reclassified as follows in accordance with IFRS 5:

	Dr €'000	Cr €'000
Asset held for sale	340	
Property, plant and equipment		340
(Being reclassification of building as an asset held for sale)		

Step 4: After classification as held for sale.
No further adjustment is necessary, as the asset's carrying amount (€340,000) does not exceed its fair value less costs to sell (€340,000).

After classification as held for sale, no further depreciation will be charged on the building, but it must continue to be monitored for impairment.

Example 3   Asset carried under IAS 16 *Revaluation Model* (write-down required)

Kompany Limited has land which has been carried under the revaluation model of IAS 16. At 31 March 2010, the land satisfies the conditions of IFRS 5 to be classified as a non-current asset held for sale. The following information relates to the asset at that date:

- cost = €250,000
- carrying value = €400,000
- fair value (i.e. market value) = €360,000
- selling costs = €20,000
- value in use = €280,000 (provided for information purposes only)

Outline how the above non-current asset should be accounted for in the financial statements of Kompany Limited.

Solution   (Tax is ignored)

Step 1: The land qualifies as an asset that should be classified as held for sale.

Step 2: Immediately before the initial classification of the asset as held for sale.

IFRS 5 requires that its carrying amount shall be measured in accordance with applicable IFRSs/IASs.

It is necessary therefore to examine the land for evidence of impairment under IAS 36.

In this instance there is an impairment of the land, as its recoverable amount (i.e. fair value less costs to sell, as value in use is not relevant) of €340,000 is less than its carrying value of €400,000.

The land is therefore written down to its recoverable amount in accordance with IAS 36:

	Dr €'000	Cr €'000
Revaluation surplus – OCI	60	
Property, plant and equipment		60

Step 3: Reclassify non-current asset as an asset held for sale.

	Dr €'000	Cr €'000
Asset held for sale	340	
Property, plant and equipment		340
(Being reclassification of building as an asset held for sale)		

Step 4: After classification as held for sale.
No further adjustment is necessary, as the asset's carrying amount (€340,000) does not exceed its fair value less costs to sell (€340,000).

After classification as held for sale, the land must continue to be monitored for impairment.

Let us assume that, on 1 July 2010, the fair value less costs to sell of the land falls to €300,000.

- There is a further impairment loss of €40,000 relating to the land.
- IFRS 5 states that an entity shall recognise an impairment loss for any subsequent write-down, i.e. where a loss occurs after the asset is classified as held for sale. Any such loss should be charged to profit or loss. Thus, the following journal entry will be required:

	Dr €'000	Cr €'000
Impairment loss – I/S	40	
Asset held for sale		40
(Being impairment of asset after classification as held for sale)		

- Any increase in value, while an asset is held for sale, should be recognised in profit or loss to the extent that it does not exceed the cumulative impairment loss that has already been recognised in profit or loss (i.e. in accordance with IFRS 5, or previously in accordance with IAS 36).

In Example 3, therefore, a recovery in the value of the asset would be credited to profit or loss up to a maximum of €40,000.

- Any revaluation surplus may be transferred to retained earnings when an asset is sold.

Example 4   Asset carried under the IAS 16 *Revaluation Model* (no write-down required)

Kompany Limited has land which has been carried under the revaluation model of IAS 16. At 31 March 2010, the land satisfies the conditions of IFRS 5 to be classified as *held for sale*. The following information relates to the asset at that date:

- NBV = €400,000
- fair value (i.e. market value) = €440,000
- selling costs = €20,000
- value in use = €280,000 (provided for information purposes only)

Outline how the above non-current asset should be accounted for in the financial statements of Kompany Limited.

Solution   (Tax is ignored)

Step 1: The land qualifies as an asset that should be classified as held for sale.

Step 2: Immediately before the initial classification as held for sale.
IFRS 5 requires that the asset's carrying amount should be measured in accordance with applicable IFRSs/IASs.

It is necessary therefore to revalue the building to fair value under IAS 16:

	Dr €'000	Cr €'000
Property, plant and equipment	40	
Revaluation surplus – OCI		40
(Being revaluation of land to fair value)		

Step 3: Reclassify non-current asset as an asset held for sale.

	Dr €'000	Cr €'000
Asset held for sale	440	
Property, plant and equipment		440
(Being reclassification of land as an asset held for sale)		

Step 4: After classification as held for sale.
After the asset is transferred to non-current assets held for sale, a further adjustment is necessary as fair value less costs to sell (i.e. €420,000) is less than the asset's carrying amount of €440,000. Thus, the selling costs must be deducted from the asset's carrying value:

	Dr €'000	Cr €'000
Impairment loss – I/S	20	
Asset held for sale		20
(Being restatement of asset held for sale to fair value less costs to sell in accordance with IFRS 5)		

Appendix 17.2

Discontinued operation

In November 2010, Sensor Limited decided to dispose of its pharmaceutical division. A prospective buyer was identified in December 2010, and a sale is highly probable before the end of 2011.

The post-tax losses of the division for the year ended 31 December 2010 amounted to €4.6M. The assets of the pharmaceutical division were classified as a disposal group under IFRS 5, and a post-tax loss of €2.2M was recorded in measuring the assets at their fair value less costs to sell.

Outline how Sensor Limited should account for the pharmaceutical division in its financial statements for the year ended 31 December 2010.

Solution   The pharmaceutical division is a component of Sensor Limited, and is classified as held for sale. It therefore qualifies as a discontinued operation, in accordance with IFRS 5.

The following should be presented as a *single amount* in the statement of comprehensive income:

- €4.6M, being the sum of the post-tax loss of the discontinued operation; plus
- €2.2M, being the post-tax impairment loss recognised on the measurement of the component division at fair value less costs to sell.

Sensor Limited
Statement of comprehensive income for the year ended 31 December 2010

	€'000
Revenue	9,100
Cost of sales	(7,230)
Gross profit	1,870
Distribution costs	(700)
Administrative expenses	(250)
Other expenses	(150)
Finance costs	(600)
Profit before tax	170
Income tax expense	(50)
Profit for the year from continuing operations	120
Loss for the year from discontinued operations	(6,800)
(Loss)/profit for the year	(6,680)
Other comprehensive income	
Revaluation surplus	400
Total comprehensive income for the year	(6,280)

QUESTIONS

17.1 Which of the following criteria are used to determine whether an asset should be categorised as 'held for sale':

(i)   The asset should be available for immediate sale.
(ii) The asset should be available for sale at a future date yet to be determined.
(iii) The sale of the asset should be highly probable.
(iv) The sale of the asset is a possibility.
(v)   There should be an active programme to locate a buyer.
(vi) There need not be an active marketing programme for the asset.

(a) (i) and (ii) only
(b) (i), (iii) and (v) only
(c) (ii), (iv) and (vi) only
(d) (iv) and (vi) only   (Chartered Accountants Ireland)

17.2 Disposal of land

On 1 November 2010, OUTSTAMP Limited decided to dispose of a block of land, which had cost €2.2M in 2007. The land had been revalued to €3.6M in the financial statements during 2009.

The market value of the land on the 1 November 2010 was €2.9M, and it was estimated that selling costs would amount to €100,000.

It was anticipated that the sale would be completed in the first half of 2011.

Required:
You are required to outline how the disposal of the land should be treated in the financial statements for the year ended 31 December 2010. Your answer should include journal entries, and should be in accordance with international accounting standards.

17.3 HARDING Group

HARDING plc ('HARDING') is the parent company of a group of companies which prepares consolidated financial statements in accordance with international accounting standards. The principal activities of HARDING are as a holding company and also as a property investment company. Throughout the year ended 31 December 2010, the holding company owned 100% of GOLF Ltd, whose principal activity is the sale of books through an Internet website. The company has been underperforming in recent years and the sale of the company is currently being negotiated.

The board of Harding plc agreed at a board meeting in November 2010 to sell GOLF to a third party as a going concern. A price has been agreed, and final negotiations are currently under way with an anticipated completion date of September 2011. Employees and customers were informed in December 2010 of the pending sale. The Group Financial Director is keen to exclude GOLF from the consolidated financial statements for the year ended 31 December 2010 on the grounds that it is no longer part of continuing group operations due to its impending sale. In previous years, GOLF was included in the group results. Summary financial information for GOLF is included below:

GOLF Ltd
Statement of comprehensive income

	2010 €M	2009 €M
Revenue	80	50
Cost of sales	(50)	(70)
Gross profit/(loss)	30	(20)
Other operating expenses	(140)	(30)
Loss before tax	(110)	(50)

The Group Financial Director would like to gain a fuller understanding of how the results of GOLF will be shown in the consolidated financial statements for the year ended 31 December 2010.

Required:

Explain how GOLF will be shown in the consolidated financial statements with reference to relevant international accounting standards. Disclosures are *not* required.

(Chartered Accountants Ireland)

17.4 GHORSE plc

GHORSE is preparing its financial statements for the year ended 31 October 2010. GHORSE identified two manufacturing units, Cee and Gee, which it had decided to dispose of in a single transaction. These units comprised non-current assets only. One of the units, Cee, had been impaired prior to the end of the reporting period, and it had been written down to its recoverable amount of €35M at 30 September 2010. The criteria in IFRS 5 *Non-Current Assets Held for Sale and Discontinued Operations*, for classification as held for sale, had been met for Cee and Gee at 30 September 2010. The following information related to the assets of the cash-generating units at 30 September 2010:

	Depreciated historical cost (i.e. value in financial statements at 30 September 2010)	Fair value less costs to sell	Value under IFRS at 30 September 2010 (i.e. value under IAS 16 and 36)
	€M	€M	€M
Cee	50	35	35
Gee	70	90	70
	120	125	105

The fair value less costs to sell had risen at the year end to €40M for Cee and €95M for Gee. The increase in the fair value less costs to sell had not been taken into account by GHORSE.

Required:

Outline the accounting treatment of the above transactions and the impact that the resulting adjustments would have on return on capital employed for the year ended 31 October 2010. (ACCA)

17.5 PARTWAY

PARTWAY is in the process of preparing its financial statements for the year ended 31 October 2010. The company's main activity is in the travel industry, mainly selling package holidays (flights and accommodation) to the general public through the Internet and retail travel agencies. During the current year the number of holidays sold by travel agencies declined dramatically and the directors decided at a board meeting on 15 October 2010 to cease marketing holidays through its chain of travel agents and sell off the related high-street premises. Immediately after the meeting, the travel agencies' staff and suppliers were notified of the situation and an announcement was made in the press. The directors wished to show the travel agencies' results as a discontinued operation in the financial statements to 31 October 2010. Due to the declining business of the travel agents, on 1 August 2010 (3 months before the year end), PARTWAY expanded its Internet operations to offer car hire facilities to purchasers of its Internet holidays.

The following are PARTWAY's summarised income statement results:

	(i) Internet €'000	(ii) Travel agencies €'000	(iii) Car hire €'000	Year ended 31 October 2010 (i) + (ii) + (iii) Total €'000	Year ended 31 October 2009 Total €'000
Revenue	23,000	14,000	2,000	39,000	40,000
Cost of sales	(18,000)	(16,500)	(1,500)	(36,000)	(32,000)
Gross profit/(loss)	5,000	(2,500)	500	3,000	8,000
Operating expenses	(1,000)	(1,500)	(100)	(2,600)	(2,000)
Profit/(loss) before tax	4,000	(4,000)	400	400	6,000

The results for the travel agencies for the year ended 31 October 2009 were: revenue €18M, cost of sales €15M and operating expenses of €1.5M.

Required:

(a) Discuss whether the directors' wish to show the travel agencies' results as a discontinued operation is justifiable.

(b) Assuming the closure of the travel agencies is a discontinued operation, prepare the (summarised) income statement of PARTWAY for the year ended 31 October 2010 together with its comparatives.

Part 6

LIABILITIES AND EQUITY

Chapter 18

Share-based payment

A share-based payment transaction is one in which an entity receives goods or services in return for:

(i) *Equity instruments.* For example, an entity may issue its own shares as payment for goods or services. This is called an *equity-settled share-based payment*. The goods or services received are measured at their **fair value**, and recorded as an asset or expense as appropriate. There is a corresponding increase in equity.

If an entity cannot reliably estimate the fair value of the goods or services received, their value, and the corresponding increase in equity should be measured by reference to the fair value of the equity instruments (e.g. shares) granted. Or,

(ii) *Incurring a liability.* In this case, an entity agrees to transfer cash or other assets, for amounts that are based on the price (or value) of its equity instruments. This is called a *cash-settled share-based payment.*

The goods or services acquired and the liability incurred should be initially measured at the fair value of the liability on the date that the goods or services are acquired. Until the liability is settled, the liability should be remeasured at the end of each reporting period, and at the date of settlement, with any changes in fair value recognised in profit or loss.

Example 1 Equity-settled share-based payment

On 1 December 2010, Trimmer Limited issued 10,000 of its equity shares to Mango Limited, in return for goods which had a fair value of €15,000. These goods were included in the inventory of Trimmer Limited at 31 December 2010, and were sold for €20,000 during 2011. Trimmer Limited has a reporting date of 31 December.

Outline how this transaction should be recorded in the financial statements of Trimmer Limited.

Solution When goods or services are received as consideration for equity instruments, the transaction should be measured at the fair value of the goods or services on the date they are received. At 31 December 2010, the goods are included in the inventory of Trimmer Limited, and are therefore an asset at that date. The goods are charged to profit or loss following their sale in 2011. This is illustrated as follows:

	Dr €'000	Cr €'000
Inventory	15	
Share capital/share premium		15
(Being goods acquired on 1 December 2010 as consideration for the issue of equity shares in the year ended 31 December 2010)		
Cost of sales – I/S	15	
Inventory		15
(Being the cost of goods sold during 2011)		
Bank/trade receivables	20	
Revenue		20
(Being goods sold during 2011)		

Example 1 revisited

Cash-settled share-based payment

Cash-settled share-based payments result in an increase in a liability. Thus, in Example 1 above, let us assume that Trimmer Limited is paying for the goods in cash, and that the amount payable is based on the fair value of 10,000 of Trimmer's equity shares at 31 December 2010. The fair value of 10,000 of Trimmer's equity shares was as follows:

€15,000 at 1 December 2010
€17,000 at 31 December 2010

Outline how this transaction should be recorded in the financial statements of Trimmer Limited.

Solution

The transaction should initially be recorded at the fair value of the goods received. The liability should subsequently be remeasured at 31 December 2010:

	Dr €'000	Cr €'000
Inventory	15	
Trade payables		15
(Being goods acquired on 1 December 2010)		
Loss on remeasurement of liability – I/S	2	
Trade payables		2
(Being loss on remeasurement of liability at 31 December 2010)		
Trade payables	17	
Bank		17
(Being payment of liability)		
Cost of sales – I/S	15	
Inventory		15
(Being the cost of goods sold during 2011)		
Bank/trade receivables	20	
Revenue		20
(Being goods sold during 2011)		

Scope

IFRS 2 applies to all entities, but only to share-based payments made for the acquisition of goods and services. Thus, it does not apply to **dividends**, the general issue of **shares**, or to the purchase of treasury shares.

An entity does not apply IFRS 2 in respect of transactions in which goods are acquired as part of a **business combination**, as defined by IFRS 3 *Business Combinations*. Nor should IFRS 2 be applied to share-based payments that fall under the scope of paragraphs 8–10 of IAS 32 *Financial Instruments: Presentation,* or paragraphs 5–7 of IAS 39 *Financial Instruments: Recognition and Measurement.*

Equity-settled share-based payment transactions

This is a transaction in which an entity receives goods or services as consideration for its own **equity instruments** (including shares or share options). Perhaps the most common example is share option schemes offered to company employees. Such schemes have been particularly prevalent in fast-growing companies, such as those in the technology sector. Typically, these schemes provide employees with the option of buying shares in the future at a pre-specified price. This gives rise to three important dates:

(i)   *Date of grant of options.* This is the date on which the directors/employees are granted the option to purchase the shares at a future point in time. For example, a company might on 1 January 2011 grant options to its directors to buy shares at €1.50 per share in the future. 1 January 2011 is the *grant date* of the options.

(ii) *Vesting date of options.* This is the date on which the directors/employees *qualify* for the options. For example, the option agreement on 1 January 2011 might stipulate that directors/employees must complete three years of service (dating from 1/1/2011). The vesting date of the options in this instance would be 1 January 2014.

(iii) *Exercise date of the options.* This is the date on which the directors/employees exercise their rights under the option agreement to purchase the shares.

The accounting treatment of share options has been a very controversial area. Attention has focused primarily on whether share options should be charged as an expense.

In a review of the literature, Alves[1] identifies the following arguments *against* the expensing of share options:

- share options do not meet the definition of an expense;
- share options are considered to be a capital transaction;
- the potential dilution of share options is already reflected adequately in the diluted **earnings per share** figure (EPS is discussed in detail in Chapter 43);
- the cost of share options cannot be estimated reliably;
- expensing share options will damage new companies, and will have severe economic consequences.

Alves quotes the following arguments in *favour of* expensing share options:

- disclosure is not a substitute for recognition;
- the argument that the cost of share options cannot be estimated reliably is weak;
- the argument that expensing share options will damage new companies is unfounded.

In IFRS 2, *Share-based Payment*, the IASB takes the view that the cost of share options should be expensed. Share options can be regarded as the payment that an entity provides in return for services provided by its employees. Thus, IFRS 2 requires that the cost of providing the share options should be expensed over the vesting period. The entity is thereby matching the cost with the benefits being derived from the option holders. IFRS 2 also requires that the cost should be measured at the fair value of the shares or share options at the **date of grant of the options.**

Example 2

On 1 January 2011, M plc issued share options, giving each of four executives the right to purchase 25,000 shares at 25 cents per share. The value of the shares on 1 January 2011 was €1. A condition of the agreement was that the executives would complete three years of service from 1 January 2011. The nominal value of the company's shares was 10 cents. It should be assumed that the fair value of each share option on 1 January 2011 equals 75 cents.

The company's share price on subsequent dates was as follows:

1 January 2012	€1.50
1 January 2013	€2
1 January 2014	€3

Outline how the share options should be accounted for by M plc.

Solution

At 1 January 2011 (i.e. the date of grant), the fair value of the options per share is 75 cents. In accordance with IFRS 2, this should be expensed over the vesting period of three years, as follows:

	Dr €'000	Cr €'000
Share option expense – I/S	25	
Equity		25
(Being estimated cost of share option scheme for year ended 31 December 2011, based on the allocation of fair value at option grant date over vesting period (4 × 25,000 × 75c/3))		
Share option expense – I/S	25	
Equity		25
(Being estimated cost of share option scheme for year ended 31 December 2012, based on the allocation of fair value at option grant date over vesting period (4 × 25,000 × 75c/3))		
Share option expense – I/S	25	
Equity		25
(Being estimated cost of share option scheme for year ended 31 December 2013, based on the allocation of fair value at option grant date over vesting period (4 × 25,000 × 75c/3))		

Changes in market conditions which occur after the grant date are not taken into account. Thus, the increase in market values on 1 January 2012, 1 January 2013 and 1 January 2014 are not taken into consideration in computing the amount of the expense that is charged.

If all of the executives exercise their options in full on 1 January 2014, they will each pay €6,250 for 25,000 shares. This would be recorded in total by M plc as follows:

	Dr	Cr
	€	€
Bank (4 × €6,250)	25,000	
Equity*	75,000	
Ordinary share capital (4 × 25,000 × 10 cents)†		10,000
Share premium (balancing figure)		90,000

* This represents the amount of equity built up over the vesting period (€25,000 per annum for three years). This is transferred to ordinary share capital when the executives exercise their options.
† Increases in ordinary share capital are at nominal value only (i.e. 10 cents per share).

■ What if options lapse during the vesting period?

The overall effect of IFRS 2 is to charge to expense the fair value (determined at grant date) of share options that vest. Thus, if one of the four executives in Example 2 were to leave on 1 January 2012, and therefore lose his/her share option rights, the above entries would be revised as follows.

Example 2 revisited

	Dr	Cr
	€'000	€'000
Share option expense – I/S	25	
Equity		25
(Being the cost of share option scheme for year ended 31 December 2011, based on the allocation of fair value at option grant date over vesting period (4 × 25,000 × 75c × 1/3))		
Share option expense – I/S	12.5	
Equity		12.5
(Being the cost of the share option scheme for 2012, based on the allocation of fair value at option grant date over the vesting period ((3 × 25,000 × 75c × 2/3) – 25,000))		
Share option expense – I/S	18.75	
Equity		18.75
(Being the cost of the share option scheme for 2013, based on the llocation of fair value at option grant date over the vesting period (3 × 25,000 × 75c × 3/3) – (12,500 + 25,000))		

Thus, the total expense over the three years is €56,250, which equates to the cost of the share options for three executives only (i.e. 3 × 75c × 25,000). Thus, unless share options vest, no expense is charged. At each period end, the number of share options that are likely to vest is reassessed, considering non-market conditions only, such as length of service and required earnings per share targets.

■ What determines fair value at the option grant date?

IFRS 2 requires that the **fair value** of equity instruments granted be based on market prices, if possible. The terms and conditions on which the equity instruments are granted should also be taken into account in determining their fair value. If market prices are not available, fair value should be estimated using a valuation technique (e.g. the binomial model) to estimate what the price of the equity instruments would have been at grant date in an arm's length transaction between knowledgeable, willing parties.

Market conditions *are* taken into consideration in calculating fair value at the option grant date. For example, an option agreement may stipulate a target share price which must be achieved before share options can be exercised. The higher this target price is, the lower the fair value of the share options is likely to be. However, as noted above, market conditions are not considered in computing the expense charged during the vesting period.

Example 3 Maestro Limited issued share options to one of its executives on 1 January 2011. The terms of the option stipulate that if the executive is still a member of the board on 1 January 2014, he will have the option to purchase 100,000 shares at €1 per share. A further prerequisite condition is that the share price must at least equal €2.50 on 1 January 2014. The fair value of the executive's share options at 1 January 2011 is estimated at €120,000.

Outline how this share option should be accounted for by Maestro Limited, on the assumption that the share price on 1 January 2014 is €2.10, and that the executive is also a member of the board at that time.

Solution On 1 January 2014, the executive has satisfied the stipulated *service* requirements, as he remains a member of the board at that date. The fair value of the share options at the option grant date (i.e. 1 January 2011) is expensed over the vesting period. The market condition which stipulates a minimum share price on 1 January 2014 will influence the computation of the option's fair value at 1 January 2011. It does not, however, affect the expensing of that fair value over the vesting period. This is the case, irrespective of the fact that the executive is unable to exercise his options, due to the minimum price of €2.50 not being achieved on 1 January 2014.

The share option will be recorded by Maestro Limited as follows:

	Dr €'000	Cr €'000
Share option expense – I/S	40	
Equity		40

(Being the annual cost of share option scheme for each of the three years ended 31 December 2013, based on the allocation of the fair value at option grant date over the vesting period (i.e. €120,000/3))

Cash-settled share-based payments

Cash-settled share-based payment transactions involve an entity receiving goods or services, and in exchange agreeing to make a cash payment (or a transfer of other assets) of an amount that is calculated by reference to the price of an equity instrument of the paying entity. Share appreciation rights are the most common form of cash-settled share-based payment transaction.

IFRS 2 requires that cash-settled share-based payment transactions should be accounted for by building up a provision of an amount, measured at fair value, that will eventually be paid over the period in which the goods or services are received. The charge recognised in the first period should be based on an initial estimate of the amount that will eventually be paid, but subsequent charges should take into account changes in that amount.

Example 4 On 1 January 2011, Halford plc issued share appreciation rights (SARs) to a number of its employees. These rights will vest after three years if the employees remain in the employment of Halford plc. Each SAR provides for a cash payment equal to the amount that the Halford share price exceeds €5. No payment will be made if the share price is at or below €5.

The cumulative fair value of the SARs worked out as follows:

31 December 2011 = €30,000
31 December 2012 = €48,000
31 December 2013 = €72,000

Outline how Halford plc should account for the share appreciation rights.

Solution The cost of the share appreciation rights will be recorded by Halford plc as follows:

	Dr €'000	Cr €'000
Expenses – I/S	10	
Provision for share appreciation payments – SOFP		10
(Being charge for 2011; 30,000 × 1/3)		
Expenses – I/S	22	
Provision for share appreciation payments – SOFP		22
(Being charge for 2012; (48,000 × 2/3) – 10,000)		
Expenses – I/S	40	
Liability for share appreciation payments – SOFP		40
(Being charge for 2013; 72,000 – (10,000 + 22,000))		

Share-based payment transactions with cash alternative

These are agreements in which either the entity or the counterparty has the choice as to whether the entity settles the transaction in cash (or other assets) or by issuing equity instruments:

(i) *If the entity has the choice*:
- Treat as a cash-settled transaction if the entity has a present obligation to settle in cash
- Treat as an equity-settled transaction if there is no present obligation to settle in cash.

(ii) *If the counterparty has the choice*:
- This gives rise to a compound financial instrument, which must be split into its debt and equity components.

Disclosures

- The nature and extent of share-based payment arrangements that existed during the period.
- A description of each type of share-based payment arrangement.
- The number and weighted average exercise prices of share options.
- The weighted average share price at the date of exercise of share options exercised during the period.

■ How the fair value of goods or services received, or the fair value of equity instruments granted during the period, was determined.

■ The effect of share-based payment transactions on the entity's profit or loss for the period and on its financial position.

Summary

(i) The accounting treatment of share-based payment depends on whether the transaction will be settled in equity, cash, or equity with a cash alternative.

(ii) *Equity-settled share-based payment:*
■ These payments give rise to an increase in a component of equity.
■ In general, the corresponding debit entry for goods or services received should be measured at the fair value of those goods or services when they are received. That fair value should be expensed unless the transaction gives rise to an asset.
■ For *transactions with employees*, the corresponding debit entry is measured at the fair value of the equity instruments granted. Fair value should be measured at the grant date and expensed over the vesting period. Fair value will be affected by market-based conditions (e.g. share price targets) but not vesting conditions (e.g. length of service or EPS targets). The charge to expense is determined by compliance with vesting conditions, but not by the outcome of market conditions.

(iii) *Cash-settled share-based payment:*
■ A provision, measured at fair value, is built up in the SOFP, over the period in which the goods or services are received.
■ The corresponding debit entry is charged as an expense or recorded as an **asset**, as appropriate.

(iv) *Share-based payment transactions with a cash alternative:*
■ The accounting treatment depends on whether the entity or the counterparty has the power to exercise a choice of payment method.

■ Reference

1. Alves, A. (2010). The controversy over accounting for stock options: a literature review. *International Research Journal of Finance and Economics,* Issue 53, pp. 7–25.

QUESTIONS

18.1 ELECTRON

ELECTRON, a public limited company, operates in the energy sector. The company has grown significantly over the last few years and is currently preparing its financial statements for the year ended 30 June 2011.

The company granted share options to its employees on 1 July 2010. The fair value of the options at that date was €3M. The options vest on 30 June 2013. The employees have to be employed at the end of the three-year period for the options to vest and the following estimates have been made.

Estimated percentage of employees leaving during vesting period at:

Estimate at grant date 1 July 2010	5%
Estimate at 30 June 2011	6%

Required:

Outline how ELECTRON plc should account for its share option scheme in its financial statements for the year ended 30 June 2011.   (ACCA)

18.2 BETH Group

BETH granted 200 share options to each of its 10,000 employees on 1 December 2009. The shares vest if the employees work for the group for the next two years. On 1 December 2009, BETH estimated that there would be 1,000 eligible employees leaving in each year up to the vesting date. At 30 November 2010, 600 eligible employees had left the company. The estimate of the number of employees leaving in the year to 30 November 2011 was 500 at 30 November 2010. The fair value of each share option at the grant date (1 December 2009) was €10. The share options have not been accounted for in the financial statements.

Required:

Outline how the BETH Group should account for the share option scheme in its financial statements for the year ended 30 November 2010.   (ACCA)

Chapter 19

Income taxes

There is a well-known saying that in life only two things are certain: death and taxes. As corporate entities have the potential to survive indefinitely, in business, only taxes can be relied on not to disappoint. The first known use of taxation was used by the pharaohs in Egypt around 3000 BC, and references to raising taxation are also contained in the Bible.

The main purpose of taxation is to provide revenue for areas such as national defence, a transport network, hospitals and schools. A second function is redistribution, where taxation is used to transfer wealth to those in society who are less well off. A third objective of taxation is repricing, which imposes levies to promote desired societal improvements. For example, tobacco is taxed to discourage smoking and carbon taxes are imposed to encourage the use of green energy sources.

The importance of taxation depends largely on the dominant economic system. For example, in capitalist economies such as the United States, taxation plays a very important role in raising revenue, and in effecting wealth redistribution and repricing. In socialist economies, such as the traditional Chinese model, taxation has been less important, as revenues have been derived from government ownership of business interests.

In accounting for taxation, entities must comply with IAS 12 *Income Taxes*. The objective of IAS 12 is to prescribe the accounting treatment for current tax and **deferred tax**.

Current tax

Current tax is the amount of tax payable or recoverable on the taxable profit or loss of an accounting period.

Accounting profit (i.e. profit before tax in the financial statements) is normally the starting point in computing the amount of current tax. Accounting profit is adjusted by the tax authorities when computing *taxable profit*.

Example 1 Mandrigo Limited earned profit before tax of €520,000 for the year ended 31 December 2010. Mandrigo owns one machine, which cost €500,000 on 1 January 2010, and has a residual value of zero. The machine has an expected useful life of five years and depreciation of €100,000 has been charged. The tax authorities permit a capital allowance of €120,000 to be claimed on this machine for 2010. Mandrigo pays corporation tax at 20%.

*Compute Mandrigo Limited's **taxable profit**, and the amount of current tax for 2010.*

Solution	Taxable profit is computed as follows:

	€
Accounting profit	520,000
Add back:	
Depreciation (disallowed expense)	100,000
	620,000
Less:	
Capital allowances	(120,000)
Taxable profit	500,000
Current tax at 20%	100,000

Accounting profit provides the starting point for the computation of current tax. However, this must be adjusted, as in Example 1 above, to reflect the rules of the tax authorities.

Current tax should be recognised as a liability to the extent that it has not been paid. Thus, Mandrigo Limited will be required to make the following journal entry at 31 December 2010:

	Dr	Cr
	€'000	€'000
Income tax charge – I/S	100	
Current tax liability – SOFP		100
(Being current tax on profit of year ended 31 December 2010)		

- A tax loss should be recognised as an asset to the extent that it enables an entity to recover current tax of a previous period.
- The current tax charge should be adjusted in respect of any underestimates or overestimates of current tax in prior periods.
- Current tax liabilities and assets should be measured using the rates/laws that have been enacted or substantively enacted by the end of the reporting period.
- Current tax assets and current tax liabilities should not be offset in the SOFP, unless an entity has the legal right and the intention to settle on a net basis.

Deferred tax

Imagine that you have located an old lawnmower in a shed that you have been clearing. Although in good working condition, the mower has only one height setting, and that setting is suitable for cutting grass with one week's summer growth. By Sunday the grass has reached the requisite height, and the mower performs well as you put it through its paces. The next day the blade is too high (or the grass too low). On Tuesday, the grass is a little higher, and by Saturday it has almost reached its required cutting height. On Sunday, the blades and the grass are at the same level and the mower is called into action once again.

From Monday to Saturday, the gap between the blade and the mower can be described as a *temporary* difference. It is temporary because, by Sunday, that gap has disappeared. However, there is also an overgrown area in the garden which the lawn mower is unable to cut. The gap between the blade height and that of the grass in the overgrown area can be described as a *permanent* difference, as the two will never be at the same level.

In financial reporting, the grass represents a firm's profits in its **financial statements**. Likewise, one can visualise the tax system as the blades which take a cut of those profits to raise government revenue.

Example 2 | **Taxable temporary difference**

Consider the case of a firm that buys land in 2009 for €1.5M, and revalues it to €2.5M on 31 December 2010. In the financial statements, the revaluation is recorded as follows:

	Dr €'000	Cr €'000
Land	1,000	
Revaluation surplus – OCI		1,000

Although a gain of €1M has been recognised in the financial statements in 2010, the authorities normally charge tax only when the land is sold. Thus, at 31 December 2010, there is a *temporary* difference between the financial statements and the tax system. This difference will disappear when the land is eventually sold.

The accrual concept requires that expenses are recognised in the same period as related income. Thus, in the financial statements at 31 December 2010 the tax charge must be recognised at the same time as the revaluation surplus. Assuming that the tax rate is 20%, the following journal entry will be required:

	Dr €'000	Cr €'000
Deferred tax charge – OCI	200	
Deferred tax provision – SOFP		200
(Being deferred tax on temporary difference at 31 December 2010)		

It should be noted that, as the revaluation surplus is recognised in OCI, so is the related tax charge.

If the land is sold in 2011 for €2.5M, the authorities will then subject the gain to tax, and the tax will then become a **current liability**. At that point the temporary difference disappears – the gain that was previously recognised in the financial statements is now also subjected to tax by the authorities. The following journal entries will be required following the sale of the land:

	Dr €'000	Cr €'000
Bank	2,500	
Land		2,500
(Being disposal of land)		
Deferred tax provision – SOFP	200	
Current tax provision – SOFP		200
(Being reclassification of deferred tax as current tax)		

On disposal of the land, the temporary difference between the financial statements prepared by the accountant, and the tax system operated by the tax authorities, ceases to exist. Deferred tax has done its job of facilitating the application of the **accrual** concept, and the deferred tax balance in the SOFP is now zero.

Tax base

The tax base of an asset or liability is its value per the tax authorities. In Example 2 above, the tax base of the land at 31 December 2010 is €1.5M, because no increase in value is recognised by the tax authorities until the land is actually sold. Temporary differences are most easily identified by comparing the tax base of assets and liabilities with their carrying value in the financial statements.

	Value of land per financial statements at 31 December 2010 €'000	Tax base at 31 December 2010 €'000	Temporary difference €'000
Land	2,500	1,500	1,000

The above difference of €1M is called a *taxable* temporary difference. This is because, at 31 December 2010, future taxable gains on the land exceed future gains to be recognised in the financial statements. Therefore, a deferred tax provision is established at 31 December 2010 (see Example 2 above).

Temporary differences can, however, also be *deductible* differences – see Example 3 below.

Example 3 Deductible temporary difference

Mandrigo Limited charged pension costs of €200,000 in computing *accounting profit* for the year ended 31 December 2010, but these costs were not paid until 2011. The tax authorities allow pension costs as a deduction from *taxable profit* when they are paid (i.e. in this case in 2011).

Outline how the pension costs should be recorded by Mandrigo Limited in its financial statements for the year ended 31 December 2010. The rate of corporation tax is 25%.

Solution

	Value per financial statements at 31 December 2010 €'000	Tax base at 31 December 2010 €'000	Temporary difference €'000
Pension costs liability	200	Nil	200

At 31 December 2010, future taxable profit is less than future accounting profit (i.e. in 2011, pension costs of €200,000 will be allowed as a deduction by the tax authorities, but the pension cost charge in the 2011 income statement will be zero). Thus, there is a *deductible* temporary difference of €200,000 at 31 December 2010, and a deferred tax asset will be recognised at that date. The following journal entries will be required in Mandrigo's financial statements for the year ended 31 December 2010:

	Dr €'000	Cr €'000
Pension costs – I/S	200	
Pension costs accrual – SOFP		200
Deferred tax asset – SOFP	50	
Deferred tax credit – I/S		50
(Being deferred tax asset relating to pension costs: €200,000 × 25%)		

Table 19.1 Assets and liabilities – implications of differences in their tax base and their carrying value in the financial statements

Asset	Liability	Temporary difference	Journal entry (based on temporary difference × tax rate)
Carrying value in financial statements > asset's tax base	Carrying value in financial statements < liability's tax base	*Taxable*	DR Deferred tax charge in statement of comprehensive income CR Deferred tax in SOFP
Carrying value in financial statements < asset's tax base	Carrying value in financial statements > liability's tax base	*Deductible*	DR Deferred tax in SOFP CR Deferred tax credit in statement of comprehensive income

Table 19.1 summarises the implications of differences between the tax base of an asset or liability and its value in the financial statements at the end of the reporting period.

Permanent differences

The differences outlined in Examples 2 and 3 above are temporary differences. They resemble the height difference between the lawnmower blade and the grass, which disappears every Sunday. Some differences, however, can be of a permanent nature, and like the height difference between the mower and the overgrown area, they never disappear. An example of a permanent difference is a penalty imposed on a firm for exceeding permitted emission levels. This is charged as an expense in the **income statements**, but may never be an allowable tax deduction under the rules of the tax authorities. Deferred tax has *no* role to play in respect of permanent differences.

Requirements of IAS 12 *Income Taxes*

Full provision basis

IAS 12 requires that deferred tax be provided in full on almost all *temporary* differences. Examples of temporary differences that have deferred tax implications include the following:

(i) Deductible temporary differences

- Retirement benefit costs which are charged as an expense when incurred but may only be allowed by the tax authorities when paid.
- Revaluation losses, which are recognised in the financial statements when they occur, but may only be allowed by the tax authorities when the assets are sold.
- Research costs charged as an expense in computing accounting profit, but which may only be allowed by the tax authorities when paid.
- Unrealised profit on intra-group sales in the consolidated accounts of a group (see Appendix 19.1).

(ii) Taxable temporary differences

- Interest income recognised in the financial statements as it is earned, which is taxed by the authorities when received.

- Revaluation gains.
- Interest capitalised in producing or constructing an asset (see IAS 23 *Borrowing Costs*). This interest is normally allowed by the tax authorities when it is incurred, but is charged against accounting profit as the related asset is **depreciated/amortised**.

(iii) Temporary differences which can be either taxable or deductible

- accelerated capital allowances, where the NBV of an asset differs from its tax WDV;
- **current assets** (e.g. investments) 'marked to market' (i.e. restated to market value) where the change in value is recorded in accounting profit, but is included in taxable profit only on realisation.

■ Measurement and recognition under IAS 12

(i)   Deferred tax assets and liabilities should be measured using the tax rates which are expected to apply when the asset is realised or the liability is settled, based on tax rates/laws that have been enacted or substantively enacted by the end of the reporting period.

(ii) Deferred tax should be recognised as income or expense, and included in net profit or loss for the period, except to the extent that the tax arises from:
- a transaction or event that is recognised outside profit or loss, either in OCI or directly in equity, or
- a business combination

(iii) *Discounting.* IAS 12 does *not* permit deferred tax assets and liabilities to be discounted.

(iv) *Deferred tax assets.* A deferred tax asset should be recognised for deductible temporary differences, unused tax losses, and unused tax credits; but only to the extent it is probable that taxable profit will be available against which they can be offset.

The carrying amount of deferred tax assets should be reviewed at the end of each reporting period. A previously unrecognised deferred tax asset should be recognised to the extent that it has become probable that future taxable profit will allow the deferred tax asset to be recovered.

(v)   *Presentation.* Deferred tax assets and liabilities should be offset only if:
- the entity has a legally enforceable right to set off current tax assets against current tax liabilities; and
- the deferred tax assets and liabilities relate to income taxes levied by the same tax authority.

■ How important is deferred tax?

The significance of deferred tax is directly related to the nature of the taxation system in a particular jurisdiction. For example, in the UK and the Republic of Ireland, the taxation system and the accounting system are relatively independent of each other. Thus, deferred tax tends to be a significant item in the SOFP of UK and ROI companies, as large temporary differences can occur. By contrast, in France and Germany, the tax system and the accounting system are more closely aligned. Consequently, deferred tax tends to be less important in these countries, and deferred tax balances in the statement of financial position are generally much smaller.

An integrated deferred tax example is outlined in Appendix 19.2.

Disclosure

(i) IAS 12

- The major components of tax expense and tax income should be disclosed separately
- Aggregate current and deferred tax relating to items charged or credited directly to equity
- Amount of income tax relating to each component of other comprehensive income
- Explanation of the relationship between tax expense/income and accounting profit
- Changes in tax rates
- Amount of deductible temporary differences, unused tax losses, and unused tax credits for which no deferred tax asset is recognised
- Aggregate amount of temporary differences associated with investments in **subsidiaries**, associates and joint ventures for which deferred tax liabilities have not been recognised
- For each type of temporary difference, and each type of unused tax losses and unused tax credits, the amount of deferred tax assets and liabilities recognised, and the amount of deferred tax income or expense recognised
- Tax expense relating to discontinued operations
- Tax consequences of **dividends** that were proposed or declared after the end of the reporting period.

(ii) IAS 1

- Liabilities and assets for current tax
- Deferred tax liabilities and assets
- Tax expense.

Summary

- Current tax is the amount of tax payable or recoverable on the taxable profit or loss of an accounting period.
- Current tax is usually recognised as an expense in the income statement, and any amount unpaid should be included as a current liability in the SOFP.
- Deferred tax allows the total tax charge to be computed on the accrual basis of accounting.
- Deferred tax should be provided on almost all temporary differences.
- Temporary differences are computed by comparing the tax base of each asset and liability (i.e. the amount attributed to the item for tax purposes) with its carrying amount in the SOFP at the end of each reporting period.
- Deferred tax assets and liabilities should not be discounted, and should only be offset if they relate to income taxes levied by the same tax authority and the entity has a legally enforceable right of offset.
- In accounting for taxation, an entity should use tax rates and laws that have been enacted or substantially enacted by the end of the reporting period.

Appendix 19.1

Consolidated financial statements and deferred tax

A consolidation adjustment will be made to exclude unrealised profit on intra-group sales from the accounting profit of the group.

However, this profit will have been included in the taxable profit of the company which sold the goods within the group, and tax will have been levied on that company.

This results in a *deductible temporary difference*, as the asset's tax base is greater than the asset's carrying value in the financial statements.

Example Mercer Limited has a 100% subsidiary undertaking, Morse Limited. During 2010, Morse sold goods for €2M to Mercer at a mark-up of 25% on cost. A quarter of these goods remained in the inventory of Mercer at 31 December 2010.

The Mercer Group pays corporation tax at 30%.

IAS 27 requires, as a consolidation adjustment, that the intra-group profit must be eliminated on the goods held in inventory by Mercer at 31 December 2010. The following journal entries will be required:

	Dr €	Cr €
Consolidated retained earnings – SOFP	100,000	
Inventory – SOFP		100,000
(Being elimination of intra-group inventory profit: €2M × $^1/_4$ × 20%)		
Deferred tax asset – SOFP	30,000	
Deferred tax credit – I/S		30,000
(Being deferred tax on unrealised profit relating to intra-group sales – see Note 1 below.)		

Note 1:

	At 31 December 2010 €
Carrying value of inventory in financial statements	400,000
Tax base of inventory	500,000
Deductible temporary difference	100,000
Deferred tax asset at 30%	30,000

Appendix 19.2

IAS 12 an integrated example

Tempura Limited operates in the medical goods industry. The following details relate to the year ended 31 March 2011:

(a) Tempura Limited pays corporation tax at 30%, six months after the year end. Profit before taxation for the year ended 31 March 2011 was €130,000. Taxable profit for the same period was €35,000.

(b) The following balances applied to the non-current assets of Tempura Limited at 31 March 2011:

Net book value	€250,000
Tax written down value	€170,000

These balances do not include the building purchased in (d) below.

(c) Tempura Limited opened a deposit account in May 2010. Deposit interest accrued, at 31 March 2011, amounted to €25,000. This interest was credited to Tempura Limited's income statement in the year ended 31 March 2011, but was not received until June 2011. Deposit interest is taxed by the tax authorities when it is received.

(d) Tempura Limited purchased a freehold building in May 2010 for €200,000. This building was revalued to €300,000 on 31 March 2011. The current capital gains tax rate is 20%.

(e) No other temporary differences exist at 31 March 2011.

(f) Tempura Limited had a provision of €22,000 for deferred tax at 31 March 2010. None of this balance relates to the building in (d) above.

Required:

You are required (using journal entries where appropriate) to outline how the above transactions should be accounted for by Tempura Limited in its financial statements for the year ended 31 March 2011.

Solution		Dr €'000	Cr €'000
	Current tax charge – I/S	10.5	
	Current tax liability – SOFP		10.5
	(Being current tax on profits of the year end 31 March 2011)		
	Interest receivable – SOFP	25	
	Interest receivable – I/S		25
	(Being deposit interest receivable at 31 March 2011)		
	Freehold buildings	200	
	Bank		200
	(Being purchase of building in May 2010)		
	Freehold buildings	100	
	Revaluation surplus – OCI		100
	(Being revaluation of building in March 2011)		
	Deferred tax charge – OCI*	20	
	Deferred tax charge – I/S	9.5	
	Deferred tax provision – SOFP		29.5
	(Being increase in deferred tax provision at 31 March 2011 – see attached deferred tax computation)		

* This is deferred tax relating to the revaluation surplus on the building.

Computation of deferred tax provision at 31 March 2011

	€
Building	
Tax base	200,000
Carrying value in financial statements	300,000
Taxable temporary difference	100,000

Item	Carrying value in financial statements	Tax base	Temporary difference
Other non-current assets	Asset of €250,000	Asset of €170,000	Taxable difference €80,000
Deposit interest	Asset of €25,000	Nil	Taxable difference €25,000

Total taxable temporary differences at 31 March 2011, excluding revaluation surplus	105,000
Deferred tax provision required at 30%	31,500
Deferred tax provision on revaluation surplus	20,000
Deferred tax provision required at 31 March 2011	51,500
Deferred tax provision at 31 March 2010	(22,000)
Increase in deferred tax provision required at 31 March 2011	29,500
Analysis of increase in deferred tax provision:	
Revaluation surplus (€100,000 × 20%)	20,000
Other (balance)	9,500
Total	29,500

Tempura Limited
statement of financial position (extract) as at 31 March 2011

Liabilities	
Current liabilities	
Trade and other payables	xxx
Current tax payable	10.5
	xxx
Non-current liabilities	
Term loan	xxx
Deferred tax	51.5
Long-term provisions	xxx
	xxxx
Total liabilities	xxxx

Tempura Limited
statement of comprehensive income (extract) for the year ended
31 March 2011

	€'000
Revenue	xxxx
Cost of sales	(xxxx)
Gross profit	xxxx
Distribution costs	(xxx)
Administrative expenses	(xxx)
Other expenses	(xxx)
Finance costs	(xxx)
Profit before tax	xxx
Income tax expense (10,500 + 9,500)	(20)
Profit for the year from	
continuing operations	xxx
Other comprehensive income	
Revaluation surplus	100
Income tax on revaluation surplus	(20)
Total comprehensive income for the year	xxx

QUESTIONS

19.1 Deferred tax can be best described as:

(a) An indefinite interest-free loan from government
(b) Tax due in more than one year
(c) Tax due when the company ceases trading
(d) Tax implied by asset and liability valuations in the statement of financial position.

(Chartered Accountants Ireland)

19.2 HARDING Group

The HARDING Group is currently considering the acquisition of PROSPECT Ltd, a property investment company. The Financial Director has been reviewing the group-deferred taxation provision and would like your advice on the impact of the following:

1. PROSPECT has a portfolio of readily marketable government securities which are held as current assets at market value in the statement of financial position, with any increase or decrease being taken to profit or loss. The gains on these investments are taxed when the investments are sold, and at present the securities are valued at €5M above cost.
2. PROSPECT intends to make an additional accrual for pension contributions of €1M. This will not be allowable for tax purposes until it is paid.

Assume a corporation tax rate of **30%**.   (Chartered Accountants Ireland)

19.3 HARDCOURT Limited

HARDCOURT Limited operates in the chemical sector. The following details relate to the year ended 31 March 2011:

(a) HARDCOURT Limited has 20,000 issued ordinary shares, and paid an interim dividend of €124,000 in September 2010.
(b) HARDCOURT Limited pays corporation tax at 30%, payable six months after the year end. Profit before taxation for the year ended 31 March 2011 was €130,000 (year end 31 March 2010 €60,000).

   Taxable profit for the year ended 31 March 2011 was €40,000 (year end 31 March 2010 €50,000).

(c) The following information relates to the plant and machinery of HARDCOURT Limited at 31 March 2011:

   Total cost to date amounted to €1.2M, accumulated depreciation being €600,000. Capital allowances claimed to date amounted to €500,000.

(d) HARDCOURT Limited opened a deposit account in May 2010. Deposit interest accrued, at 31 March 2011, amounted to €40,000. This interest was credited to HARDCOURT Limited's income statement in the year ended 31 March 2011, but was not received until June 2011.
(e) HARDCOURT Limited purchased freehold land in May 2007 for €400,000. This land was revalued to €800,000 on 31 March 2010. It was not intended to dispose of this land for the foreseeable future. The current capital gains tax rate is 20%.
(f) Development costs of €200,000 were incurred by HARDCOURT during the year ended 31 March 2010. All of these costs were capitalised in the statement of financial position at 31 March 2010, and were expensed to the income statement at the rate of 20% per annum, commencing in the year ending 31 March 2011. These development costs were allowed for taxation purposes at the time that they were incurred.
(g) HARDCOURT Limited made political donations of €40,000 during the year ended 31 March 2011. Political donations are not allowable for tax purposes.

(h) The HARDCOURT Group had a balance of €72,000 on its deferred tax account at 31 March 2010, none of which related to the land purchased in (e) above.

Required:

(a) You are required (using journal entries where appropriate) to outline how the above transactions should be accounted for in the financial statements of HARDCOURT Limited for the year ended 31 March 2011.

(b) In your opinion, what should be the principal objectives of accounting for deferred taxation in the financial statements of companies, and to what extent does IAS 12 achieve this objective?

19.4 BRUCE plc

BRUCE plc ('BRUCE'), an Irish listed company that prepares its financial statements to 31 December each year, sells products to those involved in magic and illusion.

BRUCE
Statement of financial position at 31 December 2010

	Note	Book value €'000	Tax value €'000
Assets			
Non-current assets			
Property	(1)	40,000	10,000
Plant and equipment	(1)	20,000	8,000
Development costs	(2)	4,000	–
		64,000	18,000
Current assets			
Inventory		8,000	8,000
Trade receivables		6,000	6,000
Bank and cash		2,000	2,000
		80,000	34,000
Equity and liabilities			
Capital and reserves			
€1 ordinary shares		10,000	10,000
Retained earnings		41,000	1,000
		51,000	11,000
Non-current liabilities			
Loan	(3)	8,000	9,000
Deferred income	(4)	4,000	–
Employee retirement benefit scheme	(5)	2,000	–
Deferred taxation	(6)	10,000	10,000
Current liabilities			
Trade payables		4,000	4,000
Deferred income	(4)	1,000	–
		80,000	34,000

Notes

(1) The directors of BRUCE have decided to record the company's property, plant and equipment at fair value rather than depreciated historic cost. The fair value of the property at 31 December 2010 is deemed to be €50M, while the fair value of plant and equipment on the same date is €25M.

(2) Development costs are capitalised and amortised over future periods in determining accounting profit but deducted in determining taxable profit in the period in which they are incurred.

(3) During the year ended 31 December 2010, BRUCE negotiated a new loan with repayments commencing in 2012. For accounting purposes, the loan has been recorded net of the associated transaction costs paid in 2010. These costs are allowable for tax in the year in which they are paid.

(4) The deferred income relates to a non-taxable government grant received by BRUCE.

(5) In determining accounting profit employee retirement benefit costs are deducted when the service is provided by the employees, but, in determining taxable profit, they are deducted when contributions or retirement benefits are paid by BRUCE.

(6) This represents the deferred taxation liability at 31 December **2009**. During the year ended 31 December 2010, the taxation rate changed from 25 to 20%.

Required:
Calculate the deferred taxation expense to be included in the statement of comprehensive income of BRUCE for the year ended 31 December 2010 and the deferred tax liability at that date.

(Chartered Accountants Ireland)

19.5 KESARE Group
The following statement of financial position relates to KESARE Group, a public limited company at 30 June 2011:

	€'000
Assets	
Non-current assets	
Property, plant, and equipment	10,000
Goodwill	6,000
Other intangible assets	5,000
Financial assets (cost)	9,000
	30,000
Trade receivables	7,000
Other receivables	4,600
Cash and cash equivalents	6,700
	18,300
Total assets	48,300
Equity and liabilities	
Share capital	9,000
Other reserves	4,500
Retained earnings	9,130
Total equity	22,630
Non-current liabilities	
Long-term borrowings	10,000
Deferred tax liability	3,600
Employee benefit liability	4,000
Total non-current liabilities	17,600
Current tax liability	3,070
Trade and other payables	5,000
Total current liabilities	8,070
Total liabilities	25,670
Total equity and liabilities	48,300

The following information is relevant to the above statement of financial position:

(i) The financial assets are equity investments that are classified as held for trading, but are shown in the above statement of financial position at their cost on 1 July 2010. The market value of the assets is €10.5M on 30 June 2011. Taxation is payable on the sale of the assets.

(ii) The stated interest rate for the long-term borrowing is 8%. The loan of €10M represents a convertible bond which has a liability component of €9.6M and an equity component of €0.4M. The bond was issued on 30 June 2011.

(iii) The defined benefit plan has a rule change on 1 July 2010. KESARE estimate that of the past service costs of €1M, 40% relates to vested benefits and 60% relates to benefits that will vest over the next five years from that date. The past service costs have not been accounted for.

(iv) The tax bases of the assets and liabilities are the same as their carrying amounts in the statement of financial position at 30 June 2011, except for the following:

(a)

	€'000
Property, plant and equipment	2,400
Trade receivables	7,500
Other receivables	5,000
Employee benefits	5,000

(b) Other intangible assets were development costs which were all allowed for tax purposes when the cost was incurred in 2010.

(c) Trade and other payables include an accrual for compensation to be paid to employees. This amounts to €1M and is allowed for taxation when paid.

(v) Goodwill is not allowable for tax purposes in this jurisdiction.

(vi) Assume taxation is payable at 30%.

Required:

(a) Discuss the conceptual basis for the recognition of deferred taxation using the temporary difference approach to deferred taxation.

(b) Calculate the provision for deferred tax at 30 June 2011 after any necessary adjustments to the financial statements showing how the provision for deferred taxation would be dealt with in the financial statements. (Assume that any adjustments do not affect current tax. Candidates should briefly discuss the adjustments required to calculate the provision for deferred tax.)

(ACCA)

Chapter 20

Employee benefits

IAS 19 deals with the various benefits provided by an entity to its employees. The Standard identifies four categories of employee benefits:

- short-term employee benefits (e.g. wages and salaries)
- post-employment benefits (e.g. pensions)
- other long-term employee benefits (e.g. long-term disability benefits)
- termination benefits (e.g. lump sum redundancy payments)

The overall purpose of IAS 19 is to identify the correct amount of expense to be charged by an employer in respect of services provided by employees, and to recognise a liability for any of these amounts that remain unpaid.

Short-term employee benefits

These are defined by IAS 19 as '. . . employee benefits (other than termination benefits) that are due to be settled within twelve months after the end of the period in which the employees render the related service'. These benefits include the following:

(i)   Wages, salaries and social security contributions;
(ii) Short-term compensated absences (e.g. annual leave and sick leave);
(iii) Profit sharing and bonuses, payable within 12 months of the period end;
(iv) Non-monetary benefits (e.g. medical care, accommodation and company cars).

Where an employee has provided service to an entity during an accounting period, the entity must recognise the amount of short-term employee benefits due in exchange (on an undiscounted basis) as follows:

- as an expense;
- as a liability if part or all of the amount remains unpaid at the end of the period.

■ Wages, salaries and social security contributions

The accounting treatment here generally requires a straightforward application of the principles of IAS 19.

Example 1 Gringo Limited incurred wages and salaries costs of €4.8M in respect of the year ended 31 December 2010. In addition to this amount, Gringo incurred employer's social security costs of €400,000. All amounts were paid at 31 December, with the exception of the social security costs.

Show the journal entry in respect of wages and salaries of Gringo for the year ended 31 December 2010.

	Dr €'000	Cr €'000
Wages and salaries expense – I/S	5,200	
Bank		4,800
Accrued expenses – SOFP		400

An exception to the above treatment occurs when another standard requires or permits the inclusion of employee benefits in the cost of an asset. For example, the services provided by an entity's employees might relate to the construction of an asset.

Example 2 During 2010, Gringo Limited also paid €450,000 to a group of its employees who are engaged in the construction of an extension to the company's head office building.

Outline the accounting treatment for these payments.

Solution Under IAS 23 *Borrowing Costs* the employee benefits of €450,000 are directly attributable to the construction of the head office extension. These costs should therefore be included as part of the cost of that asset as follows:

	Dr €'000	Cr €'000
Buildings	450	
Bank		450

■ Short-term compensated absences

IAS 19 outlines how an entity may compensate employees for absence for various reasons, including holidays, sickness and short-term disability, maternity leave and jury service.

Two types of short-term compensation absences are identified by IAS 19:

- *accumulating* compensating absences, where employees can carry forward entitlements if not used in full at the end of the current period; and
- *non-accumulating* compensating absences, which cannot be carried forward to future periods.

For accumulating compensating absences, an entity must recognise a liability in respect of any expected amounts payable in the following period. See Example 3 below.

Example 3 Gringo Limited allows 22 days of paid annual leave to all of its employees. Unused leave at the end of a calendar year is extended for one additional year. Annual leave which has not been taken by the end of the following year is forfeited.

At 31 December 2010, employees in Gringo Limited had a total of 300 days of unused annual leave. Thirty of these days had also been unused at 31 December 2009. The average gross cost of one day's annual leave is €130.

Outline the accounting treatment for the annual leave outstanding in Gringo Limited at 31 December 2010. It should be assumed that no amounts were accrued at 31 December 2009 in respect of unused leave.

Solution Of the annual leave outstanding at 31 December 2010, 270 days can be carried forward by Gringo's employees into 2011. This leave is defined by IAS 19 as an *accumulating* compensating absence, and an accrued expense and liability must be recognised as follows:

	Dr €	Cr €
Wages and salaries expense – I/S	35,100	
Accrued expenses – SOFP		35,100

(Being annual leave outstanding at 31 December 2010, i.e. €130 × 270)

The remaining annual leave of 30 days is forfeited as it has not been used within the permitted time frame.

■ Profit-sharing and bonus plans

IAS 19 states that an entity shall recognise the expected cost of profit-sharing and bonus payments when:

- the entity has a present obligation (legal or constructive) to make such payments as a result of past events; and
- a reliable estimate of the obligation can be made.

A constructive obligation is one that an entity may have incurred due to precedent or custom and practice. See Example 4 below.

Example 4   Gringo Limited has traditionally paid its employees a year-end bonus, based on company performance and profits for the year. At 31 December 2010, the board of Gringo decided to pay an annual bonus totalling €500,000. This amount was due and unpaid at 31 December 2010.

Outline the accounting treatment for Gringo Limited's annual bonus for 2010.

Solution   Gringo Limited has a present obligation to pay its employees an annual bonus of €500,000 in respect of the year ended 31 December 2010. The payment of an annual bonus has been company practice in Gringo for several years, and it therefore constitutes a constructive obligation.

The amount payable to employees should be recognised in the financial statements for the year ended 31 December 2010 as follows:

	Dr €'000	Cr €'000
Wages and salaries expense – I/S	500	
Accrued expenses – SOFP		500

Post-employment benefits

The main type of post-employment benefit provided to employees is a retirement benefit, such as a pension. IAS 19 identifies two types of pension plans.

■ Defined-contribution plans

In this type of plan, an entity's obligation is limited to the amount that it agrees to contribute to the fund. Thus, the amount of post-employment benefit that will be received by an employee is determined by:

- the amount of contributions paid by an entity (and perhaps also the employee); and
- investment returns arising from the contributions.

Hence, in a defined-contribution plan, actuarial risk (that benefits will be less than expected) and investment risk (that assets invested will be insufficient to meet expected benefits) fall on the employee.

Defined-benefit plans

In this type of plan, the entity has an obligation to provide the agreed benefits to current and former employees. Typically, under a defined-benefit plan, a former employee will receive a pension that is based on his/her salary around the time of retirement. If there is any shortfall in the assets of the plan, this deficit must be contributed by the employer. Consequently, actuarial risk and investment risk fall on the entity.

Accounting for defined-contribution plans

Accounting for this type of plan is straightforward, as an entity's obligation is limited to the amount that is due to be contributed. Where an employee has rendered a service to an entity during a period, the entity should recognise the following amounts in its financial statements:

- an expense;
- a liability (accrued expense), after deducting any amount already paid.

Example 5   Gringo Limited operates a defined-contribution pension plan for all employees who commenced employment with the company after 1 January 2007. The contribution due in respect of the year ended 31 December 2010 is €1.1M, of which €300,000 is unpaid at the year end.

Outline the accounting treatment for Gringo Limited's defined-contribution plan.

Solution   Gringo Limited must charge an expense of €1.1M in respect of its defined-contribution plan. An accrued expense of €300,000 must be included in the statement of financial position at 31 December 2010.

	Dr €'000	Cr €'000
Pension costs expense – I/S	1,100	
Bank		800
Accrued expenses – SOFP		300

Accounting for defined-benefit plans

Accounting for defined-benefit plans is the most complex area of IAS 19. The overall approach of the Standard is to promote stability in the income statement from year to year. IAS 19 achieves this objective by allowing fluctuations on a defined-benefit pension plan be excluded from an entity's profit or loss. Three alternative methods of accounting for such fluctuations are permitted by IAS 19. They can be recognised in:

- other comprehensive income; or
- in profit or loss; or
- they can remain unrecognised as long as they do not exceed certain thresholds.

The approach of IAS 19 can be best understood by considering Example 6 below.

Example 6 Gringo Limited operates a defined-benefit pension plan for all employees who commenced employment with the company on or before 1 January 2007.

At 31 December 2009, Gringo had included a defined-benefit liability of €3.8M in its statement of financial position. This comprises:

	€'000
Present value of defined-benefit obligation	7,700
Fair value of assets of plan	3,900
Defined-benefit liability	3,800

Actuarial losses of €980,000 were unrecognised at 31 December 2009.

The following information relates to the year ended 31 December 2010:

	€'000
Employer contributions	680
Employee contributions	340
Interest cost	290
Benefits paid during current period	480
Past service costs (all benefits vested at 31/12/2010)	300
Current service cost	460
Expected return on assets of plan	320
Fair value of assets of plan at 31 December 2010	4,400
Present value of defined-benefit obligation at 31 December 2010	8,400

Calculate the defined-benefit expense for the year ended 31 December 2010, and the defined-benefit liability/asset at 31 December 2010.

Solution (a) Defined-benefit expense

The amount of defined-benefit expense that will be charged to profit or loss for the year ended 31 December 2010 is calculated as follows:

	€'000
Interest cost (note (1))	290
Past service cost (note (2))	300
Current service cost (note (3))	460
Expected return on plan assets	(320)
Defined benefit expense charged to profit or loss	730

Note (1) – Interest cost
This is the amount by which the present value of the defined benefit obligation at the beginning of the year has increased. The benefits due to employees at the beginning of the year are now one period closer, and therefore will cost more in present value terms. The interest cost will be charged as an expense in the current year's income statement.

Note (2) – Past service cost
This is the present value of changes in the current period which alter the amount of benefits awarded for employee service in previous periods. IAS 19 requires that past service costs be recognised as an expense on a straight-line basis over the average period until the benefits become vested.

For example, a company might award a pension increase of 4% to employees who have 10 years of service. Let us assume that half of the employees have 10 years of service. For those employees, the benefits are already vested, and the cost of providing the additional pension should be charged to profit or loss immediately.

The other employees might, on average, have completed four years of service. In this case, the cost of providing the additional pension should be charged on a straight-line basis over the six years of service required for the benefits to vest.

Note (3) – Current service cost

This is the increase in the present value of the defined benefit obligation, arising from employee service in the current period.

(b) Actuarial gains and losses

Actuarial gains/losses comprise:

- *Experience adjustments* (difference between actuarial assumptions at the beginning of the current period and what has actually occurred – e.g. wage rate inflation for current period is higher than anticipated or the actual return on plan assets differs from the expected return).
- The *effects of a change in actuarial assumptions* during the current period (e.g. actuary adjusts the rate of increase of future wage inflation rate).

The amount of actuarial gains and losses for Gringo Limited is computed as follows:

Actuarial loss/gain on defined-benefit *obligation*	€'000
Present value of defined-benefit obligation on 1 January 2010	7,700
Current service cost	460
Past service cost	300
Interest cost	290
Benefits paid	(480)
	8,270
Actuarial loss (balancing figure)	130
Present value of defined-benefit obligation at 31 December 2010	8,400

Actuarial loss/gain on *assets* of pension plan	€'000
Fair value of plan assets at 1 January 2010	3,900
Expected return on plan assets	320
Employer contributions	680
Employee contributions	340
Benefits paid	(480)
	4,760
Actuarial loss (balancing figure)	(360)
Fair value of plan assets at 31 December 2010	4,400

In a single year, the amount of an actuarial gain or loss can be extremely large. For example, in 2008 the credit crisis triggered huge falls in asset prices across the globe. The collapse left a significant deficit in many defined-benefit plans, as a gulf emerged between the fair value of plan assets and the obligations they were funding.

The IAS 19 approach is to limit the impact of actuarial losses on an entity's profit or loss. The Standard provides a choice of accounting treatments for actuarial gains and losses, as follows:

(i) Recognise actuarial gains/losses in other comprehensive income as they occur

Gringo Limited can choose to recognise actuarial gains and losses in the period in which they occur, by including them in **other comprehensive income**. This would result in the following journal entry in the year ended 31 December 2010:

	Dr €'000	Cr €'000
Pension costs – OCI	490	
Defined-benefit obligation – SOFP		490
(Being total actuarial losses, i.e. 130,000 + 360,000 for year end 31 December 2010)		

(ii) Recognise actuarial gains/losses in profit or loss as they occur

Gringo Limited can choose to recognise actuarial gains and losses in the period in which they occur, by including them in **profit or loss**. This would result in the following journal entry in the year ended 31 December 2010:

	Dr €'000	Cr €'000
Pension costs – I/S	490	
Defined-benefit obligation – SOFP		490
(Being total actuarial losses, i.e. 130,000 + 360,000 for year end 31 December 2010)		

(iii) 10% Corridor

Actuarial gains and losses may be excluded from the statement of comprehensive income.

However, a portion of the actuarial gains and losses should be charged to **profit or loss** if, at the end of the **previous** reporting period, cumulative unrecognised actuarial gains and losses exceed the greater of:

- 10% of the present value of the defined benefit obligation; and
- 10% of the fair value of any plan assets at that date.

Gains and losses that exceed the 10% corridor must be charged to profit or loss, but they may be spread over the average remaining working lives of employees in the plan. This test can be applied to Gringo Limited, as follows, in respect of the year ended 31 December 2010:

	€'000
10% of present value of defined-benefit obligation at 31 December 2009	770
10% of the fair value of the plan assets at 31 December 2009	390

Thus, the maximum available threshold for actuarial losses at 31 December 2009 is €770,000. However, unrecognised actuarial losses of Gringo Limited at 31 December 2009 amounted to €980,000. Consequently, the excess actuarial losses of €210,000 must be charged to profit or loss, but they may be spread over the average remaining working lives of employees in the plan. On the assumption that the latter figure is 20 years, the following journal entry will be required in the 2010 financial statements:

	Dr €'000	Cr €'000
Pension costs – I/S	10.5	
Defined-benefit obligation – SOFP		10.5

Should Gringo choose the 'corridor' option, there will be a charge to profit or loss of €10,500, additional to that of the €730,000 charge in (a) above.

(c) Statement of financial position

The amount that an entity recognises as a defined-benefit liability will depend on the accounting treatment chosen for actuarial gains and losses in (b) above. Consider the case of Gringo Limited.

What if Gringo decides to recognise actuarial gains/losses as they occur (either in other comprehensive income or in profit or loss)?

Under this policy there will be no unrecognised actuarial losses at any time. Thus, the unrecognised losses of €980,000 at 31 December 2009, referred to previously, do *not* apply.

The defined-benefit liability will be computed as follows:

	€'000
PV of defined-benefit obligation at 31 December 2010	8,400
Fair value of plan assets at 31 December 2010	(4,400)
Defined-benefit liability in statement of financial position at 31 December 2010	4,000

What if Gringo decides to use the 10% corridor approach?

The defined-benefit liability will be computed as follows:

	€'000
Present value of defined-benefit obligation at 31 Dec. 2010	8,400
Less:	
Unrecognised actuarial losses at 31 Dec. 2010*	(1,459.5)
Fair value of plan assets at 31 December 2010	(4,400)
Defined-benefit liability in statement of financial position at 31 December 2010	2,540.5

* Unrecognised actuarial losses at 31 December 2010:

	€'000
Unrecognised actuarial losses at 31 December 2009	980
Actuarial losses arising during 2010 (130,000 + 360,000)	490
Actuarial losses recognised in year end 31 December 2010	(10.5)
	1,459.5

The journal entries for the defined benefit plan of Gringo Limited are outlined in Appendix 20.1.

(d) Which approach is most commonly used in practice to account for actuarial gains and losses?

Morais[1] carried out a study of the approach adopted in 17 European countries. The study was based on the first set of **financial statements** prepared under IFRS/IAS by 523 European companies. The overall findings were as follows:

- 49% of the companies used the corridor approach;
- 44% recorded actuarial gains and losses in other comprehensive income as they arose;
- 7% recorded actuarial gains and losses in profit or loss as they arose.

The 'other comprehensive income' option was by far the most popular alternative in the UK and the Republic of Ireland. If both of these countries are excluded from the sample, it was found that the corridor method was used by 69.5% of companies in the other European countries.

Other long-term employee benefits

Examples of other long-term employee benefits include:

- long-term compensated absences such as long-service leave;
- long-term disability benefits;
- profit-sharing and bonuses payable 12 months or more after the end of the period in which employees render the related service.

The accounting treatment of these benefits is similar to that outlined in respect of defined-benefit pension plans. An important difference, however, is that actuarial gains and losses are recognised immediately. Thus, the corridor option allowed for defined-benefit pension plans is not permitted in the case of other long-term employee benefits.

Statement of financial position

The net total of the following two amounts should be recognised as a liability:

(i) Present value of the defined-benefit obligation at the end of the reporting period;
(ii) Less the fair value of plan assets.

Statement of comprehensive income

The net total of the following amounts should be recognised as an expense or income in profit or loss, except when another standard permits or requires their inclusion in the cost of an asset:

- current service cost
- interest cost
- expected return on any plan assets
- actuarial gains and losses, which must be recognised immediately
- past service cost, which should be recognised immediately.

Termination benefits

An entity may be committed by legislation, by business practice, or by a desire to act equitably to make payments to employees when it terminates their employment.

Termination benefits do not provide an entity with future economic benefits, and they are therefore recognised as an expense immediately. Termination benefits should be recognised as a liability and an expense, however, only when the entity is demonstrably committed to:

- terminate the employment of an employee before the normal retirement date; or
- provide termination benefits as a result of an offer made in order to encourage voluntary redundancy.

An entity is demonstrably committed to a termination only when it has a detailed formal plan that has no realistic possibility of withdrawal.

Example 7 In December 2010, Gringo Limited announced a detailed plan for terminating the employment of 5% of its workforce. The termination date scheduled by the company was 1 April 2011 and it was agreed that lump sum termination benefits totalling €1.6M would be made to the staff affected.

In December 2010, Gringo Limited also announced detailed plans for voluntary redundancy. It was expected that a further 100 staff would opt for the terms offered by the company, which involve a deferred lump sum payment of €50,000 per employee payable on 1 January 2013.

Outline the accounting treatment for the termination payments scheduled by Gringo Limited. The market yield on blue chip corporate bonds at 31 December 2010 was 6%.

Solution Gringo has a detailed formal plan in place in December 2010, which will result in the termination of employment for 5% of its workforce. As there is no realistic possibility of that plan being withdrawn, Gringo is deemed to be demonstrably committed to the termination plan.

Termination payments totalling €1.6 million should be recognised as an expense and a liability in the financial statements of Gringo for the year ended 31 December 2010.

The following journal entry will be required:

	Dr €'000	Cr €'000
Termination payments expense – I/S	1,600	
Termination payments liability – SOFP		1,600

In the case of voluntary redundancy, IAS 19 requires that the measurement of termination benefits shall be based on the number of employees expected to accept the offer. IAS 19 also states that termination benefits falling due more than 12 months after the reporting period should be discounted to present value, using the market yield on high-quality corporate bonds.

Gringo is expected to make voluntary redundancy payments totalling €5M on 1 January 2013. When discounted at an annual rate of 6%, these payments have a present value of €4.45M. The following journal entry is required in the financial statements for the year ended 31 December 2010:

	Dr €'000	Cr €'000
Termination payments expense – I/S	4,450	
Provision for termination payments – SOFP		4,450

Summary

- The overall objective of IAS 19 is to identify the correct amount of expense to be charged by an employer in respect of services provided by an employer, and to recognise a liability for any of these amounts that remain unpaid.
- Short-term employee benefits provided during a reporting period should be charged to profit or loss, and recognised as a liability if unpaid.
- An employer should charge to profit or loss its agreed contribution for the period to a defined-contribution pension plan.
- An employer should charge to profit or loss the current period cost (excluding actuarial gains/losses) of a defined-benefit pension plan.

- Actuarial gains/losses in respect of defined-benefit pension plans should be:
  - included in other comprehensive income when they occur; or
  - included in profit or loss when they occur; or
  - recognised in profit or loss over the expected average remaining working lives of the participating employees, to the extent that they exceed the 10% threshold allowed by IAS 19. This is known as the 'corridor approach'.
- Other long-term benefits (e.g. long-term disability) should be accounted for in a similar way to defined-benefit plans, except that all actuarial gains and losses should be recognised immediately in profit or loss.
- Termination benefits that satisfy certain conditions should be recognised as an expense immediately, as they do not provide an entity with future economic benefits.

■ Reference

1. Morais, A. I. (2008). Actuarial gains and losses: the choice of the accounting method. *Accounting in Europe*, 5 (2), pp. 127–39.

Appendix 20.1

Journal entries for defined-benefit pension plan of Gringo Limited

	Dr €'000	Cr €'000
Defined-benefit assets	680	
Bank		680
(Being employer contributions for the year)		
Defined-benefit obligation – SOFP	480	
Defined-benefit assets		480
(Being benefits paid for the year)		
Defined-benefit assets	320	
Expected return on assets – I/S		320
(Being expected return on assets)		
Interest expense – I/S	290	
Defined-benefit obligation – SOFP		290
(Being interest cost for year)		
Current service costs – I/S	460	
Defined-benefit obligation – SOFP		460
(Being current service cost for year)		
Past service costs – I/S	300	
Defined-benefit obligation – SOFP		300
(Being past service costs for year)		

Alternative treatments of actuarial losses

(i) Recognise actuarial losses in other comprehensive income as they occur

	Dr €'000	Cr €'000
Actuarial loss – OCI	130	
Defined-benefit obligation		130
(Being actuarial loss for year on defined-benefit obligation)		
Actuarial loss – OCI	360	
Defined-benefit assets		360
(Being actuarial loss for year on defined-benefit plan assets)		

or

(ii) Recognise actuarial losses in profit or loss as they occur

	Dr €'000	Cr €'000
Actuarial loss – I/S	130	
Defined-benefit obligation		130
(Being actuarial loss for year on defined-benefit obligation)		
Actuarial loss – I/S	360	
Defined-benefit assets		360
(Being actuarial loss for year on defined-benefit plan assets)		

or

(iii) 10% corridor approach

	Dr €'000	Cr €'000
Pension costs – I/S	10.5	
Defined-benefit obligation – SOFP		10.5
(Being write-off of actuarial loss for year)		

QUESTIONS

20.1 GLOVE

On 1 June 2008, GLOVE introduced a new defined-benefit retirement plan. At 1 June 2008, there were no unrecognised actuarial gains and losses. The following information relates to the retirement plan:

	€M 31 May 2009	€M 31 May 2010
Unrecognised actuarial losses to date	3	5
Present value of obligation	20	26
Fair value of plan assets	16	20

The expected average remaining working lives of the employees in the plan is 10 years at 31 May 2009 and 31 May 2010. GLOVE wishes to defer actuarial gains and losses by using the 'corridor' approach. The defined liability is included in non-current liabilities.

Required:
Outline the accounting treatment of GLOVE's defined-benefit retirement plan for the year ended 31 May 2010. (ACCA)

20.2 ASH Limited

The following information is given about ASH Ltd's defined-benefit pension plan:

	2008 €'000	2009 €'000	2010 €'000
Current service cost	250	280	310
Benefits paid	260	300	340
Contributions paid	160	180	200
Present value of obligations at 31 December	2,430	2,826	3,200
Fair value of plan assets at 31 December	2,294	2,274	2,400
Discount rate at start of year	9%	8%	8%
Expected return on plan assets	12%	11%	11%

The present value of the obligation and the fair value of the plan assets were both €2M at 1 January 2008, and there were no actuarial gains or losses at this date. The average remaining working life of the current employees was estimated to be 10 years at 1 January 2008.

Required:

(a) In respect of each of the three years ending 31 December 2008, 2009 and 2010, outline how the pension scheme would be shown in the financial statements of ASH Ltd. It should be assumed that ASH Ltd uses the 'corridor' approach permitted by IAS 19 *Employee Benefits*.

(b) Outline the effect on the financial statements of ASH Ltd if actuarial gains or losses are recorded in *other comprehensive income* as they arise.

(c) Why might a defined-contribution scheme be preferred by an employer setting up a pension scheme for its employees?

20.3 MACALJOY plc

MACALJOY, a public limited company, is a leading support services company which focuses on the building industry. The company would like advice on how to treat certain items under IAS19 *Employee Benefits* and IAS 37 *Provisions, Contingent Liabilities and Contingent Assets*. The company operates the MACALJOY (2009) Pension Plan which commenced on 1 November 2009 and MACALJOY (1993) Pension Plan, which was closed to new entrants from 31 October 2009, but which was open to future service accrual for the employees already in the scheme. The assets of the schemes are held separately from those of the company in funds under the control of trustees. The following information relates to the two schemes.

MACALJOY (1993) Pension Plan

The terms of the plan are as follows:

(i)   Employees contribute 6% of their salaries to the plan.
(ii) MACALJOY contributes, currently, the same amount for the benefit of the employees.
(iii) On retirement, employees are guaranteed a pension which is based upon the number of years' service with the company and their final salary.

The following details relate to the plan in the year to 31 October 2010:

	€M
Present value of obligation at 1 November 2009	200
Present value of obligation at 31 October 2010	240
Fair value of plan assets at 1 November 2009	190
Fair value of plan assets at 31 October 2010	225
Current service cost	20
Pension benefits paid	19
Total contributions paid to the scheme for year to 31 October 2010	17

Actuarial gains and losses are recognised in other comprehensive income.

MACALJOY (2009) Pension Plan

Under the terms of the plan, MACALJOY does not guarantee any return on the contributions paid into the fund. The company's legal and constructive obligation is limited to the amount that is contributed to the fund. The following details relate to this scheme:

	€M
Fair value of plan assets at 31 October 2010	21
Contributions paid by company for year to 31 October 2010	10
Contributions paid by employees for year to 31 October 2010	10

The discount rates and expected return on plan assets for the two plans are:

	1 November 2009	31 October 2010
Discount rate	5%	6%
Expected return on plan assets	7%	8%

Required:

The company would like advice on how to treat the two pension plans for the year ended 31 October 2010, together with an explanation of the differences between a defined-contribution plan and a defined-benefit plan.

Chapter 21

Provisions, contingent liabilities and contingent assets

It is often said that the only certainty about the future is its uncertainty. Yet there is something strangely appealing about trying to successfully predict the outcome of future events, and bookmakers and stockbrokers make a good living from punters and investors who speculate on movements in stock prices, exchange rates, commodity prices and myriad sporting and other events.

Predicting the future is also a critical skill in many occupations and professions. Weather forecasts are made by analysing a complex combination of meteorological variables. Statisticians use demographic trends to predict future changes in population densities. Actuaries advise on pension fund values, based on forecasts of life expectancies and asset returns. Accountants, perhaps more than most, must contend with the vagaries of unexpected future events, and the measurement of **assets** and **liabilities** requires that these events are routinely forecast. This includes making estimates of the useful lives of assets, the saleability of inventory, and the solvency of an entity's customers.

Sometimes it is not possible to accurately predict the amount or timing of the cash flows associated with a liability. For example, an entity's former employee may take a legal action on the grounds of unfair dismissal. At the end of the reporting period, while awaiting an outcome, the entity must determine how likely it is that the litigant will be successful, and how much he/she will be awarded by the court. Other, more routine estimates of cash outflows must also be made, for example, in forecasting the amount of goods sold that will be returned by customers.

In dealing with matters such as these, guidance is provided by IAS 37 *Provisions, Contingent Liabilities and Contingent Assets*.

Provisions

General recognition criteria

IAS 37 defines a provision as a liability of uncertain timing or amount. A provision should be recognised when:

- an entity has a present obligation (legal or constructive) as a result of a past event;
- payment is probable; and
- a reliable estimate can be made of the amount of the obligation.

An obligating event is one that creates a legal or constructive obligation, and therefore results in an enterprise having no realistic alternative but to settle the obligation.

A constructive obligation arises if past practice creates a valid expectation on the part of a third party. For example, a store might have a long-standing policy of making refunds to customers for goods returned within 30 days.

■ Measurement of provisions

An entity should recognise as a **provision** the *best estimate* of the expenditure required to settle the present obligation at the end of the reporting period. This means that:

- *Provisions for one-off events* (e.g. restructuring, environmental clean-up, lawsuit settlements) are measured at their most likely amount.

Example 1　In December 2010, a customer took a legal action against Brent Limited, claiming breach of contract. On 12 March 2011, the date on which its financial statements were authorised for issue, Brent received legal advice that the customer was likely to be awarded €20,000.

Provision should be made at 31 December 2010 for the amount of the award that the customer is expected to receive. The following journal entry is required:

	Dr €	Cr €
Litigation costs – I/S	20,000	
Provision for litigation settlement – SOFP		20,000

- *Provisions for large populations of events* (e.g. warranties, customer refunds) are measured at a probability-weighted expected value.

Example 2　Brent Limited has a policy of making cash refunds at its customers' request. Although there is no legal obligation to do so, it is believed that the policy has promoted a greater than average level of customer loyalty to the company.

On the basis of past experience, it is estimated that cash refunds relating to 2010 sales will amount to €600,000 in 2011. Brent Limited earns an average gross margin of 40% on sales.

Outline how Brent Limited should account for its refunds policy in its 2010 financial statements.

Solution　Although there is no legal compulsion for Brent Limited to make cash refunds, this has been the established practice, so as to promote customer loyalty. On the basis that it is probable that cash refunds of €600,000 will be made during 2011, a provision should be made at 31 December 2010 for the gross margin recorded on those sales in 2010. The following journal entry is required:

	Dr €	Cr €
Provision for refunds – I/S	240,000	
Provision for refunds – SOFP		240,000

- *Discounting.* Where the effect of the time value of money is material, the amount of a provision shall be at a **discounted present value**. One should use a pre-tax discount rate that reflects the current market assessments of the time value of money and the specific risks of the liability.

Example 3　In December 2010, Brent Limited accepted responsibility for environmental damage caused by its exploration activities, and it has agreed to pay for the clean-up costs. It is estimated that these costs are likely to amount to €2M in December 2012. An appropriate pre-tax discount rate is considered to be 10%.

Outline how Brent Limited should account for the clean-up costs in its 2010 financial statements.

Solution   As Brent Limited has agreed to pay an estimated amount of €2M in respect of clean-up costs, provision should be made for these costs at 31 December 2010. Given the size of the provision, the effect of the two-year moratorium on payment is likely to be material. The clean-up costs should therefore be provided on a discounted basis as follows:

	Dr €'000	Cr €'000
Provision for clean-up costs – I/S	1,653	
Provision for clean-up costs – SOFP		1,653

(Being the present value cost of environmental clean-up: $€2M/(1.1)^2$)

■ Future events

In measuring a provision, an entity should consider **future events** as follows:

- changes in applying existing technology (e.g. savings in a planned clean-up due to availability of improved equipment);
- changes in legislation only if virtually certain to be enacted;
- gains on the expected disposal of assets should not be taken into account.

■ Reimbursements from third parties

When some or all of the expenditure required to settle a provision is expected to be reimbursed by another party, the reimbursement should be recognised as a separate asset, but only when it is virtually certain that the reimbursement will be received if the entity settles the obligation.

In the income statement, the expense relating to a provision may be presented net of the amount recognised for a reimbursement.

Example 4   On 31 December 2010, Brent Limited received written confirmation that it would receive an insurance settlement of €400,000 in respect of the environmental damage in Example 3 above.

Outline how the insurance settlement should be accounted for by Brent Limited.

Solution   As Brent Limited is guaranteed to receive the insurance settlement, it should be recognised as a separate asset, and it should be offset against the related expense in the income statement:

	Dr €'000	Cr €'000
Insurance settlement asset – SOFP	400	
Provision for clean up-costs – I/S		400

■ Remeasurement of provisions

Provisions should be reviewed and adjusted at the end of each reporting period. If an outflow is no longer probable, the provision should be credited to income.

■ Future operating losses

Provisions should *not* be recognised for future operating losses. These provide an indication, however, that certain assets of an entity may be impaired, and these assets should be tested under IAS 36 *Impairment of Assets*.

■ Onerous contracts

An onerous contract is a contract in which the unavoidable costs of meeting the obligations under the contract exceed the economic benefits expected to be received from it. The present obligation under an onerous contract should be recognised and measured as a provision.

Example 5

On 31 December 2009, Brent Limited signed a five-year lease on a premises, requiring annual payments of €100,000 in advance. During 2010, it transpired that Brent Limited has no further use for the building, and it is not possible to sub-lease the building to another tenant. At 31 December 2010 the present value cost of outstanding lease instalments amounted to €255,000.

Outline how Brent Limited should account for the lease in its financial statements for the year ended 31 December 2010.

Solution

The lease agreement is an onerous contract for Brent Limited. The discounted amount of the outstanding lease payments should be provided for at 31 December 2010.

	Dr €'000	Cr €'000
Provision for lease costs – I/S	255	
Provision for lease costs – SOFP		255

■ Restructuring

The following are examples of events that may fall under the definition of restructuring:

- sale* or termination of a line of business
- closure of business locations
- changes in management structure
- fundamental reorganisation of a company

A provision for restructuring costs is recognised only when:

- an entity has a present obligation (legal or constructive[†]) as a result of a past event;
- it is probable that an outflow of resources will be required to settle the obligation; and
- a reliable estimate can be made of the amount of the obligation.

* No obligation arises for the sale of an operation until there is a binding sale agreement.
[†] A constructive obligation to restructure arises only when an entity has a detailed formal plan, which it has begun to implement, and whose main features have been announced to those affected by it.

A restructuring provision should only include direct expenditures caused by the restructuring, not costs that are associated with the ongoing activities of an entity.

Example 6

In September 2010, Brent Limited announced that it intended to rationalise its distribution division. A detailed plan was drawn up in December 2010 for the sale of surplus non-current assets, and for the redeployment of staff. The plan was approved in principle by members of staff who will be affected by it.

It was estimated that rationalising its distribution division would necessitate a provision of €3M at 31 December 2010. This provision is analysed as follows:

	€'000
Loss on disposal of non-current assets	975
Redundancy settlements	525
Warehouse redesign costs	330
Marketing costs	570
Future operating losses	600
	3,000

No provision has been made in the financial statements at 31 December 2010.

Outline how Brent Limited should account for the rationalisation of its distribution division in its financial statements for the year ended 31 December 2010.

Solution   A provision for restructuring should only be recognised when the general recognition criteria of IAS 37 are met. In addition, IAS 37 states that an obligation to restructure arises only when an entity has:

- a detailed formal plan for the restructuring; and
- raised a valid expectation in those affected that it will carry out the restructuring by starting to implement the plan or announcing its main features to those affected by it.

These recognition criteria appear to have been satisfied in respect of Brent Limited's intention to rationalise its distribution division. In identifying costs that should be recognised within a restructuring provision, IAS 37 states that

> . . . a restructuring provision shall include only the direct expenditures arising from the restructuring, which are those that are both;
> - necessarily entailed by the restructuring; and
> - not associated with the ongoing activities of the entity.

The following amounts should therefore be provided for by Brent Limited at 31 December 2010:

	€'000
Loss on disposal of non-current assets	975
Redundancy settlements	525
	1,500

IAS 37 states that '. . . provisions shall not be recognised for future operating losses'.

Also, marketing costs should not be provided for, on the basis that they relate to the future conduct of the business and are not obligations at the end of the reporting period. Warehouse redesign costs which will be incurred by Brent Limited are excluded on the same basis.

Thus, on the basis that Brent Limited is committed to the rationalisation of its distribution division, the following entry will be required in its financial statements for the year ended 31 December 2010:

	Dr €'000	Cr €'000
Restructuring provision – I/S	1,500	
Restructuring provision – SOFP		1,500

■ Decommissioning costs

Where provision is made for decommissioning and other environmental costs, a corresponding asset will be set up at the same time, on the basis that the expenditure provides access to future economic benefits. For example, the cost of setting up an oil rig would be increased by the present value of expected decommissioning costs.

Example 7   Brent Limited constructed a new oil rig in the North Sea during 2010, at a cost of €2.5M. Construction was completed on 1 December 2010, and the oil rig, which has a zero residual value, will be depreciated at 10% per annum on a straight-line basis. A full year's depreciation is charged in the year of construction.

On completion of construction, it was estimated that the cost of decommissioning the oil rig would amount to €500,000.

Brent Limited has a weighted average cost of capital of 8%.

Outline how the construction of the oil rig should be accounted for in the financial statements of Brent Limited for the years ending 31 December 2010 and 2011.

Solution   The construction costs of the oil rig should be capitalised as part of property, plant and equipment. This should include the present value cost of decommissioning the rig, which should also be recognised as a provision. The following journal entries will be required:

	Dr €'000	Cr €'000
Year ending 31 December 2010		
Property, plant and equipment	2,500	
Bank		2,500
Property, plant and equipment	250	
Provision for decommissioning – SOFP		250
(Being the present value of decommissioning costs, at 31 December 2010, based on a WACC of 8%: €500,000 × 0.5*)		
Depreciation expense – I/S	275	
Accumulated depreciation		275
(Being depreciation for 2010: €2.75M × 10%)		
Year ending 31 December 2011		
Depreciation expense – I/S	275	
Accumulated depreciation		275
(Being depreciation for 2011)		
Decommissioning expense – I/S	20	
Provision for decommissioning – SOFP		20
(Being unwinding of discount†)		

* It is assumed that decommissioning will take place at the time that the asset is fully depreciated. The present value factor for year 9 at 8% = 0.5.
† The cost of decommissioning is one year closer at 31 December 2011. Therefore, the increase in present value cost equals (€500,000/(1.08)^8) less (€500,000/(1.08)^9) = €20,009.

For examples of provisions see Appendix 21.1.

Contingent liabilities and contingent assets

Contingent liabilities

IAS 37 defines a **contingent liability** as:

- *a possible obligation arising from past events, which is dependent on whether an uncertain future event occurs, or*
- *a present obligation, where payment is not probable, or which cannot be measured reliably.*

Contingent liabilities should *not* be recognised, but should be disclosed, unless the possibility of a transfer of economic benefits is remote.

Example 8 In November 2010, legal action was instigated against Brent Limited by one of its suppliers. On 12 March 2011, when its financial statements were authorised for issue, the company's legal advisers were of the view that an award of up to €150,000 could be made against Brent Limited. However, it was not considered likely that the supplier's action would be successful.

This is a contingent liability, as there is a possible obligation arising from past events. Details should be disclosed in Brent Limited's financial statements for the year ended 31 December 2010.

Contingent assets

IAS 37 defines a **contingent asset** as

a possible asset, arising from past events, where an inflow of economic benefits depends on the outcome of an uncertain future event.

Contingent assets should *not* be recognised in an entity's financial statements. They should, however, be disclosed if an inflow of economic benefits is probable. Should the realisation of economic benefits be virtually certain, then the related asset is not a contingent asset, and its recognition is appropriate.

Disclosures

For each class of provision, an entity should disclose:

- carrying amount at the beginning and the end of the period;
- additional provisions made in the period;
- amounts used (i.e. incurred and charged) during the period; and
- the increase during the period in the discounted amount arising from the passage of time.

For each class of provision, a brief description should outline:

- nature
- timing
- uncertainties
- major assumptions
- expected reimbursements.

Where disclosure of the above information is expected to seriously prejudice the position of the entity in a dispute with other parties, an entity need not disclose the information, but it shall disclose the general nature of the dispute and the reason why the information has not been disclosed.

Summary

- A provision is a liability of uncertain timing or amount. A provision should be recognised when:
  - an entity has a present obligation as a result of a past event;
  - payment is probable; and
  - a reliable estimate can be made of the amount of the obligation.
- An entity should recognise as a provision the best estimate of the expenditure required to settle the present obligation.
- Provisions should be discounted to present value when the effect of the time value of money is material.
- Provisions should be reviewed and adjusted at the end of each reporting period. If an outflow is no longer probable, the provision should be credited to income.
- Contingent liabilities should *not* be recognised, but should be disclosed, unless the possibility of a transfer of economic benefits is remote.
- Contingent assets should *not* be recognised in an entity's financial statements. They should, however, be disclosed if an inflow of economic benefits is probable.

Appendix 21.1

Examples of provisions

Details	Present obligation as the result of a past event?	Probable outflow of resources which can be measured reliably?	Provision required?
Warranty	Obligating event is the sale of defective goods	Yes	Yes
Contaminated land An oil company has been contaminating land for several years. At 31 December 2010 it is virtually certain that draft legislation will be enacted shortly after the year end	The obligating event is the contamination of the land	Yes	Yes. A provision is required for the best estimate of the costs of clean-up
Contaminated land and constructive obligation An oil company causes contamination in a country where there is no legislation requiring clean-up. The company has a widely published environmental policy of cleaning up any contamination caused	Obligating event is the contamination of the land, which gives rise to a constructive obligation	Yes	Yes. A provision is recognised for the best estimate of the costs of clean-up
Refunds policy	Obligating event is the sale of the product, which gives rise to a constructive obligation	Yes	Yes. A provision is recognised for the estimated cost of refunds

Details	Present obligation as the result of a past event?	Probable outflow of resources which can be measured reliably?	Provision required?
Closure of division – no implementation before end of reporting period The board of an entity decided on 12 December 2010 to close a division. Decision not communicated before 31 December 2010 to any of those affected, and no other steps taken to implement the decision	There has been no obligating event, so there is no obligation	No	No provision is recognised
Closure of division – communication/ implementation before the end of the reporting period	Obligating event is the communication of the decision to customers and employees, which gives rise to a constructive obligation from that date	Yes	Yes. A provision is recognised for the best estimate of the closure costs
Staff retraining as a result of changes in EU legislation At the end of the reporting period, no retraining of staff has taken place	No obligating event (i.e. retraining) has taken place	No	No provision is required
Repairs and maintenance (no legal requirement) A furnace has a lining that needs to be replaced every five years for technical reasons. At 31 December 2010, the lining has been in use for three years	There is no present obligation to replace the furnace lining	No	No provision is recognised
Repairs and maintenance (legal requirement) An airline is required by law to overhaul its aircraft once every three years	There is no present obligation, because the entity could avoid the future expenditure by its future actions, e.g. by selling the aircraft	No	No provision is recognised

QUESTIONS

21.1 Refunds policy

O'NEILL RETAIL has introduced a new policy in 2010 of refunding purchases by dissatisfied customers if goods are returned within one month with a proof of purchase. This facility is now well known among the customer base and has proved popular with customers, prompting an increase in sales. It is anticipated that approximately 5% of goods will be returned. The sales for December 2010 were €550,000 with the average margin being 20%. Mr O'Neill would like to know the correct accounting treatment and necessary disclosures for the new refunds policy.

Required:

Advise O'NEILL RETAIL as to the recommended accounting treatment relating to the new refund policy, setting out any journals required and all relevant disclosures relating to the financial statements for the year ended 31 December 2010. (Chartered Accountants Ireland)

21.2 IRISHLINK

Two of the depots used by IRISHLINK, one in Cork and one in Donegal, are held under two separate leases, both of which were signed on 1 January 2010.

The Cork depot is included in the draft financial statements for the year ended 31 December 2010 at its depreciated historical cost of €4.8M. Under the terms of the 10-year lease, the depot must be restored to its original condition at the end of the lease period. IRISHLINK estimates that the present value of these restoration costs at 31 December 2010 is €2.5M as a result of structural changes that have been made to the depot. Therefore the company would like to provide €250,000 each year to cover these costs. The directors of IRISHLINK believe that the lease has a recoverable amount of €6.5M at 31 December 2010.

The Donegal depot is held under a five-year operating lease, and this depot must be returned in good condition at the end of the lease term. IRISHLINK estimates that the present value of carrying out the necessary redecoration work at the end of the lease period will be €1M. However, as a result of uninsured water damage in December 2010, IRISHLINK will need to spend €400,000 in 2011 repairing the damage; but this should reduce the anticipated redecoration expenditure at the end of the lease period by an equivalent amount.

Required:

Explain how each of the leases should be reflected in the financial statements of IRISHLINK for the year ended 31 December 2010. (Chartered Accountants Ireland)

21.3 Divisional reorganisation

The TARGET group continually evaluates the business performance of the group companies to ensure focus, effort and resources are concentrated on those areas that can generate maximum return for the group. Experience and results over the last 18 months have clearly indicated that the Pharmaceutical Division of TARGET ENGINEERING is proving to be less profitable than the Food Processing Division but is utilising the same resources and capital.

As a result, during November 2010, a Divisional Reorganisation Plan was formulated to focus the future trading activities of TARGET ENGINEERING exclusively on customers in the food processing sector. This Divisional Reorganisation Plan will have an impact on the staff, non-current assets and other resources which to date have been dedicated to the Pharmaceutical Division.

The details of the plan have already been discussed with, and communicated to, the relevant employees and their union representatives. It is widely known by the company's competitors, customers and suppliers that TARGET ENGINEERING is no longer tendering for future contracts in the pharmaceutical sector. The timetable within the Divisional Reorganisation Plan assumes implementation commencing in February 2011 with completion by June 2011.

235

The key features of the Divisional Reorganisation Plan are as follows:

- 30 staff facing compulsory redundancy at a cost to the company of €500,000;
- 20 staff retasked to the Food Processing Division – training costs to convert €50,000;
- investment in new systems to support expanded Food Processing Division €100,000.

None of the costs have been incurred yet but TARGET's financial director anticipates that he will create a restructuring provision in the financial statements of the coming year, i.e. 31 December 2011, for €650,000 to cover, in full, the costs of implementing the plan.

Required:
Set out the impact, if any, of the Divisional Reorganisation Plan on the financial statements of TARGET ENGINEERING for the year ended 31 December 2010.   (Chartered Accountants Ireland)

Part 7

CONSOLIDATED FINANCIAL STATEMENTS

Chapter 22

Consolidated financial statements

Imagine that you have won the lotto, and you decide to realise your dream of owning a business empire of your own. Shortly afterwards you pay €10M to purchase 10% of the equity share capital of a company called Holdall Limited, whose affairs you have been monitoring for some time.

In February 2011, Holdall acquires a boating company called Sail Limited – paying €2M for 80% of that company's equity share capital.

The following month, Holdall buys 100% of a bus company called Double Decker Limited for €2.5M, and in May it buys all of the shares in Tracks Limited, a railway company, for €3M. As you sip your cappuccino, you are enjoying being rich, and you cannot wait to find out how much profit your companies will earn for the year. All have a 31 December year end, so in late February you eagerly await news of your investments.

In March 2012, you receive a brown envelope, containing the financial statements of Holdall Limited, and a letter from chief executive, Sharon Williams. However, neither the financial statements nor the letter says anything about the profits of Sail, Double Decker or Tracks. You wait a further week, but there is still no news. Puzzled, you contact the manager of Double Decker for an explanation. He informs you, over the phone, that he posted the company's **financial statements** the previous week.

> 'I didn't get them,' you say.
> 'Well they were sent,' he replies indifferently.
> 'Sent where?'
> 'Let's see. 127 Willow Avenue'.
> 'That's not my address!'
> '127 Willow Avenue is Holdall Limited's registered office, sir.'
> 'Why didn't you send them to *me*?' you ask crossly.
> 'Do you own shares in Double Decker, sir?'
> 'No, but . . .'
> 'Only shareholders receive the financial statements, sir.'

You contact Sharon Williams, who says that the accountant is working on the financial statements of the group. They should be available some time tomorrow.

> 'The group? What's the group?' you ask, scratching your head.
> 'It's all four companies together – Holdall, Sail, Double Decker and Tracks. The group financial statements contain a single set of figures for all the companies in the group.'
> 'That's handy!' you reply with a sigh of relief.
> 'Yes, it means that you only have to read one set of financial statements to see how all of the companies are performing.'
> 'At last things are starting to make sense!'

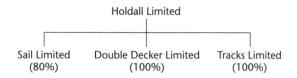

You speak to the accountant of Holdall Limited, who draws a diagram to represent the group.

Parents and subsidiaries

'Holdall is a parent,' he explains, 'and the other three companies are subsidiaries.'

'So a parent is a company that has one or more subsidiaries', you add, making your question sound more like a statement.

'Exactly!'

'And a subsidiary is a company that is controlled by another company.'

'Correct.'

'So, to exercise control, Holdall must own more than 50% of another company's voting shares.'

'Not necessarily,' the accountant explains. 'Control also exists when the parent owns half or less of the voting power, when there is:

- power over more than half of the voting rights by virtue of an agreement with other investors;
- power to govern the financial and operating policies of the entity;
- power to appoint or remove the majority of the members of the board of directors; or
- majority voting power at meetings of the board of directors.'

'For example, let's assume that Holdall Limited owns 40% of the equity shares of a company called Airline Limited. And Holdall Limited also has the power to appoint 6 of the 10 members of the board of directors of Airline Limited. Is Airline Limited a subsidiary of Holdall Limited?'

You shrug your shoulders and smile, wondering how the accountant knows of your plans for world domination of the transport sector.

'Well, although Holdall owns only 40% of the equity shares of Airline, it has the power to appoint the majority of Airline's board of directors. So, in fact Airline is a subsidiary of Holdall.'

'You're making this up, right?'

'Certainly not,' replies the accountant. 'These rules are clearly outlined in IAS 27.'

'IAS what?'

'IAS 27. *Consolidated and Separate Financial Statements.*'

Presentation of consolidated financial statements

'So **consolidated financial statements** are prepared for the shareholders of the parent company. Is that right?'

'Quite right,' replies the accountant.

'And a parent always has to present consolidated financial statements?'

'Yes, unless of course:

- the parent is itself a wholly owned subsidiary;
- the parent is a partially owned subsidiary, and its other owners do not object to consolidated financial statements not being prepared;
- the parent's debt or equity instruments are not traded in a public market.'

'But none of those exceptions apply in the case of Holdall.'

'Quite right. So Holdall will *have* to present consolidated financial statements.'

'Just as I thought!' you say with a smile.

Consolidation procedures

■ Date of consolidated financial statements

'Obviously, all the companies in a group must have the same year end.'

'Ideally, yes,' replies the accountant.

'What if they don't?'

'Holdall, Sail, Double Decker and Tracks all have a year end of 31 December. Right?'

'Yes, of course.'

'Now, suppose that the new subsidiary, Airline Limited, prepares financial statements up to 31 October.'

'Okay, so what happens then?'

'Well, IAS 27 requires Airline to prepare additional financial statements up to 31 December, unless it's impracticable to do so.'

'What if it is? Impracticable I mean.'

'That's okay as long as the end of Airline's reporting period does not differ by more than three months from the rest of the group.'

'So, Airline's financial statements up to 31 October could be used.'

'Yes, because the difference from the group's year end of 31 December is less than three months.'

'But what if Airline burns down in November or December? Wouldn't that be a bit misleading?'

'I wasn't finished,' says the accountant with a sigh. 'Adjustments would have to be made for the effects of significant transactions or events that occur between 31 October and 31 December.'

'Like Airline being burned down?'

'Yes, like Airline being burned down!' confirms the accountant, the strain beginning to show on his face.

■ Accounting policies

'Consolidated financial statements must be prepared using uniform accounting policies for all companies in a group,' adds the accountant, anxious to reassert his control.

'Huh?'

'Suppose that companies in the Holdall Group all use FIFO to account for inventories.'

'What's FIFO?'

'First-in-first-out,' replies the accountant, his voice taking on a superior tone. 'Now suppose that the new subsidiary, Airline Limited, accounts for inventories using a weighted average cost formula.'

'What happens then?' you ask, covering your mouth to stifle a yawn.

'The inventories of Airline must be adjusted to a FIFO basis, for inclusion in the consolidated financial statements of the Holdall Group.'

■ Intra-group items

'I suppose you know that intra-group balances, transactions, income and expenses must be eliminated in full.'

The accountant interprets your silence as a *no* and begins to explain what he means.

'Well, let's have another look at the Holdall group,' he says, pointing at the diagram he had drawn previously. 'Suppose that Tracks Limited owes €1M to a customer as a legal settlement. Would that concern you?'

'You bet it would – a million euro!' You gasp and emit a long whistle.

'Well you'd be right to be concerned, and of course the €1M would appear in the group financial statements as a liability.'

'It's just as well that you're making this stuff up!'

'Now, what if Tracks owed €1M to *Double Decker*?'

'Well, that wouldn't make much difference, would it? I mean Holdall owns both of them anyway. So if one of them owes money to the other, why should I care?'

'That's right. From a group perspective money owed by Tracks to Double Decker is irrelevant.'

'It's an intra-group balance. Is that what you mean?'

'Exactly, and it's cancelled when preparing the group financial statements. €1M will be deducted from the trade payables of Tracks and from the trade receivables of Double Decker.'

'I suppose that's in IAS 27 as well?'

Nodding his head, the accountant adjusts his cufflinks so that both point upwards at an identical angle.

'Now, I've got a question for you,' and leaning forward in your chair, your face widens into a smile.

The accountant stares dismissively, thinking it unlikely you could know a question that he would be unable to answer.

'When accountants die, why are they buried 20 feet under the ground?'

He looks at you quizzically, his mouth open, but nothing comes out. You pause for a moment, and then, rising from your chair, you turn to face him as you leave the room.

'Because deep down you're nice guys!'

Chapter 23

Consolidated statement of financial position

Imagine that you are an athlete competing in the decathlon event. You obtain a points score for each individual event that you complete (e.g. long jump, 800 metres, hammer) and these individual scores are added together to make up your overall total. This overall total is what will determine your ranking against other athletes.

The preparation of a consolidated statement of financial position is similar in many respects. Consolidation involves adding together each item (e.g. land and buildings, inventory, trade receivables) of the parent and all subsidiaries in a group and consolidating them into a group statement of financial position. This is illustrated in Figure 23.1, which shows the SOFP of a parent and its three subsidiary companies being incorporated into a single SOFP for the group.

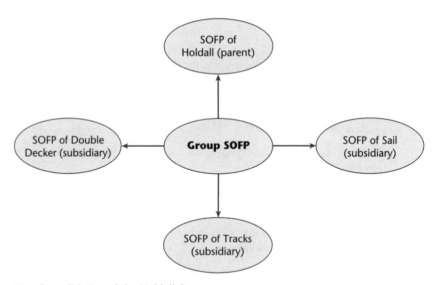

Figure 23.1 Consolidation of the Holdall Group

Consolidated statement of financial position at date of acquisition

Example 1 On 1 January 2011, P Ltd acquired 100% of the equity shares of S Ltd for €400,000 in cash. The statement of financial position of each company immediately after the acquisition is shown below:

	P Ltd €	S Ltd €
Assets		
Non-current assets		
Land and buildings	600,000	200,000
Investment in S Ltd	400,000	–
	1,000,000	200,000
Current assets		
Inventory	400,000	260,000
Trade receivables	250,000	150,000
	1,650,000	610,000
Current liabilities		
Trade payables	(120,000)	(100,000)
Bank overdraft	(80,000)	(110,000)
Net assets	1,450,000	400,000
Equity		
Ordinary share capital	200,000	100,000
Retained earnings	1,250,000	300,000
	1,450,000	400,000

Prepare a consolidated statement of financial position of the P Limited Group at 1 January 2011.

Solution

	P Ltd €	S Ltd €	Adj. €	Group €
Assets				
Non-current assets				
Land and buildings	600,000	200,000		800,000
Investment in S Ltd	*400,000*	–	–400,000	–
	1,000,000	200,000		800,000
Current assets				
Inventory	400,000	260,000		660,000
Trade receivables	250,000	150,000		400,000
	1,650,000	610,000		1,860,000
Current liabilities				
Trade payables	(120,000)	(100,000)		(220,000)
Bank overdraft	(80,000)	(110,000)		(190,000)
Net assets	1,450,000	400,000		1,450,000
Equity				
Ordinary share capital	200,000	*100,000*	–100,000	200,000
Retained earnings	1,250,000	*300,000*	–300,000	1,250,000
	1,450,000	400,000		1,450,000

The consolidated SOFP will be prepared using only the group amounts (i.e. the final column above). The following amounts, shown in **bold italics** above, are cancelled on consolidation:

- *Investment in S Ltd €400,000.* This is the amount paid by P Ltd for S Ltd. While it is an asset of P Ltd, it is not an asset of the group. In the consolidated SOFP, it is replaced by the net assets of S Ltd of €400,000.
- *Ordinary share capital of S Ltd €100,000.* These shares are held by P Ltd rather than by a party external to the group. Therefore, from a group perspective this amount is irrelevant and it is cancelled on consolidation.

■ *Retained earnings of S Ltd €300,000*. The retained earnings of a subsidiary at the date of acquisition may be distributed to P Ltd as a dividend. However, P Ltd is not permitted to distribute these outside of the group. Therefore, these retained earnings are irrelevant from a group perspective, and they are cancelled on consolidation.

It is important to note that the above amounts are cancelled only when preparing a consolidated SOFP of the group. These amounts are *not* adjusted in the *individual* financial statements of either P Ltd or S Ltd. Hence, they are known as *consolidation adjustments*.

■ Goodwill arising on acquisition

In Example 1 above, the amount paid by P Ltd (€400,000) equals the net assets of S Ltd at the date of acquisition. It is more common, however, that an acquirer, in order to gain control, will pay more than the amount of a target company's net assets. This gives rise to **goodwill** arising in the *group* SOFP, and in accordance with IFRS 3 *Business Combinations* goodwill is measured as the difference between:

(i) the aggregate of:
  ■ the acquisition-date fair value of consideration paid;
  ■ the amount of any **non-controlling interest** in the acquiree;
  ■ in a business combination achieved in stages, the acquisition-date fair value of the acquirer's previously held *equity interest* in the acquiree; and
(ii) the net of the acquisition-date amounts of the identifiable assets acquired and the liabilities assumed, measured in accordance with IFRS 3.

Example 2 On 1 January 2011, P Ltd acquired 100% of the equity shares of S Ltd for €700,000 cash. The statement of financial position of each company immediately after the acquisition is shown below. The fair value of the land and buildings of S Ltd at 1 January 2011 was €300,000.

	P Ltd €	S Ltd €
Assets		
Non-current assets		
Land and buildings	600,000	200,000
Investment in S Ltd	700,000	–
	1,300,000	200,000
Current assets		
Inventory	400,000	260,000
Trade receivables	250,000	150,000
	1,950,000	610,000
Current liabilities		
Trade payables	(120,000)	(100,000)
Bank overdraft	(380,000)	(110,000)
Net assets	1,450,000	400,000
Equity		
Ordinary share capital	200,000	100,000
Retained earnings	1,250,000	300,000
	1,450,000	400,000

Prepare a consolidated statement of financial position of the P Limited Group at 1 January 2011.

Note: The SOFP of S Ltd is unchanged from Example 1 above. The SOFP of P Ltd shows two changes:

■ Investment in S Ltd has increased by €300,000 to €700,000.
■ Bank overdraft has increased by €300,000 to €380,000.

Solution		P Ltd	S Ltd	Adj.	Group
		€	€	€	€
Assets					
Non-current assets					
	Land and buildings	600,000	300,000		900,000
	Investment in S Ltd	*700,000*	–	–700,000	–
	Goodwill	–	–		200,000
		1,300,000	300,000		1,100,000
Current assets					
	Inventory	400,000	260,000		660,000
	Trade receivables	250,000	150,000		400,000
		1,950,000	710,000		2,160,000
Current liabilities					
	Trade payables	(120,000)	(100,000)		(220,000)
	Bank overdraft	(380,000)	(110,000)		(490,000)
	Net assets	1,450,000	500,000		1,450,000
Equity					
	Ordinary share capital	200,000	*100,000*	–100,000	200,000
	Retained earnings	1,250,000	*300,000*	–300,000	1,250,000
	Revaluation surplus	–	*100,000*	–100,000	–
		1,450,000	500,000		1,450,000

The SOFP of S Ltd shows land and buildings revised to its fair value at acquisition date of €300,000.

Amounts shown in **bold italics** above are cancelled on consolidation. Assets cancelled amount to €700,000 and equity cancelled amounts to €500,000. The difference gives rise to goodwill of €200,000 which is included as an intangible asset in the SOFP of the group.

Goodwill arising on consolidation is computed as follows:

	€
Fair value of consideration paid	700,000
Fair value of identifiable net assets acquired	(500,000)
Goodwill arising on acquisition	200,000

Goodwill will be carried as a non-current intangible asset in the consolidated SOFP of the P Ltd Group. It must be tested annually for impairment.

■ Bargain purchase

In the event that goodwill is *negative*, this represents a bargain purchase. A bargain purchase might occur, for example, if the owners of an acquiree are forced into a liquidation sale of their business. Any resulting gain is recognised, by the acquirer, in profit or loss.

Example 3 On 1 January 2010, Holdall Ltd purchased 100% of the equity shares of Tracks Ltd for a cash payment of €2M. The fair value of the assets of Tracks at that time was €3M, and Tracks also had liabilities of €400,000.

Outline the effect of this business combination on the consolidated SOFP of the Holdall Group.

Solution	€'000
Consideration paid	2,000
Less fair value of identifiable net assets acquired	2,600
Goodwill	(600)

The acquisition of Tracks Ltd represents a bargain purchase, and the gain of €600,000 is recognised in profit or loss of the Holdall Group in the year ended 31 December 2010. Before recognising a gain on a bargain purchase, IFRS 3 requires that the acquirer ensure it has correctly identified all of the assets acquired and all of the liabilities assumed.

Consolidated statement of financial position in post-acquisition periods

Examples 1 and 2 above have dealt with the preparation of a consolidated SOFP at the date of acquisition. In subsequent periods, the principal issue to be addressed relates to post-acquisition profits and losses of **subsidiaries**.

Profits of a subsidiary earned in the post-acquisition period can be distributed to the **parent** as a **dividend**, and these profits can be further distributed by the parent outside of the group (i.e. to the parent's shareholders). Therefore, retained earnings of a subsidiary that arise after acquisition should be added to group-retained earnings when preparing the consolidated SOFP. Likewise, accumulated losses incurred by a subsidiary in post-acquisition periods should be deducted from the retained earnings of the group.

Example 4 Assume the identical facts as in Example 2 above, except that S Ltd has retained profits of €250,000 for the year ending 31 December 2011. There is a corresponding increase in net assets of S Ltd of €250,000, and it is assumed that this relates wholly to an increase in trade receivables.

As the retained earnings of €250,000 are post-acquisition, they should be added to group-retained earnings in the consolidated SOFP.

The consolidated SOFP of the P Ltd Group is prepared as follows at 31 December 2011:

	P Ltd €	S Ltd €	Adj. €	Group €
Assets				
Non-current assets				
Land and buildings	600,000	300,000		900,000
Investment in S Ltd	700,000	–	–700,000	–
Goodwill	–	–		200,000
	1,300,000	300,000		1,100,000
Current assets				
Inventory	400,000	260,000		660,000
Trade receivables	250,000	400,000		650,000
	1,950,000	960,000		2,410,000
Current liabilities				
Trade payables	(120,000)	(100,000)		(220,000)
Bank overdraft	(380,000)	(110,000)		(490,000)
Net assets	1,450,000	750,000		1,700,000

	P Ltd	S Ltd	Adj.	Group
	€	€	€	€
Equity				
Ordinary share capital	200,000	100,000	–100,000	200,000
Retained earnings	1,250,000	550,000*	–300,000	1,500,000
Revaluation surplus	–	100,000	–100,000	–
	1,450,000	750,000		1,700,000

* This includes €300,000 of pre-acquisition retained earnings of S Ltd and €250,000 of its post-acquisition retained earnings. Pre-acquisition amounts are cancelled on consolidation.

Non-controlling interest

Sometimes a parent company only acquires part of a subsidiary. For example, X Ltd might acquire 75% of the equity shares of Y Ltd. As X controls Y, this gives rise to a parent–subsidiary relationship. The 25% shareholding in Y that is not owned by X is referred to as the **non-controlling interest (NCI)**.

The consolidated SOFP of the X Ltd Group will include 100% of the assets and liabilities of subsidiary Y. It will be necessary, however, to show that 25% of those assets belong to the NCI, and that the NCI also bears its 25% share of the subsidiary's liabilities.

Example 5 On 1 January 2011, P Ltd acquired 75% of the equity shares of S Ltd for €700,000 cash. The statement of financial position of each company immediately after the acquisition is shown below. The fair value of the land and buildings of S Ltd at 1 January 2011 was €300,000.

These facts are identical to those in Example 2 above, except that P Ltd has acquired only 75% of S Ltd shares. Non-controlling interests are measured at their proportionate share of the identifiable net assets of S Ltd.

	P Ltd	S Ltd
	€	€
Assets		
Non-current assets		
Land and buildings	600,000	200,000
Investment in S Ltd	700,000	–
	1,300,000	200,000
Current assets		
Inventory	400,000	260,000
Trade receivables	250,000	150,000
	1,950,000	610,000
Current liabilities		
Trade payables	(120,000)	(100,000)
Bank overdraft	(380,000)	(110,000)
Net assets	1,450,000	400,000
Equity		
Ordinary share capital	200,000	100,000
Retained earnings	1,250,000	300,000
	1,450,000	400,000

Prepare a consolidated statement of financial position of the P Limited Group at 1 January 2011.

Solution		P Ltd	S Ltd	Adj.	Group
		€	€	€	€
Assets					
Non-current assets					
Land and buildings		600,000	300,000		900,000
Investment in S Ltd		*700,000*	–	–700,000	–
Goodwill		–	–		325,000
		1,300,000	300,000		1,225,000
Current assets					
Inventory		400,000	260,000		660,000
Trade receivables		250,000	150,000		400,000
		1,950,000	710,000		2,285,000
Current liabilities					
Trade payables		(120,000)	(100,000)		(220,000)
Bank overdraft		(380,000)	(110,000)		(490,000)
Net assets		1,450,000	500,000		1,575,000
Equity					
Ordinary share capital		200,000	*100,000*	–100,000	200,000
Retained earnings		1,250,000	*300,000*	–300,000	1,250,000
Revaluation surplus		–	*100,000*	–100,000	–
		1,450,000	500,000		1,450,000
Non-controlling interests		–	–		125,000
		1,450,000	500,000		1,575,000

Amounts shown in **bold italics** above are cancelled on consolidation.

The only changes in the solution, compared with Example 2, relate to goodwill and non-controlling interest.

- **Non-controlling interest** is computed as follows:

	€
Fair value of identifiable net assets at date of acquisition × 25% =	125,000

- **Goodwill** arising on consolidation is computed as follows:

	€
Fair value of consideration paid	700,000
Non-controlling interest	125,000
	825,000
Less fair value of identifiable net assets acquired	(500,000)
Goodwill arising on acquisition	325,000

■ Measurement of non-controlling interests

In Example 4 above, NCI is computed as a percentage of the identifiable net assets of S Ltd at the date of acquisition. As a result, the consolidated SOFP only includes P Ltd's share of goodwill arising on acquisition.

IFRS 3 *Business Combinations* also permits NCI at the date of acquisition to be calculated as a percentage of the fair value of the entity that is acquired. For example, let us assume that the fair value of S Ltd as a whole at the acquisition date is €600,000. NCI will therefore equal €150,000 (i.e. €600,000 × 25%).

- **Goodwill** is now computed as follows:

	€
Fair value of consideration paid	700,000
Non-controlling interest (25% of fair value of S at acquisition: €600,000 × 25%)	150,000
	850,000
Less fair value of identifiable net assets at acquisition	(500,000)
Goodwill arising on acquisition	350,000

The goodwill of €350,000 arising on acquisition now equals 100% of the goodwill arising on the acquisition of S Ltd, and not just the parent company's share. This method of measuring NCI at the date of acquisition takes the entity view, rather than that of the parent company. It is consistent with the *physical* capital maintenance concept outlined in the IASB framework.

The above alternatives only affect the measurement of non-controlling interest at the date of acquisition. Subsequent changes in non-controlling interest are treated in the same way under both methods.

Preference shares

In addition to equity shares, a subsidiary may also issue **preference shares**. Preference shares held by a parent are cancelled on consolidation. Preference shares of a subsidiary that do not belong to a parent are included in non-controlling interest in the consolidated SOFP.

Example 6 On 1 January 2011, P Ltd acquired 75% of the equity shares and 40% of the preference shares S Ltd for €700,000 cash. The statement of financial position of each company immediately after the acquisition is shown below. The fair value of the land and buildings of S Ltd at 1 January 2011 was €300,000.

Non-controlling interests are measured at their proportionate share of the identifiable net assets of S Ltd.

	P Ltd	S Ltd
	€	€
Assets		
Non-current assets		
Land and buildings	600,000	200,000
Investment in S Ltd	700,000	–
	1,300,000	200,000
Current assets		
Inventory	400,000	260,000
Trade receivables	250,000	200,000
	1,950,000	660,000
Current liabilities		
Trade payables	(120,000)	(100,000)
Bank overdraft	(380,000)	(110,000)
Net assets	1,450,000	450,000
Equity		
Ordinary share capital	200,000	100,000
Preference share capital	–	50,000
Retained earnings	1,250,000	300,000
	1,450,000	450,000

Prepare a consolidated statement of financial position of the P Limited Group at 1 January 2011.

Solution	P Ltd	S Ltd	Adj.	Group
	€	€	€	€
Assets				
Non-current assets				
Land and buildings	600,000	300,000		900,000
Investment in S Ltd	*700,000*	–	–700,000	–
Goodwill	–	–		305,000
	1,300,000	300,000		1,205,000
Current assets				
Inventory	400,000	260,000		660,000
Trade receivables	250,000	200,000		450,000
	1,950,000	760,000		2,315,000
Current liabilities				
Trade payables	(120,000)	(100,000)		(220,000)
Bank overdraft	(380,000)	(110,000)		(490,000)
Net assets	1,450,000	550,000		1,605,000
Equity				
Ordinary share capital	200,000	*100,000*	–100,000	200,000
Preference share capital	–	*50,000*	–50,000	–
Retained earnings	1,250,000	*300,000*	–300,000	1,250,000
Revaluation surplus	–	*100,000*	–100,000	–
	1,450,000	550,000		1,450,000
Non-controlling interests	–	–		155,000
	1,450,000	550,000		1,605,000

Amounts shown in **bold italics** above are cancelled on consolidation.

- **Non-controlling interest** is computed as follows:

	€
(Ordinary share capital + retained earnings + FV adjustment) × 25%	
= (€100,000 + €300,000 + €100,000) × 25%	125,000
Preference share capital × 60% (i.e. €50,000 × 60%)	30,000
	155,000

- **Goodwill** arising on consolidation is computed as follows:

	€
Fair value of consideration paid	700,000
Non-controlling interest	155,000
	855,000
Less fair value of identifiable net assets acquired	(550,000)
Goodwill arising on acquisition	305,000

Elimination of unrealised profits

It is not unusual for companies within a group to sell goods to one another. If, at the end of the accounting period, some of these goods are held as assets within the group, it will be necessary to eliminate any profit that was recognised on their transfer. Otherwise, consolidated profit could be artificially inflated by the continuous transfer of goods within the group.

Example 7 Holdall Limited owns 80% of Sail Limited. During the year ending 31 December 2011, Sail Ltd sold goods to Holdall for €1.8M. This included a mark-up of 25% on cost. At 31 December 2011, a third of these goods were included in the inventory of Holdall Ltd.

Outline how these transactions should be accounted for in the consolidated statement of financial position of Holdall Ltd at 31 December 2011.

Solution IAS 27 *Consolidated and Separate Financial Statements* requires that unrealised profit on intra-group transactions must be eliminated in full. Thus, although Holdall Ltd only has an 80% interest in Sail Ltd, all unrealised profit must be eliminated. As the goods were sold by Sail to Holdall, it will be necessary for the NCI to bear its share of the adjustment. This would not arise if the goods were sold by the parent company to its subsidiary, as the profit would then be earned by the parent.

Unrealised intra-group profit is computed as follows at 31 December 2011:

$$€1.8M \times 1/3 \times 20\%* = €120,000$$

* 25% on cost = 20% on selling price.

The following consolidation adjustments are made in the group financial statements of Holdall Ltd:

Inventory is reduced by €120,000
Consolidated retained earnings is reduced by €96,000 (i.e. €120,000 × 80%)
Non-controlling interest is reduced by €24,000 (i.e. €120,000 × 20%)

The following journal adjustment is made in the consolidated financial statements:

	Dr €	Cr €
Retained earnings	96,000	
Non-controlling interest	24,000	
Inventory		120,000

Intra-group balances

IAS 27 also requires that intra-group balances should be cancelled when preparing a consolidated SOFP. Intra-group balances may arise as a result of the sale of goods or services on credit, or because one group company lends to another.

If items (e.g. cash or goods) are in transit between companies at the end of the reporting period, the balances in the individual companies' books will not be equal. In this case, the cash or goods that are in transit should be shown as an asset in the consolidated SOFP.

Example 8 Double Decker Ltd and Tracks Ltd are both wholly owned subsidiaries of Holdall Ltd. Double Decker supplies goods on credit to Tracks and the following balances were shown in the companies' financial statements at 31 December 2010:

	Double Decker	Tracks
	€	€
Inter-company trade receivables (due from Tracks)	25,000	
Inter-company trade payables (due to Double Decker)		20,000

The difference between the two balances relates to goods of €5,000 invoiced at cost by Double Decker on 30 December 2010. These goods were received by Tracks on 2 January 2011.

Outline how the above inter-company balances should be accounted for in the consolidated statement of financial position at 31 December 2010.

Solution   The following consolidation adjustments should be made to the SOFP of the Holdall Group:

- inter-company balances of both companies should be cancelled;
- goods in transit of €5,000 should be included as inventory.

Therefore, the following journal adjustment will be required in the group financial statements:

	Dr	Cr
	€	€
Intra-group trade payables	20,000	
Inventory	5,000	
Intra-group trade receivables		25,000

Summary

- The SOFP of a parent and its subsidiaries are amalgamated to form a group SOFP.
- Goodwill arises at the acquisition date when the fair value of the consideration paid is different to the fair value of the identifiable net assets acquired.
- The shareholding in a subsidiary that is not owned by its parent is known as non-controlling interest. IFRS 3 permits two alternative approaches for measuring non-controlling interest at the acquisition date.
- Unrealised intra-group profit must be eliminated in full in the consolidated SOFP. If sales have been made by a subsidiary to its parent, then non-controlling interests, if any, must bear their share of this adjustment.
- Intra-group balances must be cancelled in the consolidated SOFP of a group.

QUESTIONS

23.1 TOY plc

TOY plc, a 60% owned subsidiary of BOY plc ('BOY'), sold €25,000,000 of goods to BOY during the year ended 31 December 2010 at a mark-up on cost of 20%. At 31 December 2010, BOY still held €12,000,000 of these goods in inventory. The consolidated balance sheet intra-group profit elimination entries, in accordance with IAS 27 *Consolidated and Separate Financial Statements*, would be:

			€	€
(a)	Dr	Consolidated retained earnings	2,000,000	
	Cr	Inventory		2,000,000
(b)	Dr	Consolidated retained earnings	1,200,000	
	Dr	Non-controlling interests	800,000	
	Cr	Inventory		2,000,000
(c)	Dr	Consolidated retained earnings	2,400,000	
	Cr	Inventory		2,400,000
(d)	Dr	Consolidated retained earnings	1,440,000	
	Dr	Non-controlling interests	960,000	
	Cr	Inventory		2,400,000

(Chartered Accountants Ireland)

23.2 FRY plc

FRY plc owns 80% of the ordinary share capital of both SAUSAGE Ltd and BACON Ltd. The statements of financial position of the three companies at 31 December 2010 indicated:

	Fry plc €M	Sausage Ltd €M	Bacon Ltd €M
€1 ordinary shares	10,000	5,000	5,000
Retained earnings	12,000	20,000	(10,000)
	22,000	25,000	(5,000)

FRY plc measures non-controlling interests at their proportionate share of the net identifiable assets of subsidiaries. The non-controlling interest in the consolidated statement of financial position of FRY plc at 31 December 2010 is:

(a) €4,000M
(b) €5,000M
(c) €7,000M
(d) €8,400M

(Chartered Accountants Ireland)

23.3 PARENT Limited

The statements of financial position of PARENT Ltd and its two subsidiaries STAR Ltd and SPRING Ltd as at the 31 December 2010 are as follows:

	Parent Ltd €000		Star Ltd €000		Spring Ltd €000
Non-current assets					
Property and equipment	4,761		521		411
Investment in Star Ltd	600				
Investment in Spring Ltd	575				
	5,936				
Current Assets					
Inventories	1,532		222		187
Trade receivables	1,947		258		202
Cash at bank	239	3,718	30	510	13	402
		9,654		1,031		813
Equity					
Ordinary share capital		5,000		500		300
Revaluation reserve		2,500		–		100
Retained earnings		547		320		250
		8,047		820		650
Liabilities					
Trade payables		1,607		211		163
		9,654		1,031		813

The following information is also available:

- Parent Ltd acquired 60% of Star Ltd on 1 January 2009 when Star Ltd had retained earnings of €280,000. The fair value of the property and equipment of Star Ltd on that date was €30,000 more than the book value. This valuation has not been reflected in the books of Star Ltd. *Ignore the effect of the revaluation on depreciation.*
- Parent Ltd acquired 90% of the shares of Spring Ltd on 1 January 2010, when Spring Ltd had a revaluation reserve of €60,000 and retained earnings of €230,000. The fair value of Spring Ltd's assets and liabilities on that date was equal to their book value.
- Goodwill arising on acquisition in relation to Star Ltd has suffered an impairment loss of 50% since the date of acquisition. The impairment loss for Spring Ltd is 25% since acquisition.
- The following intra-group balances exist on 31 December 2010:
  - Star Ltd owes Parent Ltd €15,000;
  - Spring Ltd owes Parent Ltd €25,000;
  - Spring Ltd owes Star Ltd €8,000.
- Goods purchased for €8,000 from Parent Ltd are included in Star Ltd's inventory at 31 December 2010. Parent Ltd had invoiced these goods to Star Ltd at cost plus 60%.

Required:

(a) Prepare a consolidated statement of financial position for the group at 31 December 2010.

(b) Distinguish between the concept of 'control' and 'ownership' as used in relation to the statement of financial position.

23.4 The PITTA Group

The summarised statements of financial position of PITTA plc and its subsidiary company, SCONE Ltd, at 31 December 2010 were as follows:

	PITTA plc		SCONE Ltd	
	€M	€M	€M	€M
Non-current assets				
Tangible assets at NBV		1,380		640
Investment in SCONE at cost		980		–
Current assets				
Inventory	900		600	
Debtors	750		280	
Bank	390		140	
	2,040		1,020	
Current liabilities				
Trade payables	700		400	
Taxation	300		100	
	1,000		500	
Working capital		1,040		520
Provision for deferred tax		(400)		(300)
Net assets		3,000		860
Financed by				
Ordinary share capital (€1 each)		800		150
Share premium		900		–
Retained earnings		1,300		710
		3,000		860

The following information is relevant:

(i) On 15 November 2010, PITTA plc made an offer for the entire share capital of SCONE Ltd. On the 31 December 2010 the offer was declared unconditional as to acceptances, and on the same date all of the remaining shareholders of SCONE Ltd accepted the offer of PITTA plc.

(ii) The consideration for this acquisition was 320 million shares in PITTA plc. The market value of PITTA shares on 31 December 2010 was €3 (€2.80 on 15 November 2010). Additionally, a further €300 million cash will be paid on 31 December 2012 if certain profit targets are achieved by SCONE Ltd. The board of directors of PITTA is confident that these targets will be achieved. No amount has been provided by PITTA in respect of this deferred consideration.

(iii) The following acquisition expenses were incurred by PITTA plc:

	€M
Professional fees	15
Maintenance of Acquisition Dept.	5

The above costs have been included as part of the cost of investment in SCONE Ltd.

(iv) Since the year end it has come to light that SCONE Ltd failed to provide for losses of €20M, which should have been provided in accordance with IAS 37 *Provisions, Contingent Liabilities and Contingent Assets*.

(v) At 31 December 2010, SCONE Ltd expected to be successful as the plaintiff in a court action. On investigation, the directors of PITTA plc estimate that an amount of €10M is likely to be received in March 2011.

(vi) Land and buildings of SCONE Ltd included in the accounts at €200M at 31 December 2010 are valued at €300M on an existing use basis.

(vii) The directors of PITTA plc are of the opinion that, in the context of the overall group position, a provision for deferred tax of €50M at 31 December 2010, would be adequate in respect of SCONE Ltd.

(viii) The directors of PITTA plc intend to carry out a significant reorganisation of the operations of SCONE Ltd. The total costs of this programme, including rationalisation costs, are estimated at €100M.

(ix) Should PITTA plc wish to raise borrowed funds, a fixed rate of 10% (relevant discount factor 0.827) is currently being quoted in respect of a two-year loan.

Required:

You are required to show all the necessary journal entries for PITTA plc and SCONE Ltd, and prepare the consolidated statement of financial position of the PITTA Group at 31 December 2010.

23.5 MURAKWAI plc

You have recently qualified as a chartered accountant and are currently on secondment with MURAKWAI plc ('MURAKWAI') to assist with the preparation of the company's financial statements for the year ended 31 December 2010. The financial accountant of MURAKWAI has presented you with the following information:

**Draft consolidated statement of comprehensive income for
the year ended 31 December 2010**

	€'000
Revenue	10,500
Cost of sales	(6,500)
Gross profit	4,000
Operating expenses	(2,000)
Operating profit	2,000
Finance costs	(500)
Share of profit of associate	650
Profit before tax	2,150
Income tax expense	(450)
Profit for period	1,700

Draft statement of financial position at 31 December 2010

	€'000 2010	€'000 2009
Assets		
Non-current assets		
Property, plant and equipment	7,700	3,800
Goodwill	500	–
Investment in associate	1,850	1,800
Current assets		
Inventory	1,440	980
Trade receivables	1,560	1,230
Bank and cash	55	90
	13,105	7,900

	€'000	€'000
	2010	2009
Equity and liabilities		
Capital and reserves		
€1 ordinary shares	2,000	1,000
Share premium	2,000	–
Retained earnings	5,950	4,700
Non-current liabilities		
Finance lease	480	300
Current liabilities		
Trade payables	1,280	900
Taxation	410	360
Proposed dividends	450	400
Property, plant and equipment payable	170	30
Finance lease	165	130
Accrued finance costs	200	80
	13,105	7,900

Additional information:

(1) On 30 June 2010 MURAKWAI purchased all of the ordinary share capital of SCOTT Ltd ('SCOTT'). The acquisition was financed as follows:

Cash paid €2M
Issue of 1 million €1 ordinary shares

The market value of MURAKWAI's €1 ordinary shares on 30 June 2010 was €3 per ordinary share. The fair value of SCOTT's net assets was the same as their book value and the acquisition of SCOTT has been included in the draft consolidated financial statements for the year ended 31 December 2010 shown above. The directors of MURAKWAI believe that the goodwill arising on the acquisition of SCOTT had been impaired at 31 December 2010 and have reflected this in operating expenses in the draft consolidated income statement for the year ended 31 December 2010 shown above. The statement of financial position of SCOTT at 30 June 2010 showed the following:

	€'000
Assets	
Non-current assets	
Property, plant and equipment	3,000
Current assets	
Inventory	800
Trade receivables	1,500
Bank and cash	100
	5,400
Equity and liabilities	
Capital and reserves	
€1 ordinary shares	1,000
Retained earnings	3,200
Current liabilities	
Trade payables	1,200
	5,400

(2) In January 2010, the directors of MURAKWAI decided to record all of the company's property, plant and equipment at valuation. Following a professional valuation in January 2010, property, plant and equipment were valued at €9M. This has not yet been reflected in the draft consolidated financial statements shown above. MURAKWAI charges depreciation on all property, plant and equipment on a straight-line basis over five years to operating expenses. It is company policy to charge a full year's depreciation in the year of acquisition and none in the year of disposal.

(3) On 1 December 2010, when the exchange rate was €1 equal to $2, MURAKWAI sold goods to an American company for the first time. The sale amounted to $168,000. The customer paid for the goods on 23 January 2011 when the exchange rate was €1 equal to $1.90. At 31 December 2010, €1 was equal to $2.10. Although inventory and cost of sales have been adjusted to reflect this transaction, the sale has not yet been reflected in the draft consolidated financial statements for the year ended 31 December 2010 shown above.

(4) In December 2010, the directors of MURAKWAI proposed dividends of €450,000, and these are included in current liabilities at 31 December 2010. Past experience suggests that these dividends will be approved by the shareholders at the annual general meeting in March 2011.

(5) In March 2011 one of MURAKWAI's customers commenced legal action against the company, alleging that a contract completed in November 2010 had not been carried out in accordance with the terms and conditions of the contract. The directors of MURAKWAI refute the allegations and their legal advisers believe that the company has a 60% chance of successfully defending the action. If the customer is successful, damages and legal fees are expected to be approximately €1M. If MURAKWAI successfully defends the claim, non-recoverable legal fees will amount to €150,000. No adjustment has been made for this in the draft consolidated financial statements for the year ended 31 December 2010 shown above. It is expected that the case will be resolved before the end of 2011.

(6) There were no disposals of property, plant and equipment during the year ended 31 December 2010. Additions to property, plant and equipment during the year ended 31 December 2010, excluding those acquired from SCOTT, include €400,000 which were acquired under finance lease. The depreciation charge of €1.2M, which is included in the draft statement of comprehensive income for the year ended 31 December 2010, is based upon the historic cost of property, plant and equipment.

(7) Dividends of €600,000 were received from the associate during the year ended 31 December 2010.

Required:

Prepare the consolidated statement of comprehensive income of MURAKWAI for the year ended 31 December 2010 and the consolidated statement of financial position at that date.

(Chartered Accountants Ireland)

Chapter 24

Consolidated statement of comprehensive income

This statement combines the results of a parent and all of its subsidiaries into a single statement of comprehensive income. This is done by adding together each company's revenue, cost of sales, etc. to give the group total for each item. The following adjustments are required.

Intra-group items

Sales that take place within a group do not constitute sales to parties external to the group. They must therefore be eliminated when preparing the consolidated statement of comprehensive income.

Example 1 Tracks Limited is a wholly owned subsidiary of Holdall Limited. During the year ended 31 December 2010, Tracks Limited sold goods to Holdall Limited for €1.2M.

Outline how these sales should be accounted for in the consolidated statement of comprehensive income of the Holdall Group for the year ended 31 December 2010.

Solution Sales of Tracks have increased by €1.2M. Holdall's cost of sales has also increased by €1.2M. As these transactions have not taken place with a party *outside* of the Holdall Group, they must be eliminated when preparing the consolidated statement of comprehensive income. Therefore, group revenue and group cost of sales should both be reduced by €1.2M.

The following consolidation adjustment is required:

	Dr €m	Cr €m
Revenue	1.2	
Cost of sales		1.2

It is also necessary to eliminate any unrealised profit on intra-group sales. Some of the goods purchased by Holdall from Tracks may be still retained in Holdall's inventory at the end of its reporting period. Any profit earned by Tracks on these goods has not been earned *outside* of the group (i.e. by a sale to an external party). It must therefore be eliminated when preparing the consolidated statement of comprehensive income of the Holdall Group.

Example 1 revisited Let us assume that Tracks earned a profit of €300,000 on the goods sold to Holdall during 2010, and that one-third of these goods are still in Holdall's inventory at 31 December 2010.

Outline how this profit should be accounted for in the consolidated statement of comprehensive income of the Holdall Group for the year ended 31 December 2010.

Solution   At 31 December 2010, Holdall's inventory includes one-third of the goods purchased from Tracks. Profit earned by Tracks on the sale of those goods has not been realised by a sale to an external party. It must therefore be eliminated when preparing the consolidated financial statements of the Holdall Group for the year ended 31 December 2010.

Group cost of sales is increased by €100,000 to eliminate the unrealised profit from the consolidated statement of comprehensive income. Inventory at 31 December 2010 is also reduced by €100,000, so that inventory is valued at its cost to the group (i.e. the amount paid for the goods by Tracks). It is a requirement of IAS 2 that inventory should be valued at the lower of cost and net realisable value – see Chapter 11.

Thus, the following consolidation adjustment is required:

	Dr €'000	Cr €'000
Cost of sales	100	
Inventory		100

Other intra-group transactions must also be cancelled in the consolidated statement of comprehensive income. Examples of such transactions include debenture interest and management charges.

Example 2   Holdall Limited purchased €1M 10% debentures in Tracks Limited on 1 January 2010. Interest on these debentures has been charged and credited in the income statement of Tracks and Holdall respectively for the year ended 31 December 2010.

On 31 December 2010, Holdall charged Tracks with management expenses of €150,000.

Outline how the debenture interest and management expenses should be accounted for in the consolidated statement of comprehensive income of the Holdall Group.

Solution   Both the debenture interest and the management expenses are intra-group items, and neither relate to transactions with a party that is external to the group. Therefore, both items should be cancelled in the consolidated statement of comprehensive income of the Holdall Group.

The following consolidation adjustments are required:

	Dr €'000	Cr €'000
Debenture interest receivable – consolidated I/S	100	
Debenture interest expense – consolidated I/S		100
Management income – consolidated I/S	150	
Management expense – consolidated I/S		150
(Being reversal, for consolidation purposes, of entries made by Holdall and Tracks)		

Non-controlling interests

Sometimes a **parent** only owns part of the shares of a **subsidiary**. In this case, the consolidated statement of comprehensive income must separately identify the amount of group profit that is attributable to **non-controlling interests**. This is computed as a percentage of:

- group profit for the year, and separately
- group total comprehensive income for the year

Example 3 Holdall Limited owns 80% of the ordinary share capital of Sail Limited. All of Holdall Limited's other subsidiaries are wholly owned. The following is an extract from the consolidated statement of comprehensive income of the Holdall Group for the year ended 31 December 2010:

	Holdall €m	Sail €m	Group €m
Profit before tax	145	55	200
Income tax expense	(25)	(5)	(30)*
Profit for the year	120	50	170
Other comprehensive income:			
Gains on property revaluation	10	10	20*
Total comprehensive income for the year	130	60	190
Profit attributable to:			
Owners of the parent			160
Non-controlling interests (€50M × 20%)			10
			170
Total comprehensive income attributable to:			
Owners of the parent			178
Non-controlling interests (€60M × 20%)			12
			190

* Includes 100% of Sail.

Dividends

Dividends paid to external parties should be included in the statement of changes in equity of a group. Only dividends paid by a parent company to its own shareholders qualify in this regard.

■ Dividends paid by a subsidiary to its parent

Dividends paid by a subsidiary to its parent are intra-group dividends, and must be cancelled when preparing the consolidated statement of comprehensive income.

Example 4 In July 2010, Tracks Limited paid an ordinary dividend of €80,000, all of which was distributed to its parent company, Holdall Limited.

Outline how this dividend should be accounted for in the consolidated statement of comprehensive income of the Holdall Group.

Solution Holdall will have recorded the dividend as income in its statement of comprehensive income. Tracks will have accounted for the dividend as a reduction of retained earnings in its statement of changes in equity.

The following consolidation adjustment is required to reverse the above treatment:

	Dr €'000	Cr €'000
Dividend income – I/S	80	
Retained earnings – SOCIE		80

■ Dividends paid by a subsidiary to non-controlling interests

These dividends are paid to external parties who are outside the group. They are reflected in the consolidated financial statements of a group as:

- a reduction of retained earnings
- a reduction in the bank balance

This will be entered in the subsidiary's books in the normal way, and a consolidation adjustment is not required.

Subsidiary acquired during the reporting period

When a subsidiary is acquired during a **reporting period**, only its post-acquisition profit should be included in the consolidated statement of comprehensive income. A subsidiary's pre-acquisition profit is not available for distribution outside of the group, and therefore it is excluded from the consolidated statement of comprehensive income.

Example 5 On 30 June 2010, Holdall Limited acquired 100% of the equity share capital of Double Decker Limited. The profit of Double Decker was earned evenly over the year ended 31 December 2010.

On the basis that Double Decker's profit was earned evenly during the year, half of its profits for 2010 can be deemed to arise in the post-acquisition period. Thus, half of Double Decker's revenue, cost of sales, administrative expenses, etc. will be included in the consolidated statement of comprehensive income.

Preparation of consolidated statement of comprehensive income

Example 6 P Ltd acquired 75% of the ordinary share capital of S Ltd on 1 January 2009. The statements of comprehensive income of P and S for the year ended 31 December 2010 are as follows:

	P Ltd €'000	S Ltd €'000
Revenue	2,940	1,040
Cost of sales	(1,210)	(560)
Gross profit	1,730	480
Distribution costs	(200)	(100)
Administrative expenses	(350)	(60)
Finance costs	(80)	(20)
Dividend received from S Ltd	40	–
Profit before tax	1,140	300
Income tax expense	(180)	(68)
Profit for the year	960	232
Other comprehensive income:		
Gains on property revaluation	220	90
Total comprehensive income for the year	1,180	322

During the year ended 31 December 2010, S Ltd sold goods to P Ltd for €400,000 including a mark-up of 25% on cost. A quarter of these goods were included in the inventory of P Ltd at 31 December 2010.

Prepare the consolidated statement of comprehensive income of the P Ltd Group for the year ended 31 December 2010.

Solution

Consolidated statement of comprehensive income of the P Ltd Group for the year ended 31 December 2010

	P Ltd €'000	S Ltd €'000	Adjustment €'000	Group €'000
Revenue	2,940	1,040	−400 (note 1)	3,580
Cost of sales	(1,210)	(580) (note 2)	−400 (note 1)	(1,390)
Gross profit	1,730	460		2,190
Distribution costs	(200)	(100)		(300)
Administrative expenses	(350)	(60)		(410)
Finance costs	(80)	(20)		(100)
Dividend received from S	40	–	(40) (note 3)	–
Profit before tax	1,140	280		1,380
Income tax expense	(180)	(68)		(248)
Profit for the year	960	212	(40)	1,132
Other comprehensive income:				
Gains on property revaluation	220	90		310
Total comprehensive income for the year	1,180	302	(40)	1,442
Profit attributable to:				
Owners of the parent				1,079
Non-controlling interests (note 4)				53
				1,132
Total comprehensive income attributable to:				
Owners of the parent				1,366.5
Non-controlling interests (note 5)				75.5
				1,442

Notes
1. Intra-group sales are €400,000, and this has been recorded by S Ltd as sales and by P Ltd as cost of sales. However, only sales made to external parties can be recognised as **group** sales. Therefore, in preparing the group statement of comprehensive income,
   - sales must be reduced by €400,000;
   - cost of sales must be reduced by €400,000.
2. Intra-group profit of €20,000 must be eliminated (i.e. €400,000 × 1/4 × 20%). This has been earned by S Ltd on goods that have yet to be sold outside of the group. As this profit has not been earned by the group, it must be cancelled. This is done by adding €20,000 to the cost of sales of S Ltd.
3. The dividend received by P Ltd from S Ltd is an intra-group dividend. As it has not been paid to a party external to the group, it must be cancelled when preparing the group statement of comprehensive income.
4. Non-controlling interest in profit for the year of S Ltd is computed as follows:

   (Profit of S Ltd for the year × 25%) = (€212,000 × 25%) = €53,000

5. Non-controlling interest in total comprehensive income for the year is computed as follows:

   (Total comprehensive income of S Ltd for the year × 25%) = (€302,000 × 25%) = €75,500

Summary

- The consolidated statement of comprehensive income combines the results of a parent and its subsidiaries into a single statement.
- Intra group items, such as dividends paid by a subsidiary to its parent, should be eliminated when preparing the consolidated statement of comprehensive income.
- Non-controlling interest is the percentage of a subsidiary that is not owned by a parent company. NCI should be shown separately in respect of:
  - group profit for the year; and
  - group total comprehensive income for the year.
- If a subsidiary is acquired during the reporting period, only its post-acquisition profit should be included in the consolidated statement of comprehensive income.

QUESTIONS

24.1 and 24.2 HIT and MISS

HIT plc (HIT) purchased all of the ordinary share capital of MISS Ltd (MISS) on 1 July 2010. The income statements of the two companies for the year ended 31 December 2010 showed the following:

	HIT €'000	MISS €'000
Revenue	5,000	2,865
Cost of sales	(3,500)	(1,980)

The revenue of HIT includes sales to MISS during the six-month period from 1 July 2010 to 31 December 2010, amounting to €900,000. All sales are made at cost plus 33$^1/_3$%. The inventory of MISS at 31 December 2010 includes goods invoiced by HIT at €90,000.

24.1 The revenue to be disclosed in the consolidated statement of comprehensive income of the HIT Group for the year ended 31 December 2010 is:

(a) €5,532,500
(b) €5,782,500
(c) €6,082,500
(d) €7,215,000

24.2 The cost of sales to be disclosed in the consolidated statement of comprehensive income of the HIT Group for the year ended 31 December 2010 is:

(a) €3,212,500
(b) €3,612,500
(c) €4,617,500
(d) €4,670,000

24.3 PIRATE Group

The following are the financial statements of PIRATE plc and SAINT Ltd for the year ended 31 December 2010:

Statement of comprehensive income for the year ended 31 December 2010

	PIRATE plc €'000	SAINT Ltd €'000
Revenue	14,000	9,750
Cost of sales	8,400	5,850
Gross profit	5,600	3,900
Operating expenses	(1,970)	(1,100)
Interest payable	(350)	(180)
Profit before tax	3,280	2,620
Income tax expense	(1,350)	(1,050)
Profit for the year	1,930	1,570
Retained earnings brought forward	5,716	3,815
Retained earnings carried forward	7,646	5,385

Statement of financial position at 31 December 2010

	PIRATE plc €'000	SAINT Ltd €'000
Non-current assets		
Tangible assets	10,350	9,520
Investment in Saint Ltd	5,485	
	15,835	9,520
Current assets		
Inventory	1,600	1,020
Trade receivables	970	600
Cash	6,031	170
	8,601	1,790
Trade payables: amounts falling due within one year	(1,290)	(1,125)
	23,146	10,185
Ordinary shares (€1)	14,500	4,000
Share premium	1,000	800
Retained earnings	7,646	5,385
	23,146	10,185

The following information is relevant:

(i) PIRATE plc acquired 70% of the ordinary shares of SAINT Ltd on 1 January 2009 when SAINT Ltd had the following reserves:

	€'000
Share premium	800
Retained earnings	2,400

(ii) At 1 January 2009 the tangible non-current assets of SAINT Ltd exceeded their book value by €300,000. This surplus has not been reflected in the financial statements of SAINT Ltd. At that date the average remaining useful life of non-current assets was 10 years.

(iii) During the current year SAINT Ltd sold goods to PIRATE plc at invoice value €360,000, on which SAINT Ltd made a mark-up of 20%. One-half of these goods remained in the inventory of PIRATE Plc at 31 December 2010.

(iv) Goodwill was impaired by €94,000 during 2009. There was no further impairment in 2010.

(v) Non-controlling interests are valued at their proportionate share of the identifiable net assets.

Required:

Prepare the consolidated statement of comprehensive income and the consolidated statement of financial position of the PIRATE Group for the year ended 31 December 2010. Show the required journal entries and necessary adjustments.

24.4 TRUMPTON plc

On 1 July 2010, TRUMPTON plc ('TRUMPTON') purchased 75% of the ordinary share capital of CAMBERWICK Ltd. ('CAMBERWICK') when the fair value of CAMBERWICK's net assets was the same as their book value. The trial balances of TRUMPTON and CAMBERWICK as at 31 December 2010 are as follows:

	Dr €'000	Cr €'000
TRUMPTON		
Property, plant and equipment – cost	500,000	
Investment in CAMBERWICK	150,000	
Inventory at 1 January 2010	250,000	
Trade receivables	200,000	
Current account with CAMBERWICK	50,000	
Bank and cash	75,000	
Purchases	800,000	
Selling and distribution costs	125,000	
Administrative expenses	80,000	
€1 ordinary shares		200,000
Retained earnings at 1 January 2010		500,000
Revenue		1,250,000
Property, plant and equipment – accumulated depreciation at 1 January 2010		100,000
Trade payables		180,000
	2,230,000	2,230,000
CAMBERWICK		
Property, plant and equipment – cost	250,000	
Inventory at 1 January 2010	80,000	
Trade receivables	100,000	
Bank and cash	40,000	
Purchases	600,000	
Selling and distribution costs	75,000	
Administrative expenses	35,000	
€1 ordinary shares		50,000
Retained earnings at 1 January 2010		120,000
Revenue		850,000
Property, plant and equipment – accumulated depreciation at 1 January 2010		50,000
Trade payables		65,000
Current account with TRUMPTON		45,000
	1,180,000	1,180,000

Additional information:

1. The activities of TRUMPTON and CAMBERWICK occur evenly throughout the year. There were no changes to the capital structure of either company during the year ended 31 December 2010, and neither of the companies paid or proposed dividends during this period.

2. There were no additions to property, plant and equipment during the year ended 31 December 2010 by either company. Both companies provide for depreciation on a straight-line basis over 10 years, charging depreciation to administrative expenses.

3. Income tax due on profits for the year ended 31 December 2010 is as follows:

TRUMPTON   €41M.
CAMBERWICK   €27M.

4. On 28 December 2010, CAMBERWICK sent a cheque to TRUMPTON for €5M. This was not received by TRUMPTON until 3 January 2011.

5. The inventory of TRUMPTON and CAMBERWICK at 31 December 2010 was valued at €260M and €100M respectively.

Required:

Prepare the consolidated statement of comprehensive income of TRUMPTON group for the year ended 31 December 2010 and the consolidated statement of financial position at that date.

(Chartered Accountants Ireland)

Chapter 25

Business combinations

A **business combination** takes place when an acquirer obtains control of one or more businesses. This will involve a payment being made, normally in cash or in the form of the acquiring company's equity capital. In return, the acquiring business will obtain ownership of **assets** and will usually assume responsibility for the **liabilities** of the business that is acquired.

Example 1 On 1 January 2010, Hornet Limited purchased 100% of the equity shares of Spider Limited for a cash payment of €3M. The fair value of the assets of Spider at that time was €2.6M, and Spider also had liabilities of €0.5M.

Outline the effect of this business combination on the consolidated financial statements of Hornet Limited.

Solution Hornet has paid €3M to acquire the identifiable net assets of Spider, which have a fair value of €2.1M (i.e. €2.6M – €0.5M). Therefore, goodwill of €0.9M arises, and this will be recognised as an intangible asset in the consolidated SOFP of the Hornet Group. The impact of the business combination on the consolidated financial statements can be summarised as follows:

	Dr €m	Cr €m
Assets	2.6	
Liabilities		0.5
Bank		3.0
Goodwill	0.9	

The acquisition method

IFRS 3 *Business Combinations* requires that an entity should account for each business combination by applying the acquisition method. This involves:

- **Identifying the acquirer**: for each business combination, one of the combining entities must be identified as the acquirer. In Example 1 above, Hornet Limited is the acquirer.
- **Determining the acquisition date**.

The acquisition date is the date on which the acquirer obtains control of the acquiree. This is usually the date on which the acquirer pays the consideration, and acquires control over the assets and liabilities of the acquiree. In Example 1 above, the acquisition date is 1 January 2010.

Recognition and measurement of assets and liabilities acquired

IFRS 3 requires an acquirer to **recognise**, separately from **goodwill**, the identifiable assets acquired, the liabilities assumed and any **non-controlling interest** in the acquiree. The identifiable assets acquired and the liabilities assumed should normally be **measured** at their acquisition-date fair values.

Recognition conditions

To qualify for recognition an item must:

- at the acquisition date, meet the definitions of assets and liabilities in the *Framework for the Preparation and Presentation of Financial Statements*;
- be part of the business acquired.

The following are implications of applying the above recognition conditions.

Example 2 **Post-acquisition reorganisation costs**

Following its acquisition of Spider, Hornet plans to exit from one of Spider's activities, and to terminate the employment of some of Spider's workforce. This reorganisation is expected to cost €500,000.

Outline how these reorganisation costs should be accounted for as part of the business combination.

Solution Hornet may expect, at the acquisition date, to incur the above costs, but it is not *obliged* to do so. Thus, these costs are not liabilities at the acquisition date. They should instead be recognised as expenses in Hornet's post-combination financial statements.

Example 3 **Unrecorded asset**

On 1 January 2010, Hornet Limited paid €4.2M to acquire 100% of the equity share capital of Sideshow Limited. The fair value of the net identifiable assets included in Sideshow's SOFP at the acquisition date amounted to €3.1M. In addition, Sideshow had an internally generated brand which, though not included in its SOFP, had a fair value of €400,000 on 1 January 2010.

Outline the effect of this business combination on the consolidated financial statements of Hornet Limited.

Solution Although the internally generated brand is not included in the SOFP of Sideshow, it nonetheless complies with the definition of an asset, per the IASB's *Framework.** In accordance with IFRS 3, therefore, the brand should be included as an asset arising as part of the business combination, and its effect can be summarised as follows:

	Dr €m	Cr €m
Net identifiable assets	3.1	
Brand asset	0.4	
Bank		4.2
Goodwill	0.7	

* The IASB *Framework* defines an asset as a resource controlled by an entity as a result of past events, and from which future economic benefits are expected to flow to the entity.

■ Measurement principle

The identifiable assets acquired and the liabilities assumed should be **measured** at their acquisition-date fair values.

Example 4

On 1 January 2010, Hornet Limited acquired 100% of the equity shares of Splinter Limited for €3.6M in cash. The book value of total assets in the SOFP of Splinter at that date was €2.8M, and Splinter's total liabilities amounted to €1M. Buildings, which were included in Splinter's SOFP at €800,000, had a fair value of €1.5M.

Outline the effect of this business combination on the consolidated financial statements of Hornet Limited.

Solution

Hornet has paid €3.6M to acquire identifiable net assets that have a fair value of €2.5M (i.e. €2.8M – €1M + fair value adjustment of €700,000). The impact of the business combination on the consolidated financial statements of Hornet can be summarised as follows:

	Dr €m	Cr €m
Assets	3.5	
Liabilities		1.0
Bank		3.6
Goodwill	1.1	

IFRS 3 specifies certain exceptions to the recognition and measurement principles of the Standard. These exceptions are outlined in Appendix 25.1.

Measurement period

If the initial accounting for a business combination is incomplete by the end of the reporting period in which the combination occurs, the acquirer should use provisional values in its financial statements. Adjustments to provisional values should be made for up to one year, in respect of facts and circumstances that existed at the acquisition date.

No adjustments are permitted after one year, except to correct an error in accordance with IAS 8 *Accounting Policies, Changes in Accounting Estimates and Errors*.

Example 5

Hornet Limited acquired 100% of the equity shares of Slice Limited on 1 January 2010, when the value of the identifiable net assets of Slice Limited was provisionally estimated at €4.5M. In June 2010, Slice Limited's tax liability for 2009 was finalised, at an amount that was €100,000 in excess of what had been provided at the acquisition date.

In February 2011, an unrecorded liability of €50,000 was discovered, relating to the purchase of goods in 2009.

Outline how the above events should be accounted for in the consolidated financial statements of the Hornet Group.

Solution

The finalisation of Slice Limited's tax liability in June 2010 occurs within 12 months of the acquisition date. It is therefore a measurement period adjustment and Slice Limited's net identifiable assets at acquisition date should be reduced to €4.4M.

The discovery of the unrecorded liability of €50,000 is made more than 12 months after the acquisition date. Therefore, unless it is considered a material error, in accordance with IAS 8 retrospective adjustment is *not* permitted, and it should be charged to profit or loss in 2011.

Acquisition-related costs

These are costs that the acquirer incurs to effect a **business combination**. They include finders' fees, legal, accounting and other professional fees. The issue costs of debt or equity securities should be recognised in accordance with IAS 32 and IAS 39. All other acquisition-related costs should be charged as expenses in the period in which they are incurred.

Subsequent measurement and accounting

In general, an acquirer shall apply other applicable IFRSs in subsequent periods when accounting for assets acquired, liabilities assumed and equity instruments issued in a business combination. However, IFRS 3 provides specific guidance in respect of the following issues.

■ Reacquired rights

An acquirer may reacquire a right that it had previously granted to an acquiree. For example, an acquirer may reacquire the rights of an acquiree to use certain technology under a licensing agreement. A reacquired right, recognised as an intangible asset, should be amortised over the remaining contract period.

Example 6 On 1 January 2010, Hornet Limited acquired 100% of the equity share capital of Snooze Limited. On that date, the SOFP of Snooze included an intangible asset of €480,000, representing licensing rights to intellectual property that had been purchased from Hornet on 1 January 2008 for €800,000. The terms of the licensing contract permitted Snooze the unlimited use of the asset for a five-year period, commencing on 1 January 2008.

Outline how the intellectual property should be accounted for by Hornet Limited in its consolidated financial statements.

Solution The intellectual property rights should be included as an intangible asset of €480,000 in the consolidated SOFP at 1 January 2010. The asset should be amortised over three years from that date.

■ Contingent consideration

Contingent consideration should be measured at fair value at the acquisition date. The amount of contingent consideration may change as the result of a post-acquisition event (e.g. meeting an earnings target). In this case, the accounting treatment depends on whether the consideration is in the form of equity or some other asset such as cash. If it is equity, the original estimate is not remeasured, and settlement is accounted for within equity.

If the contingent consideration is classified as an asset or a liability that:

(i) is a financial instrument and is within the scope of IAS 39, it should be measured at fair value, with any resulting gain or loss recognised in profit or loss or in OCI in accordance with IAS 39;

(ii) is not within the scope of IAS 39, it should be accounted for in accordance with IAS 37 or other IFRSs as appropriate.

A change in the **fair value** of contingent consideration may be the result of additional information that the acquirer obtained after the acquisition date about facts and circumstances that existed at the acquisition date (e.g. clarification of an acquiree's tax liability). Such a change is a measurement period adjustment and the amount of consideration should be amended retrospectively.

Example 7 Hornet Limited acquired 100% of the equity share capital of Sugar Limited on 1 January 2010. Hornet paid €2M for the shares of Sugar, and an additional amount of €1M was payable if Sugar's earnings for 2010 exceeds €10M.

Outline the accounting treatment of the contingent consideration, on the assumption that Sugar exceeds the earnings target of €10M.

Solution The fact that Sugar Limited exceeds the earnings target of €10M for 2010 is a post-acquisition event. As the contingent consideration is in the form of cash, the additional consideration of €1M should be charged to profit or loss in 2010 as follows:

	Dr €'000	Cr €'000
Acquisition cost – I/S	1,000	
Trade and other payables		1,000

Accounting for investments in subsidiaries in the separate financial statements of a parent

IAS 27 requires that a **parent** present consolidated financial statements unless:

- the parent is itself a wholly owned **subsidiary**;
- the parent is a partially owned subsidiary, and its other owners do not object to consolidated financial statements not being prepared; and
- the parent's debt or equity instruments are not traded in a public market.

A parent that is exempted from presenting consolidated financial statements can present separate financial statements as its primary **financial statements**. Separate financial statements are defined by IAS 27 as financial statements in which:

. . . the investments are accounted for on the basis of the direct equity interest rather than on the basis of the reported results and net assets of the investees.

In its separate financial statements, a parent should account for a subsidiary either:

- at cost, or
- in accordance with IAS 39

Example 8 On 1 January 2010, Pare Limited purchased 60% of the equity shares in Straw Limited at a cost of €1.5M in cash. Pare is a wholly owned subsidiary and does not prepare consolidated financial statements.

Outline how the purchase of shares in Straw Limited should be recorded by Pare Limited. It should be assumed that Pare Limited accounts for investments in subsidiaries at cost in its separate financial statements.

Solution **(i) Accounting for subsidiary at cost**
Straw Limited is controlled by Pare Limited, following the latter's acquisition of 60% of Straw's equity shares. In the separate financial statements of Pare Limited, the purchase of Straw Limited will be recorded as an asset at cost as follows:

	Dr €'000	Cr €'000
Investment in Straw Limited	1,500	
Bank		1,500

Subsequently, Pare Limited should record any dividends that it receives from Straw, and any impairment losses relating to its investment.

(ii) Accounting for subsidiary in accordance with IAS 39
IAS 39 requires that financial assets should be recorded at fair value, which usually equals the amount of consideration paid. Thus, in the separate financial statements of Pare Limited, the purchase of Straw Limited will be recorded as an asset at fair value as follows:

	Dr €'000	Cr €'000
Financial asset	1,500	
Bank		1,500

As Straw Limited is an unquoted company, Pare's investment will be classed as an available for sale financial asset, rather than an asset held for trading.

Pare Limited should continue to record its investment in Straw at fair value, unless its fair value cannot be reliably measured. Any changes in fair value should be recognised in other comprehensive income (except for impairment losses which should be charged to profit or loss).

■ Dividends

In its separate financial statements, a parent should record **dividends** from a subsidiary in profit or loss. The dividend should be recorded when the entity's right to receive the dividend is established.

Example 9 On 1 July 2010, Pare Limited received a dividend of €60,000 from its subsidiary, Straw Limited.

Outline how this dividend should be treated in the separate financial statements of Pare Limited.

Solution The dividend received from Straw Limited should be recorded in the profit or loss of Pare Limited in the year ended 31 December 2010. This treatment is appropriate irrespective of whether the dividend is paid out of Straw Limited's pre-acquisition or post-acquisition profits.

	Dr €'000	Cr €'000
Bank	60	
Dividend income – I/S of Pare Limited		60

Disclosures

An acquirer must disclose information that enables users of its financial statements to evaluate the nature and financial effect of a **business combination** that occurs either during the current reporting period, or after the end of the reporting period but before the financial statements are authorised for issue.

The following is a summary of the disclosures that are required:

- name and description of the acquiree;
- acquisition date;
- percentage of voting interests acquired;
- primary reasons for the business combination, and a description of how the acquirer obtained control of the acquiree;
- a qualitative description of the factors that make up the goodwill recognised;
- acquisition-date fair value of the total consideration transferred;
- contingent consideration arrangements and indemnification assets;
- details of acquired receivables;
- amounts recognised for each major class of asset acquired and liabilities assumed;
- total amount of goodwill that is expected to be deductible for tax purposes;
- details of a bargain purchase;
- details of a business combination achieved in stages;
- details of the acquiree's post-acquisition revenue and profit or loss.

Summary

- Business combinations should be accounted for using the acquisition method.
- Assets acquired and liabilities assumed in a business combination are usually measured at their acquisition-date fair values.
- Provisional values should be used if the initial accounting for a business combination is incomplete at the end of the reporting period in which a business combination occurs.
- Appropriate adjustments to provisional values should be made for up to one year.
- The issue costs of debt or equity securities should be recognised in accordance with IAS 32 and 39. All other acquisition-related costs should be charged as expenses in the period in which they are incurred.
- A parent that is exempted from presenting consolidated financial statements can present separate financial statements as its primary financial statements.

Appendix 25.1

Exceptions to the recognition and measurement principles of IFRS 3

(i) Contingent liabilities

IFRS 3 requires that an acquirer should recognise a contingent liability assumed in a business combination if it is a present obligation that arises from past events and its fair value can be measured reliably.

Example

Hornet Limited acquired 100% of the equity shares of Squid Limited on 1 January 2010 for cash consideration of €2M. The fair value of the identifiable net assets of Squid at that date was €1.6M. Squid was also the defendant in a court action relating to an injury suffered by an employee. Squid accepts that it has an obligation to compensate the employee for damages amounting to €1M. At 1 January 2010, however, due to a technical flaw in the legal papers presented by the employee's legal advisers, it was estimated that Squid had a 70% chance of winning the action.

Outline the effect of this business combination on the consolidated financial statements of Hornet Limited.

Solution

Squid has a present obligation, arising from past events in this case. The obligation only gives rise to a contingent liability, however, as there is a 70% probability that the judgment will be in favour of Squid. In accordance with IFRS 3, therefore, a provision of €300,000 (i.e. €1M × 30%) must be made at 1 January 2010 in respect of the court proceedings against Squid Limited.

The impact of the business combination on the consolidated financial statements of Hornet can be summarised as follows:

	Dr €m	Cr €m
Identifiable net assets*	1.3	
Bank		2.0
Goodwill	0.7	

* Net of provision for legal proceedings of €0.3M.

(ii) Income taxes

An acquirer shall recognise and measure a deferred tax asset or liability, arising in a business combination, in accordance with IAS 12 *Income Taxes*.

(iii) Employee benefits

An acquirer shall recognise and measure a liability (or asset), related to the acquiree's employee benefit arrangements, in accordance with IAS 19 *Employee Benefits*.

(iv) Reacquired rights

An acquirer may reacquire a right that it had previously granted to an acquiree. For example, an acquirer may reacquire the right of an acquiree to use certain technology under a licensing agreement. IFRS 3 requires that the acquirer shall measure the value of a reacquired right on the basis of the remaining contractual term of the related contract.

(v) Share-based payment awards

The rules of IFRS 2 should be applied in measuring a liability or an equity instrument related to the replacement of an acquiree's share-based payment awards with those of the acquirer.

(vi) Assets held for sale

The acquirer shall measure an acquired non-current asset held for sale in accordance with IFRS 5 *Non-Current Assets Held for Sale and Discontinued Operations.*

QUESTIONS

25.1 BIRD Limited

BIRD Ltd purchased 100% of the ordinary share capital of NEST Ltd on 31 December 2010. The consideration for the purchase was the issue of 100,000 €1 ordinary shares with a fair value of €2.20 each. The net assets of NEST at 31 December 2010 were:

	Book value	Fair value
	€	€
Goodwill	5,000	5,000
Identifiable net assets:		
Patents	14,000	20,000
Plant and equipment	120,000	138,000
Net current assets	30,000	30,000

The goodwill arising on the acquisition of NEST is:
(a) €7,000
(b) €12,000
(c) €27,000
(d) €32,000

(Chartered Accountants Ireland)

25.2 BOLTON Ltd

During the year ended 31 December 2009, BOLTON Ltd estimated that the carrying amount of goodwill had been impaired and wrote it down by €100,000. In 2010, the directors of BOLTON Ltd reassessed goodwill and it was decided that the previously impaired goodwill still existed. The appropriate accounting treatment in the 2010 financial statements is to:

(a) reverse the previous goodwill impairment loss.
(b) recognise the revalued amount of goodwill by an adjustment against the asset revaluation surplus.
(c) ignore the reversal.
(d) increase goodwill by an adjustment to retained earnings.

(Chartered Accountants Ireland)

25.3 HOLLY Limited

On 1 March 2009 the HARDING Group acquired a subsidiary company, HOLLY, for a consideration of €10M. At the time of completion of the 2009 financial statements, a final valuation of net assets was not available, and goodwill was provisionally based on a net asset value of €8M. The final valuation became available in December 2010 and shows a net asset value of €7M. The group financial director has asked you to advise as to the effect of this information on the consolidated financial statements for the year ended 31 December 2010.

(Chartered Accountants Ireland)

25.4 PRICELESS Group

PRICELESS purchased 70% of SCRAMBLE on 1 July 2010 for €28M. The fair value of the net identifiable assets of SCRAMBLE at that date was €38.8M.

Required:

Calculate the amount of goodwill arising on the acquisition of SCRAMBLE and the amount of non-controlling interests:

(a) If non-controlling interests are measured at their proportionate share of identifiable net assets; and

(b) If non-controlling interests are measured at fair value.

Chapter 26

Changes in ownership interest

This chapter examines the acquisition and disposal of shares in a **subsidiary**. A distinction is made between share acquisitions and disposals that:

- result in a **parent** company gaining or losing control; and
- do *not* result in a parent company gaining or losing control.

Acquisition of shares

A business combination achieved in stages

Sometimes an acquirer may hold an equity interest in an acquiree, prior to gaining control. For example, Entity A might own 25% of the equity shares of Entity B, which is accounted for as an associate, under the equity method, in accordance with IAS 28. Entity A later acquires the remaining 75% of B, giving Entity A control over Entity B.

At acquisition date (i.e. the date it obtains control), Entity A is required to remeasure, at fair value, its previously held equity interest in Entity B. The resulting gain or loss, if any, should be recognised in profit or loss. **Thus, gaining control triggers remeasurement.**

Example 1 On 1 January 2009, Hornet Limited purchased 30% of the equity shares of Alton Limited for €2M. Alton earned profit of €1M for the year ended 31 December 2009, and paid no dividend. On 1 January 2010, Hornet acquired the remaining 70% of Alton for a further cash payment of €6.3M. The fair value of the identifiable net assets of Alton Limited at 1 January 2010 was €7M.

Outline the effect of this business combination on the consolidated financial statements of Hornet Limited.

Solution On 1 January 2009, Alton will be included as an investment in associate of €2M in the consolidated SOFP of Hornet. Under the equity method, this asset will be increased by €300,000 (i.e. 30% of profit for the year), to €2.3M at 31 December 2009.

Hornet paid €6.3M for the remaining 70% on 1 January 2010, thereby gaining control of Alton on that date.

The fair value at acquisition date of Hornet's previously held stake in Alton is computed as €2.7M (i.e. €6.3M × 3/7) on 1 January 2010. A gain of €400,000 (i.e. €2.7M – €2.3M) is therefore recorded on its remeasurement to fair value.

The accounting treatment in the consolidated financial statements can be summarised as follows:

	Dr €'000	Cr €'000
Investment in associate	2,000	
Bank		2,000
(Being purchase of 30% of Alton on 1/1/2009)		
Investment in associate	300	
Consolidated retained earnings		300
(Being Hornet Group's share of post-acquisition retained earnings of Alton)		
Investment in associate	400	
Gain on remeasurement – consolidated I/S **(W1)**		400
(Being gain on remeasurement of previous investment of 30% in Alton on date of attaining control)		
Identifiable net assets	7,000	
Bank		6,300
Investment in associate (€2M + €0.3M + €0.4M)		2,700
Goodwill **(W2)**	2,000	
(Being application of acquisition accounting in accordance with IFRS 3)		

Workings   **W1: Profit on derecognition of investment in associate**

	€'000
Cost of original 30% stake	2,000
Hornet's share of associate's post-acquisition retained profit (€1M × 30%)	300
Carrying value of investment in associate at date of attaining control	2,300
Fair value of investment in associate on attaining control (W2)	2,700
Gain on remeasurement to fair value at date of attaining control	400

W2: Goodwill on acquisition

	€'000
Fair value of consideration paid for 7/10 of Alton	6,300
Fair value of previously held equity investment at date of attaining control:	
€6.3M × 3/7	2,700
Fair value of entity as a whole at date of attaining control	9,000
Fair value of identifiable net assets acquired	(7,000)
Goodwill arising on acquisition	2,000

■ Purchase of additional equity shares *after* control is obtained

Sometimes an acquirer, having already obtained a majority stake in an acquiree, may decide to purchase additional shares. For example, Entity C may own 65% of the equity share capital of Entity D, and later decide to purchase an additional 15%. As Entity C's 65% stake represents a controlling interest, the purchase of additional shares is treated as a transaction between owners. It does *not* trigger the remeasurement of C's previous holding, and no gain or loss is recognised.

Example 2   Hornet Limited acquired 60% of the equity share capital of Second Limited on 1 January 2008 for cash consideration of €3M. On 1 January 2010, Hornet purchased an additional 20% of equity in Second for €1.5M. Identifiable net assets were included in the SOFP of Second on 1 January 2010 at €6M.

Explain how Hornet's purchase of 20% of shares in Second is accounted for in its consolidated financial statements.

Solution Prior to its purchase of a 20% stake on 1 January 2010, Hornet already holds a controlling interest in Second. Thus, the purchase of the additional shares is treated as a transaction between owners, as follows:

	Dr €'000	Cr €'000
Non-controlling interest (20% × €6M)	1,200	
Bank		1,500
Adjustment to parent's equity – in SOCIE (balancing figure)	300	

Disposal of shares in a subsidiary

■ Loss of control

A parent may lose control of a subsidiary by disposing of part of its ownership interest. For example, a parent that owns 100% of the shares of a subsidiary may dispose of 60% of its shares. A parent can also lose control of a subsidiary in other ways; for example, it may no longer have the power to appoint a majority of members to the board of directors.

If a parent loses control of a subsidiary, in its consolidated financial statements it:

(i)   derecognises the assets (including any goodwill) and liabilities of the subsidiary, at their carrying amounts at the date when control is lost;

(ii) derecognises the carrying amount of any non-controlling interests in the former subsidiary;

(iii) recognises the fair value of consideration received;

(iv) recognises any investment retained at its fair value at the date when control is lost;

(v)   recognises any resulting difference as a gain or loss attributable to the parent.

Example 3 Pare Limited purchased 80% of the shares of Banan Limited for €200,000 cash on 1 January 2010. At that date, Banan Limited had the following net assets, stated at fair value:

Non-current assets of €90,000
Current assets of €40,000
Liabilities of €30,000

Banan Limited had profit of €100,000 for the year ended 31 December 2010. Therefore, net assets also increased by €100,000 to €200,000 at 31 December 2010.

Non-controlling interests are measured at their proportionate share of the identifiable net assets of Banan Limited.

Assume that Pare sells its entire 80% stake in Banan Limited for €410,000 on 31 December 2010.

Required:
Explain how the above transactions will be recorded in the consolidated financial statements of the Pare group.

Solution The **purchase** of shares by Pare on 1 January 2010 is recorded in the consolidated financial statements as follows:

	Dr €'000	Cr €'000
Non-current assets	90	
Current assets	40	
Liabilities		30
Bank		200
Non-controlling interest*		20
Goodwill (balancing figure)	120	
(Being acquisition of Banan Limited)		
Net assets	100	
Consolidated retained earnings		80
Non-controlling interest		20
(Being profit of Banan Limited for 2010)		

* Non-controlling interest at 1 January 2010 is computed as $(90,000 + 40,000 - 30,000) \times 20\% = 20,000$.

The **disposal** of Pare's entire 80% stake in Banan represents a loss of control. It is recorded as follows in the consolidated financial statements:

	Dr €'000	Cr €'000
Bank	410	
Goodwill		120
Net assets		200
Non-controlling interest	40	
Profit on disposal – I/S (balancing figure)		130

If material, the profit on disposal should be separately disclosed in the income statement, or in the notes, in accordance with IAS 1.

■ Disposals that do *not* result in a loss of control

A parent can dispose of some of its shares without losing control over a subsidiary. For example, if a parent owns 100% of the shares of a subsidiary, and disposes of 25%, it still retains control, by virtue of its retention of a 75% stake in the subsidiary.

IAS 27 requires that changes which do not result in the loss of control should be accounted for as equity transactions (i.e. transactions between owners). The carrying amounts of the controlling interest and the non-controlling interest should be adjusted to reflect the change in their interest in the subsidiary.

Example 4 Assume the same facts as in Example 3 above, except that Pare Limited disposes of only a quarter of its shareholding in Banan on 31 December 2010 for cash consideration of €100,000.

Required:
Explain how the above transaction will be recorded in the consolidated financial statements of the Pare group.

			Dr €'000	Cr €'000

Solution

The purchase of the 80% stake in Banan will be recorded in the same way as in Example 3 above.

However, on 31 December 2010, following the sale of a quarter of its 80% shareholding, Banan continues to be a subsidiary of Pare. Thus, there is **no loss of control**.

When control is retained, a transaction is treated as occurring between owners. There is no profit/loss on disposal, and goodwill remains unchanged.

	Dr €'000	Cr €'000
Bank	100	
Non-controlling interest*		40
Adjustment to parent's equity – in SOCIE		60

* The increase in non-controlling interest is computed as 20% of the net assets of Banan Limited on 31 December 2010 (i.e. €200,000 × 20%).

Summary

(i) Acquisition of shares

- When a business combination is achieved in stages, an acquirer is required to remeasure at fair value, on the date that control is obtained, its previous equity interest in an acquiree. Any gain or loss on remeasurement should be recognised in profit or loss. Thus, gaining control triggers remeasurement in the consolidated financial statements.
- An acquirer may purchase additional shares in an acquiree after control has already been obtained. The purchase of the additional shares is treated as a transaction between owners. It does *not* trigger the remeasurement of the acquirer's previous shareholding, and no gain or loss is recognised in the consolidated financial statements.

(ii) Disposal of shares in a subsidiary

- If a parent loses control of a subsidiary, a profit or loss on disposal of the shares is recognised in the consolidated financial statements.
- If a parent disposes of shares in a subsidiary without losing control, it should be accounted for as a transaction between owners. No profit or loss is recognised in the consolidated financial statements, and the non-controlling interest should be adjusted to reflect the change in their interest in the subsidiary.

QUESTIONS

26.1 Part disposal of O'NEILL RESTAURANT

The O'NEILL Group of companies is a successful wholesale and retail group. The group structure is straightforward, with O'NEILL ENTERPRISES Ltd owning 100% of O'NEILL RETAIL Ltd and 60% of O'NEILL RESTAURANT Ltd. In its separate financial statements, O'NEILL ENTERPRISES Ltd accounts for subsidiaries at cost.

O'NEILL RESTAURANT was incorporated seven years ago, at a total cost of €10,000. In its initial few years, the company traded well and built up an established clientele. However, it then entered a period of decline and its turnover and profitability suffered. A new restaurant manager was recruited four years ago, and he has worked very hard since then to develop the customer base and to increase the turnover and profitability of the company.

In 2009, he was headhunted by a competitor, and in a bid to keep him *in situ*, Mr O'Neill offered him an opportunity to purchase a stake in the company. At 31 December 2009, the manager purchased 40% of the company at a price of €200,000. He is keen to purchase a further 30% of the company and a consideration of €175,000 has been negotiated with a completion date of 31 December 2010. No entries relating to the 30% purchase have been reflected in the statement of financial position.

The carrying value of the identifiable net assets of O'NEILL RESTAURANT at 31 December 2010 was €156,000.

The fair value of the remaining investment (i.e. 30%) in O'NEILL RESTAURANT at 31 December 2010 was €175,000.

Required:

Mr O'Neill, the managing director of the O'NEILL Group, would like to understand the impact of this further sale on the separate financial statements of O'NEILL ENTERPRISES, and on the consolidated financial statements for the year ended 31 December 2010. He would also like to know how O'NEILL RESTAURANT will be treated in the consolidated financial statements for the year ended 31 December 2011.   (Chartered Accountants Ireland)

26.2 Purchase and disposal of shares

Sections (ii), (iii) and (iv) below are each based on section (i) and they should be considered separately.

(i) Acquisition of subsidiary

P Limited purchased 80% of the shares of S Limited for €200,000 cash on 1 January 2010. At that date, S Limited had the following net assets, stated at fair value:

- non-current assets of €90,000
- current assets of €40,000
- Liabilities of €30,000

S Limited had profit of €100,000 for the year ended 31 December 2010.

The fair value of the identifiable net assets of S Limited at 31 December 2010 was €200,000. Non-controlling interests are measured at their proportionate share of those net assets.

Required:

Provide the journal entries to show how S Limited should be recorded in the consolidated financial statements of P Limited.

(ii) Disposal with loss of control

Assume that P Limited sells its entire 80% stake in S Limited for €410,000 on 31 December 2010.

Required:

Provide the journal entries to show how the disposal of S Limited should be recorded in the consolidated financial statements of P Limited.

(iii) Disposal that does *not* result in a loss of control

Assume that P sells 20% of S Limited shares for €100,000 on 31 December 2010 (i.e. sells 25% of its 80% shareholding).

Required:

Provide the journal entries to show how the disposal of part of P's shareholding in S Limited should be recorded in the consolidated financial statements of P Limited.

(iv) Disposal of shares resulting in a subsidiary becoming an associate

Assume that P sells 40% of S Limited shares for €250,000 on 31 December 2010 (i.e. sells half of its 80% shareholding). The fair value of P Limited's remaining stake in S was €250,000 on 31 December 2010.

Required:

Outline how the disposal of part of P's shareholding in S Limited should be recorded in the consolidated financial statements of P Limited.

Chapter 27

Investments in associates

An **associate** is an entity over which an investor has significant influence, and which is neither a **subsidiary** nor a joint venture. Significant influence is the power to participate in the financial and operating policy decisions of the investee. If an investor holds, directly or indirectly (e.g. through subsidiaries), 20% or more of the voting power of an investee, it is normally presumed that the investor has significant influence.

The existence of *significant influence* by an investor is usually shown by one or more of the following ways:

(a) representation on the board of directors;
(b) participation in policy-making processes, including participation in decisions about dividends;
(c) material transactions between the investor and the investee;
(d) interchange of managerial personnel; or
(e) provision of essential technical information.

Example 1 On 31 March 2010, Blue Limited purchased 25% of the equity shares of Yellow Limited. Blue has the power to nominate two directors to the board of Yellow Limited, and it participates in Yellow's policy-making decisions.

Explain the status of Yellow in relation to Blue.

Solution It is presumed that Blue exercises significant influence over Yellow as it holds 20% or more of its equity share capital, and it:

- has representation on the board of directors of Yellow; and
- participates in Yellow's policy-making decisions.

Therefore, Yellow is an associate of Blue.

Although control over 20% or more of the voting power is the accepted norm for an investment to be regarded as an associate, a smaller holding will be sufficient if the investor clearly demonstrates that it has significance influence over the investee. Conversely, an investor that controls 20% or more of the voting power of an investee may be able to demonstrate that it does *not* have significant influence. Appendix 27.1 provides an interesting example of the latter case, relating to Ryanair's 29.8% shareholding in Aer Lingus.

■ Third-party holdings

A substantial or majority stake by another investor does *not* preclude an investor from having significant influence. In Example 1 above, it is possible that the remaining 75%

of shares in Yellow are held by an outside, independent investor. As the Blue group exercises significant influence, however (e.g. through board representation), Yellow is still classified as an associate of the group.

Accounting for investments in associates

This area is regulated by IAS 28 *Investments in Associates*. With limited exceptions, IAS 28 requires that an investment in an associate should be accounted for in the investor's financial statements using the **equity method**. This also applies in the case of investors who do not have subsidiaries, and who are therefore not required to present consolidated financial statements.

The equity method involves the following accounting treatment.

■ Statement of financial position

- the associate is initially recognised as an investment (i.e. an **asset**) at cost;
- the investor's share of the associate's profit arising after the date of acquisition is added to the investment. A share of losses is deducted;
- the amount of any distributions received from the associate is deducted;
- the investor's share of the associate's other comprehensive income (e.g. revaluation of an asset) is added/deducted.

■ Statement of comprehensive income

- the investor's share of the profit or loss of the associate for the year is recognised in the investor's profit or loss;
- the investor's share of other comprehensive income for the year (if any) is included in the investor's other comprehensive income.

Example 2 | Blue plc is the parent of a number of companies which form the Blue Group. On 1 January 2010 Blue plc paid €2.5M to acquire 30% of the equity share capital of Orange Limited. The fair value of Orange Limited's identifiable net assets at that date was €7M.

During the year ended 31 December 2010 Orange earned profit after tax of €100,000 and paid an equity dividend of €40,000. On 31 December 2010 Orange revalued a land site from €1M to €1.3M.

Outline how the above transactions should be accounted for in the consolidated financial statements of Blue plc for the year ended 31 December 2010. Show illustrative extracts from the consolidated financial statements.

Solution | **Consolidated statement of financial position of Blue plc**

Orange is an associate of Blue, and it will initially be recognised as an asset at cost of €2.5M. Blue's share of Orange's profit after tax (€30,000) is added, as is Blue's share (€90,000) of the revaluation surplus. The dividend of €12,000 received from Blue is deducted. Thus, a non-current asset of €2,608,000 will be shown in the consolidated statement of financial position as *investment in associate*.

None of the individual assets or liabilities of the associate will appear in the consolidated statement of financial position.

Consolidated statement of comprehensive income of Blue plc

This statement includes Blue's share of Orange's profit after tax (i.e. €30,000). The illustrative financial statements of IAS 1 show this figure appearing immediately above the group's *profit before tax* figure.

Blue's share of Orange's revaluation surplus (i.e. €90,000) is included as part of the group's other comprehensive income, along with a separate record of the related deferred tax charge.

The consolidated revenue and expense items equal the total of Blue plc and its subsidiaries. None of the associate's revenue or expenses is included in the group financial statements.

Illustrative extracts from the consolidated financial statements follow.

Consolidated statement of financial position as at 31 December 2010

	€'000
Assets	
Non-current assets	
Property, plant and equipment	xxx,xxx
Goodwill	xx,xxx
Other intangible assets	xx,xxx
Investment in associate	2,608
	xxx,xxx

Consolidated statement of comprehensive income for the year ended 31 December 2010

	€'000
Revenue	xx,xxx
Cost of sales	(xx,xxx)
Gross profit	xx,xxx
Other income*	xxx
Distribution costs	(xxx)
Administrative expenses	(xxx)
Other expenses	(xxx)
Finance costs	(xxx)
Share of profit of associate	30
Profit before tax	x,xxx
Income tax expense	(xxx)
Profit for the year	x,xxx
Other comprehensive income:	
Cash flow hedges	xxx
Gains on property revaluation	xxx
Actuarial gains on defined benefit pension plans	xxx
Share of other comprehensive income of associate	90
Income tax relating to components of other comprehensive income	(xxx)
Other comprehensive income for the year, net of tax	xxx
Total comprehensive income for the year	**x,xxx**

* Dividends received from Orange should not be included in Blue's consolidated income. It already includes a share of Orange's profit, and it is out of this profit that the dividend is paid. Therefore, to include the dividend as income would be double counting.

Goodwill arising on acquisition of shares in an associate

Goodwill is computed as the difference between the cost of the investment and the investor's share of the net **fair value** of the associate's identifiable assets and liabilities. In Example 2 above, goodwill is computed as follows:

	€'000
Consideration paid	2,500
Investor's share of fair value of associate's identifiable net assets and liabilities (€7M × 30%)	(2,100)
Goodwill	400

Goodwill is not separately shown, but is included in the carrying value of the investment. Thus, in this example, at the date that the shares in Orange are acquired, the investment in the associate is recognised as an asset of €2.5M, which includes Blue's share of Orange's net assets (i.e. €2.1M) + goodwill of €400,000:

	Dr €'000	Cr €'000
Investment in associate	2,500	
Bank		2,500

In the case of **negative goodwill** arising, it is included as income in computing the investor's share of the associate's profit or loss in the period in which the investment is acquired. Thus, if the consideration paid in the above example was €2M, negative goodwill of €100,000 would arise. The acquisition of shares in the associate would then be recorded as follows:

	Dr €'000	Cr €'000
Investment in associate	2,100	
Bank		2,000
Negative goodwill (included in the investor's I/S as share of the associate's profit or loss)		100

Exceptions to the use of the equity method

An investment in an associate must be accounted for using the equity method except when:

(a) the investment is classified as held for sale in accordance with IFRS 5;
(b) IAS 27 exempts a parent that also has an investment in an associate from having to present consolidated financial statements;
(c) the investor is a wholly or partially owned subsidiary, whose debt or equity instruments are not publicly traded, and whose parent company produces consolidated financial statements that comply with IFRS.

Upstream and downstream transactions

These are transactions between an investor and its associate. An example of an *upstream* transaction is the sale of assets from an associate to the investor. *Downstream* transactions are, for example, sales of assets from the investor to its associate. **IAS 28 requires that any unrealised profit on these transactions is eliminated, to the extent of the investor's interest in the associate.**

Example 3 | **Upstream transaction**

Blue plc owns 30% of the equity shares in its associate company, Orange Limited. During the year ended 31 December 2010, Orange sold goods to Blue for €3M, which included a profit of €1M. A quarter of these goods are still held in the inventory of Blue at 31 December 2010.

Explain how the above transaction should be treated in the consolidated financial statements of Blue plc.

Solution | Blue's share of unrealised profit in this case amounts to €75,000 (i.e. €1M × 25% × 30%). In the consolidated statement of comprehensive income of Blue plc, the share of profit from Orange is reduced by €75,000. The asset *investment in associate* is also reduced by €75,000 in the consolidated SOFP.

	Dr €'000	Cr €'000
Share of profit of associate – I/S	75	
Investment in associate		75
(Being elimination in the consolidated financial statements of Blue's share of unrealised profit)		

Example 4 | **Downstream transaction**

Assume the same facts as in Example 3 above, except that the sale of goods is from Blue plc to its associate, Orange Limited.

Explain how this transaction should be treated in the consolidated financial statements of Blue plc.

Solution | The investor's equity share of unrealised profit should be eliminated to the extent of Blue's interest in Orange. This is effected by increasing the cost of sales. The same amount is deducted from *investment in associate* in the consolidated SOFP.

	Dr €'000	Cr €'000
Cost of sales	75	
Investment in associate		75

Reporting periods and accounting policies

The rules in IAS 28, in respect of associates, are similar to those of IAS 27 relating to subsidiaries.

■ Reporting periods

If the end of the investor's **reporting period** differs from that of its associate, the associate should prepare financial statements as of the same date of those of the investor, unless it is impracticable to do so.

In any case the difference between the end of the reporting period of the associate and that of the investor should not exceed three months. Adjustments should be made for the effects of significant transactions or events that occur in the interim period.

■ Accounting policies

Uniform accounting policies should be used. When the associate's accounting policies differ from those of the investor, adjustments should be made to those of the associate when its **financial statements** are used by the investor in applying the **equity method**.

Losses of an associate

An investor's share of losses of an associate may equal or exceed the carrying amount of the associate in the investor's financial statements. Should this occur, the investor will cease to recognise its share of any further losses, unless the investor has a legal or constructive obligation or has made payments on behalf of the associate.

Example 5   On 1 January 2008, Blue plc paid €2M to acquire 30% of the equity share capital of White Limited. The accumulated losses of White for the three years ended 31 December 2010 amounted to €10M.

Explain how the above transactions should be accounted for in the financial statements of Blue plc.

Solution   Initially, the investment in White will be recorded at cost, as follows:

	Dr €'000	Cr €'000
Investment in associate	2,000	
Bank		2,000

In accordance with IAS 28, Blue should apply the equity method in accounting for its associate, White Limited. Thus, Blue's share of White's post-acquisition losses will be recorded in Blue's statement of comprehensive income, and also deducted from the carrying amount of the investment.

Blue's share of the post-acquisition losses of White amounts to €3M. During the three years ended 31 December 2010, Blue records these losses only up to the amount of the carrying value of its investment in White.*

	Dr €'000	Cr €'000
Share of associate's losses – I/S of Blue plc	2,000	
Investment in associate		2,000

Now, suppose that White earns after-tax profits of €6M in 2011. In this event, Blue can begin to recognise its share of those profits (i.e. €1.8M) only after its share equals the share of White's losses that have not been recognised (i.e. €1M). Thus, Blue will recognise €0.8M as its share of White's profits in its statement of comprehensive income in 2011.

	Dr €'000	Cr €'000
Investment in associate	800	
Share of associate's profits – I/S of Blue plc		800

* After Blue's interest in White is reduced to zero, additional losses are provided for only to the extent that Blue has incurred legal or constructive obligations or made payments on behalf of White.

Impairment losses

The entire carrying amount of an investment in an associate should be tested for **impairment**, whenever there is any indication that impairment may have occurred.

Separate financial statements of an investor

An interest in an associate should be accounted for in an investor's separate financial statements at cost or under the rules of IAS 39. See Chapter 25 for further details of separate financial statements.

Disclosure requirements of IAS 28

- the fair value of investments in associates for which there are published prices;
- summarised financial information of associates, including the aggregated amounts of assets, liabilities, revenues and profit or loss;
- the reason why the presumption that an investor does not have significant influence is overcome if the investor holds less than 20% of the investee's voting power;
- the reasons why the presumption that an investor has significant influence is overcome if the investor holds 20% or more of the investee's voting power;
- the reporting period of an associate when this differs from that of the investor, and the reason for using a different date or different period;
- any significant restrictions on the ability of associates to transfer funds to the investor;
- any unrecognised share of losses of an associate;
- the fact that an associate is not accounted for using the equity method;
- summarised financial information of associates that are not accounted for using the equity method.

Summary

- An associate is an entity over which an investor has significant influence, and which is neither a subsidiary nor a joint venture.
- Investments in associates are usually accounted for in the investor's financial statements using the equity method.
- Any unrealised profits on transactions between an associate and an investor are eliminated to the extent of the investor's interest in the associate.
- An investor and associate should use the same accounting policies and have the same reporting period.

Appendix 27.1

Extract from the financial statements of Ryanair Holdings plc

■ **Example of a significant equity shareholding not treated as an associate**

Note 4 Available for sale financial assets (extract)

	At March 31	
	2009	2008
	€'000	€'000
Investment in Aer Lingus	93,150	311,462

During the 2009 fiscal year the company acquired a further stake in Aer Lingus plc, an Irish airline, at a cost of €4.2M, bringing Ryanair's total holding in Aer Lingus to 29.8% . . . This investment is classified as available-for-sale, rather than as an investment in an associate, because the company does not have the power to exercise any influence over the entity.

The company's determination that it does not have any influence over Aer Lingus has been based on the following factors, in particular:

(i) Ryanair does not have any representation on the Aer Lingus board of directors, not does it have a right to appoint a director.

(ii) Ryanair does not participate in Aer Lingus' policy-making decisions, nor does it have a right to participate in such policy-making decisions.

(iii) There are no material transactions between Ryanair and Aer Lingus, there is no inter-change of personnel between the two companies and there is no sharing of technical information between the companies.

(iv) Aer Lingus and its principal shareholder (Irish government: 25.1%; employee share ownership plan: 14.2%) have openly opposed Ryanair's investment or participation in the company.

(v) On 13 August 2007 and 4 September 2007, Aer Lingus refused Ryanair's attempt to assert its statutory rights to requisition a general meeting (a legal right of any 10% shareholder under Irish law).

QUESTIONS

27.1 BREAD plc

BREAD plc owns 80% of the ordinary share capital of BUTTER Ltd, which owns 75% of the ordinary share capital of JAM Ltd. BREAD plc also owns 30% of the ordinary share capital of CRUST Ltd. All four companies own equity-voting shares in SANDWICH Ltd as follows:

	%
BREAD	14
BUTTER	11
JAM	8
CRUST	12

When deciding whether SANDWICH Ltd is an associate of BREAD plc in accordance with IAS 28 *Investments in Associates*, what is the relevant percentage shareholding?

(a) 29%
(b) 31%
(c) 33%
(d) 45%   (Chartered Accountants Ireland)

27.2 Sale of site

BINGLEY Limited, which is a property development company, is a wholly owned subsidiary of DARCY plc, and is a member of the DARCY group of companies. BINGLEY holds an 18% interest in another property development company, COLLINS. COLLINS has several other corporate shareholders. The majority of its shares are held by a property investment company unconnected with the DARCY group. BINGLEY is represented on the board of directors of COLLINS and, via this representation, participates in all major decisions required to be taken in the management of the company.

BINGLEY regularly supplies COLLINS with development land and, during the year ended 31 December 2010, BINGLEY sold a development site to COLLINS at its open market value of €2M. BINGLEY had purchased the site during the same year for €1.8M.

Required:

Outline the correct accounting treatment and disclosure of the interest in COLLINS, and the sale of land to that company, in the consolidated financial statements of the DARCY group for the year ended 31 December 2010. Journals are *not* required.   (Chartered Accountants Ireland)

27.3 PRICE Group

The following are the financial statements of PRICE plc, SCAM Ltd and ASK Ltd for the year ended 31 December 2010:

Statement of comprehensive income for the year ended 31 December 2010

	PRICE plc €'000	SCAM Ltd €'000	ASK Ltd €'000
Revenue	56,000	39,000	27,480
Cost of sales	33,600	23,400	10,480
Gross profit	22,400	15,600	17,000
Operating expenses	7,880	4,400	2,480
Operating profit	14,520	11,200	14,520
Interest payable	1,400	720	280
Profit before tax	13,120	10,480	14,240
Income tax expense	5,400	4,200	1,680
Profit for the year	7,720	6,280	12,560
Retained earnings b/f	22,864	15,260	13,200
Retained earnings c/f	30,584	21,540	25,760

Statements of financial position at 31 December 2010

	PRICE plc €000	SCAM Ltd €000	ASK Ltd €000
Non-current assets			
Tangible assets	41,400	38,080	64,800
Investment in SCAM Ltd	21,940		
Investment in ASK Ltd	22,000		
	85,340	38,080	64,800
Current assets			
Inventories	6,400	4,080	3,120
Trade receivables	3,880	2,400	1,960
Cash	2,124	680	80
	12,404	7,160	5,160
Amounts falling due within one year			
Trade and other payables	(5,160)	(4,500)	(3,400)
Net assets	92,584	40,740	66,560
Ordinary shares (€1)	58,000	16,000	34,800
Share premium	4,000	3,200	6,000
Retained earnings	30,584	21,540	25,760
	92,584	40,740	66,560

The following information is relevant:

(i) PRICE Plc acquired 70% of the ordinary shares of SCAM Ltd on 1 January 2009 when SCAM's reserves were:

	€'000
Share premium	3,200
Retained earnings	9,600

(ii) At 1 January 2009 the tangible non-current assets of SCAM Ltd exceeded their book value by €1.2M. This surplus has not been reflected in the financial statements of SCAM Ltd. At that date the average remaining useful life of non-current assets was 10 years.

(iii) PRICE plc acquired 40% of the ordinary shares of ASK Ltd on 1 January 2010 when the balance on Ask Ltd's share premium account was €6M and its retained earnings were €13.2M.

(iv) During the current year, SCAM Ltd sold goods to PRICE plc at invoice value €1.44M, on which SCAM Ltd made a mark-up of 20%. One-half of these goods were still in the inventory of PRICE plc at 31 December 2010.

(v) Goodwill on acquisition of SCAM Ltd has become impaired by €188,000 per annum since the date of acquisition. The premium arising on investment in ASK Ltd has become impaired by €80,000 since the date of investment.

Required:

Prepare the consolidated statement of comprehensive income of the PRICE plc Group for the year ended 31 December 2010 and a consolidated statement of financial position at that date. In your answer show the required journal entries and necessary adjustments.

Chapter 28

Interests in joint ventures

A joint venture is a contractual arrangement whereby two or more parties undertake an economic activity that is subject to joint control.

Example 1 X Ltd, Y Ltd and Z Ltd join forces to form Alpha Ltd. Each company owns an equal share of Alpha, which has been set up to exploit opportunities in the Greek stationery market. X, Y and Z participate in the management of Alpha, and liaise in relation to matters of policy.

Outline the status of Alpha Ltd in the financial statements of X, Y and Z.

Solution X, Y and Z have established Alpha to exploit opportunities in the Greek stationery market. This is an example of two or more parties undertaking an economic activity that is subject to joint control. Therefore, Alpha is a joint venture and X, Y and Z are venturers.

Forms of joint venture

IAS 31 identifies three forms of joint venture:

- jointly controlled operations
- jointly controlled assets
- jointly controlled entities.

Jointly controlled operations

A jointly controlled operation involves the use of the **assets** and other resources of a venturer, rather than the establishment of a separate entity. Each venturer uses its own property, plant and equipment and carries its own inventories. It also incurs its own expenses and liabilities and raises its own finance.

An example of a jointly controlled *operation* is when two or more venturers combine their operations, resources and expertise to manufacture, market and distribute jointly a particular product, such as an aircraft. Different parts of the manufacturing process are carried out by each of the venturers. Each venturer bears its own costs and takes a share of the revenue from the sale of the aircraft.

IAS 31 states that in respect of its interests in jointly controlled operations, a venturer shall recognise in its financial statements:

- the assets it controls and the liabilities that it incurs; and
- the **expenses** it incurs and its share of the income that it earns from the sale of goods or services by the joint venture.

Example 2 On 1 January 2010, Magnum Limited entered into a joint venture arrangement with Calypso Limited. This agreement involved the manufacture and distribution of an electrically powered automobile engine. Magnum Limited agreed to source the necessary raw materials and to design and construct an engine casing that would accommodate an electrically powered motor unit. Calypso Limited agreed to develop and manufacture the required unit. It was agreed that sales revenue would be split on a 50 : 50 basis.

During 2010, Magnum Limited purchased machinery costing €300,000. The machine has a zero residual value, and is depreciated over five years on a straight-line basis, a full year's depreciation being charged in the year of purchase. Other costs incurred, and paid in full by Magnum Limited during 2010, amounted to €400,000. Sales revenues for 2010 amounted to €200,000, and Magnum had inventories on hand at 31 December 2010 which had cost €30,000.

Outline how Magnum Limited should account for its joint venture with Calypso Limited.

Solution This is a jointly controlled operation, as defined by IAS 31. Magnum Limited should record the following items in its financial statements for the year ended 31 December 2010:

- the assets it controls; and
- the expenses that it incurs and its share of the income that it earns from the sale of units by the joint venture.

The following journal entries will be required for Magnum Limited:

	Dr €'000	Cr €'000
Machinery	300	
Bank		300
Depreciation expense – I/S	60	
Accumulated depreciation – SOFP		60
Cost of sales/expenses – I/S	400	
Bank		400
Bank/trade receivables	100	
Revenue – I/S		100
(Being 50% share of revenue for year end 31/12/2010)		
Inventory – SOFP	30	
Cost of sales		30

■ Jointly controlled assets

Some joint ventures involve the joint control of one or more assets, which are used to obtain benefits for the venturers. Each venturer may take a share of the output from the assets and bear an agreed share of expenses incurred.

This form of joint venture does not involve the establishment of a separate entity.

Example 3 On 1 May 2010, Magnum Limited jointly purchased an investment property with Ringo Limited. The property, which cost €600,000, is equally owned by both companies. Net rental income for the eight months ended 31 December 2010 amounted to €25,000, all of which was received. The fair value of the property at 31 December 2010 was €800,000.

Outline the accounting treatment for this property in the financial statements of Magnum Limited for the year ended 31 December 2010.

Solution This property is a jointly controlled asset. IAS 31 states that, in respect of jointly controlled assets, a venturer shall recognise in its financial statements:

- its share of the jointly controlled asset
- any liabilities it has incurred, and
- any income and expenses relating to the asset

IAS 40 *Investment Property* permits a choice of either a **fair value** model or a cost model for investment property. On the assumption that Magnum Limited opts for the fair value model, its share of the gain arising during the eight months ended 31 December 2010 should be included in profit or loss.

The following journal entries will be required for Magnum Limited:

	Dr €'000	Cr €'000
Investment property	300	
Bank		300
Bank	12.5	
Rental income – I/S		12.5
Investment property	100	
Revaluation gain – I/S		100

■ Jointly controlled entities

(i) Definition

A jointly controlled entity involves the establishment of a corporation, partnership or other entity in which each venturer has an interest.

Example 4 On 1 October 2010, Magnum Limited and Calyso Limited set up a new company, Scale Limited, to service the after-sales service of its electrically powered engines. Magnum and Calypso each hold 50% of the shares in Scale Limited.

Scale Limited is a jointly controlled entity, in which Magnum and Calypso are venturers.

(ii) Accounting treatment for jointly controlled entities

IAS 31 allows two alternative treatments:

- proportionate consolidation
- equity method of accounting

Proportionate consolidation
This involves the following treatment in the venturer's **financial statements**:

- the SOFP should include its share of the assets that the venturer controls jointly, and its share of the liabilities for which it is jointly responsible;
- the venturer's income statement should include its share of the income and expenses of the jointly controlled entity.

Equity method
This involves the following treatment in the venturer's financial statements:

- the venturer's SOFP should initially include its investment at cost. This is increased or decreased to recognise the venturer's share of the post-acquisition profit or loss of the joint venture.

- its share of the profit or loss of the joint venture is recognised in the venturer's profit or loss.

See example in Appendix 28.1.

Exceptions to the use of proportionate consolidation and the equity method
As stated above, IAS 31 permits the use of either proportionate consolidation or the **equity method** in accounting for jointly controlled entities. However, certain exceptions apply – see Appendix 28.2.

(iii) Transactions between a venturer and a jointly controlled entity

Transfers from a venturer to a joint venture
When a venturer contributes or sells assets to a joint venture, while the assets are retained by the joint venture, the venturer should recognise only that portion of the gain or loss that is attributable to the interests of the other venturers.

However, the venturer should recognise the full amount of any loss when the contribution or sale provides evidence of a reduction in the net realisable value of current assets or an impairment loss.

Example 5

On 1 November 2010, Magnum Limited sold goods to its joint venture, Scale Limited, for €300,000. The sales price included a profit margin of 50%, and a quarter of the goods were held in inventory by Scale Limited at 31 December 2010. Scale received three months' credit.

Magnum owns 50% of the shares of Scale, and exercises joint control with the other venturer, Calypso Limited.

Outline how the sale of these goods to Scale Limited should be accounted for in the financial statements of Magnum Limited.

Solution

To the extent that Scale has retained the goods in inventory at 31 December 2010, Magnum should only recognise the portion of the profit that is attributable to the interests of the other venturer, Calypso Limited.

Thus, the following journal entries will be made by Magnum in respect of the sale to Scale Limited:

	Dr €'000	Cr €'000
Trade receivables	300	
Revenue		300
(Being sale of goods by Magnum to Scale)		
Cost of sales	150	
Inventory – SOFP		150
(Being Magnum's cost of goods sold to Scale)		
Profit before tax	18.75	
Inventory*		
OR		18.75
Investment in joint venture†		

(Being elimination of Magnum's share of the profit on goods sold which are retained in inventory by Scale at 31 December 2010: €300,000 × 50% × 50% × 25%, i.e. selling price × profit margin × Magnum's share × percentage of goods held in inventory)

* The credit entry is to inventory if Scale is included in Magnum's financial statements using proportionate consolidation.
† The credit entry is to investment in joint venture if Scale is included in Magnum's financial statements using the equity method.

Transfers from a joint venture to a venturer

When a venturer purchases assets from a joint venture, the venturer should not recognise its share of the profits of the joint venture until it resells the assets to an independent party.

A venturer should recognise its share of any losses in the same way as profits, except that losses should be recognised immediately when they represent a reduction in the net realisable value of current assets or an impairment loss.

Example 6 | **Sale of asset by a jointly controlled entity to a venturer**

On 1 October 2010, Magnum Limited purchased goods from Scale Limited for €400,000, at a mark-up of 50% on cost. A quarter of these goods were retained in inventory by Magnum at 31 December 2010. Magnum received three months' credit.

Outline how the purchase of goods from Scale Limited should be accounted for in the financial statements of Magnum Limited.

Solution | Magnum Limited should record its share of Scale Limited's profit on these goods only to the extent that they have been resold by Magnum.

Thus, the following journal entries will be made by Magnum in respect of the purchase of goods from Scale Limited:

	Dr €'000	Cr €'000
Cost of sales	400	
Trade payables		400
(Being goods purchased from Scale)		
Profit before tax	16.7	
Inventory – SOFP		16.7

(Being elimination of Magnum's share of Scale's profit on goods sold which are retained in inventory by Magnum at 31 December 2010: €400,000 × 50% × 33^1/₃% × 25%, i.e. selling price × Magnum's share × profit margin × percentage of goods held in inventory)

(iv) Jointly controlled entities where an investor does not have joint control

An investor in a jointly controlled entity that does not have joint control should account for the investment in accordance with IAS 39 or, if it has significant influence in the joint venture, in accordance with IAS 28.

(v) Separate financial statements of a venturer

An interest in a jointly controlled entity should be accounted for in a venturer's separate financial statements at cost or under the rules of IAS 39. See Chapter 25 for further details of separate financial statements.

Disclosures

A venturer is required to disclose the following information in respect of its interests in joint ventures:

- details of **contingent liabilities**
- commitments
- a listing and description of interests in significant joint ventures

■ the method used to recognise its interests in jointly controlled entities

New standard for joint ventures

A new standard called *Joint Arrangements* is expected to replace IAS 31 during 2011. This standard will replace IAS 31. It is expected that the new standard will require the equity method to be used in accounting for jointly controlled entities. In that case, the use of proportionate consolidation would no longer be permitted.

Summary

- A joint venture is a contractual arrangement whereby two or more parties undertake an economic activity that is subject to joint control.
- IAS 31 identifies three forms of joint venture:
  - jointly controlled operations
  - jointly controlled assets
  - jointly controlled entities
- A jointly controlled **operation** involves the use of the assets and other resources of a venturer, rather than the establishment of a separate entity. Each venturer uses its own property, plant and equipment and carries its own inventories. It also incurs its own expenses and liabilities and raises its own finance.
- Some joint ventures involve the joint control of one or more **assets**, which are used to obtain benefits for the venturers. Each venturer may take a share of the output from the assets and bear an agreed share of expenses incurred.
- A jointly controlled **entity** involves the establishment of a corporation, partnership or other entity in which each venturer has an interest. IAS 31 allows two alternative treatments for jointly controlled entities:
  - proportionate consolidation
  - equity method of accounting

  It is expected that a new IASB standard, called *Joint Arrangements*, will no longer permit the use of proportionate consolidation in accounting for a jointly controlled entity.
- When a venturer sells assets to a jointly controlled entity, while the assets are retained by the joint venture, the venturer should recognise only that portion of the gain or loss that is attributable to the interests of the other venturers.
- When a venturer purchases assets from a jointly controlled entity, the venturer should not recognise its share of the profits of the joint venture until it resells the assets to an independent party.

Appendix 28.1

Comparison of proportionate consolidation and the equity method

On 1 January 2010, Magnum Limited and Calypso each invested €1M in setting up Minor Limited. Magnum and Calypso both own 50% of the equity shares in Minor, and they exercise joint control over its economic activities.

The following information is extracted from Minor Limited's financial statements for the year ended 31 December 2010:

Statement of comprehensive income for the year ended 31 December 2010

	€'000
Revenue	800
Cost of sales	(200)
Gross profit	600
Distribution expenses	(50)
Other expenses	(40)
Profit before tax	510
Income tax expense	(60)
Profit for the year	450

Statement of financial position at 31 December 2010

	€'000
Assets	
Non-current assets	
Land and buildings	1,150
Current assets	
Inventory	900
Trade receivables	700
Total assets	2,750
Equity and liabilities	
Share capital	2,000
Retained earnings	450
Total equity	2,450
Current liabilities	
Trade payables	300
Total equity and liabilities	2,750

Outline how the above transactions should be accounted for in the financial statements of Magnum Limited for the year ended 31 December 2010. Show illustrative extracts from the financial statements.

Solution   Minor Limited is a jointly controlled entity, in which Magnum and Calypso are venturers. In the financial statements of Magnum, its investment in Minor can be accounted for using either of two approaches:

- proportionate consolidation; or
- equity method

(i) Proportionate consolidation

- the SOFP should include its share of the assets that the venturer controls jointly, and its share of the liabilities for which it is jointly responsible;
- the venturer's income statement should include its share of the income and expenses of the jointly controlled entity.

Illustrative extracts from the financial statements follow.

**Statement of financial position of Magnum Limited at
31 December 2010**

	€'000
Assets	
Non-current assets	
Land and buildings (includes €575,000 of JV)	xx,xxx
Plant and equipment	xx,xxx
	xx,xxx
Current assets	
Inventory (includes €450,000 of JV)	xx,xxx
Trade receivables (includes €350,000 of JV)	xx,xxx
Bank	xx,xxx
Total assets	xxx,xxx
Current liabilities	
Trade payables (includes €150,000 of JV)	xx,xxx
Equity	
Share capital	xx,xxx
Retained earnings (includes €225,000 of JV)	xx,xxx

**Statement of comprehensive income of Magnum Limited for the year ended
31 December 2010**

	€'000
Revenue (includes €400,000 of JV)	xx,xxx
Cost of sales (includes €100,000 of JV)	(xx,xxx)
Gross profit	xx,xxx
Distribution costs (includes €25,000 of JV)	(xxx)
Administrative expenses	(xxx)
Other expenses (includes €20,000 of JV)	(xxx)
Finance costs	(xxx)
Profit before tax	x,xxx
Income tax expense (includes €30,000 of JV)	(xxx)
Profit for the year	x,xxx

(ii) Equity method

■ The venturer's SOFP should initially include its investment at cost. This is increased or decreased to recognise the venturer's share of the post-acquisition profits or losses of the joint venture.

■ Its share of the profit or loss of the joint venture is recognised in the venturer's profit or loss.

Illustrative extracts from the financial statements follow.

Statement of financial position of Magnum Limited at 31 December 2010

	€'000
Assets	
Non-current assets	
Land and buildings	xx,xxx
Plant and equipment	xx,xxx
Investment in joint venture (i.e. €1M + €225,000)	1,225
	xx,xxx
Current assets	
Inventory	xx,xxx
Trade receivables	xx,xxx
Bank	xx,xxx
Total assets	xxx,xxx
Current liabilities	
Trade payables	xx,xxx
	xxx,xxx
Equity	
Share capital	xx,xxx
Retained earnings (includes €225,000 of JV)	xx,xxx
Total equity	xxx,xxx

Statement of comprehensive income of Magnum Limited for the year ended 31 December 2010

	€'000
Revenue	xx,xxx
Cost of sales	(xx,xxx)
Gross profit	xx,xxx
Distribution costs	(xxx)
Administrative expenses	(xxx)
Other expenses	(xxx)
Finance costs	(xxx)
Share of profit of joint venture	225
Profit before tax	x,xxx
Income tax expense	(xxx)
Profit for the year	x,xxx

Appendix 28.2

Exceptions to the use of proportionate consolidation or the equity method for jointly controlled entities

(i) Interests in jointly controlled entities that are classified as held for sale should be accounted for in accordance with IFRS 5.

(ii) When an investor ceases to have joint control over an entity, it should account for any remaining investment in accordance with IAS 39, provided that the former jointly controlled entity does not become a subsidiary or associate.

(iii) If a parent is exempted from preparing consolidated financial statements by paragraph 10 of IAS 27, it can prepare separate financial statements as its primary financial statements. Either IAS 39 or the cost method can be used in the separate financial statements when accounting for a jointly controlled entity.

(iv) Proportionate consolidation or the equity method do not have to be used if all of the following apply:

- the venturer is itself a wholly owned subsidiary, or is a partially owned subsidiary and its owners do not object to proportionate consolidation or the equity method not being used;
- the venturer's debt or equity instruments are not traded in a public market;
- the venturer did not file, nor is in the process of filing, its financial statements for the purposes of issuing financial instruments in a public market;
- the ultimate or any intermediate parent of the venturer produces consolidated financial statements available for public use that comply with IFRSs.

QUESTIONS

28.1 BINGLEY Limited

BINGLEY Limited, which is a property development company, is a wholly owned subsidiary of DARCY plc, and is a member of the DARCY group of companies. During the year ended 31 December 2010, BINGLEY entered into a contract with an unconnected property development company under which a new company, PHILLIPS, was formed.

BINGLEY owns 50% of the shares in PHILLIPS, with the other 50% being held by the other party to the agreement. PHILLIPS was formed for the purpose of undertaking a major commercial property development project, which neither of its shareholders could undertake alone due to its size and the working capital investment required. The two companies therefore decided to undertake the project jointly via a new company. The contractual arrangement between the two shareholders is such that PHILLIPS will be managed by them jointly for the duration of the development project, and all profits or losses will be divided equally between them once the project is complete. It is anticipated that the project will take two to three years to complete.

Required:

Explain how the interest in PHILLIPS should be accounted for in the consolidated financial statements of DARCY. Journals and disclosure notes are *not* required.   (Chartered Accountants Ireland)

28.2 SUREGUARD Ltd

As part of the commercial development of the MAGNA group, MAGNA HOLDINGS has been strategically seeking expansion into new but related business areas. On 1 January 2010 MAGNA HOLDINGS, together with another company, STANDARD SECURITY, formed a new company, SUREGUARD Ltd ('SUREGUARD'), to bid for security contracts at ports, airports and other public and private buildings. Strategically, this is believed to represent a good 'fit', with MAGNA HOLDINGS delivering the equipment, infrastructure and finance for the contracts whilst STANDARD SECURITY sources the security manpower and day-to-day management to deliver the operational requirements of the contracts. During its first full year of trading SUREGUARD has successfully commenced a number of major contracts at retail stores and regional airports and the initial performance of the company has been slightly ahead of expectations.

SUREGUARD has share capital of €200,000, of which MAGNA HOLDINGS holds 70%, with 30% held by STANDARD SECURITY. Both MAGNA HOLDINGS and STANDARD SECURITY are fully involved in the strategic development of SUREGUARD and each company has two seats on the executive board. Voting rights of the company are split equally between the two investors and, although not subject to any written agreement, it has been agreed and practised to date that either party can exercise a veto over key decisions. The intention is that in future years if the company trades profitably then the two investor companies will receive dividends from SUREGUARD.

From your audit work you are also aware that MAGNA SECURITY, a 100% subsidiary of MAGNA HOLDINGS, has sold equipment to SUREGUARD. This equipment was invoiced to SUREGUARD in February 2010 at €1.4M sales value and is being carried forward at this amount less depreciation. The cost to MAGNA SECURITY of these items was €1M. A debtor remains in the books of MAGNA SECURITY at 31 December 2010 of €250,000 in respect of this transaction.

Required:

(i) Explain how the investment in SUREGUARD should be treated and disclosed in the separate company financial statements of MAGNA HOLDINGS and in the consolidated financial statements of the MAGNA group for the year ended 31 December 2010.

It should be assumed that, in its separate financial statements, MAGNA HOLDINGS accounts for investments in associates, joint ventures and subsidiaries at cost.

(ii) Set out the journals required to reflect your recommended accounting treatment under (i), together with any journals and disclosures arising from transactions between MAGNA SECURITY and SUREGUARD during the year ended 31 December 2010.   (Chartered Accountants Ireland)

Chapter 29

Consolidated statement of cash flows

The principles underlying the preparation of the statement of cash flows for an individual entity were outlined in Chapter 8. This chapter focuses on the *consolidated* stage of that statement, and examines the treatment of the following areas:

- acquisition of a **subsidiary** during the period;
- **non-controlling interests**;
- impairment of **goodwill**;
- investments that are equity-accounted;
- disposal of a subsidiary during the period.

Acquisition of a subsidiary

The amount of consideration paid (net of any cash or overdrafts of the subsidiary at acquisition date) is included as an outflow under *cash flows from investing activities* in the year in which a subsidiary is acquired.

Example 1

Marge Limited acquired 75% of the shares of Homer Limited for cash consideration of €4M on 1 January 2011. Homer Limited has identifiable net assets of €2.8M at the acquisition date, which included:

- bank balance €300,000
- plant and equipment €2.1M
- inventory €400,000

Required:
Outline how the acquisition of Homer Limited will be recorded in the consolidated statement of cash flows of Marge Limited.

Solution

Consolidated statement of cash flows of Marge Limited for the year ended
31 December 2010 (extract)

	€'000
Cash flow from investing activities	
Purchase of subsidiary*	(3,700)
Net decrease in cash and cash equivalents†	(xxxx)

* Cash paid of €4M less Homer's bank balance of €300,000.
† The acquisition of Homer will decrease the cash and cash equivalents of the Marge Group by €3.7M.

One must be careful to avoid double-counting when calculating the change in the group's assets and liabilities for the period. For example, when computing the amount of plant and equipment purchased, €2.1M must be deducted from plant and machinery in the consolidated SOFP at 31 December 2010, so as to cancel the effect of the acquisition of Homer. Similarly, group inventory at 31 December 2010 should exclude inventory of €400,000 obtained through the acquisition of Homer.

Non-controlling interests

Dividends paid to non-controlling interests are external to the group, and these dividends will be included as a *financing* cash flow or as an *operating* cash flow.

Example 2 Bash Limited acquired 75% of Street Limited on 1 February 2010, when the fair value of the identifiable net assets of Street Limited was €3.6M. Bash Limited's reporting period ends on 31 December, and non-controlling interests are measured (at acquisition) at their proportionate share of identifiable net assets.

The following information is available from the consolidated statement of financial position of Bash:

- non-controlling interests at 1 January 2010 were €5.2M
- non-controlling interests at 31 December 2010 were €7M.

Total comprehensive income attributable to non-controlling interests for the year ended 31 December 2011 was €1.6M.

Dividends paid to non-controlling interests are computed as follows:

	€'000
Non-controlling interests at 1 January 2010	5,200
Non-controlling interest in profits for 2010	1,600
Increase in non-controlling interests arising from the acquisition of Street Limited (€3.6M × 25%)	900
Dividends paid to non-controlling interests	(700) Balancing figure
Non-controlling interests at 31 December 2010	7,000

Impairment of goodwill

The impairment of goodwill is not a cash flow. Therefore, in the statement of cash flows, any impairment of goodwill during the current period should be added back to profit before taxation, when computing *cash generated from operations*.

Investments which are equity-accounted

IAS 28 requires that associates are accounted for using the equity method. IAS 31 requires that joint ventures be accounted for using either the equity method or proportional consolidation.

Only **dividends** received from investments that are equity-accounted should be included in the consolidated statement of cash flows. These dividends should be included under *cash flows from investing activities*.

Example 3   On 1 January 2010, Call Limited purchased 25% of the equity share capital of Centre Limited for €1.5M. Call has the power to appoint two directors to the board, and exercises significant influence over Centre.

Centre Limited earned profit of €600,000 for the year ended 31 December 2010, net of income tax. At 31 December 2010, the investment in Centre is included in the consolidated SOFP of the Call Group at €1.6M.

Required:

Outline how Centre Limited should be included in the consolidated statement of cash flows of the Call Group.

Solution   Centre Limited is an associate of Call Limited. Any dividends received from Centre should be included under *cash flows from investing activities* in the consolidated statement of cash flows of the Call Group. Dividends received can be computed as follows:

	€'000
Investment in associate at 1 January 2010	1,500
Share of profit for the year (600,000 × 25%)	150
Dividend received	(50) Balancing figure
Investment in associate at 31 December 2010	1,600

Disposal of a subsidiary during the period

When a parent disposes of a subsidiary, the proceeds of disposal (net of cash and cash equivalents held by the subsidiary at the disposal date) are shown as a cash inflow under *cash flows from investing activities* in the consolidated statement of cash flows. Thus, the effect of the disposal is the opposite of that of an acquisition.

In the case of a disposal, it is also necessary to eliminate the profit or loss on disposal when computing *cash generated from operations*.

Example 4   On 1 January 2009, P Limited purchased 100% of the ordinary shares of S Limited. Goodwill arising on acquisition amounted to €100,000. On 31 December 2010, P Limited disposed of its entire shareholding in S Limited for cash consideration of €2.5M. The carrying value of the identifiable net assets of S Limited in the consolidated SOFP at the date of disposal was €2.1M, which included a bank balance of €250,000 and plant and equipment of €1.4M.

Required:

Outline how the disposal of S Limited should be recorded in the consolidated statement of cash flows of P Limited.

Solution   The proceeds of disposal (€2.5M), less S Limited's bank balance at the date of disposal (€250,000) will be recorded as a cash inflow of €2.25M under *cash flows from investing activities* in the consolidated statement of cash flows of P Limited.

The profit on disposal of €300,000 (i.e. €2.5M – net assets of €2.1M – goodwill of €100,000) will be deducted from profit before tax when computing *cash generated from operations*.

**Consolidated statement of cash flows of P Limited for the year ended
31 December 2010 (extract)**

	€'000
Cash flow from investing activities	
Sale of subsidiary*	2,250
Net increase in cash and cash equivalents†	(xxxx)

* Cash received of €2.5M, less S Limited's bank balance of €250,000 at date of disposal.
† The sale of S will increase cash and cash equivalents of the P Group by €2.25M.

When calculating the change in the group's assets and liabilities for the period, one must be careful to avoid double-counting. For example, when computing the amount of plant and equipment purchased during the period, €1.4M must be added to the group balance at 31 December 2010, so as to adjust for the effect of plant & equipment lost because of the sale of S.

If, in Example 4 above, consideration for the sale of S Limited was received entirely in equity shares (instead of cash), then the result in the consolidated statement of cash flows of P would be as follows:

	€'000
Cash flow from investing activities	
Sale of subsidiary‡	(250)

‡ No cash or cash equivalents are received as consideration by P Limited when S Limited is sold. However, the €250,000 bank balance of S at the time of disposal is lost when S is sold. Therefore, the sale of S results in a net cash outflow of €250,000.

Summary

This chapter has examined the consolidated statement of cash flows. It has focused on the following areas, which relate specifically to the financial statements of a group:

- acquisition of a subsidiary during the period;
- non-controlling interests;
- impairment of goodwill;
- investments that are equity-accounted;
- disposal of a subsidiary during the period.

QUESTIONS

29.1 CAPE plc

CAPE plc ('CAPE') prepares its financial statements to 31 December each year.

During 2010 CAPE purchased 75% of the ordinary share capital of BONNET Limited for €90,000 in cash. The fair value of the net assets of BONNET at the date of acquisition was:

	€'000
Plant and equipment	80
Inventory	15
Trade receivables	15
Bank and cash	2
Trade payables	(32)
Net assets	80

Extracts from the group's consolidated financial statements are shown below.

Cape plc
Consolidated statement of comprehensive income for the year ended 31 December 2010

	Notes	2010 €'000	2009 €'000
Revenue		3,600	3,200
Cost of sales		(2,700)	(2,400)
Gross profit		900	800
Administrative expenses	(1)	(300)	(250)
Finance charges		(60)	(50)
Share of profit of associate		75	60
Profit before tax		615	560
Income tax expense		(150)	(140)
Profit for the year		465	420
Attributable to:			
Owners of the parent		372	336
Non-controlling interests		93	84
		465	420

Cape plc
Consolidated statement of financial position at 31 December 2010

	Notes	2010 €'000	2009 €'000
Assets			
Non-current assets			
Property	(1)	–	100
Plant and equipment	(2)	360	320
Goodwill	(3)	30	20
Investment in associate		120	45
		510	485
Current assets			
Inventory		200	170
Trade receivables		250	220
Bank and cash		30	25
		990	900

	Notes	2010 €'000	2009 €'000
Equity and liabilities			
Ordinary share capital		100	100
Revaluation reserves		–	45
Retained earnings		510	190
		610	335
Non-controlling interests		90	110
		700	445
Non-current liabilities			
Obligations under finance leases		100	80
Current liabilities			
Trade payables		40	215
Taxation		100	120
Obligations under finance leases		50	40
		990	900

Additional information:

(1) Included in administrative expenses for the year ended 31 December 2010 is a gain of €50,000 arising from the sale of the property during the year. The property had been revalued some years previously, with the surplus being credited to revaluation reserves. It is group policy to charge a full year's depreciation in the year of acquisition and none in the year of disposal.

(2) During the year ended 31 December 2010, CAPE entered into new finance lease agreements in respect of all the plant and equipment additions for the year. The amount financed by way of the leases amounted to €75,000.

(3) During 2010, dividends of €97,000 were paid to the shareholders of CAPE.

Required:

Prepare the consolidated statement of cash flows of CAPE plc for the year ended 31 December 2010.

(Chartered Accountants Ireland)

Part 8

MISCELLANEOUS ACCOUNTING ISSUES

Chapter 30

Events after the reporting period

Important events sometimes occur between the end of an entity's **reporting period** and the date on which its **financial statements** are authorised for issue. These are known as *events after the reporting period.* The question that arises is whether the financial statements of the previous period should be adjusted, or whether details of such events should merely be disclosed in the notes.

Adjusting events

These are events after the reporting period that provide further evidence of conditions that existed at the end of the reporting period. This includes an event which indicates that the **going concern** assumption in relation to the whole or part of the enterprise is not appropriate. Financial statements should be adjusted for **adjusting events**.

In the following examples, it should be assumed that Bailey Limited has prepared its financial statements for the year ended 31 December 2010, and that they are authorised for issue on 10 March 2011.

Example 1 **Settlement of a court case that confirms the entity had a present obligation at the end of the reporting period**

A director of Bailey Limited was dismissed in November 2010, and instituted court proceedings against the company in December 2010. At 31 December 2010, provision was made for an amount of €200,000 in respect of the former director's claim. In February 2011, the case was settled out of court, the director being awarded €350,000, including costs. This amount was paid in April 2011.

The out-of-court settlement provides further evidence of conditions existing at the end of the reporting period. Consequently, the settlement is an adjusting event after the reporting period. An additional amount of €150,000 should be provided at 31 December 2010.

	Dr €'000	Cr €'000
Redundancy settlement – I/S	150	
Trade and other payables – SOFP		150
(Being increase in provision for redundancy settlement at 31 December 2010)		

Example 2 **Bankruptcy of a customer after the reporting period**

A customer who owed €100,000 to Bailey Limited at 31 December 2010, was declared bankrupt in January 2011.

The bankruptcy of the customer in January 2011 is indicative that a loss existed at 31 December 2010. Thus, trade receivables at 31 December 2010 must be adjusted as follows:

	Dr €'000	Cr €'000
Bad debts – I/S	100	
Trade receivables		100
(Being the write-off of a debt at 31 December 2010, as an adjusting event after the reporting period)		

Example 3 | **Sale of inventories after the reporting period**

Inventories of Bailey Limited, which had a carrying value of €300,000 at 31 December 2010, were disposed of in February 2011 for €180,000.

The sale of the inventories in February 2011 provides evidence of their net realisable value at 31 December 2010. The sale constitutes an adjusting event after the reporting period.

	Dr €'000	Cr €'000
Cost of sales	120	
Inventory – SOFP		120
(Being reduction in value of inventory to its net realisable value at 31 December 2010)		

Example 4 | **The determination after the reporting period of the proceeds from assets sold**

In December 2010, Bailey Limited sold a subsidiary undertaking which it had owned for several years. The consideration was agreed as being at least €3M, and to be no greater than €4M, the price being ultimately determined by the profits of the subsidiary for the year ended 31 December 2010. Profits of the subsidiary, determined in late January 2011, were in line with expectations and the final consideration was settled as €3.5M.

In preparing its financial statements for the year ended 31 December 2010, the finalisation of the disposal price of the subsidiary will be an adjusting event after the reporting period. The disposal proceeds of the subsidiary, as recorded in the 2010 financial statements, will be €3.5M.

Example 5 | **The discovery of an error which shows that the financial statements are incorrect**

In January 2011, Bailey Limited discovered that an invoice from a supplier for €300,000 had been recorded in error as €30,000 in December 2010.

The discovery of this error is an adjusting event after the reporting period, and the following adjustment will be made in the 2010 financial statements:

	Dr €'000	Cr €'000
Cost of sales	270	
Trade payables		270
(Being correction of understatement of trade payables)		

Non-adjusting events

These are events that are indicative of conditions that arose *after* the reporting period. An entity should *not* adjust its financial statements for **non-adjusting events** after the reporting period.

An entity must disclose the following for each material category of non-adjusting events:

- the nature of the event; and
- an estimate of its financial effect, or a statement that such an estimate cannot be made.

■ Non-adjusting events that would generally result in disclosure

- A major business combination after the reporting period
- Announcing a plan to discontinue an operation
- Major purchases of **assets**
- Classification of assets as held for sale
- Major disposals of assets
- Destruction of a major production plant by fire after the reporting period
- Announcing, or commencing, the implementation of a major restructuring
- Abnormally large changes after the reporting period in asset prices or foreign exchange rates
- Entering into significant commitments or **contingent liabilities**, for example by issuing significant guarantees.

Example 6   **Decline in market value of investments after the reporting period**

Bailey Limited had non-current asset investments at 31 December 2010, which were included in the statement of financial position at a valuation of €560,000. The investments fell in value after the year end, and were valued at €350,000 on 12 March 2011, when the company's financial statements were authorised for issue.

The change in value of the investments is a non-adjusting event after the reporting period. Bailey Ltd should continue to value the investments at €560,000 in its SOFP at 31 December 2010. Details of the fall in value of the investments should be disclosed if it is considered material.

Example 7   **Dividends**

In January 2011, the board of directors of Bailey Limited declared a dividend of 5 cents per share in respect of the year ending 31 December 2010.

The declaration of a dividend after the reporting period is a non-adjusting event after the reporting period. Thus, no record of this dividend will appear in the financial statements of Bailey Limited for the year ending 31 December 2010.

Going concern

An entity shall *not* prepare its financial statements on a going concern basis if management determines after the reporting period either that:

- it intends to liquidate the entity or cease trading; or
- it has no realistic alternative but to do so.

Disclosures

- Date when the financial statements were *authorised for issue* and who gave that authorisation.

- If the entity's owners or others have the *power to amend* the financial statements after issue, the entity shall disclose that fact.
- For non-adjusting events, an entity should disclose the nature of the event, and an estimate of its financial effect or a statement that such an estimate cannot be made.
- Information received after the reporting period about conditions that existed at the end of the reporting period.

Summary

- Events after the reporting period are those events that occur between the end of the reporting period and the date when the financial statements are authorised for issue.
- The financial statements should be adjusted when these events provide further evidence of conditions that existed at the end of the reporting period.
- The financial statements should not be prepared on a going concern basis if management determines after the reporting period either that it intends to liquidate the entity or to cease trading, or that it has no realistic alternative but to do so.
- Non-adjusting events are events that are indicative of conditions that arose after the end of the reporting period. The financial statements should *not* be adjusted.

QUESTIONS

30.1 OSCAR

On 23 January 2011, OSCAR entered into a contract with PETERSON Ltd for the sale of OSCAR's administrative offices for €20M. The offices were recorded in the company's balance sheet at 31 December 2010 at €15M. Under the terms of the contract, OSCAR will lease back the offices for a period of 20 years at an open market rental. The directors intend to use the proceeds to expand overseas.

Required:
Explain how this transaction should be treated in OSCAR's 2010 financial statements.

30.2 ELECTRON

ELECTRON has a good relationship with its shareholders and employees. It has adopted a strategy of gradually increasing its dividend payments over the years. On 1 August 2010, the board proposed a dividend of 5 cents per share for the year ended 30 June 2010. The shareholders will approve the dividend along with the financial statements at the general meeting on 1 September 2010 and the dividend will be paid on 14 September 2010. The directors feel that the dividend should be accrued in the financial statements for the year ended 30 June 2010 as a 'valid expectation' has been created.

Required:
Outline how the dividend should be treated by ELECTRON in its financial statements for the year ended 30 June 2010.

30.3 HILMINE Limited

The accounting year end for HILMINE Ltd is 31 May 2010. The following matters need to be considered before the financial statements for the year ended 31 May 2010 can be finalised:

(i) The company is currently suing one of its suppliers for failure to supply goods according to contract. Legal advice suggests that HILMINE Ltd will probably win the case and will be awarded damages to the amount of €2M.

(ii)   The company operates an opencast mine and is legally obliged to restore the environment when mine workings are complete. This is expected to occur in 12 years' time. The estimated cost of rectifying the environmental damage caused so far is €6M. The estimated total cost of rectifying the damage caused until mine workings are complete is €25M.

(iii) On 24 May 2010 HILMINE Ltd decided to close down one of its mines. This would involve redundancy payments of €750,000. At 31 May 2010, the decision has not been announced and has not yet been acted upon.

Required:

Explain how these matters should be dealt with in the financial statements of HILMINE Ltd for the year ended 31 May 2010.

30.4 TRADING Limited

The following events occurred after 31 December 2010 but before the financial statements for TRADING Ltd for the year end 31 December 2010 were authorised for issue:

(i)   The company made a takeover bid for another company.

(ii)   It was discovered that a motor vehicle shown as an asset in the statement of financial position at 31 December 2010 had been stolen on 10 January 2011.

(iii) The company made a major investment in land and buildings.

(iv)   The company announced a major restructuring plan.

Required:

Classify each of the above events as adjusting or non-adjusting, and explain how each should be dealt with in TRADING Ltd's financial statements for the year ended 31 December 2010. It may be assumed that all the events are considered material.

30.5 BRANCH plc

(a) What is the difference between an 'adjusting event' and a 'non-adjusting event' under IAS 10 *Events after the Reporting Period*?

(b) BRANCH plc provisionally drew up its accounts for the year ending 31 December 2010 as follows:

**Draft statement of comprehensive income for the year ended
31 December 2010 (summarised)**

	€'000
Profit before tax	824
Income tax expense	208
Profit for the year	616

Draft statement of financial position at 31 December 2010

	€'000	€'000
Non-current assets		7,312
Current assets	2,212	
Creditors falling due within one year	2,088	
Net current assets		124
Total assets less current liabilities		7,436
Creditors falling due after more than one year		640
Net assets		**6,796**
Capital and reserves		
Called-up share capital		3,400
Share premium		2,596
Retained earnings		800
Total equity		**6,796**

Before the accounts were authorised for issue by the directors of BRANCH plc the following items were discovered:

(i) Included in non-current assets are two properties, A and B, with written-down values of €120,000 and €160,000 respectively. Property A was sold on 17 December 2010 at a price to be determined by an independent valuer. On 9 January 2011 the price was agreed at €138,000. Property B was subsequently sold on 4 January 2011 at a price of €126,000.

(ii) Items of inventory included in current assets at €40,000 at 31 December 2010 were sold on 2 January 2011 for €37,000.

(iii) Other items of inventory valued at €20,000 were sold on 10 January 2011 for €34,000 to a customer who subsequently went into liquidation on 19 January 2011. It was noted that as at 31 December 2010 this customer owed BRANCH plc €23,000.

(iv) On 2 January 2011, a fire occurred at one of the company's warehouses, and inventory included in the statement of financial position at 31 December 2010 at €90,000 was severely damaged.

(v) On 11 March 2011, 300 employees of the 400-strong workforce took strike action. The strike is anticipated to be of a short-term nature.

Required:
You are required to redraft the summarised financial statements of BRANCH plc, taking account of the above items. You may assume that tax on ordinary activities remains unchanged in the redrafted accounts.

30.6 TENTACLE

The following material information has arisen since the reporting date, but prior to the financial statements of TENTACLE for the year ended 31 March 2011 being authorised for issue:

(i) The notification of bankruptcy of a customer. The balance of the trade receivable due at 31 March 2011 was €23,000 and at the date of the notification it was €25,000. No payment is expected from the bankruptcy proceedings.

(ii) Sales of some items of product W32 were made at a price of €5.40 each in April and May 2011. Sales staff received a commission of 15% of the sales price on this product. At 31 March 2011, TENTACLE had 12,000 units of product W32 in inventory included at cost of €6 each.

(iii) TENTACLE is being sued by an employee who lost a limb in an accident while at work on 15 March 2011. The company is contesting the claim as the employee was not following the safety procedures that he had been instructed to use. Accordingly the financial statements contain a note of contingent liability of €500,000 for personal injury damages. In a recently decided case where a similar injury was sustained, a settlement figure of €750,000 was awarded by the court. Although the injury was similar, the circumstances of the accident in the decided case are different from those of TENTACLE's case.

(iv) TENTACLE is involved in the construction of a residential apartment building. It is being accounted for using the percentage of completion basis in IAS 11 *Construction Contracts.* The recognised profit at 31 March 2011 was €1.2M based on costs to date of €3M as a percentage of the total estimated costs of €6M. Early in May 2011, TENTACLE was informed that due to very recent industry shortages, building materials will cost €1.5M more than the estimate of total cost used in the calculation of percentage of completion. TENTACLE cannot pass on any additional costs to the customer.

Required:
State and quantify how items (i)–(iv) above should be treated when finalising the financial statements of TENTACLE for the year ended 31 March 2011. (ACCA)

Chapter 31

Leases

A lease is a contract which involves the user of an **asset** (i.e. the lessee) paying its owner (i.e. the lessor) in return for the use of the asset. The principal accounting issue that arises is whether the asset should be recognised in the **statement of financial position** of the lessee.

Guidance is provided by the IASB *Framework*, which states that an asset should be recognised when:

- it is probable that the future economic benefits will flow to the entity; and
- the asset has a cost or value that can be measured reliably.

The *Framework* also stipulates that transactions should be accounted for and presented in accordance with their substance and economic reality and not just their legal form.

Thus, when a lessee is expected to obtain the future economic benefits from an asset, even though *not* its legal owner, the lessee should recognise the asset and the related liability in its statement of financial position.

This is arguably the best-known example of the application of *substance over form*. This principle requires that the accounting treatment of a transaction should reflect its commercial reality rather than follow the strict legal interpretation. Thus, when a lessee obtains the de facto, but not the legal ownership of an asset, for accounting purposes the asset is regarded as being owned by the lessee.

The rules for accounting for leases are contained in IAS 17 *Leases*.

Key definitions and classification of leases per IAS 17

■ Finance lease

A **finance lease** is a lease that transfers substantially all the risks and rewards of ownership of an asset to the lessee. Title may or may not eventually pass. A finance lease typically involves a financial institution (the lessor), purchasing an asset which it then leases to another entity (the lessee). This is illustrated in Figure 31.1, which shows

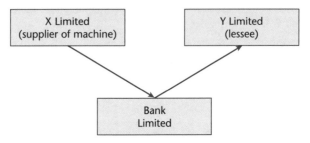

Figure 31.1 **Finance lease**

Accounting by lessees

a machine purchased by Bank Limited from X Limited. The machine is then leased to Y Limited.

See Appendix 31.1 for further details of finance leases.

Example 1 On 1 January 2010, Bank Limited leased a machine to Bridge Limited. Under the terms of the agreement, Bridge will make three annual lease payments of €40,000, followed by six annual payments of €1. The fair value of the machine at 1 January 2010 was €100,000, and it had an estimated useful life of five years. Residual value is zero.

How should this lease be classified in the financial statements of Bridge Limited?

Solution The lease term is for a total period of nine years, which exceeds the asset's expected useful life of five years. During the secondary lease term of six years, Bridge Limited will make only nominal annual payments of €1. It should also be noted that Bridge's payments will be the only return that Bank Limited will make, and that the residual value of the machine is zero.

Thus, although legal title to the asset does not pass to the lessee, Bridge Limited is, **in substance**, the owner of this machine. Therefore, the agreement should be classified as a finance lease.

■ Operating lease

An **operating lease** is a lease other than a finance lease.

Example 2 On 1 January 2010, Grange Autos Limited leased a new car to Morse Limited for a period of six months.

In this case, the duration of the lease agreement is substantially less than the useful life of the asset. The amount that Grange Autos receives from Morse will be substantially less than the fair value of the car. Thus, as Grange Autos Limited retains effective ownership of the asset, the lease is classified as an operating lease.

■ Land and buildings

In classifying a lease of land and buildings, the minimum lease payments should be allocated between land and buildings in proportion to their relative fair values:

- **Land** is normally classified as an **operating** lease, unless title passes to the lessee at the end of the lease term.
- **Buildings** are classified as a finance lease *or* an operating lease, by applying the classification criteria of IAS 17.

Accounting by lessees

■ Finance leases

At the inception of the lease, a finance lease should be recorded as an asset and a liability, at the lower of:

- the **fair value** of the asset, and
- the **present value** (PV) of the minimum lease payments

321

Example 3 On 1 January 2010, X Limited leased a machine from Bank Limited on the following terms:

	€
Cash cost	130,000
Lease interest	20,000
	150,000

The primary lease term is for three years, with annual lease instalments of €50,000 payable in advance. X Limited can continue to lease the machine for a secondary period of three years for an annual rental of €1. The PV of the minimum lease payments is €130,000.

The machine has an estimated useful life of five years and a zero residual value. X Limited incurred professional advisory fees of €2,000 in arranging the lease agreement.

Outline how this lease agreement should be recorded in the financial statements of X Limited. Interest should be computed on an actuarial basis.

Solution The lease term runs for the full economic life of the machine, and the PV of the minimum lease payments amounts to all of the fair value of the leased asset. Thus, it is clear that, in substance, X Limited is the owner of the machine, and that this is a finance lease which should be recorded in the books of X Ltd as follows:

	Dr	Cr
	€	€
Machinery*	132,000	
Deferred interest[†] – SOFP	20,000	
Lease obligation[‡] – SOFP		150,000
Bank		2,000
(Being initial record of finance lease)		

In the SOFP of X Limited, the lease obligation should be shown as a liability of €130,000 (€150,000 – €20,000). It should *not* be offset against the leased asset.

* **Machinery** held under a finance lease should be depreciated using the same policy as for owned machinery. If there is no reasonable certainty that the lessee will obtain ownership at the end of the lease, then the asset should be depreciated over the shorter of the lease term or the life of the asset. Any initial direct costs of the lessee (e.g. professional advisory fees) are added to the amount recognised as an asset.
[†] **Deferred interest** is the amount of future interest outstanding. This will be charged as an expense in the lessee's income statement over the term of the lease agreement. At each reporting date, the remaining deferred interest is offset against the lease obligation, in order to identify the amount of **capital** outstanding on the lease. Capital outstanding is recognised as a liability in the lessee's SOFP, and split into its current and non-current portions.
[‡] Payments on a finance lease should be apportioned between the finance charge and the reduction of outstanding capital. The finance charge should be allocated so as to produce a constant periodic rate of interest on the remaining balance of the liability.

Journal entries

Assuming that X Ltd depreciates machinery at 20% on a straight-line basis, it will make the following entries for 2010 in respect of the lease agreement:

	Dr	Cr
	€	€
Depreciation expense – I/S	26,400	
Accumulated depreciation		26,400
(Being depreciation of machine at 20% per annum on a straight-line basis)		

	Dr €	Cr €
Lease interest – I/S **(see Appendix 31.2)**	13,000	
Deferred interest – SOFP		13,000
(Being lease interest charge for 2010)		
Lease obligation – SOFP	50,000	
Bank		50,000
(Being lease payments in 2010)		

**Extract from statement of comprehensive income for the year ended
31 December 2010**

	€
Depreciation	26,400
Finance charge	13,000

Extract from statement of financial position at 31 December 2010

Non-current assets	
Cost	132,000
Accumulated depreciation	(26,400)
Net book value	105,600
Non-current liabilities	
Finance lease	43,000
Current liabilities	
Finance lease	37,000
Accruals*	13,000

* Lease interest accrued at 31 December 2010.

■ Operating leases

Operating lease payments should normally be recognised as an expense in the lessee's income statement, on a straight-line basis over the lease term.

Example 4   On 1 January 2010, Short Limited leased a building for two years from Rich Limited, at a rental of €25,000 per annum, payable in advance.

This is an operating lease. Therefore, neither the asset nor the lease liability will be recorded by Short Limited. The following entry will be made in 2010:

	Dr €'000	Cr €'000
Lease charges – I/S	25	
Bank/trade payables		25
(Being lease rental for 2010)		

■ Sale and leaseback transactions

This involves an entity selling a valuable asset (e.g. a building in a prime location), which it then leases back from the purchaser. Typically, the purchaser would be a financial institution, such as a bank or an insurance company.

(i) Where the sale and leaseback transaction results in a finance lease

Any excess of the sales proceeds over the carrying amount of the asset is deferred and **amortised** over the lease term.

Example 5 | R Limited transferred the ownership of its office buildings to an insurance company in a sale and leaseback agreement. The premises had cost R Limited €300,000 several years ago, and had been revalued to €500,000 in its last financial statements. The proceeds of sale were €750,000, and the premises had been leased back to R Limited for substantially all of its entire useful life.

Accounting treatment in books of R Ltd:

	Dr €'000	Cr €'000
Bank	750	
Buildings		500
Deferred income – SOFP		250
Revaluation surplus	200	
Retained earnings		200
(Being transfer of unrealised surplus to realised reserves)		

The deferred income of €250,000 should be recorded as income by R Limited over the lease term. The building will now be brought back into R Limited's SOFP, as in Example 3 above.

(ii) Where the sale and leaseback transaction results in an operating lease

If it is clear that the transaction is carried out at fair value, any profit or loss on sale should be recognised immediately.

Assuming that Example 5 above were to result in an *operating* lease, the following entries would be recorded in the books of R Limited:

	Dr €'000	Cr €'000
Bank	750	
Buildings		500
Gain on disposal of building – I/S		250
Revaluation surplus	200	
Retained earnings		200

If the sale price is less than fair value the profit or loss should be recognised immediately, except that if a loss is compensated for by future rentals at below market price, it should be amortised over the period of use.

If the sale price is above fair value, the excess should be deferred and amortised over the period of use; and if the fair value at the time of the transaction is less than the carrying amount, a loss equal to the difference should be recognised immediately.

Accounting by lessors

Finance leases

At the commencement of the lease term, the lessor should record the lease in its SOFP as a receivable, at an amount equal to the net investment in the lease.

The lessor should recognise finance income based on a pattern reflecting a constant periodic rate of return on the lessor's net investment outstanding in respect of the finance lease.

Example 6   On 1 January 2010, Bank Limited leased a machine to X Limited on the following terms:

	€
Cash cost	130,000
Lease interest	20,000
	150,000

The primary lease term is for three years, with annual lease instalments of €50,000 payable in advance. X Limited can continue to lease the machine for a secondary period of three years for an annual rental of €1.

On 1 January 2010, Bank Limited's net investment in the lease amounted to €130,000. This is a finance lease, and it should be recorded in the books of Bank Ltd as follows:

	Dr	Cr
	€	€
Lease payments receivable – asset SOFP	150,000	
Bank		130,000
Deferred income – SOFP		20,000
(Being initial entry for finance lease in the books of Bank Ltd)		

Note that only the **capital** component of lease payments receivable of €130,000 (€150,000 – €20,000) will be shown as an asset in the SOFP of Bank Ltd at the inception of the lease.

The following entries will be recorded in 2010:

	Dr	Cr
	€	€
Bank	50,000	
Lease payments receivable – SOFP		50,000
(Being lease payments received in 2010)		
Deferred income – SOFP	13,000	
Lease income – I/S		13,000
(Being lease income included in income statement in 2010 – see Appendix 31.2)		

Extract from the statement of comprehensive income of Bank Limited for the year ended 31 December 2010

	€
Lease income	13,000

Extract from the statement of financial position of Bank Limited at 31 December 2010

Current assets

Lease payments receivable*	93,000

* Lease payments receivable at 31 December 2010 = future lease payments outstanding (i.e. €100,000) less interest content (i.e. €7,000 – see Appendix 31.2).

Manufacturers or dealer lessors

Some companies both lease and sell the same type of asset. For example, General Motors have in the past sold and leased the cars which they manufacture.

For **finance leases**, this type of lessor should include selling profit or loss in the same period as it would for an outright sale.

Example 7 IBM leases a computer, for its entire useful life, to Rocket Limited, on the following basis:

- five annual lease payments of €1,000 in arrears;
- IBM's cost of producing the computer is €2,500;
- IBM's normal cash selling price is €4,000.

At its inception, this finance lease will be recorded in IBM's financial statements as follows:

	Dr €	Cr €
Lease payments receivable – SOFP*	5,000	
Revenue – I/S		4,000
Deferred income – SOFP*		1,000
Cost of sales	2,500	
Inventory – SOFP		2,500

* These amounts will be offset, to give a net lease payments receivable asset in the SOFP of €4,000.

■ Operating leases

Assets held for **operating leases** should be presented in the statement of financial position of a **lessor** according to the nature of the asset.

Lease income should normally be recognised over the lease term on a straight-line basis.

Example 8 On 1 January 2010, Rich Limited purchased a building for €600,000, which it immediately leased to Short Limited for two years, at a rental of €25,000 per annum, payable in advance.

	Dr €	Cr €
Building	600,000	
Bank		600,000
(Being purchase of building by Rich Limited on 1 January 2010)		
Bank/receivables	25,000	
Lease income – I/S		25,000
(Being lease income on operating lease for 2010)		

Disclosure

By lessees

(i) Finance leases

- Carrying amount for each class of asset at the end of the reporting period
- Reconciliation between total minimum lease payments and their present value for:
  - the next year
  - years 2–5 inclusive
  - later than five years
- Contingent rents recognised as an expense
- A general description of the lessee's material leasing arrangements.

(ii) Operating leases

- Total of minimum lease payments under non-cancellable operating leases for:
  - the next year
  - years 2–5 inclusive
  - later than five years
- a general description of the lessee's significant leasing arrangements.

By lessors

(i) Finance leases

- A reconciliation between the gross investment in the lease at the end of the reporting period and the PV of minimum lease payments
- Gross investment in the lease and the PV of minimum lease payments receivable at the end of the reporting period for:
  - the next year
  - years 2 to 5 inclusive
  - later than five years
- Unearned finance income
- Unguaranteed residual values
- Accumulated allowance for uncollectible minimum lease payments receivable
- A general description of the lessor's material leasing arrangements.

(ii) Operating leases

- Minimum lease payments under non-cancellable operating leases in aggregate and for:
  - the next year
  - years 2–5 inclusive
  - later than five years
- A general description of the lessor's material leasing arrangements.

New standard on leasing

A new standard on leasing is due to be published during 2011. It is expected that this will result in a new single approach to accounting for leases. This will effectively eliminate the concept of an operating lease, and mean that all leased assets will have to appear in the statement of financial position of a lessee. This is likely to have a significant impact on those sectors which make extensive use of operating leases (e.g. the airline industry).

It is intended that the new standard will apply to lease contracts on a retrospective basis. Therefore, existing lease contracts will be affected. However, the new standard is not expected to be effective for several years, thus allowing companies with significant levels of operating leases to adapt to the change.

Summary

- A *finance lease* is a lease that transfers substantially all the risks and rewards of ownership of an asset to the lessee. A finance lease should be recorded as an asset and a liability in the financial statements of a lessee. The leased asset should be replaced by an amount receivable in the statement of financial position of the lessor.
- An *operating lease* is a lease other than a finance lease. The leased asset should remain in the statement of financial position of the lessor. Annual lease instalments should be recorded as income by the lessor and as an expense by the lessee.
- A new leasing standard to be published in 2011 is expected to eliminate the concept of an operating lease, resulting in all leased assets being included in the statement of financial position of a lessee.
- The accounting treatment of a sale and leaseback transaction depends on whether the agreement is a finance lease or an operating lease.

Appendix 31.1

Classification of a lease as a finance lease

1. **Situations that would normally lead to a lease being classified as a finance lease include the following:**

   - the lease transfers ownership of the asset to the lessee by the end of the lease term;
   - the lessee has the option to purchase the asset at a price which, at the inception of the lease, makes it reasonably certain that the option will be exercised;
   - the lease term is for the major part of the economic life of the asset;
   - at the inception of the lease, the PV of the minimum lease payments amounts to at least substantially all of the fair value of the leased asset;
   - the leased assets are of a specialised nature, such that only the lessee can use them without major modifications.

2. **Other situations which might also lead to classification as a finance lease are:**

   - if the lessee is entitled to cancel the lease, the lessor's losses associated with the cancellation are borne by the lessee;
   - gains or losses from fluctuations in the residual value of the asset fall to the lessee;
   - the lessee has the ability to continue to lease the asset for a secondary period, at a price that is substantially lower than market rent.

Appendix 31.2

Allocation of lease payments between capital and interest in Examples 3 and 6

(i) Actuarial method

IAS 17 requires that lease interest should be allocated to each period during the lease term, so as to produce a constant periodic rate of interest on the remaining balance of the liability. This is called the actuarial method, and it is used in this solution.

To apply the actuarial method in Example 3, we first compute the discount rate that will make the lease payments (i.e. 50,000 × 3) equal to the fair value of the leased asset (i.e. 130,000).

$$€130,000 = 50,000 + \frac{50,000}{(1 + r)^1} + \frac{50,000}{(1 + r)^2}$$

As the lease payments are in advance, the first payment which is made at time zero has a PV factor of 1.

We solve for r, which equals 16.25% (approx). This is called the interest rate implicit in the lease. Each lease payment is then divided into:

- interest component (i.e. interest paid at beginning of period, which was accrued at end of previous period); and
- capital component, which is the lease payment made in the period less its interest content.

In Example 3:

Year end	Opening balance due	Capital repayment at beginning of period	Lease interest for period at 16.25%	Closing balance due
31.12.10	130,000	(50,000)*	13,000[†]	93,000
31.12.11	93,000	(37,000)[‡]	7,000[§]	43,000
31.12.12	43,000	(43,000)[¶]	Nil	Nil

* The first lease payment is made on 1 January 2010 (i.e. T_0), and this comprises 100% capital, as no interest has accrued at this date.
[†] Interest for 2010 = (130,000 − 50,000) × 16.25% = 13,000.
[‡] Capital repayment on 1 January 2011 = 50,000 − 13,000 (i.e. lease payment less interest accrued at end of 2010, paid on 1 January 2011).
[§] Interest for 2011 = (93,000 − 50,000) × 16.25% = 7,000 (rounded).
[¶] Capital repayment on 1 January 2012 = 50,000 − 7,000 (i.e. lease payment less interest accrued at end of 2011, paid on 1 January 2012).

Total capital repaid by 31 December 2012 = €130,000 (i.e. 50,000 + 37,000 + 43,000)
Total lease interest charged by 31 December 2012 = €20,000 (i.e. 13,000 + 7,000)

(ii) Sum of digits method

The sum of digits method provides a reasonable approximation of the actuarial method, and IAS 17 permits it to be used in practice. It involves the following procedure:

- Each lease payment is assigned a digit. Digit 1 is assigned to the last payment, digit 2 to the second-last payment and so on. If payments are made in advance, no digit is assigned to the last period as no capital is outstanding for the last period.
- The digits are added together to give the 'sum of digits'.
- The lease interest element of each payment is computed by dividing the total lease interest charge by the sum of the digits and multiplying by the digit assigned to that payment.

This can be applied to Example 3 above as follows.

The total number of lease payments in the primary lease period is 2 (the last payment is ignored as instalments are in advance). Therefore, the sum of digits is 3 (i.e. 2 + 1), and interest is computed as follows:

Lease interest for year ending 31 December 2010 = €20,000 × 2/3 = €13,333
Lease interest for year ending 31 December 2011 = €20,000 × 1/3 = €6,667

These figures are quite close to those computed under the actuarial method above.

QUESTIONS

31.1 CLARENCE Limited

CLARENCE Ltd ('CLARENCE') entered into a new finance lease agreement on 1 January 2010 for the purchase of a new machine. The terms of the agreement were as follows:

Cash price of machine	€340,000
Annual payments	€80,000 beginning on 1 January 2010
Lease term	5 years

Using the sum of digits, CLARENCE's obligation under the finance lease, net of future finance obligations, at 31 December 2010 is:

(a) €260,000
(b) €284,000
(c) €316,000
(d) €320,000

(Chartered Accountants Ireland)

31.2 FINO

On 1 April 2010, FINO increased the operating capacity of its plant. Due to a lack of liquid funds it was unable to buy the required plant which had a cost of €350,000. On the recommendation of the finance director, FINO entered into an agreement to lease the plant from the manufacturer. The lease required four annual payments in advance of €100,000, commencing on 1 April 2010. The plant would have a useful life of four years and would be scrapped at the end of this period. The finance director, believing the lease to be an operating lease, commented that the agreement would improve the company's return on capital employed (compared to outright purchase of the plant).

Required:

Discuss the validity of the finance director's comment and describe how IAS 17 *Leases* ensures that leases such as the above are faithfully represented in an entity's financial statements.   (ACCA)

31.3 New customer

HARRINGTON MOTORS has been approached by a local firm, SMITH MOTORS Ltd, which currently has an arrangement with one of HARRINGTON's competitors, in relation to its fleet of 30 company cars. The cars are currently traded in every three years, with a one-off payment being made at the date of trade-in for each car. The owner of the local firm has decided to consider alternative methods of financing his fleet, and would like to consider easing his cash-flow burden by means of contract hire.

In order to provide this service, HARRINGTON MOTORS would need to purchase 30 new cars from the relevant manufacturers and to trade these in every three years. However, the company believes that it should get a good deal on trade-ins due to its long-standing relationships with the relevant manufacturers.

The hire period would commence on 1 April 2010 and run for three years. The payment schedule would be as follows:

1 April 2010	€200,000
1 April 2011	€100,000
1 April 2012	€75,000

Required:

Advise HARRINGTON MOTORS as to the accounting treatment and disclosure of the cars held for rental under the proposed contract hire arrangement.   (Chartered Accountants Ireland)

31.4 Acquisition of industrial saw

On 1 January 2010 BENNETT acquired an industrial saw from AB FINANCE Ltd on a finance lease. The lease payments are €5,000 per annum for four years with an option to extend payments for a further two years at €500 per annum. The first payment was made upon delivery and subsequent payments are made annually in advance. The interest rate agreed for the lease is 12% per annum and the machine will have an estimated life of four years.

Required:

Outline the correct accounting treatment of the finance lease in the financial statements of BENNETT for the year ended 31 December 2010. Show the relevant extracts in the statement of comprehensive income and statement of financial position. Disclosure notes are *not* required.

(Chartered Accountants Ireland)

31.5 GRASMERE Limited

GRASMERE Limited prepares accounts to 31 March each year. On 1 April 2010, the company acquired an asset by means of a finance lease. The fair value of the asset on this date was €40,000 and the company was required to make six half-yearly lease payments of €7,674 each. The first payment was payable on 1 April 2010. The rate of interest implicit in the lease was 6% per half year. The asset has an estimated useful life of three years.

Calculate the total finance charge payable by GRASMERE Limited, and show how this is allocated over the lease term using:

(i)   The sum of digits method;
(ii) The actuarial method.

On the assumption that the actuarial method is used, show the impact of the finance lease on the financial statements of GRASMERE Ltd for the years ended 31 March 2011, 2012 and 2013.

31.6 DEF Ltd

DEF Ltd entered into a lease arrangement on 1 January 2010 with the following stipulations:

Cost of asset	€25,000
Estimated useful life	5 years
Lease term	5 years
Lease payments	€6,500 payable in advance
Interest rate implicit in the lease	15.2%

(a) You are required to show the necessary accounting treatment to record the details of this lease arrangement for the first three years.

(b) On 1 June 2010, DEF Ltd signed, as a tenant, an operating lease for a warehouse which it intends to use as a distribution point. However, the warehouse needed to be fitted out before it could be used. The monthly rental for the warehouse is €100,000, commencing 1 June 2010. The fitting out was completed on 1 December 2010, and the warehouse became operational on this date. The directors of DEF Ltd want to capitalise the rent paid during the six months' fitting-out period, together with the cost of fixtures and fittings.

Is the accounting treatment proposed by the directors of DEF Ltd acceptable?

Chapter 32

Revenue

Profit is frequently used as a measure of performance or as the basis for other measures, such as ROI or EPS. Profit is computed as income less expenses, the latter including such items as cost of sales, depreciation, and impairment losses.

Income encompasses revenue and gains, the distinction being that revenue arises in the course of the ordinary activities of an entity whereas gains do not. Thus, *gains*, which include items such as profit on disposal of non-current assets, are usually displayed separately in the income statement.

Revenue is the gross inflow of economic benefits arising from the ordinary activities of an enterprise. Gross, in this context, means before deducting expenses. Revenue should, however, be stated net of VAT that is payable.

The components of profit are outlined in Figure 32.1.

This chapter focuses on the recognition and measurement of revenue, which is dealt with in IAS 18 *Revenue*.

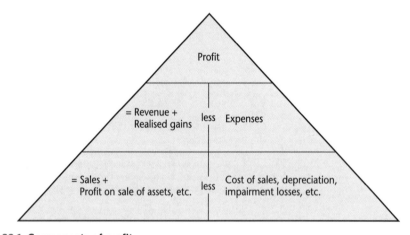

Figure 32.1 **Components of profit**

Scope

IAS 18 applies to revenue arising from the following:

- the sale of goods;
- the rendering of services; and
- the use by others of an entity's assets, yielding interest, royalties and **dividends**.

Measurement of revenue

Revenue should be measured at the **fair value** of the consideration receivable. An exchange for goods and services of a similar nature and value is not regarded as a transaction giving rise to revenue. However, an exchange for dissimilar goods and services is regarded as generating revenue.

If the inflow of cash or cash equivalents is deferred, discounting is appropriate. This would occur, for example, if a seller extends interest-free credit (beyond normal credit terms) to a buyer, or is charging interest at below the market rate.

See examples 1–4 in Appendix 32.1.

Categories of revenue

Sale of goods

Revenue arising from the sale of goods should be recognised when all of the following conditions have been satisfied:

- the seller has transferred to the buyer the significant risks and rewards of ownership;
- the seller retains neither continuing managerial involvement to the degree usually associated with ownership nor effective control over the goods sold;
- the amount of revenue can be measured reliably;
- it is probable that the economic benefits associated with the transaction will flow to the seller; and
- the costs incurred or to be incurred in respect of the transaction can be measured reliably.

See examples 5–8 in Appendix 32.1.

Rendering of services

Provided that all of the following conditions are met, revenue should be recognised by reference to the stage of completion of the transaction at the end of the reporting period (the percentage-of-completion method):

- the amount of revenue can be measured reliably;
- it is probable that the economic benefits will flow to the seller;
- the stage of completion at the end of the reporting period can be measured reliably; and
- the costs incurred, or to be incurred, in respect of the transaction can be measured reliably.

If the above criteria are *not* met, revenue arising from the rendering of services should be recognised only to the extent of the expenses recognised that are recoverable (a *cost-recovery approach*).

See examples 9–12 in Appendix 32.1.

Interest, royalties and dividends

Provided it is probable that the economic benefits will flow to the entity, and the amount of revenue can be measured reliably, revenue should be recognised as follows:

(i) *Interest.* Using the effective interest rate method as outlined in IAS 39 *Financial Instruments: Recognition and Measurement.*

(ii) *Royalties*. On an accrual basis in accordance with the substance of the relevant agreement.

(iii) *Dividends*. When the shareholder's right to receive payment is established.

See examples 13–15 in Appendix 32.1.

Customer loyalty programmes

Customer loyalty programmes are used to provide customers with incentives to buy an entity's goods and services. If a customer buys goods or services, the entity grants the customer award credits (often described as 'points').

IFRIC* Interpretation 13 requires that award credits be accounted for as a separately identifiable component of a sales transaction, and should be measured at their **fair value** (i.e. the amount for which they could be sold separately).

An entity should recognise the award credits as revenue when they are redeemed and the entity has fulfilled its obligations to supply the awards.

Example 1 Flyco Limited was established as a new airline in January 2010. During 2010, ticket sales amounted to €20M, all of which had been received in cash by the year end.

Flyco Limited operates a frequent flyer scheme, and customers receive a free flight when they have 100 points accumulated. At 31 December 2010, the fair value of customers' frequent flyer points outstanding was estimated at €400,000. Credits to the value of €60,000 had been redeemed by customers during 2010.

Outline how Flyco Limited should account for the frequent flyer scheme in its financial statements.

Solution Revenue recognised for 2010 should be stated net of the fair value of frequent flyer points which, at 31 December 2010, are yet to be redeemed by customers.

Thus, the following journal entry is required:

	Dr €'000	Cr €'000
Bank	20,000	
Revenue – I/S		19,600
Deferred income – SOFP		400
(Being ticket sales for the year ended 31 December 2010)		

Disclosure

An entity shall disclose:

(i) the accounting policies for the recognition of revenue.

(ii) the amount of each significant category of revenue, including:

- the sale of goods;
- the rendering of services;
- interest;
- royalties;
- dividends.

(iii) the amount of revenue from exchanges of goods or services in each of the categories in (ii) above.

* IFRICs are issued by the IFRS Interpretations Committee, which has 14 members and interprets international standards on behalf of the IASB.

New standard on revenue

The IASB is expected to publish a new standard called *Revenue from Contracts with Customers* during 2011. This standard will replace IAS 18. The new standard will require revenue to be recognised as performance obligations are satisfied. Performance obligations are enforceable promises to transfer goods or services to a customer. This will mean, for example, that revenue relating to the provision of services will no longer be recognised on a percentage of completion basis.

Summary

- *Revenue* is the gross inflow of economic benefits arising from the ordinary activities of an enterprise.
- Revenue should be measured at the fair value of the consideration received or receivable.
- Revenue should be recognised as income when it meets the following criteria:
  - it is probable that the economic benefits associated with the transaction will flow to the entity; and
  - the amount of revenue can be measured reliably.
- Additional recognition criteria are separately identified for revenue from:
  - the sale of goods;
  - the rendering of services; and
  - interest, royalties and dividends.

Appendix 32.1

Examples

■ Measurement of revenue

Example 1   X Limited sells goods for €121,000 cash, including VAT of 21%.

VAT is a liability owed to the tax authorities. It is not income, and it should not be included in revenue.

	Dr €'000	Cr €'000
Cash	121	
Revenue		100
VAT		21

Example 2   Y Limited sells goods for €10,000 as agent on behalf of another company, and retains a 10% commission charge.

	Dr €'000	Cr €'000
Bank	10	
Revenue – I/S		1
Trade payables		9

IAS 18 requires the above treatment when goods are sold by an entity in an agency relationship. In this event, only the commission element of the transaction is recognised as revenue.

Example 3   Brock Limited is an Internet technology company. During 2010, Brock exchanged advertising services, having a value of €5,000, with another Internet company. The exchange was effected by each company being permitted to place advertisements on each other's site to the value of €5,000.

IAS 18 states that an exchange of goods or services of a similar nature and value is not regarded as a transaction that generates revenue. Thus, Brock Limited should not record revenue from this transaction.

Example 4   Lots Limited, a property development company, sells a land site for €1M. The site had been acquired several years previously for €100,000.

Sanitaire Limited, a company in the chemical industry, sold a development site for €300,000, which had been acquired previously for €140,000.

These transactions will be accounted for as follows:

	Dr €'000	Cr €'000
Bank	1,000	
Revenue – I/S		1,000
Cost of sales	100	
Inventory – SOFP		100
(Being sale of development site by Lots Limited)		
Bank	300	
Property, plant and equipment		140
Profit on disposal – I/S		160
(Being profit on sale of development site by Sanitaire Limited)		

Example 4 emphasises the fact that only goods and services which an entity normally sells should be regarded as revenue. Thus, the sale of the land site is correctly recorded as revenue by Lots Limited, which is a property development company. For Sanitaire Limited, which operates in the chemical industry, the sale of a development site is not part of that company's ordinary operations. The sale should not therefore be recorded as revenue.

■ Sale of goods

Example 5 **Sale or return**

A distributor sells cars to a garage on sale or return for €300,000. Under the terms of the agreement, the garage can return the cars to the distributor and receive a full refund. It is not possible to estimate reliably how many cars will be returned.

The risks and rewards of ownership have not passed to the garage in this example. Should the cars remain unsold, it is the distributor who will suffer in terms of obsolescence risk, etc. Thus, no sale should be recorded by the distributor, who should continue to carry the cars as inventory in its statement of financial position.

Example 6 **Refunds**

A retailer offers a 12-month guarantee on all goods sold, whereby a customer can return any product and receive a full refund. Sales for 2010, excluding VAT, amounted to €800,000. It has been found, in the normal course of business, that 2% of goods sold are returned. All goods returned can be resold, and the average profit margin on sales is 25%.

The retailer retains only a very limited amount of risk in respect of the goods sold. Therefore revenue should be recognised, and an accrual made for goods likely to be returned.

	Dr €'000	Cr €'000
Bank	800	
Revenue – I/S		800
Increase in warranty provision – I/S	4	
Warranty provision* – SOFP		4

* €800,000 × 25% × 2%.

Example 7 **Warranty**

A software house supplies customised packages for the medical goods industry. Title to the customer passes on installation of the package, but a further three-month warranty period applies, during which all problems with the system must be eliminated at the expense of the software house. It is not possible to estimate reliably the cost of this work in each case.

Although legal title has passed to the customer, the risks and rewards still remain with the software house, and the amount of revenue cannot be measured reliably. Revenue should not be recognised until after the three-month warranty period has expired.

Example 8 **Deferred payment sale**

Bronze Limited sold goods on 31 December 2010 for €20,000, and allowed a year's interest-free credit. The product normally sells for €18,182 cash on delivery.

The interest rate implicit in the sale transaction is 10% (i.e. the rate that discounts the nominal amount of the transaction (i.e. €20,000) to the current cash sales price of the goods).

Bronze Limited will record the sale at its fair value of €18,182 (i.e. €20,000/1.1) in the year ended 31 December 2010. The difference between the nominal amount and the fair value of the consideration is recognised as interest revenue in the year ending 31 December 2011.

	Dr	Cr
	€	€
Trade receivables	18,182	
Revenue – I/S		18,182
(Being revenue recognised at 31 December 2010)		
Trade receivables	1,818	
Interest revenue – I/S		1,818
(Being interest revenue for the year ending		
31 December 2011)		
Bank	20,000	
Trade receivables		20,000
(Being consideration received on 31 December 2011)		

■ Rendering of services

Example 9 **Film production**

On 1 July 2010 Galbraith Film Studios commenced the production of a film which is scheduled for completion on 30 June 2011. Production was 50% complete by 31 December 2010. Galbraith is receiving a fixed fee of €1.6M for the entire project.

Galbraith should record revenue from this project on a stage-of-completion basis. Thus, assuming that production is on target, 50% of the fee should be recorded as revenue for the year ended 31 December 2010. The following journal entry will be required at that time:

	Dr	Cr
	€'000	€'000
Trade receivables	800	
Film production fees – I/S		800

Example 10 **Fire alarm maintenance**

Incendo Limited has had a contract, since 1 January 2010, for the monthly maintenance of fire alarm equipment in all of the office buildings of Hotspur Limited. The monthly fee for this service is €6,000.

This contract satisfies the criteria to be recognised as revenue. At each month end, Incendo Limited will recognise revenue of €6,000 as income:

	Dr €'000	Cr €'000
Bank/trade receivables	6	
Service fees – I/S		6

Example 11 **Advertising contract**

An advertising agency has a contract with a client for a two-year period. Fees are dependent on the client's sales levels, the fee increasing at a rate of 5% of the increase in the client's sales level. During 2010, the client's sales levels increased by €1M.

The IAS 18 criteria for recognising revenue from the rendering of services have been met, and on a percentage-of-completion basis, the following journal entry should be made by the advertising agency:

	Dr €'000	Cr €'000
Trade receivables	50	
Advertising fees – I/S		50

Example 12 **Underwriting contract**

An underwriter has agreed to accept a 'costs only fee', in the event that a client's share price should fall below a minimum level at the close of business on the first day of issue. The issue is scheduled to take place three months after the underwriter's year end of 31 December 2010, and it is difficult to say whether the minimum price will be exceeded.

At 31 December 2010, the underwriter had incurred costs of €100,000, which can be certified as being directly related to the share issue.

The amount of revenue from the underwriting contract cannot be measured reliably. When this occurs, revenue should be recognised only to the extent of the expenses recognised that are recoverable.

Thus, the following journal entry should be made by the underwriting firm in its 2010 financial statements:

	Dr €'000	Cr €'000
Trade receivables	100	
Underwriting fees – I/S		100
(Being recoverable costs recognised as revenue)		

■ Interest, royalties and dividends

Example 13 Interest

Major Limited purchased loan stock in B Limited on 1 January 2011 for €10,000. The loan stock carries no interest and will be redeemed on 31 December 2013 for €13,310.

The effective interest rate is 10% per annum, and the loan stock is accounted for as follows using the *effective interest rate method*:

	Dr €	Cr €
Financial asset	10,000	
Bank		10,000
(Being purchase of loan stock on 1 January 2011)		
Financial asset	1,000	
Interest receivable – I/S		1,000
(Being interest at 10% for year end 31 December 2011)		
Financial asset	1,100	
Interest receivable – I/S		1,100
(Being interest at 10% for year end 31 December 2012 i.e. (10,000 + €1,000) × 10%)		
Financial asset	1,210	
Interest receivable – I/S		1,210
(Being interest at 10% for year end 31 December 2013 i.e. (10,000 + €1,000 + €11,000) × 10%)		
Bank	13,310	
Financial asset		13,310
(Being encashment of loan stock at maturity)		

Example 14 Royalties

Margot Limited earned royalties of €90,000 for the year ended 31 December 2010 on intellectual property rights which had been subcontracted to a third party. Half of the amount due was unpaid at the period end.

The royalty income receivable by Margot Limited should be accounted for on an accrual basis as follows:

	Dr €	Cr €
Bank	45,000	
Trade and other receivables – SOFP	45,000	
Royalty income – I/S		90,000

Example 15 Dividends

Bronze Limited held shares in Tenco Bank Limited, which declared a dividend of 20 cents per share on 3 February 2011, in respect of the year ended 31 December 2010.

The right of Bronze Limited was established after 31 December 2010. Thus the dividend of 20 cents per share will be recorded by Bronze Limited in its financial statements for the year ending 31 December 2011.

QUESTIONS

32.1 OSCAR

Due to increased competition, particularly from overseas, OSCAR began selling goods on a sale or return basis during 2010. Under the terms of the sale, customers are able to return items within 30 days from the date of sale. Payment for goods not returned within this 30-day period is required within 28 days thereafter. During 2010, a number of OSCAR's customers exercised their right of return. OSCAR typically sells goods on this basis at cost plus 25%. The sales figure in the draft financial statements for the year ended 31 December 2010 is based upon goods supplied to customers by 31 December 2010. Sales on a sale or return basis in November and December 2010 were €1,250,000 and €1,500,000 respectively.

Required:
Explain the implications of this policy for OSCAR's 2010 financial statements.

(Chartered Accountants Ireland)

32.2 Recognition of revenue

Explain the criteria that suggest revenue should generally be recognised at the point of sale.

(Chartered Accountants Ireland)

32.3 ELECTRON

ELECTRON, a public limited company, operates in the energy sector. ELECTRON buys and sells oil and currently has a number of oil trading contracts. The contracts to purchase oil are treated as non-current assets and amortised over the contracts' durations. On acceptance of a contract to sell oil, 50% of the contract price is recognised immediately, with the balance being recognised over the remaining life of the contract. The contracts always result in the delivery of the commodity.

Required:
Discuss the accounting treatment of oil trading contracts by ELECTRON.

(ACCA)

32.4 NORMAN plc

One of the hotels owned by NORMAN is a hotel complex which includes a theme park, a casino and a golf course as well as a hotel. The theme park, casino and hotel were sold in the year ended 31 May 2011 to CONQUEST, a public limited company, for €200M but the sale agreement stated that NORMAN would continue to operate and manage the three businesses for their remaining useful life of 15 years. The residual interest in the business reverts back to NORMAN after the 15-year period. NORMAN would receive 75% of the net profit of the businesses as operator fees and CONQUEST would receive the remaining 25%. NORMAN has guaranteed to CONQUEST that the net minimum profit paid to CONQUEST would not be less than €15M.

NORMAN has recently started issuing vouchers to customers when they stay in its hotels. The vouchers entitle the customers to a €30 discount on a subsequent room booking within three months of their stay. Historical experience has shown that only one in five vouchers is redeemed by the customer. At the company's year end of 31 May 2011, it is estimated that there are vouchers worth €20M which are eligible for discount. The income from room sales for the year is €300M and NORMAN is unsure how to report the income from room sales in the financial statements.

(ACCA)

32.5 ROUTER plc

ROUTER operates in the entertainment industry. It recently agreed with a television company to make a film which would be broadcast on the television company's network. The fee agreed for the film was €5M with a further €100,000 to be paid every time the film is shown on the television company's channels. It is hoped that it will be shown on four occasions. The film was completed

343

at a cost of €4M and delivered to the television company on 1 April 2011. The television company paid the fee of €5M on 30 April 2011, but indicated that the film needed substantial editing before they were prepared to broadcast it, the costs of which would be deducted from any future payments to ROUTER. The directors of ROUTER wish to recognise the anticipated future income of €400,000 in the financial statements for the year ended 31 May 2011.

Required:

Outline how the above transactions should be dealt with in the financial statements of ROUTER for the year ended 31 May 2011. (ACCA)

Chapter 33

Government grants and disclosure of government assistance

The importance of government grants is largely dependent on the nature of the economic system in which an entity operates. In capitalist economies, the stock market and private sector borrowing are the main sources of external finance, whereas in a socialist economy the government has a far more central role in the provision of funding.

Irrespective of the prevailing economic system, government grants may be perceived as being significant from a political perspective. In fact, during the US investment tax credit controversy of the early 1960s, a rare government intervention was triggered by Opinion 2 of the Accounting Principles Board (the predecessor of **FASB**) which proposed that a tax credit,* to stimulate the purchase of machinery, be subtracted from the cost of the related asset. The Kennedy administration, however, insisted that companies should be permitted to include the tax credit in current income, and the government-appointed SEC intervened to allow either accounting method to be used.

The issue, from a government perspective, was to utilise the tax credit to stimulate economic growth and job creation. The administration believed that this would be best achieved by allowing companies to record the tax credit in income and thereby allow companies to report higher earnings figures.

It is important, therefore, that government grants and other government assistance be properly regulated, if only to avoid a repetition of accounting decisions being made for political reasons. IAS 20 *Accounting for Government Grants and Disclosure of Government Assistance* addresses these issues.

Accounting for government grants

Initial recognition and presentation

Government grants should be recognised when there is reasonable assurance that:

- an entity will comply with any conditions attached to the grant; and
- the grant will be received.

---

* Under US legislation at that time, a tax credit was a reduction of current tax due.

Accounting treatment of government grants related to assets

■ Initial record

Government grants related to assets should be presented in the statement of financial position either by:

- setting up the grant as deferred income; or
- deducting the grant from the carrying amount of the asset.

Example 1   On 1 January 2009, Mercer Limited received a grant of €100,000 towards a machine costing €500,000. Mercer Limited depreciates machinery at 10% per annum on a straight-line basis. Two alternative approaches are acceptable for the initial recognition of the grant:

	Dr €'000	Cr €'000
Bank	100	
Deferred income – SOFP		100
(Being separate treatment of grant in statement of financial position)		

or

	Dr €'000	Cr €'000
Bank	100	
Property, plant and equipment		100
(Being grant offset against asset)		

■ Recognition as income

Government grants should be recognised as income by matching them with the related costs which they are intended to compensate.

Example 2   In accounting for the grant in Example 1 above, Mercer Limited will make the following annual entries:

	Dr €'000	Cr €'000
Depreciation expense – I/S	50	
Accumulated depreciation		50
Deferred income – SOFP	10	
Other income – I/S		10
(Being annual entries when grant and asset have been kept separate in the statement of financial position)		

or

	Dr €'000	Cr €'000
Depreciation expense	40	
Accumulated depreciation		40
(Being annual entry when grant has been offset against asset in the statement of financial position)		

Accounting treatment of government grants related to income

A grant related to income may be reported separately as 'other income' or deducted from the related expense.

Example 3 Lange Limited has been guaranteed a government grant of €20,000 as the reimbursement of training costs which have been expensed during 2010. The grant will be recorded as income in 2010 either by:

- including the grant under a separate heading, such as other income; or
- offsetting the grant against training costs.

	Dr €'000	Cr €'000
Receivables – SOFP	20	
Other income – I/S		20

or

	Dr €'000	Cr €'000
Receivables – SOFP	20	
Training expenses – I/S		20

Non-monetary government grants

A government grant may take the form of a transfer of a non-monetary **asset**, such as land or other resources. It is usual to assess the **fair value** of the asset, and to record both the asset and the grant at this amount. An alternative is to record both at a nominal amount.

Repayment of government grants

A government grant which becomes repayable should be treated as the revision of an accounting estimate, as defined by IAS 8.

Repayment of grants relating to assets

- If the grant was initially recorded as deferred income, the balance of deferred income should be reduced by the amount that is repayable.
- If the grant was initially used to reduce the carrying value of the asset, its repayment should be recorded as an increase in the asset's carrying value.

   The cumulative additional depreciation that would have been recognised to date as an expense, in the absence of the grant, should be recognised immediately as an expense.

Example 4 Assume that the grant of €100,000 in Example 1 above became repayable on 1 January 2010 (i.e. one year after grant was received).

(i) If the grant was originally recorded as *deferred income*, the following entries will be required:

	Dr €'000	Cr €'000
Deferred income – SOFP	90	
Provision for grant repayment – SOFP		90
(Being repayment offset against remaining balance on deferred income)		
Grant repayment expense – I/S	10	
Provision for grant repayment – SOFP		10
(Being excess of grant repayment over balance remaining on deferred income, i.e. €100,000 – €90,000)		

(ii) If the grant was originally *deducted from the carrying value of the asset*, the following entries will be required:

	Dr €'000	Cr €'000
Property, plant and equipment	100	
Provision for grant repayment – SOFP		100
(Being increase of carrying amount of asset)		
Depreciation expense – I/S	10	
Accumulated depreciation		10
(Being depreciation originally avoided due to grant being offset against asset, now charged as an expense)		

■ Repayment of grants relating to income

Repayment should first be applied against any unamortised deferred credit set up in respect of the grant. Any excess should be recognised immediately as an expense.

Example 5 Assume that, on 1 January 2011, the training expenses grant of €20,000 (Example 3 above) became repayable. The following entry will be required:

	Dr €'000	Cr €'000
Grant repayment expense – I/S	20	
Provision for grant repayment – SOFP		20

Disclosure of government grants

IAS 20 requires the following to be disclosed:

- Accounting policy for grants, including method of presentation in the statement of financial position
- Nature and extent of grants recognised in the financial statements
- Unfulfilled conditions and contingencies attaching to recognised grants.

IAS 20 also requires the disclosure of the benefits of government assistance, whose value cannot be reasonably measured. Examples are technical or marketing advice.

Summary

- Government grants should be recognised when there is reasonable assurance that:
  - an entity will comply with any conditions attached to the grant; and
  - the grant will be received.
- Government grants related to assets should be presented in the SOFP either by:
  - setting up the grant as deferred income; or
  - deducting the grant from the carrying amount of the asset.
- Grants related to income should be reported separately as 'other income', or deducted from the related expense.
- If a government grant becomes repayable, it should be treated as the revision of an accounting estimate.

QUESTIONS

33.1 NORMAN plc

NORMAN has obtained a significant amount of grant income for the development of hotels in Europe. The grants have been received from government bodies and related to the size of the hotel which has been built by the grant assistance. The intention of the grant income was to create jobs in areas where there was significant unemployment. The grants received of €70M will have to be repaid if the cost of building the hotels is less than €500M.

Required:

Discuss how the above income would be treated in the financial statements of NORMAN for the year ended 31 May 2010.

33.2 Grant assistance

During the year ended 31 December 2010, BENNETT received a government grant to partially finance the purchase of some items of plant and machinery required for a planned expansion of the manufacturing side of the business. Expenditure of up to €1.5M of plant and machinery was approved by the government department involved, with the grant being approved for 60% of the total expenditure. The full amount of the grant had been received by 31 December 2010.

The conditions on which the grant was approved were that the expenditure would relate to the purchase of specific items of plant and machinery and that an additional 10 members of staff would be hired.

At 31 December 2010, BENNETT had hired 12 extra staff members and had purchased €1.2M of the specified plant and machinery. It is the intention of the directors, if cash flow permits, to purchase a further €600,000 worth of plant and machinery in the year ending 31 December 2011.

The plant and machinery purchased will be depreciated at 8% per annum on a straight-line basis. It is the company's policy to depreciate assets fully in the year of acquisition, regardless of the date of purchase.

The directors of BENNETT feel that it is important to show grant assistance received separately in the financial statements. To date, the only accounting entry in relation to the grant received has been to record it as a separate item within deferred income in the draft financial statements of the company for the year.

Required:

Outline the correct accounting treatment, including any relevant journals, of the government grant received by the company in the financial statements for the year ended 31 December 2010. Draft the disclosure notes required.

(Chartered Accountants Ireland)

Chapter 34

The effects of changes in foreign exchange rates

International business has grown in importance in recent years and most business entities now have transactions that are denominated in one or more foreign currencies. This can result in foreign exchange risk. For a company in the eurozone, this can arise, for example, by exporting goods to the UK and invoicing in pounds sterling. The same company might import materials from the US, and agree to pay in US dollars.

This raises the issue as to how such transactions should be accounted for, in terms of recording and measuring foreign currency revenues, expenses, receivables and payables.

Recording foreign currency transactions

■ Identifying an entity's functional currency

IAS 21 requires that a foreign currency transaction be recorded in an entity's **functional currency**.

Functional currency is defined as the currency of the primary environment in which an entity operates. This is normally the currency in which an entity receives and pays out cash. The following factors should be considered as the primary factors in determining an entity's functional currency:

(i) The currency:
  - that mainly influences sales prices (often the currency in which sales prices are denominated and settled); and
  - of the country whose competitive forces and regulations mainly determine its sales prices.
(ii) The currency that mainly influences labour, material and other costs (often the currency in which such costs are denominated and settled).

The following factors may also provide evidence of an entity's functional currency:

- the currency in which funds from financing activities (i.e. issuing debt and equity) are generated;
- the currency in which receipts from operating activities are usually retained.

Example 1 Cramwell Limited sells most of its goods in the eurozone, with sales invoices being denominated in euro. Sixty percent of the company's costs are incurred in euro, through manufacturing plants based in France and Spain. The remaining production costs are denominated in pounds sterling, through production plants located in the UK.

As the vast majority of Cramwell Limited's revenues, and 60% of its costs, are denominated in euro, the euro is the company's functional currency. Therefore, all of Cramwell's transactions should be recorded in euro, with transactions in other currencies being translated into euro in accordance with IAS 21.

■ Recording transactions in an entity's functional currency

Foreign currency transactions should be recorded, on initial recognition, in an entity's functional currency. This is done by applying the spot rate of exchange between the functional currency and the foreign currency at the date of the transaction.

Example 2 Cramwell Limited purchased goods on credit for £80,000 on 1 October 2010. The spot rate of exchange on that date was:

€1 = £0.8670

The functional currency of Cramwell Limited is the euro, and the transaction should be recorded in that currency as follows:

	€'000	€'000
Purchases	92,272	
Trade payables		92,272
(Being goods purchased in pounds, translated into euro: £80,000/0.8670)		

An entity may have several transactions in a foreign currency during a period. For example, let us assume that Cramwell Limited has weekly sales of £100,000 during the first quarter of 2010. The exchange rate between the euro and sterling was stable during the first quarter, and the average rate was €1 = £0.8568.

IAS 21 permits the use of an average rate for all transactions occurring during a period, as long as exchange rates do not fluctuate significantly. Thus, it would be appropriate for Cramwell Limited to use the average exchange rate for the first quarter of 2010 to record sales made during that period.

■ Monetary items and non-monetary items

IAS 21 makes an important distinction in relation to the recording of monetary items and non-monetary items.

(i) Monetary items

Monetary items are defined as units of currency held, and **assets** and **liabilities** to be received or paid, in a fixed or determinable number of units of currency. An example is trade payables which arise when goods are purchased on credit.

Example 3 Cramwell Limited purchased machinery on 1 October 2010 for $100,000 from a US supplier. These goods were paid for on 15 January 2011. Cramwell Limited has an accounting year end of 31 December.

Spot rates of exchange were as follows:

1 October 2010	€1 = $1.457
31 December 2010	€1 = $1.501
15 January 2011	€1 = $1.509

The above transaction is initially accounted for by Cramwell Limited on 1 October 2010 as follows:

	Dr €	Cr €
Machinery	68,634	
Trade payables		68,634
(Being machinery purchased on 1 October 2010, translated into euro at the spot rate on that date: 100,000/1.457)		

IAS 21 requires that at the end of each **reporting period**, foreign currency *monetary items* be translated using the *closing rate*. Monies owed by Cramwell Limited to its US supplier at 31 December 2010, are a monetary item, and should be translated into euro at 31 December 2010.

Any exchange difference that arises should be recognised in profit or loss.

	Dr €	Cr €
Trade payables	2,012	
Gain on translation of trade payables – I/S		2,012
(Being gain on translation of monetary item, computed as follows: (100,000/1.457) – (100,000/1.501))		

The exchange rate on 15 January 2011 is a non-adjusting event after the reporting period.

(ii) Non-monetary items

Non-monetary items are those that neither exhibit the right to receive, nor an obligation to deliver, fixed or determinable amounts of units of a currency. Examples of non-monetary items are inventory and plant and equipment.

IAS 21 requires that **non-monetary items that are measured at historical cost** in a foreign currency should be translated using the exchange rate at the date of the transaction. See Example 3 (revisited) below.

 Example 3 revisited The machinery purchased by Cramwell Limited on 1 October 2010 is a non-monetary asset, which is carried at historical cost. Using the exchange rate at the date of purchase, it will be included in the financial statements at 31 December 2010 as a non-current asset of €68,634 (i.e. 100,000/1.457).

IAS 21 requires that **non-monetary items measured at fair value** in a foreign currency should be translated using the exchange rates at the date when the fair value was determined.

■ Inventory and impairment of assets

(i) Inventory

IAS 2 *Inventories* requires that inventory be valued at the lower of cost and **net realisable value**. In comparing cost and net realisable value, IAS 21 requires that inventories purchased in foreign currencies be measured as follows:

- *Cost* should be translated into an entity's functional currency, using the rate in force at the date the inventory was purchased.

- *Net realisable value* should be translated using the exchange rate at the date when the NRV was determined (e.g. the end of the reporting period).

(ii) Impairment of assets

IAS 36 states that if the recoverable amount of an asset is less than its carrying amount, the carrying amount of the asset shall be reduced to its recoverable amount.

IAS 21 requires that the respective values be measured as follows:

- The *carrying amount* should be translated at the exchange rate when that amount was determined (i.e. the date of the transaction).
- The *recoverable amount* should be translated at the exchange rate at the date when that value was determined (e.g. the end of the reporting period).

Use of a presentation currency other than the functional currency

Most entities are likely to use their **functional currency** to present their **financial statements**. Thus, an entity whose functional currency is the euro will generally present its financial statements in euro. IAS 21, however, allows entities to use a different presentational currency. For example, an entity whose functional currency is the euro may present its financial statements both in euro and US dollars.

The following procedure applies when translating from the functional currency to the presentation currency:

(a) assets and liabilities in the statement of financial position should be translated at the closing rate at the end of the reporting period;
(b) income and expenses in the statement of comprehensive income should be translated at the exchange rates at the dates of the transactions;*
(c) all resulting exchange differences should be recognised in other comprehensive income.

* An average rate may be used as long as exchange rates have not fluctuated significantly during the period.

Separate translation procedures apply where an entity's functional currency is the currency of a hyperinflationary economy.

Translation of a foreign operation

If an entity has a foreign operation (e.g. a **subsidiary**, associate, joint venture or branch), it will be necessary to translate the financial statements of that operation into the currency used in the entity's own financial statements.

The rules for translation are the same as those outlined above for the use of a presentation currency other than an entity's functional currency.

Example 4 Cramwell Limited has a number of subsidiaries located in the eurozone, all of which present their financial statements in euro. Cramwell also owns 30% of the equity shares of a Japanese associate, which prepares its financial statements in yen.

Outline what steps are required before the financial statements of the Japanese company can be included with those of Cramwell Group.

Solution   The financial statements of the Japanese associate must be translated into euro, before they can be included, on an equity basis (as required by IAS 28), with those of the Cramwell Group.

Example 5   On 1 January 2010, Cramwell Limited set up a 100% owned subsidiary, Subset Limited, in the United States. Cramwell invested $4M of equity capital in Subset.

Extracts from the financial statements of Subset are presented as follows:

Statement of comprehensive income for the year ended 31 December 2010

	$'000
Revenue	8,600
Expenses	(4,900)
Profit for the year	3,700

Statement of financial position at 31 December 2010

	$'000
Building	2,000
Inventory	1,000
Trade receivables	3,400
Bank	2,500
	8,900
Trade payables	1,200
Share capital	4,000
Retained earnings	3,700
	8,900

The following exchange rates applied during the year:

1 January 2010	€1 = $1.50
31 December 2010	€1 = $1.40
Average rate for year ended 31 December 2010	€1 = $1.45

Required:
Translate the financial statements of Subset Limited into euro.

Solution

Statement of financial position as at 31 December 2010

	$'000	Rate	€'000
Building	2,000	1.40	1,428.6
Inventory	1,000	1.40	714.3
Trade receivables	3,400	1.40	2,428.6
Bank	2,500	1.40	1,785.7
	8,900		6,357.2
Trade payables	1,200	1.40	857.2
Share capital	4,000	1.50	2,666.7
Retained earnings	3,700	1.45	2,551.7
Other components of equity	–	Balancing figure	281.6
	8,900		6,357.2

Statement of comprehensive income for the year ended 31 December 2010

	$'000	Rate	€'000
Revenue	8,600	1.45	5,931.0
Expenses	(4,900)	1.45	(3,379.3)
Profit for the year	3,700		2,551.7
Other comprehensive income			
Exchange gain on			
translating foreign operation			281.6
Total comprehensive income for the year			2,833.3

The exchange gain on translating the foreign operation is computed as follows:

(a) translating profit for the year at the average exchange rate for 2010, and the corresponding amount of net assets at the closing rate on 31 December 2010:

i.e. ($3.7M/1.40) − ($3.7M/1.45) = a translation gain of €91,100 (rounded)

(b) translating the opening net assets at a closing rate that differs from the previous closing rate:

i.e. ($4M/1.40) − ($4M/1.50) = a translation gain of €190,500 (rounded)

Thus the overall exchange gain on translation of Subset Limited is €281,600 (i.e. €91,100 + €190,500). This exchange gain is *not* recognised in profit or loss, but is included in other comprehensive income. The cumulative amount of exchange differences is also presented as a separate component of equity in the statement of financial position.

Summary

- Foreign currency transactions should be recorded initially at the spot rate of exchange in an entity's functional currency.
- At the end of each reporting period, foreign currency *monetary* items should be translated using the closing rate.
- Non-monetary items measured at historical cost in a foreign currency should be translated using the exchange rate at the date of the transaction.
- Non-monetary items, measured at fair value in a foreign currency, should be translated using the exchange rates at the date when the fair value was determined.
- IAS 21 sets out the procedures that apply when an entity uses a currency, other than its functional currency, to present its financial statements.
- IAS 21 also deals with the translation of the financial statements of a foreign operation into the currency in which an entity prepares its own financial statements.

QUESTIONS

34.1 IRISHLINK

On 1 January 2010 IRISHLINK received a 15-month interest-free loan, denominated in US dollars, of US$100,000 from an American company. The loan translated to €50,000 at this date. IRISHLINK repaid the loan on 31 March 2011 at a cost of €55,000. IRISHLINK'S functional currency is the euro.

Required:

Show how the loan should be accounted for in the financial statements of IRISHLINK for the years ending 31 December 2010 and 2011. Relevant exchange rates are shown below.

1 January 2010	$1 = €2.00
31 December 2010	$1 = €2.50

(Chartered Accountants Ireland)

34.2 ASTON

ASTON has a year end of 31 December 2010. On 25 October 2010 ASTON bought goods from a Mexican supplier for 286,000 pesos. ASTON's functional currency is the dollar.

The goods remained in inventory at the year end.

25 October 2010	$1 = 11.16 pesos
16 November 2010	$1 = 10.87 pesos
31 December 2009	$1 = 11.02 pesos

Required:

Show the accounting entries for the transactions in each of the following situations:

(a) on 16 November 2010, ASTON pays the Mexican supplier in full;

(b) the supplier remains unpaid at the year end.

34.3 BRANDA plc

(a) BRANDA plc buys and sells computer equipment. BRANDA's functional currency is the pound sterling. The following information is available for foreign transactions entered into by BRANDA plc during the month ended 31 December 2010:

1 December	buys goods on credit from COMPUSIST Ltd for $60,000
5 December	sells goods on credit to HAMPER Ltd for $80,000
5 December	pays COMPUSIST Ltd $40,000 on account
10 December	buys machinery on credit from MANHATTAN Inc. for $160,000
10 December	receives $50,000 on account from HAMPER Ltd
10 December	borrows $120,000 from a US bank
22 December	pays MANHATTAN Inc. $160,000 for the machinery.

The relevant exchange rates are as follows:

1 December	£1 = $2.00
5 December	£1 = $2.20
10 December	£1 = $2.40
22 December	£1 = $2.50
31 December	£1 = $2.60.

You are required to calculate the profit or loss on foreign currency transactions to be reported in the financial statements of BRANDA plc for the year ended 31 December 2010.

(b) Outline the main differences between functional currency and presentation currency for a reporting entity. Also, set out the factors which a reporting entity will consider in determining its functional currency.

Chapter 35

Borrowing costs

The key issue that arises is whether borrowing costs relating to the acquisition, construction or production of an **asset** should be expensed or capitalised as part of the cost of the asset. This issue is addressed by IAS 23 *Borrowing Costs*.

Definitions

Borrowing costs are interest and other costs incurred in connection with the borrowing of funds.

A *qualifying asset* is an asset that necessarily takes a substantial period of time to get ready for its intended use or sale. Any of the following could be a qualifying asset:

- property, plant and equipment
- inventories
- power generation facilities
- intangible assets
- investment property

Scope

The following assets are excluded from the scope of IAS 23:

- a qualifying asset measured at **fair value**, for example a biological asset accounted for under IAS 41 *Agriculture*;
- inventories produced in large quantities on a repetitive basis.

Recognition

■ Borrowing costs incurred in respect of qualifying assets

An entity should capitalise borrowing costs that are directly attributable to the acquisition, construction or production of a qualifying asset as part of the cost of that asset.

Example 1   Blimp Limited commenced the construction of a new manufacturing plant on 1 January 2010. Construction was completed on 1 November 2010, and borrowing costs incurred during the construction period amounted to €120,000.

These borrowing costs relate to a qualifying asset and they should be capitalised as part of the new plant as follows:

	Dr €'000	Cr €'000
Property, plant and equipment	120	
Bank		120

(i) Borrowing costs eligible for capitalisation

Borrowing costs eligible for capitalisation are those borrowing costs that would have been avoided if the expenditure on the qualifying asset had not been made:

- where funds are borrowed *specifically* to obtain a qualifying asset, eligible costs are the actual costs incurred less any income earned on the temporary investment of such borrowings;
- where funds are part of a *general pool*, the eligible amount is determined by applying a capitalisation rate to the expenditure on that asset. The capitalisation rate will be the weighted average cost of borrowings incurred on the general pool.

(ii) Commencement, suspension and cessation of capitalisation

- Capitalisation of interest should *commence* when all of the following conditions are satisfied:
  - expenditures are being incurred;
  - borrowing costs are being incurred; and
  - activities necessary to prepare the asset for its intended use are in progress.

  Some costs incurred prior to the commencement of physical production may be included – for example, technical and administrative work, such as the costs of obtaining work permits for construction employees.

  However, borrowing costs incurred during a holding period (e.g. while land acquired for building purposes is held without development activity) may *not* be capitalised.
- Capitalisation should be *suspended* during periods in which active development is interrupted.
- Capitalisation should *cease* when substantially all of the activities necessary to prepare the asset for its intended use or sale are complete.

  If only minor modifications are outstanding, this indicates that substantially all of the activities are complete.

Where construction is completed in stages, and a completed stage can be used while other construction continues, the capitalisation of borrowing costs relating to that stage should cease when it is substantially complete (e.g. a business park comprising several buildings, each of which can be used individually).

Example 2 On 1 February 2010, Blimp Limited commenced the construction of a new head office building. The new building was scheduled for completion on 31 July 2010, but due to a work stoppage from 1 May to 31 July, the building was eventually completed on 31 October 2010.

The costs paid by Blimp Limited are summarised as follows:

Item	1 February 2010 €'000	1 May 2010 €'000	31 October 2010 €'000	Total €'000
Site clearance	100	–	–	100
Legal fees	35	–	–	35
Construction and fitting out	–	800	950	1,750
Total	135	800	950	1,885

From 1 February 2010, Blimp Limited paid the amounts outlined above, based on architects' certificates obtained at each due date. To finance the construction, Blimp Limited used bank funds obtained for general company use. The interest rate charged on these funds was bank base rate plus 3%. On 1 February 2010, the bank base rate was 5%, and this increased to 6% on 1 August 2010.

The total costs of €1.885M were capitalised as part of buildings by Blimp Limited at 31 October 2010.

Outline how Blimp Limited should apply the requirements of IAS 23 Borrowing Costs *in accounting for its new head office building.*

Solution

Borrowing costs that are directly attributable to the construction of a qualifying asset should be capitalised as part of the cost of that asset.

Capitalisation should, however, be **suspended** during periods in which active development is interrupted. In the case of Blimp Limited therefore, no costs should be capitalised during the period of work stoppage, 1 May–31 July 2010.

Capitalisation should **cease** when substantially all of the activities necessary to prepare the asset for its intended use or sale are complete, which in Blimp's case is 31 October 2010.

The amount of borrowing costs to be capitalised should therefore be computed as follows:

Item	Eligible cost	Timescale from commencement on 1 February to date of completion on 31 October (excluding work stoppage period of 3 months)	Annual equivalent*
	€'000		€'000
Site clearance	100	6 months	50
Legal fees	35	6 months	17.5
Construction and fitting out	800	3 months	200
Construction and fitting out	950	0 months	Nil
Total	1,885		267.5

* The purpose of converting each expenditure item to an annual equivalent is to facilitate the use of the annual interest rate for all items.

To the extent that an entity borrows funds generally and uses them for the purpose of obtaining a qualifying asset, the entity shall determine the amount of borrowing costs eligible for capitalisation by applying a capitalisation rate to the expenditures on the asset. The capitalisation rate should be the weighted average of the borrowing costs that are outstanding during the period.

The interest rate was 8% from 1 February to 30 April, and 9% from 1 August to 31 October. Therefore, the weighted average rate for the relevant period under review (excluding the three-month work stoppage) was 8.5%.

When this is applied to the annualised costs of €267,500, the borrowing costs to be capitalised amount to €22,738. The following journal entry is therefore required:

	Dr €	Cr €
Buildings	22,738	
Bank		22,738

Other borrowing costs

Other borrowing costs (i.e. those that do *not* relate to qualifying assets) should be recognised as an expense.

Example 3 During 2010, Blimp Limited incurred borrowing costs of €130,000 in respect of the general running of its business. None of these costs relate to qualifying assets, as defined by IAS 23.

These costs should be recognised as an expense as follows:

	Dr €'000	Cr €'000
Finance costs – I/S	130	
Bank		130

Transitional provisions

Under the transitional rules of IAS 23, a change in accounting policy shall only apply to borrowing costs relating to qualifying assets for which the commencement date for capitalisation is on or after the effective date of that standard (i.e. 1 January 2009). Thus, retrospective adjustment is not required in respect of interest incurred prior to 1 January 2009.

However, an entity may designate any previous date as the effective date, and apply the standard to borrowing costs incurred after that date.

Example 4 On 1 January 2008, Blimp Limited commenced the construction of a tunnel, linking its two principal manufacturing plants. The project was due for completion on 30 June 2010. Interest costs of €80,000 were incurred during the first year, and these were written off as an expense by Blimp in its financial statements for the year ended 31 December 2008.

From 1 January 2009, interest costs were capitalised as part of the asset, in accordance with IAS 23.

Outline what adjustment, if any, is required by Blimp Limited in respect of its interest costs.

Solution   The construction of the tunnel is a qualifying asset, and the capitalisation of interest costs from 1 January 2009 represents a change in accounting policy. In accordance with the transitional requirements of IAS 23, however, Blimp is not required to adjust its financial statements in order to capitalise interest incurred prior to 1 January 2009. It may, however, opt to do so if it wishes.

Disclosure

The financial statements shall disclose:

- amount of borrowing costs capitalised during the period; and
- capitalisation rate used to determine the amount of borrowing costs eligible for capitalisation.

Summary

- Borrowing costs that are directly attributable to the acquisition, construction or production of a qualifying asset should be included as part of the cost of that asset.
- Borrowing costs eligible for capitalisation are those borrowing costs that would have been avoided if the expenditure on the qualifying asset had not been made.
- Capitalisation of borrowing costs should **commence** when:
  - expenditures are being incurred;
  - borrowing costs are being incurred; and
  - activities necessary to prepare the asset are in progress.
- Capitalisation of borrowing costs should be **suspended** during periods in which active development is interrupted.
- Capitalisation should cease when substantially all of the activities necessary to prepare the asset for its intended use are complete.
- Other borrowing costs are recognised as an expense.

QUESTIONS

35.1 STORM Limited

STORM Ltd ('STORM') borrowed €400,000 on 1 January 2009. Annual interest of €23,600 is payable on 31 December each year. The loan is repayable on 31 December 2009 at a premium of €100,000. The effective periodic interest rate is 10% per annum.

The finance charge in the income statement of STORM for the year ended 31 December 2010 and the balance sheet liability at that date should be:

	Finance charge	Statement of financial position liability
	€	€
(a)	23,600	352,800
(b)	36,000	320,000
(c)	40,000	324,000
(d)	41,640	434,440

(Chartered Accountants Ireland)

35.2 YELLOW

In January 2010 YELLOW commenced a programme to extend and modernise the company's manufacturing facilities. The programme cost €1M and YELLOW financed the work through a mixture of general and specific debt. The directors estimate that 50% of the programme was financed by general debt and 50% by specific debt. YELLOW's current borrowing rate is 10% per annum, while the specific debt carries an interest rate of 15% per annum. The programme was completed in December 2010.

Required:

Explain how YELLOW should account for the borrowing costs in the financial statements for the year ended 31 December 2010.   (Chartered Accountants Ireland)

35.3 OSCAR

On 1 February 2010, OSCAR commenced the construction of a new storage and distribution facility. The directors anticipate that the facility will be ready for use in January 2010. The construction is being financed entirely by a two-year 10% €20M loan which was drawn down in February 2010. OSCAR incurred and paid issue costs of €72,000 in connection with the loan. During 2010 OSCAR incurred and paid interest charges of €1.8M in respect of the loan, and earned and received interest of €225,000 from the short-term investment of the borrowings.

Required:

(a) Explain how OSCAR should account for the interest costs.

(b) Illustrate the accounting treatment on OSCAR's 2010 financial statements, and provide the journal entries.   (Chartered Accountants Ireland)

35.4 TARGET HOLDINGS

On 1 January 2010 TARGET HOLDINGS acquired a site adjacent to its main production facility for the development of a head office building. On 1 January 2010, final plans were agreed and clearance of the site commenced. Construction continued for approximately a further nine months until the building was available for occupation and came into use on 1 October 2010.

The various costs incurred by TARGET HOLDINGS associated with the construction during 2010 are summarised in the table below:

Element	1 Jan. 2010 €'000	31 Jan. 2010 €'000	31 Mar. 2010 €'000	30 Sept. 2010 €'000	Total €'000
Acquisition of site	2,700	–	–	–	2,700
Legal fees	90	–	–	–	90
Architects' fees	100	60		60	220
Site clearance and preparation	–	240	–	–	240
Construction and fitting out	–	–	480	1,200	1,680
General administration overhead allocation	–	–	100	100	200
Total	**2,890**	**300**	**580**	**1,360**	**5,130**

From 31 January 2010 onwards the costs, as indicated in the above table (excluding the general administration overhead allocation), were certified by architects' certificates issued on each date. These were paid by TARGET HOLDINGS on the date of issue using funds drawn down from the company's overdraft facility.

In order to fund the purchase of the site and development of the head office building, TARGET HOLDINGS arranged an extension to its bank overdraft facility from €4M to €8M for a period up to 31 December 2010. An arrangement fee in respect of this extension of €28,700 was charged by the company's bankers and debited from the account on 1 January 2010. The interest rate charged on the facility throughout the year was bank lending base rate plus 4%. On 1 January 2010 base rates were 5% increasing to 5.75% on 31 March 2010, at which level they remained until December 2010. The use of the extended bank overdraft was intended as a temporary funding mechanism to cover the period of construction only.

In the non-current assets of TARGET HOLDINGS at 31 December 2010 the building has been capitalised at a total cost of €4,820,000, comprised as follows:

- acquisition of site €2.7M
- site clearance and preparation €240,000
- construction and fitting-out €1.6M
- general administration overhead allocation capitalised €200,000.

All the other costs noted in the above table have been expensed to the statement of comprehensive income. No depreciation has been charged to date on the head office building in this financial year (2010), although the depreciation policy of the company in respect of land and buildings is to write them off, straight line, over 50 years from the date of coming into use.

Interest capitalisation

Derek Rogers, a co-founder of the TARGET Group, is an engineer but throughout the trading history of the group he has taken board-level responsibility for company accounts and financial issues, in conjunction with the in-house bookkeeper/accountant. During the course of the audit Derek has indicated to you that he is aware of other companies which have capitalised interest charges on construction projects and he would like the advice of the company auditors in this respect with regard to the head office building.

Required:

Set out the circumstances in which interest on borrowings should be capitalised and calculate the appropriate amount of interest that should be capitalised in the financial statements of TARGET HOLDINGS in the year ended 31 December 2010, together with any appropriate disclosures.

(Chartered Accountants Ireland)

Chapter 36

Related party disclosures

It is important that a user of an entity's **financial statements** be aware of parties with whom the entity is related, and of transactions that have taken place with those parties during the **reporting period**. For example, if an entity is a subsidiary, its policies and decision-making powers are effectively controlled by its parent company. Thus, an awareness of a **parent–subsidiary** relationship is an important disclosure that should be made in both companies' financial statements.

Similarly, an entity may extend a loan to one of its directors at a discounted interest rate. Once again, disclosure of this transaction is important if the information provided in the entity's financial statements is to be considered as complete.

IAS 24 *Related Party Disclosures* deals with these and other related issues.

Objective of IAS 24

The objective of IAS 24 is to draw attention to the possibility that an entity's financial statements may have been affected by the existence of related parties, and by material transactions and outstanding balances with such parties.

What is a related party transaction?

A related party transaction is a transfer of resources, services, or obligations between related parties, regardless of whether a price is charged. The following are examples of transactions that are disclosed if they are with a related party:

- purchases or sales of goods
- purchases or sales of property and other assets
- rendering or receiving of services
- leases
- transfers of research and development

Who are related parties?

(a) An entity is related to a reporting entity if any of the following applies:
- both entities are members of the same group (thus, a parent and a subsidiary are related parties, as are fellow subsidiaries);
- one entity is an associate or joint venture of the other;

- one entity is an associate or joint venture of a company in a group of which the other entity is a member;
- both entities are joint ventures of the same third party;
- one entity is a joint venture of a third entity, and the other entity is an associate of the third entity;
- the entity is a post-employment benefit plan for the benefit of employees of the entity, or of any entity that is a related party of the entity;
- the entity is controlled or jointly controlled by a person identified in (b) below.

(b) A person, or a close family member of the person, is related to a reporting entity if that person:

- has control or joint control over the reporting entity;
- has significant influence over the reporting entity; or
- is a member of the key management personnel of the reporting entity or its parent.

See examples in Appendix 36.1.

The following are *not* related parties:

- two enterprises simply because they have a director or key manager in common;
- two venturers who share joint control over a joint venture;
- providers of finance, trade unions, public utilities, and government departments and agencies in the course of their normal dealings with an enterprise;
- a customer, supplier, franchisor, distributor, or general agent, simply because an entity transacts a significant volume of business with such a party.

Disclosure

■ Related party transactions

If there have been material transactions between related parties, an entity must disclose separately, for each category of related parties, the information necessary for an understanding of the potential effect of the transactions on the financial statements.

This will include:

- the nature of the related party relationship;
- the amount of the transactions;
- the amount of outstanding balances, including commitments;
- provisions for doubtful debts related to the amount of outstanding balances;
- the expense recognised during the period in respect of bad or doubtful debts due from related parties.

■ Relationships between parents and subsidiaries

Irrespective of whether there have been transactions between a parent and a subsidiary, an entity must disclose the name of its parent and, if different, the ultimate controlling party.

If neither the entity's parent nor the ultimate controlling party produces financial statements available for public use, the name of the next most senior parent that does so must also be disclosed.

■ **Management compensation**

Disclose key management personnel compensation in total and for each of the following categories:

- short-term employee benefits
- post-employment benefits
- other long-term benefits
- termination benefits, and
- share-based payment

Key management personnel are those persons having authority and responsibility for planning, directing and controlling the activities of the entity, directly or indirectly, including all directors (whether executive or otherwise) of that entity.

See examples in Appendix 36.2.

Summary

- A related party transaction is a transfer of resources, services or obligations between related parties, regardless of whether a price is charged.
- IAS 24 provides details of parties who are identified as being related.
- An entity must disclose details of material transactions with related parties.
- An entity must disclose the name of its parent and, if different, the ultimate controlling party.

Appendix 36.1

Identifying related parties

Example 1 **Parent and subsidiaries**

Magnum Limited controls two subsidiaries, Simple Limited and Small Limited.

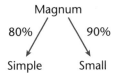

- Magnum and Simple are related parties as they are members of the same group;
- Magnum and Small are related parties on a similar basis;
- Simple and Small are related parties on a similar basis.

Example 2 **Associates**

Magnum Limited owns 25% of the equity shares in each of its associates, Alton Limited and Ash Limited.

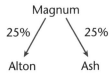

- Magnum and Alton are related parties, as Alton is an associate of Magnum;
- Magnum and Ash are related parties as Ash is an associate of Magnum;
- Alton and Ash are *not* related parties;
- Alton is a related party of both Simple and Small (see Example 1 above), because Simple and Small are members of the same group as Magnum;
- Ash is also a related party of both Simple and Small, on a similar basis.

Example 3 **Joint ventures**

Magnum Limited and another entity, Barb Limited, share joint control over Jack Limited and Jill Limited.

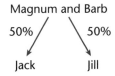

- Magnum and Jack are related parties, as Jack is a joint venture of Magnum;
- Magnum and Jill are related parties on a similar basis;

- Jack and Jill are related parties, as both are joint ventures of Magnum;
- Magnum and Barb, who are both venturers, are *not* related parties;
- Jack is a related party of both Simple and Small (see Example 1), because Simple and Small are members of the same group as Magnum;
- Jill is a related party of Simple and Small on a similar basis;
- Jack is a related party of both Alton and Ash (see Example 2), as they are joint venture and associates respectively of the same other entity (i.e. Magnum);
- Jill is a related party of both Alton and Ash on the same basis;
- Barb is a related party of both Jack and Jill.

Example 4   Member of key management personnel

On 1 December 2010, Magnum Limited extended a loan of €200,000 to Roy Scapens, who is a brother of Magnum director Tom Scapens.

- Magnum and Tom Scapens are related parties as the latter is a member of Magnum's key management personnel;
- Magnum and Roy Scapens are related parties as the latter is a close family member of one of Magnum's key management personnel.

Example 5   Customer

During 2010, Magnum Limited sold a large quantity of goods to Brice Limited. Neither company holds shares in the other.

The fact that Magnum has transacted a significant amount of business with Brice during 2010 does not necessarily mean that the two companies are related parties. Further evidence, such as a significant holding of shares by one company in the other, would be required in order to conclude that a related party relationship exists.

Appendix 36.2

Disclosure of related party transactions

Example 1 Magnum Limited has two subsidiaries, Simple Limited and Small Limited.

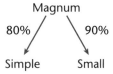

During 2010, Simple sold goods to Small for a total of €1.5M. Small owed €300,000 to Simple at 31 December 2010 in respect of these goods.

Simple and Small are members of the same group of companies. Thus, they are related parties and the sale of goods is a related party transaction. Subject to materiality considerations, disclosures will be required under IAS 24 as follows.

(i) Disclosures in the financial statements of Simple Limited and Small Limited

- The nature of the related party relationship (the fact that Simple and Small are members of the Magnum Group of companies);
- The amount of the transactions (sale of goods during 2010 for €1.5M);
- The amount of outstanding balances (Small owes €300,000 to Simple at 31 December 2010);
- The fact that Magnum is each entity's parent company.

(ii) Disclosures in the consolidated financial statements of the Magnum Group

The sale of goods between Simple and Small will be cancelled as a consolidation adjustment when the financial statements of the Magnum Group are prepared. Thus, no disclosure is required.

Example 2 Magnum Limited has an associate called Alton Limited, in which it owns 25% of the equity shares. Magnum also has a subsidiary, Simple Limited.

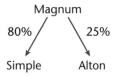

In November 2010, Alton Limited sold a land site to Simple Limited for €2M cash.

(i) Disclosures in the financial statements of Simple Limited and Alton Limited

As Alton is an associate of Magnum, and Simple is a member of the Magnum Group of companies, Alton and Simple are related parties. Therefore, subject to materiality considerations, details of this transaction should be disclosed in the financial statements of both Alton and Simple.

- The nature of the related party relationship (the fact that Alton is an associate of Magnum and that Simple is a member of the Magnum Group);
- The amount of the transaction (purchase of a land site for €2M by Simple from Alton).

(ii) Disclosures in the consolidated financial statements of the Magnum Group

Subject to materiality considerations, the following disclosures will be required in the financial statements of the Magnum Group:

- The nature of the related party relationship (the fact that Alton is an associate of the Magnum Group);
- The amount of the transaction (purchase of a land site for €2M from Alton Limited).

QUESTIONS

36.1 BELFORD Group

The BELFORD Group of companies comprises a parent company, BELFORD Limited, and two wholly owned subsidiaries, SIMPLEX Limited and SAMPLER Limited. BELFORD also has a 25% stake in the equity share capital of ASTERIX Limited. During the year ended 31 December 2010, the following transactions took place:

(i) SIMPLEX Limited sold €1M of goods to SAMPLER Limited at a margin of 20% on selling price. None of these goods were in the inventory of SAMPLER Limited at 31 December 2010.

(ii) On 30 April 2010, BELFORD Limited sold a land bank to one of its directors, Patricia O'Flynn, for €2.5M. The land, which was surplus to requirements, had cost €1.3M in 2003. A valuation certificate from a firm of auctioneers stated that the market value of the land at 30 April 2010 was €3M. The land had been revalued to €2M in the financial statements at 31 December 2009.

(iii) In July 2010, SIMPLEX Limited obtained goods from ASTERIX Limited for €400,000, ASTERIX earning half of its normal profit margin on the sale of similar goods.

Required:

(a) You are required to draft the journal entries for transaction (ii) above. Ignore tax.

(b) For each of the transactions (i)–(iii), outline what disclosures will be required in the financial statements of the BELFORD Group, and of each of the individual companies.

36.2 ATLANTIC Limited

ATLANTIC Ltd has two subsidiaries, SCANDOT Ltd and DALE Ltd. The share capital of ATLANTIC comprises €100,000 of 50 cent ordinary shares and is held as follows:

Mr Matthew Williams	60%
Mr Patrick Clarke	40%

Mr Williams is the Chairman and Managing Director of ATLANTIC and Mr Clarke is also a member of the board.

Mr Williams is Managing Director of SCANDOT which he formed in the mid 1990s in conjunction with his partner Patrick Clarke. Mr Clarke is the Financial Director.

The ordinary share capital of SCANDOT is owned 100% by ATLANTIC.

Sale of freehold land

SCANDOT's original manufacturing site was vacated in 2006 and has remained unoccupied. On 31 December 2010, SCANDOT sold this site to ASHTON Ltd for €1M. The latter company, which is owned and managed by Matthew Williams and his son, intends to develop the potential of the site as a location for an out-of-town shopping centre.

The net book value of the site in the books of SCANDOT at 31 December 2010 was €1.5M and the market value at that date was estimated to be €2M. This sale has not been reflected in the financial statements of SCANDOT for the year ended 31 December 2010.

Required:

Outline how the above transaction should be recorded in the financial statements of SCANDOT and the consolidated financial statements of ATLANTIC for the year ended 31 December 2010.

(Chartered Accountants Ireland)

36.3 MAXPOOL plc

MAXPOOL plc owned 60% of the shares in CHING Limited. BAY plc owned the remaining 40% of the €1 ordinary shares in CHING Ltd. The holdings of shares were acquired on 1 January 2009.

CHING Ltd sold a factory outlet site to BAY at a price determined by an independent surveyor on 30 November 2009.

371

On 1 March 2010, MAXPOOL plc purchased a further 30% of €1 ordinary shares of CHING Ltd from BAY plc, and purchased 25% of the ordinary shares of €1 of BAY plc.

On 30 June 2010, CHING Ltd sold the whole of its fleet of vehicles to BAY plc at a price determined by a vehicle auctioneer.

Required:

Explain the implications of the above transactions for the determination of related party relationships and disclosure of such transactions in the financial statements of the MAXPOOL Group plc, CHING Ltd, and BAY plc for the years ending 31 December 2009 and 31 December 2010. (ACCA)

Chapter 37

Financial reporting in hyperinflationary economies

The last two decades have seen inflation at low single-digit levels in most of the developed world. However, this has not been the case universally, and in some countries inflation has continued to spiral out of control. High levels of inflation present a variety of challenges to an economy, one of which is the comparability of financial information over time. A company's impressive sales growth figures may, for example, in reality reflect changes in the general price level, rather than any real increase in the volume of goods or services supplied.

IAS 29 outlines the characteristics of an economy which are indicative of hyperinflation:

- the general population prefers to keep its wealth in non-monetary assets (e.g. property) or in a stable foreign currency;
- the general population regards monetary amounts (e.g. trade receivables) in terms of a stable foreign currency. Prices may be quoted in that currency;
- sales and purchases on credit are made in prices that compensate for the expected loss of purchasing power during the credit period;
- interest rates, wages and prices are linked to a price level; and
- the cumulative inflation rate over three years is approaching or exceeds 100%.

The restatement of financial statements

IAS 29 requires that an entity whose **functional currency** is that of a hyperinflationary economy, must state its **financial statements** in terms of the measuring unit current at the end of the **reporting period**. An entity's functional currency is defined by IAS 21 *The Effects of Changes in Foreign Exchange Rates* as the currency of the primary economic environment in which the entity operates.

Example 1 The functional currency of Cromper Limited is the bengolian peso. Inflation in Bengolia has averaged 40% over the last three years.

Outline the implications of the above information for Cromper Limited when preparing its financial statements for the year ended 31 December 2010.

Solution Cromper is operating in a hyperinflationary economy, and its financial statements should be stated in terms of the measuring unit at 31 December 2010. Amounts in its financial statements, including comparatives, must be stated at price levels effective at the end of the reporting period. Thus, if inflation has been 40% in the year ended 31 December 2010, land purchased on 1 January 2010 for 1 million bengolian pesos will be stated at 1.4 million bengolian pesos at 31 December 2010.

Presentation of the information required by IAS 29 as a supplement to unrestated financial statements is not permitted. Furthermore, separate presentation of the financial statements before restatement is discouraged.

Procedures for the restatement of financial statements

■ First period in which IAS 29 is applied

At the *beginning* of the first period in which IAS 29 is applied:

- the components of owners' equity (except retained earnings and any revaluation surplus) are restated by applying a general price index from the dates that the components were contributed or otherwise arose;
- any revaluation surplus is eliminated;
- retained earnings will be the balancing figure in the restated statement of financial position.

■ End of the first period and all subsequent periods

The following rules apply for the restatement of historical cost financial statements under IAS 29. It should be assumed that the entity's functional currency is that of a hyperinflationary economy, and that its financial statements have been prepared for the year ended 31 December 2010.

Item	Rule for restatement
Statement of financial position	
Monetary items (e.g. cash, trade receivables, and trade payables)	Monetary items are not restated because they are already expressed in terms of the monetary unit current at 31 December 2010
Assets and liabilities linked by agreement to changes in prices (e.g. index-linked government bonds held as an asset)	These items are adjusted in accordance with the agreement, and carried at that adjusted amount at 31 December 2010
Non-monetary assets and liabilities carried at amounts current at the end of the reporting period (e.g. inventory stated at net realisable value, and property assets stated at fair value)	These items are not restated
All other non-monetary assets and liabilities (e.g. plant and machinery carried at historical cost less depreciation, and inventory carried at cost)	These items are adjusted by applying the change in a general price index, from the date of acquisition to 31 December 2010. For example, an entity purchases land on 1 January 2007 for 1M bengolian pesos. Annual inflation has been 40% since the acquisition date. The land will be restated to 3.84M (i.e. $1M \times (1.4)^4$) at 31 December 2010
	The restated amount of non-monetary assets should be reduced when it exceeds its recoverable amount. For example, at 31 December 2010, the above land may have a fair value less costs to sell of 3M bengolian pesos. Its value in use might be 3.2M bengolian pesos. The recoverable amount of the land is therefore 3.2M, and it should be restated at that amount, rather than 3.84M

Item	Rule for restatement
Non-monetary assets revalued at times other than their acquisition date or that of the statement of financial position	The carrying amounts should be restated from the date of revaluation
	For example, land purchased in 2006, is revalued on 1 January 2009 to 2M bengolian pesos. The land should be restated at 3.92M (i.e. 2M $\times$ (1.4)^2) bengolian pesos at 31 December 2010
Owners' equity (e.g. share capital, retained earnings)	All components of owners' equity* are restated by applying a general price index from the beginning of the period, or the date of contribution if later
	* Including any revaluation surplus arising after the beginning of the first year in which the financial statements are restated
Statement of comprehensive income	All items should be expressed in terms of the measuring unit at 31 December 2010
	Thus, all amounts need to be restated by applying the change in the general price index from the dates when the items of income and expense were initially recorded
Gain or loss on restatement	A gain or loss is likely to arise on the restatement of the financial statements under IAS 29. This will occur primarily because, unlike other items in the financial statements, *monetary* assets and liabilities are not restated
	In times of inflation, an entity that borrows 10M bengolian pesos on 1 January 2007, will still owe 10M bengolian pesos at 31 December 2010, assuming that no capital repayments have been made. However, the *real* value of the loan will have fallen significantly, due to an annual rate of inflation of 40%
	IAS 29 requires that the gain/loss on the restatement of an entity's financial statements should be included in profit or loss for the period

■ Corresponding figures

IAS 29 requires that comparative amounts should be restated by applying a general price index, so that the comparative financial statements are presented in terms of the measuring unit at the end of the current reporting period.

Example 2 The functional currency of Cromper Limited is the bengolian peso. Inflation in Bengolia has been running at 40% in each of the last three years.

Outline the implications of the above information for Cromper Limited when preparing comparative information in its financial statements for the year ended 31 December 2010.

Solution IAS 29 requires that Cromper restate its comparative amounts, based on the measuring unit current at 31 December 2010.

For example, let us assume that Cromper purchased land for 1M bengolian pesos on 1 January 2008. When preparing its financial statements for the year ended 31 December 2010, land will be stated at 2.74M (i.e. 1M $\times$ (1.4)^3) bengolian pesos both at 31 December 2010 and 2009.

■ Consolidated financial statements

A parent that reports in the currency of a hyperinflationary economy may have subsidiaries that also report in the currencies of hyperinflationary economies. The financial statements of any such subsidiary should be restated by applying a general price index of the country in whose currency it reports, before they are included in the consolidated financial statements issued by its parent.

■ Summary

- IAS 29 identifies the characteristics of an economy which are indicative of hyperinflation.
- An entity, whose functional currency is that of a hyperinflationary economy, must state its financial statements in terms of the measuring unit current at the end of the reporting period.
- The presentation of the information required by IAS 29 as a supplement to unrestated financial statements is not permitted. Also the separate presentation of the financial statements before restatement is discouraged.
- IAS 29 outlines the procedures for the restatement of an entity's financial statements in the first period in which IAS 29 is applied.
- IAS 29 also describes the procedures for the restatement of financial statements at the end of the first period and all subsequent periods.

Part 9

FINANCIAL INSTRUMENTS

Chapter 38

Capital instruments, reduction of capital and distributable profits

When arranging its financing needs, a company normally uses a combination of equity and debt funding. Debt is usually the cheapest source of finance, as interest is tax deductible, and debt holders have a preferential claim on a company's assets, which reduces their risk. Equity is a more expensive source of finance, as dividends are not tax deductible and equity shareholders only have an entitlement to a company's assets when all other prior claims have been met.

This chapter first outlines how each source of finance is classified as being either a liability or equity. The importance of this distinction is highlighted by considering its effect on a potential provider of funds. The accounting treatment of equity shares is outlined, for an issue of shares at par and at a premium. Capital reduction, including the purchase by a company of its own shares, is also explained.

This chapter also explains the rules for computing the amount of its profits that a company can distribute. Finally, the rules for offsetting a financial asset and a financial liability are outlined.

What is a financial instrument?

IAS 32 *Financial Instruments: Presentation* defines a financial instrument as a contract that results in one entity obtaining a financial asset and another entity taking on an increase in its financial liabilities or its equity.

Example 1 Thorpe Limited raised a loan of €2M on 1 January 2010 from Bank of the World.

Outline how the loan should be presented in the financial statements of Thorpe and Bank of the World.

Solution The loan is a financial instrument that gives rise to a financial asset for Bank of the World, which is owed €2M. For Thorpe Limited, it is a financial liability, as €2M is owed to Bank of the World. The loan will be recorded as follows:

	€'000	€'000
Financial statements of Bank of the World		
Loan receivable (financial asset)	2,000	
Bank		2,000
Financial statements of Thorpe Limited		
Bank	2,000	
Loan (financial liability)		2,000

Example 2 On 1 January 2011, Thorpe Limited issued 10,000 of its 10 cent ordinary shares to Park Limited. Consideration of €30,000 was received from Park Limited.

Outline how the share issue should be presented in the financial statements of Thorpe Limited and Park Limited.

Solution The share issue is a financial instrument that gives rise to a financial asset for Park Limited, and an increase in equity for Thorpe Limited. The share issue will be recorded as follows:

	€'000	€'000
Financial statements of Park Limited		
Investment in Thorpe (financial asset)	30,000	
Bank		30,000
Financial statements of Thorpe Limited		
Bank	30,000	
Ordinary share capital		1,000
Share premium		29,000

The presentation of financial instruments is regulated by IAS 32, which establishes principles for:

- presenting financial instruments as liabilities or equity; and
- offsetting financial assets and financial liabilities.

Key variables are defined in Appendix 38.1, and the scope of IAS 32 is outlined in Appendix 38.2.

Classification of financial instruments

Equity instruments

IAS 32 states that a financial instrument is an equity instrument only if it includes no contractual obligation to deliver cash or another financial asset to another entity.
   Ordinary shares are an example of an equity instrument as:

- they cannot legally be repaid to the shareholders; and
- dividends can be paid but there is no obligation on an entity to do so.

Financial liabilities

A loan raised by an entity from a bank is a financial liability, as it involves a contractual obligation to deliver cash to another entity. A debt owed to a provider of goods or services (i.e. a trade payable) is a financial liability for the same reason.

Substance over form

IAS 32 states that the substance of a financial instrument, rather than its legal form, determines its classification in an entity's statement of financial position. Substance and legal form are often consistent, but not always. For example, some financial instruments that take the legal form of equity are in substance liabilities. Others may combine features associated with both equity instruments and financial liabilities.

The factors to be considered in classifying financial instruments as equity or liabilities are considered in Examples 3–5 below.

Example 3 **Redeemable preference shares**

Thorpe Limited issued €2.5M 9% redeemable preference shares on 1 January 2010. An annual dividend is payable. The shares are redeemable at par on 1 January 2014.

Thorpe Limited has a contractual obligation to deliver cash to the holders of the preference shares, as an annual dividend and on redemption at 1 January 2014. The preference shares are therefore classified as a financial liability. Any dividends on these shares should be treated as interest expense in Thorpe Limited's income statement, and any unpaid dividends at the end of the reporting period must be provided for.

Example 4 **Non-redeemable preference shares**

On 1 January 2009, Thorpe Limited issued €2M non-redeemable preference shares. Dividend payments are at the discretion of Thorpe Limited.

As the preference shares are non-redeemable, and dividend payments are at the discretion of Thorpe Limited, there is no contractual obligation to deliver cash to the holders of the preference shares. Therefore, the €2M non-redeemable preference shares are classified as a component of equity.

Example 5 **Compound financial instruments**

On 1 January 2010, Thorpe Limited issued €1M 7% convertible bonds at par. The bonds will pay interest annually on 31 December, and they are due for redemption at par on 31 December 2012. Alternatively, the bondholders can opt to convert their bonds into 30 ordinary shares of €1 each for every €100 of convertible bonds on 31 December 2012.

The market interest rate on a similar bond, with no conversion option, was 8% on 1 January 2010.

Outline how Thorpe Limited should account for the issue of the convertible bonds.

Solution Some financial instruments may contain some characteristics of equity and some characteristics of a liability. The convertible bonds issued by Thorpe Limited are an example of such an instrument.

IAS 32 requires that compound financial instruments should be separated into their financial liability and equity components and that these should be identified as follows:

- The *fair value of the liability component* should be computed first. On initial recognition, this will equal the present value of the cash flows payable by Thorpe Limited, up to and including redemption. The discount rate used should be the market interest rate applied to similar instruments with no conversion option.
- The *fair value of the equity component* is calculated by deducting the fair value of the liability component from the fair value of the financial instrument as a whole. This represents the amount that the holders of the convertible bonds are willing to pay for the conversion rights.

Fair value of liability component

	Present value
	€
Interest on 31 December 2010 (70,000/1.08)	64,815
Interest on 31 December 2011 (70,000/ (1.08)^2)	60,014
Interest on 31 December 2012 (70,000/ (1.08)^3)	55,568
Capital redemption on 31 December 2012 (1M/(1.08)^3)	793,833
Total liability component	974,230
Equity component (balancing figure)	25,770
Proceeds of the bond issue	1,000,000

The accounting entry to record the issue of the convertible bonds is shown below.

	Dr	Cr
	€	€
Bank	1,000,000	
Convertible bonds – financial liability in SOFP		974,230
Convertible bond reserve – SOFP		25,770
(Being issue of convertible bonds on 1 January 2010)		

Interest of €70,000 is paid annually by Thorpe Limited (i.e. €1M at the coupon rate of 7%). Finance cost in the income statement, however, is charged at a rate of 8% on the carrying value of the liability component of the instrument. In 2010, the interest charge amounts to €77,938 (i.e. €974,230 × 8%). In 2011 and 2012, there is an additional charge due to the amortisation of the equity option in previous periods. The total finance cost over the period 2010–2012 will exceed the coupon interest paid by €25,770.

The accounting entries in respect of interest are outlined below:

	Dr	Cr
	€	€
Finance costs – I/S	77,938	
Bank		70,000
Convertible bonds – additional finance cost		7,938
(Being interest for year ended 31 December 2010; Effective interest charged to I/S = €77,938 (i.e. €974,230 × 8%))		

Finance costs – I/S	78,573	
Bank		70,000
Convertible bonds – additional finance cost		8,573
(Being interest for year ended 31 December 2011; Effective interest charged to I/S = €78,573 (i.e. (€974,230 + €7,938) × 8%))		

Finance costs – I/S	79,259	
Bank		70,000
Convertible bonds – additional finance cost		9,259
(Being interest for year ended 31 December 2012; Effective interest charged to I/S = €79,259 (i.e. (€974,230 + €7,938 + €8,573) × 8%))		

On maturity, the bonds will either be converted into ordinary shares, or the bondholders will be repaid their original capital of €1M. The following accounting entries will apply.

Conversion

	Dr	Cr
	€	€
Convertible bonds	1,000,000	
Convertible bond reserve	25,770	
Ordinary share capital (€1M/100) × 30		300,000
Share premium (balancing figure)		725,770
(Being conversion of the bonds into ordinary shares)		

or

Repayment

Convertible bonds	1,000,000	
Bank		1,000,000
(Being repayment of bondholders' capital)		
Convertible bond reserve	25,770	
Retained earnings		25,770
(As the bonds have been liquidated, the amount originally recorded as the equity component of the instrument is released to retained earnings)		

Importance of distinguishing between financial liabilities and equity instruments

A key objective of IAS 32 is to ensure that there is a clear distinction between financial liabilities and equity instruments in an entity's financial statements. The importance of this distinction is outlined in Examples 6 and 7 below.

Example 6 The statement of financial position of Thorpe Limited shows that the company has financial liabilities (e.g. trade payables, loans) of €6M, none of which are secured by a charge against the company's assets. Thorpe Limited also has total equity (e.g. share capital and retained earnings) of €7M.

Bank of the World is considering whether to provide additional unsecured loan finance of €3M to Thorpe Limited.

Advise Bank of the World as to whether it should advance an additional loan of €3M to Thorpe Limited.

Solution

	€M
Total assets of Thorpe if loan of €3M is advanced (6M + 7M + 3M)	16
Total unsecured creditors (€6M + €3M)	(9)
Excess assets to which creditors have a prior claim over equity shareholders	7

The assets of Thorpe Limited would have to fall by more than €7M, before they would be insufficient to fully cover the amounts due to creditors, which include the loan of €3M from Bank of the World. On this basis, Bank of the World has a substantial level of asset backing for its proposed loan, and it can have reasonable assurance that the loan will be repaid.

Example 7 Assuming the same facts as in Example 6 above, outline the implications for Bank of the World if €5.5M of Thorpe Limited's existing loans had been incorrectly classified as equity capital in its statement of financial position.

Solution		€M
Total assets of Thorpe if loan of €3M is advanced		16
Total unsecured creditors (€6M + €5.5M + €3M)		(14.5)
Excess assets to which creditors have a prior claim over equity shareholders		1.5

The reclassification of €5.5M of equity capital as loans leaves Bank of the World with a much-reduced level of asset backing for its proposed loan. Should the assets of Thorpe Limited fall by more than €1.5M, they will be insufficient to cover all of the amounts owed to creditors. Should Bank of the World advance the loan, there is therefore a significant risk that Thorpe Limited will default.

Accounting for *equity* instruments

Ordinary shares are the most common example of an equity instrument. Ordinary shares are often referred to as equity shares, and they entitle holders to the residual profits of a business after all fixed payments (e.g. interest and preference dividends) have been paid. Ordinary shareholders also own the assets of a business, after all outside claims (e.g. loans and preference shares) have been satisfied.

Issue of shares at nominal value

The nominal value of a company's ordinary shares is its face value for legal purposes. This is sometimes referred to as its par value. The issue of shares at par is recorded as follows.

Example 8 On 1 January 2008, Thorpe Limited issued 100,000 ordinary shares at par. The nominal value of each ordinary share is 10 cents.

The issue of shares by Thorpe Limited will be recorded as follows:

	Dr €'000	Cr €'000
Bank	10	
Ordinary share capital		10

Issue of shares at a premium

Ordinary shares are usually issued at an amount that is higher than their nominal value. However, share capital continues to be recorded at the nominal value of the shares issued. The excess of the issue price over nominal value is included in **share premium**.

Example 9 On 1 January 2010, Thorpe Limited issued 200,000 of its 10 cent ordinary shares at €1 each. This share issue will be recorded by Thorpe Limited as follows:

	Dr €'000	Cr €'000
Bank	200	
Ordinary share capital (200,000 × 10 cent)		20
Share premium		180

■ Purchase of own shares

A company may have several reasons for buying back its own shares. These include:

- To support its share price, at a time when its shares may be perceived to be trading at a discount. This can allow shareholders to realise a larger capital gain if they decide to encash part or all of their shareholding.
- To frustrate a hostile takeover bid.
- A lack of attractive investment opportunities.
- To set aside shares whose issue may be required under convertible bonds or employee share option agreements.

Example 10 On 1 July 2010, Thorpe Limited reacquired 60,000 of its own shares for cash consideration of €120,000.

When an entity purchases its own shares, they are known as treasury shares. The amount paid for the treasury shares is deducted from retained earnings, within equity, and it cannot be recognised as a financial asset. The purchase is recorded as follows:

	Dr €'000	Cr €'000
Treasury shares	120	
Bank		120
(Being purchase of treasury shares on 1 July 2010. These treasury shares should be deducted from equity in Thorpe Limited's SOFP)		

Thorpe Limited's statement of financial position will reflect the purchase of its shares as follows:

	€'000
Ordinary share capital	xxx
Share premium	x,xxx
Retained earnings	xxx
Treasury shares	(120)
Total equity	x,xxx

No gain or loss should be recorded in profit or loss relating to the purchase, sale, issue or cancellation of an entity's own equity instruments. This is because these are transactions with an entity's owners, and they do not involve a gain or loss to the entity. See Example 11 below.

Example 11 On 1 December 2010, Thorpe Limited sold 30,000 of its treasury shares for €80,000.

Treasury shares should be credited with €60,000, which is the amount previously paid by Thorpe Limited for the shares that are now being sold (i.e. €120,000 × 30,000/60,000). The excess proceeds are credited to share premium.

	Dr €'000	Cr €'000
Bank	80	
Treasury shares		60
Share premium		20
(Being resale of treasury shares on 1 December 2010)		

■ Reduction of capital to eliminate accumulated losses

A company with accumulated losses is not permitted to pay a dividend. This may act as a disincentive to shareholders to contribute additional capital to the business. In this situation a company may decide to reduce its share capital in order to eliminate its accumulated losses. This may require that a special resolution is passed by its shareholders, or that the company receives the permission of the courts. The accounting treatment is illustrated in Example 12 below.

Example 12 On 1 January 2010, Thorpe Limited had accumulated losses of €250,000. It was decided to reduce the nominal value of the company's 1 million ordinary shares from €1 to 75 cents, so as to eliminate Thorpe Limited's accumulated losses. The following accounting entries are required:

	Dr €'000	Cr €'000
Ordinary share capital	250	
Accumulated losses		250
(Being reduction of share capital to eliminate accumulated losses on 1 December 2010. This will result in a reduction of €250,000 in share capital in the SOFP, and a retained earnings figure of zero)		

■ Capital reconstruction scheme

If a company has consistently recurring losses, its assets may not be sufficient to meet the amount of its liabilities. If the company has better future prospects, however, its debt holders may be persuaded to participate in a reconstruction scheme to put the company's financial statements on a more solid footing. This is illustrated in Example 13 below.

Example 13 The accumulated losses of Ring Limited at 31 December 2010 amounted to €800,000, and the board of directors decided to put in place a viable business plan to restore the company to profitability. As part of a reconstruction scheme it was decided to eliminate the accumulated losses, and to reduce the carrying value of plant and machinery by €100,000.

On the basis that the liquidation of Ring Limited would have resulted in a substantial loss for the company's bondholders, as part of the reconstruction scheme they agreed to accept a reduction of €200,000 in the amount due to them. The remaining losses were to be absorbed by a reduction in Ring Limited's ordinary share capital.

The following entry is required to effect the reconstruction:

	Dr €'000	Cr €'000
Bonds	200	
Ordinary share capital (balancing figure)	700	
Accumulated losses		800
Plant and machinery		100

As a result of the reconstruction, the carrying value of the assets of Ring Limited is restated to their recoverable amount (or lower). Accumulated losses have been eliminated, thus permitting a dividend to be paid to the shareholders out of future profits. On the basis that they will benefit from the company's future profitability, the bondholders have supported the reconstruction, albeit that they have agreed to a reduction in the amount owed to them. The bondholders will, however, normally be able to demand a higher coupon rate than before.

Distributable profits

Equity investors buy shares in the expectation that they will earn a return on their investment. That return can be achieved as an increase in a company's share price, or in the form of a dividend, or both. A shareholder who wishes to receive a dividend should ensure that a company in which he intends to invest has profits that can be distributed.

Creditors also have an interest in a company's distributable profits. The payment of a dividend to shareholders reduces a company's cash assets, leaving less available to pay amounts owed to creditors.

■ What are distributable profits?

Firstly, it should be noted that distributions are made by individual companies and not by groups. The group accounts are therefore not relevant for the purposes of determining a company's profits available for distribution. The amount of a company's distributable profit is determined by legislation. Although company legislation does not define distributable profit, it addresses specific issues that may arise. In general, distributable profits can be defined as the amount of accumulated realised profits less accumulated realised losses.

Accumulated means the amount of profit or loss that has arisen over time, since the date of a company's incorporation. *Realised* profits are profits realised in the form of cash or other assets, the ultimate cash realisation of which can be assessed with reasonable certainty.

Example 14 The following balances relate to Bridge Limited, a private company, at 31 December 2010.

	€'000
Share capital	100
Share premium	460
Revaluation surplus	200
Unrealised losses	(140)
Realised profits	300
	920

Required:

(a) Calculate the distributable profit of Bridge Limited at 31 December 2010.

(b) If Bridge Limited was a public company, would the amount of its distributable profit be different?

Solution Bridge Limited has distributable profit of €300,000 at 31 December 2010. This is the amount of its realised profits at that date.

If Bridge Limited was a public company, its distributable profit would be €160,000 (i.e. realised profits less unrealised losses).

■ Realised and unrealised profits and losses

Company legislation does not define realised profits. It does, however, set out the following rules:

Revaluations

- A revaluation surplus is an unrealised profit.
- On disposal of a revalued asset, any previously unrealised surplus becomes realised.
- When a depreciable non-current asset is revalued upwards, this results in a higher periodic depreciation charge. In computing realised profit, however, depreciation should be based only on the cost of the asset.

Miscellaneous

- A provision is a realised loss.
- Development costs carried forward as an asset are treated as an unrealised loss. They become a realised loss when the asset is amortised in later periods.
- The purchase of shares to be held as treasury shares must be made out of distributable profits, which are reduced by the amount of the purchase price of the shares.
- Profits and losses resulting from the recognition of changes in fair values are realised profits and losses, to the extent that they are readily convertible into cash.

Example 15 An excerpt from the financial statements of Dyson Limited at 31 December 2010 is shown below.

	€'000
Non-current assets	
Buildings	800
Development costs	400
Other net assets	200
Net assets	1,400
Equity	
Share capital	100
Share premium	500
Revaluation surplus*	200
Retained earnings	600
Total equity	1,400

* On 31 December 2008, buildings were revalued upwards by €200,000. Dyson Limited depreciates buildings at 2% per annum on a straight-line basis.

Required:

(a) Calculate the distributable profit of Dyson Limited at 31 December 2010.

(b) If Dyson Limited was a public company, how would the amount of its distributable profit differ?

Solution (a) The distributable profit of Dyson Limited is calculated as follows:

	€'000
Retained earnings	600
Depreciation adjustment*	8
Distributable profit	608

* When computing distributable profit, depreciation should be based on buildings at cost. Depreciation charged on a revaluation surplus should therefore be added back for the purposes of computing distributable profit. Therefore, the distributable profit of Dyson Limited is increased by €8,000 (i.e. €200,000 × 2% × 2 years).

(b) If Dyson Limited was a public company, development costs of €400,000 would have to be deducted in computing distributable profit. Development costs are an unrealised loss, which in the case of a public company must be deducted in computing distributable profit. Dyson Limited would therefore have distributable profits of €208,000 (i.e. €608,000 − €400,000).

Offsetting a financial asset and a financial liability

To offset a financial asset and a financial liability, an entity must have a currently enforceable legal right to offset the recognised amounts.

Example 16 Thorpe Limited had funds of €200,000 on demand deposit with its bank on 31 December 2010. On the same date, the company had a bank overdraft of €320,000. Thorpe Limited has written confirmation from its bank that these amounts can be offset against each other.

Thorpe's demand deposit of €200,000 is a financial asset. The bank overdraft of €320,000 is a financial liability. As Thorpe Limited has bank confirmation that the two amounts can be offset, a net amount of €120,000 can be included as a current liability at 31 December 2010.

Summary

- A financial instrument is a contract that gives rise to a financial asset of one entity and a financial liability or equity instrument of another entity.
- A key objective of IAS 32 is to ensure that there is a clear distinction between financial liabilities and equity instruments.
- A financial instrument is an equity instrument only if it includes no contractual obligation to deliver cash or another financial asset to another entity.
- A financial liability involves a contractual obligation to deliver cash or another financial asset to another entity.
- Some financial instruments contain both an equity element and a liability element. These are called compound financial instruments. IAS 32 requires that compound financial instruments should be separated into their financial liability and equity components.
- Share capital is recorded at its nominal value in the statement of financial position.
- If a company purchases its own shares, these are known as treasury shares, and they are deducted from retained earnings in the statement of financial position.
- A reduction in ordinary share capital may be effected in order to eliminate a company's accumulated losses.
- A capital reconstruction scheme may present an opportunity to restructure a company's statement of financial position, with the agreement of its stakeholders.
- The distributable profit of a private company equals the amount of its cumulative realised profits, less cumulative realised losses. In the case of a public company, this is reduced by the amount of cumulative *unrealised* losses.
- A financial asset and a financial liability should not be offset unless an entity has a legal right to do so.

Appendix 38.1

Definition of key variables

A *financial instrument* is any contract that gives rise to a financial asset of one entity and a financial liability or equity instrument of another entity.

A *financial asset* is any asset that is:

(a) cash;
(b) an equity instrument of another entity (e.g. shares held in another company);
(c) a contractual right:
- to receive cash or another financial asset from another entity; or
- to exchange financial assets or financial liabilities with another entity;
(d) a contract that will or may be settled in the entity's own equity instruments.

A *financial liability* is any liability that is:

(a) a contractual obligation:
- to deliver cash or another financial asset to another entity; or
- to exchange financial assets or financial liabilities with another entity under conditions that are potentially unfavourable to the entity; or
(b) a contract that will or may be settled in the entity's own equity instruments.

An *equity instrument* is any contract that evidences a residual interest in the assets of an entity after deducting all of its liabilities.

Appendix 38.2

Scope of IAS 32

IAS 32 applies to all types of financial instruments, except:

- Interests in subsidiaries, associates or joint ventures that are accounted for in accordance with IAS 27 *Consolidated and Separate Financial Statements,* IAS 28 *Investments in Associates* or *IAS 31 Interests in Joint Ventures.*

    However, in some cases, IAS 27, IAS 28 or IAS 31 permit an entity to account for a subsidiary, associate or joint venture using IAS 39. In those cases, the entity should also apply the requirements of IAS 32.
- Employers' rights and obligations under employee benefit plans to which IAS 19 *Employee Benefits* applies.
- Most insurance contracts as defined in IFRS 4 *Insurance Contracts,* and most financial instruments to which IFRS 2 *Share-based Payment* applies.

QUESTIONS

38.1 PINGWAY

PINGWAY issued a €10M 3% convertible loan note at par on 1 April 2009 with interest payable annually in arrears. Three years later, on 31 March 2012, the loan note is convertible into equity shares on the basis of €100 of loan note for 25 equity shares, or it may be redeemed at par in cash at the option of the loan note holder.

One of the company's financial assistants observed that the use of a convertible loan note was preferable to a non-convertible loan note as the latter would have required an interest rate of 8% in order to make it attractive to investors. The assistant has also commented that the use of a convertible loan note will improve the profit as a result of lower interest costs, and as it is likely that the loan note holders will choose the equity option, the loan note can be classified as equity which will improve the company's high gearing position.

The present value of €1 receivable at the end of the year, based on discount rates of 3 and 8%, can be taken as:

	3%	8%
	€	€
End of year 1	0.97	0.93
2	0.94	0.86
3	0.92	0.79

Required:
Comment on the financial assistant's observations and show how the convertible loan note should be accounted for in PINGWAY's financial statements for the year ended 31 March 2010.   (ACCA)

38.2 WELLMAY

On 1 April 2009, an 8% convertible loan note with a nominal value of €600,000 was issued by WELLMAY at par. It is redeemable on 31 March 2010 at par or it may be converted into equity shares of WELLMAY on the basis of 100 new shares for each €200 of loan note. An equivalent loan note without the conversion option would have carried an interest rate of 10%. Interest of €48,000 has been paid on the loan and charged as a finance cost.

The present value of €1 receivable at the end of each year, based on discount rates of 8 and 10% are:

	8%	10%
End of year 1	0.93	0.91
2	0.86	0.83
3	0.79	0.75
4	0.73	0.68

Required:
Outline how the issue of the convertible loan note should be accounted for by WELLMAY in its financial statements for the year ended 31 March 2010.   (ACCA)

38.3 BRICER Ltd

On 1 January 2011, BRICER Ltd issued €250,000 of non-redeemable preference shares. The preference shares carry a fixed dividend of 6%, which can be deferred in perpetuity at the option of BRICER Ltd. If the shares are not redeemed by BRICER Ltd by 1 January 2015, the dividend will increase to 15%.

Required:
Outline how BRICER Ltd should account for the preference shares.

38.4 FLUCE plc

FLUCE plc issued €5M of 8% non-redeemable loan stock on 1 January 2011. FLUCE has the option of deferring the interest payments in perpetuity. It has always been the policy of FLUCE plc to pay interest on similar loan stock in the past.

Required:

Outline how FLUCE plc should account for the non-redeemable loan stock.

Chapter 39

Financial instruments – recognition and measurement

The measurement of financial instruments has been a very controversial area in recent years, as the global financial crisis has focused the world's attention on the financial assets of corporations such as Lehman Brothers. Some commentators, including John McCain, the Republican candidate for the US presidency in 2008, have blamed accounting rules for contributing to and worsening the crisis. At issue was the 'mark-to-market' rule, which requires that financial assets be carried at current market value.

'Assets should not be marked to unrealistic fire-sale prices,' argued William Isaac, former Federal Deposit Insurance Corporation chairman, in the *Wall Street Journal*. McCain's contention, and Isaac's, was that in a falling stock market, reducing the reported value of financial assets inevitably puts further downward pressure on stock prices.

In the face of mounting pressure, the reaction of accounting regulators was swift, with both FASB and the IASB taking action to relax the much criticised 'mark-to-market' requirements. The amendment allowed certain financial assets, carried at fair value, to depart on rare occasions from the fair value measurement basis.

As stability has returned to the financial markets, the IASB has issued IFRS 9 to consolidate its requirements for the reporting of financial assets. Entities currently have a choice of recognising and measuring financial assets under the requirements of either IAS 39 or IFRS 9. However, IFRS 9 must be applied for periods beginning on or after 1 January 2013, with earlier adoption being permitted.

IFRS 9 is being introduced in three phases. The first phase covers *classification and measurement*, and details are outlined below. Phase two concerns *impairment methodology*, and phase three relates to *hedge accounting*.

Financial assets

■ Definition

A financial asset is any asset that is:

- cash;
- an equity instrument of another entity (i.e. shares held by one entity in another entity);
- a contractual right:
  - to receive cash or another financial asset from another entity; or
  - to exchange financial assets or financial liabilities with another entity on a basis that is potentially favourable to the reporting entity.

An entity should **recognise** a financial asset in its SOFP when, and only when, the entity becomes party to the contractual provisions of the instrument.

Example 1   R Limited sells goods to T Limited on credit for €8,000 on 1 June 2011. The goods are paid for on 1 September 2011.

    The sale should be recorded by R Limited on 1 June 2011, when a contract is established for the sale of the goods to T Limited. It is not appropriate to wait until the settlement date to record the transaction.

■ Classification

IFRS 9 requires that all financial assets must be allocated into one of two classifications:

- assets measured at amortised cost, or
- assets measured at fair value

■ Initial measurement

All financial assets should initially be measured at fair value, plus transaction costs when fair value changes are not reported in profit or loss.

Example 2   P Limited purchases shares in another company for €8,000. Transaction costs amount to €600. The shares are accounted for at fair value through profit or loss (FVTPL).

	Dr	Cr
	€	€
Financial asset	8,000	
Transaction costs – I/S	600	
Bank		8,600

The transaction costs are charged as an expense in the income statement, as the financial asset is accounted for at FVTPL.

Example 3   R Limited purchases loan stock of another company for €8,000. R. Limited does not account for the loan stock at FVTPL. The transaction is recorded as follows:

	Dr	Cr
	€	€
Financial asset	8,600	
Bank		8,600

The inclusion of the transaction costs in the amount of the financial asset is appropriate as the loan stock is *not* measured at fair value through profit or loss. Thus, it is appropriate to include attributable transaction costs as part of the financial asset.

■ Subsequent measurement

Equity instruments

Equity investments must be measured at fair value in an entity's SOFP. Quoted prices in an active market provide the best evidence of fair value. Changes in fair value are recognised in profit or loss. The only exception applies in respect of equity investments *not* held for trading: an entity may, at the time of initial recognition, make an irrevocable decision to record fair value changes on such investments in *other comprehensive income*.

Example 4 Timber Limited purchased equity shares in another entity on 1 January 2011 for €100,000. The shares, which are held for trading, had a fair value of €90,000 at 31 December 2011.

	Dr	Cr
	€	€
Financial asset	100,000	
Bank		100,000
(Being purchase of equity shares on 1 January 2011)		
Fair value loss – I/S	10,000	
Financial asset		10,000
(Being restatement of equity investment to its fair value at 31 December 2011)		

If the equity shares were *not* held for trading, Timber Limited could, on 1 January 2011, have opted to recognise fair value changes in other comprehensive income. In this event, the second journal entry in Example 4 above would be revised as follows:

	Dr	Cr
	€	€
Fair value loss – OCI	10,000	
Financial asset		10,000
(Being restatement of equity investment to its fair value at 31 December 2011)		

Consequently, only dividend income will be recognised in profit or loss, should Timber Limited opt to record fair value changes in OCI.

Debt instruments

A debt instrument that complies with the business model *and* cash flow characteristics requirements of IFRS 9 should be measured at amortised cost. All other debt instruments must be measured at **fair value** through profit or loss.

Business model
An entity must hold the debt instrument to collect the contractual cash flows, and not to realise changes in fair value.

Example 5 On 1 January 2011, Major Limited purchased loan stock in Bruce Limited for €10,000. The loan stock carries no interest and will be redeemed on 31 December 2013 for €13,310. Major Limited intends to hold the loan stock until maturity.

This debt investment satisfies the business model requirement of IFRS 9, as Major's intention is to hold the loan stock until maturity, rather than to realise changes in its fair value.

Cash flow characteristics
The cash flows from the investment should be solely payments of principal and interest. The investment in Example 5 above only provides Major Limited with the repayment of principal and a redemption premium in lieu of interest for the period. Thus, this investment satisfies the cash flow requirements of IFRS 9.

As Major Limited's investment in Bruce satisfies both of the IFRS 9 requirements, it is classified at amortised cost and the redemption premium is recorded in profit or loss over the investment term using the effective interest rate.

The effective interest rate is the rate at which the discounted redemption payment equals the amount initially received. In Example 5, the effective interest rate is 10% as €10,000 = (€13,310/(1.1)^3).

The following accounting entries are required:

	Dr €	Cr €
Financial asset	10,000	
Bank		10,000
(Being purchase of loan stock on 1 January 2011)		
Financial asset	1,000	
Finance income – I/S		1,000
(Being interest at 10% for year end 31 December 2011)		
Financial asset	1,100	
Finance income – I/S		1,100
(Being interest at 10% for year end 31 December 2012, i.e. (10,000 + €1,000) × 10%)		
Financial asset	1,210	
Finance income – I/S		1,210
(Being interest at 10% for year end 31 December 2013, i.e. (10,000 + €1,000 + €1,100) × 10%)		
Bank	13,310	
Financial asset		13,310
(Being redemption of loan stock at maturity)		

Fair value option

An entity may, at initial recognition, designate a debt instrument as measured at fair value through profit or loss, if doing so eliminates or significantly reduces a measurement or recognition inconsistency. This option is available even if a debt investment satisfies both the business model and cash flow requirements of IFRS 9.

Reclassification

IFRS 9 requires that an entity reclassify its debt instruments if there is a change in its business model for managing its financial assets. Any reclassification is made prospectively from the date of reclassification.

Example 6 A financial services firm decides to shut down its retail mortgage business. It no longer accepts new business and the firm is actively marketing its loan portfolio for sale.

The business model of the financial services firm has changed, and it is no longer the intention to retain its loan assets so as to derive contractual payments of principal and interest. Thus, the loan assets should be reclassified from amortised cost to FVTPL, and fair value changes should be recorded in profit or loss from the reclassification date.

■ Derecognition of financial assets

A financial asset should be derecognised if:

- an entity has transferred the asset to another party; and
- substantially all of the risks and rewards of ownership of the asset have been transferred.

Example 7 On 31 December 2011, Marsh Limited transferred ownership of its trade receivables to Trump Limited in return for an up-front payment of €1.5M. Trump Limited, however, continues to have recourse to Marsh Limited for any bad debts.

Marsh Limited has transferred ownership of its trade receivables to Trump Limited, the latter company having the rights to the future cash inflows expected from the asset. Marsh Limited continues, however, to incur a substantial risk in respect of the trade receivables, as Trump Limited has recourse to Marsh for any bad debts. Therefore, Marsh Limited should continue to recognise the trade receivables as a financial asset in its statement of financial position. The asset should, however, be reduced as the amounts outstanding from customers are collected by Trump Limited.

Financial liabilities

Classification of financial liabilities

Two classes of financial liabilities are recognised by IFRS 9:

- financial liabilities at fair value through profit or loss (FVTPL)
- financial liabilities at amortised cost

Recognition of financial liabilities

An entity should recognise a financial liability when the entity becomes a party to the contractual provisions of the instrument.

Example 8 R Limited purchases goods from T Limited on credit for €8,000 on 1 June 2011. The goods are paid for on 1 September 2011.

The liability should be recorded by R Limited on 1 June 2011, when a contract is established for the purchase of the goods from T Limited. It is not appropriate to wait until the settlement date to record the transaction.

Initial measurement of financial liabilities

Initially, financial liabilities should be measured at fair value, minus transaction costs for financial liabilities at amortised cost. Fair value will normally be the cost of goods/services received.

Example 9 Needy Limited raised a bank loan of €100,000 on 1 January 2011. Needy Limited incurred an arrangement fee of €1,000.

The bank loan is classified as a financial liability at amortised cost. It should initially be recognised at fair value less transaction costs. The loan will therefore be recorded as follows on 1 January 2011:

	Dr €	Cr €
Bank	99,000	
Loan		99,000
(Being loan raised on 1 January 2011)		

■ Measurement subsequent to initial recognition

After their initial measurement, financial liabilities held for trading are recorded at FVTPL.

All other liabilities are measured at amortised cost, unless an entity uses the fair value option.

An entity can opt to measure financial liabilities at FVTPL if:

- it would eliminate or significantly reduce a measurement or recognition inconsistency; or
- the liability is part of a group of financial liabilities that is managed and evaluated on a fair value basis.

Most financial liabilities, however, are measured at **amortised cost.** Thus, the accounting treatment is similar to that employed for financial assets in Example 5 above. This is revisited in Example 10 below.

Example 10   Major Limited issued loan stock on 1 January 2011 for €10,000. The loan stock pays no interest and will be redeemed on 31 December 2013 for €13,310. The effective interest rate is 10% per annum.

The loan stock is a financial liability in the financial statements of Major Limited.

	Dr	Cr
	€	€
Bank	10,000	
Loan stock – SOFP		10,000
(Being issue of loan stock on 1 January 2011)		
Interest payable – I/S	1,000	
Loan stock – SOFP		1,000
(Being interest at 10% for year end 31 December 2011)		
Interest payable – I/S	1,100	
Loan stock – SOFP		1,100
(Being interest at 10% for year end 31 December 2012 i.e. (€10,000 + €1,000) × 10%)		
Interest payable – I/S	1,210	
Loan stock		1,210
(Being interest at 10% for year end 31 December 2013 i.e. (€10,000 + €1,000 + €1,100) × 10%)		
Loan stock	13,310	
Bank		13,310
(Being repayment of loan stock at maturity)		

■ Derecognition of financial liabilities

A financial liability should be derecognised when it is extinguished. This occurs on 31 August 2011 in Example 11 below, when Marge Limited has paid all amounts due to Cecil Limited.

Example 11   Marge Limited purchases goods from Cecil Limited on 1 June 2011 for €20,000. Payment for half of the goods is due on 31 July, the balance being payable on 31 August.

	Dr €'000	Cr €'000
Purchases	20	
Trade payables		20
(Being goods purchased on 1 June 2011)		
Trade payables	10	
Bank		10
(Being payment for half of the goods on 31 July)		
Trade payables	10	
Bank		10
(Being payment for half of the goods on 31 August)		

Derivatives

All derivatives are measured at fair value. Changes in fair value are recognised in profit or loss, unless an entity has elected to treat the derivative as a hedging instrument.

Summary

- Entities currently have a choice of recognising and measuring financial assets and financial liabilities under the requirements of either IAS 39 or IFRS 9. However, IFRS 9 must be applied for periods beginning on or after 1 January 2013, with earlier adoption permitted.

Financial assets
- Financial assets must be classified as assets measured at amortised cost, or assets measured at fair value.
- Financial assets should initially be measured at fair value, plus transaction costs when fair value changes are not reported in profit or loss.
- Equity instruments must subsequently be measured at fair value, with fair value changes being recognised in profit or loss. However, fair value changes on equity instruments not held for trading may be reported in other comprehensive income, subject to an irrevocable decision being made at the time of initial recognition.
- Debt instruments that satisfy the business model and cash flow characteristics tests of IFRS 9 must be measured at amortised cost. An entity may, however, at initial recognition, designate a debt instrument as measured at fair value through profit or loss, if doing so eliminates a measurement or recognition inconsistency.
- A financial asset should be derecognised if an entity has transferred the asset to another party, and substantially all of the risks and rewards of ownership of the asset have been transferred.

Financial liabilities
- Financial liabilities are classified as being at fair value through profit or loss (FVTPL), or at amortised cost.

- Initially, financial liabilities should be measured at fair value, minus transaction costs for financial liabilities at amortised cost.
- After initial recognition, financial liabilities held for trading are recorded at FVTPL. All other liabilities are measured at amortised cost, unless an entity chooses the fair value option.
- Financial liabilities should be derecognised when they are extinguished.

QUESTIONS

39.1 SPLURGE plc
On 30 September 2010, SPLURGE plc purchased 1% of the equity share capital of MINT plc for €25M. Transaction costs were €20,000. On 31 December 2010, the fair value of SPLURGE's investment in MINT was €26.5M.

Required:
Outline how the investment in MINT should be accounted for in the financial statements of SPLURGE plc.

39.2 TRAMP plc
On 1 February 2010, TRAMP plc purchased 2% of the equity shares of LADY plc for €6M. The value of these shares did not change until after 31 December 2010. TRAMP sold its shareholding in LADY on 1 November 2011 for €7M.

Required:
Outline how the investment in LADY should be accounted for in the financial statements of TRAMP plc.

39.3 GRINGLE plc
On 1 March 2010, GRINGLE plc purchased 1% of the equity share capital of MAID Ltd for €2M. The investment was not held for trading, and on 1 March 2010, GRINGLE made an irrevocable decision to record any change in fair value in other comprehensive income. On 31 December 2010, the fair value of GRINGLE's investment in MAID was €2.3M.

Required:
Outline how the investment in MAID should be accounted for in the financial statements of GRINGLE plc.

39.4 SMITH Ltd
SMITH Limited purchased goods from JONES Limited for €150,000 on 1 September 2010. SMITH paid for the goods on 1 December 2010.

Required:
Outline how the above transaction should be accounted for in the financial statements of SMITH Ltd.

Chapter 40

Financial instruments: disclosures

The proliferation of financial instruments in recent years has presented a formidable challenge to regulatory bodies such as the IASB. The rules for the presentation of financial instruments in financial statements are outlined in IAS 32, and their recognition and measurement are regulated by IAS 39 and IFRS 9. Given the complexity of certain financial instruments, it is important that entities provide disclosure in their financial statements that enable users to evaluate:

- the **significance** of financial instruments for the entity's financial position and performance; and
- the **nature and extent of risks** arising from financial instruments to which the entity is exposed, and how the entity manages those risks.

These disclosure issues are addressed in IFRS 7 *Financial Instruments: Disclosures.*

Scope

IFRS 7 should be applied to all entities and all financial statements except:

(i) interests in **subsidiaries**, **associates** or joint ventures that are accounted for under IAS 27, IAS 28 or IAS 31 respectively. However, in some cases these standards permit an entity to use IAS 39 and IFRS 9 in accounting for an interest in a subsidiary, associate or joint venture. In those cases, IFRS 7 will apply.
(ii) employers' rights and obligations arising from employee benefit plans, to which IAS 19 *Employee Benefits* applies.
(iii) some insurance contracts as defined in IFRS 4 *Insurance Contracts.*
(iv) most financial instruments, contracts and obligations under share-based payment transactions to which IFRS 2 *Share-based Payment* applies.

Significance of financial instruments

The principal disclosures to enable users to evaluate the significance of financial instruments for an entity's financial position and performance are as follows.

■ Carrying amounts in statement of financial position

The carrying amount of the following financial assets and financial liabilities should be disclosed either in the statement of financial position or in the notes:

- financial **assets** measured at **fair value** through profit or loss;
- financial **liabilities** at fair value through profit or loss;
- financial assets and liabilities measured at amortised cost.

■ Collateral

(i) The carrying amounts of financial assets that an entity has pledged as collateral.

(ii) The terms and conditions of the pledge.

■ Statement of comprehensive income

The following amounts relating to items of income, **expense**, gains or losses should be disclosed either in the statement of comprehensive income or in the notes:

(i) Net gains or net losses on:
  - financial assets or financial liabilities at fair value through profit or loss;
  - financial assets and liabilities measured at amortised cost.

(ii) Total interest income and expense for financial assets or financial liabilities that are not at fair value through profit or loss.

(iii) Any impairment loss for each class of financial asset.

■ Other disclosures

Accounting policies

Disclosure is required of the measurement bases and other accounting policies used in respect of financial instruments, when these are relevant to an understanding of the financial statements.

Hedge accounting

The following information should be disclosed for each type of hedge described in IAS 39:

- a description of each type of hedge;
- a description of the financial instruments designated as hedging instruments, and their fair values;
- the nature of the risks being hedged.

Fair value

The fair value of each class of financial assets and financial liabilities should be disclosed in a way that permits a comparison with their carrying amounts.

Fair value measurements should be classified using a fair value hierarchy with the following levels:

- quoted prices in active markets for identical assets or liabilities (Level 1);
- inputs, excluded quoted prices within Level 1, that are observable for the asset or liability (Level 2);
- inputs that are not based on observable market data (Level 3).

For fair value measurements recognised in an entity's SOFP, the following information should be disclosed for each class of financial instrument:

- the level in the fair value hierarchy into which the fair value measurements are categorised;

- any significant transfers between Levels 1 and 2;
- for fair value measurements in Level 3, a reconciliation of opening and closing balances.

Nature and extent of risks arising from financial instruments

IFRS 7 focuses mainly on three types of risk that arise from financial instruments, and how they have been managed.

(i) Credit risk

Credit risk is

the risk that one party to a financial instrument will cause a financial loss for the other party by failing to discharge an obligation.

(ii) Liquidity risk

Liquidity risk is

the risk that an entity will encounter difficulty in meeting obligations associated with financial liabilities.

(iii) Market risk

Market risk is

the risk that the fair value or future cash flows of a financial instrument will fluctuate because of changes in market prices.

Market risk comprises currency risk, interest rate risk and other price risk.

For each type of risk, IFRS 7 requires the following disclosures:

- details of an entity's exposure to the risk and how it arises;
- an entity's objectives, policies and processes for managing the risk;
- methods used to measure the risk;
- summary quantitative data about an entity's exposure to that risk at the end of the reporting period.

Specific disclosures are required in respect of credit risk, liquidity risk and market risk as follows:

(a) Credit risk:
- the entity's maximum exposure to credit risk;
- information about the credit quality of financial assets that are not impaired;
- an age analysis of financial assets that are overdue but not impaired;
- an analysis of financial assets that are impaired.

(b) Liquidity risk:
- a maturity analysis for financial liabilities, and a description of how an entity manages the related liquidity risk.

(c) Market risk:
- a sensitivity analysis for each type of market risk to which an entity is exposed at the end of the reporting period.

Part 10

FINANCIAL ANALYSIS

Chapter 41

Financial analysis

Health checks are a part of everyday life. Our cars are brought to a mechanic to be serviced, and from time to time we must fulfil the requirement of an MOT/NCT test. Most of us, particularly as we grow older, attend to our personal well-being by having our blood pressure and cholesterol levels checked to ensure that our bodies are functioning efficiently. We also routinely service items such as gas boilers, burglar alarms and other electrical appliances in our homes.

The need for a business to have a regular check-up is no different, and financial analysis can be defined as a holistic appraisal of a firm's **financial** well-being. The IASB *Framework* states that the objective of financial statements is to provide users with information to facilitate decision-making. Thus, our focus in this chapter is on the use of **financial statements** for decisions such as buying or selling shares, or merging with or acquiring another business. That is not to say that other sources of information, such as the state of a firm's order book, or its market share are not important. It is merely to acknowledge that financial statements provide valuable information for making economic decisions, and it is appropriate to focus on that information in a textbook on financial reporting.

Limitations of financial statements

In utilising financial statements for the purpose of financial analysis, the user should be aware of their limitations.

■ Completeness

As financial statements generally record only the result of financial transactions, they can not succeed in presenting a complete picture of a business. For example, the level of staff morale and efficiency of personnel, which are of great importance to a firm, cannot be quantified and are therefore not reflected in the financial statements.

■ Historic information

Financial statements provide a summary of a firm's historic financial transactions. Therefore, they contain little of a predictive nature that would be valuable for decision-making purposes. Reliability and certification requirements also result in the financial statements being issued some time after the end of the reporting period, thus impacting on their timeliness, and further limiting their usefulness for decision-making purposes.

■ Comparability

Financial analysis normally uses accounting ratios to summarise the information in a firm's financial statements. For example, the net profit margin is a useful indicator of profitability. However, financial ratios are of limited value on a stand-alone basis. If a ratio is to be meaningful, there must be some yardstick against which to compare it. Such a benchmark could be obtained by using the following sources of reference.

Cross-sectional analysis

This involves a comparison of a firm's accounting ratios with other firms in the same industry. For example, the profit margin of a supermarket multiple, such as Tesco, can usefully be compared with that of Asda or Lidl. This will assist in evaluating a firm's competitiveness and performance across its industry.

Time-series analysis

This involves a comparison of a firm's own accounting ratios over time. Thus, Tesco could evaluate its profit margin in 2010 against what was achieved in 2009 and earlier years. Time-series analysis facilitates trend analysis, whereby a firm's performance over time can be critically evaluated.

■ Timing of statement of financial position

The SOFP provides a picture of a business at a moment in time. One must be careful, however, in interpreting ratios that are based on a firm's SOFP. For example, if a company which produces umbrellas has a year end of 30 April, its inventory figure will be artificially low. By contrast, a similar company with a year end of 31 October will carry a high inventory level as it prepares for the winter season.

■ Management deficiencies

Argenti,[1] writing about business failure, maintains that by the time information is included in the financial statements, it is too late to prevent corporate failure. It is more beneficial, he argues, to assess top management for evidence of deficiencies which will ultimately result in a firm's demise.

Adjusting financial statements

The financial statements of a firm may need to be adjusted in respect of significant events that occur during a reporting period, or because of changes in a firm's measurement techniques or accounting policies. For example, a company with a 31 December year end might acquire a large **subsidiary** on 1 December 2010. Only the post-acquisition profits of the subsidiary (i.e. 31 days) can be included in the consolidated profits of the group for 2010. However, all of the subsidiary's **assets** and **liabilities** will be included in full in the consolidated SOFP.

Consider the impact of this acquisition on a ratio such as **return on investment** (ROI), which can be defined as:

$$\frac{\text{Operating profit}}{\text{Total assets}} \times 100$$

Operating profit is the profit that a business earns from its core activities, before taxation and before deducting finance costs. This is sometimes known as PBIT (i.e. profit before interest and taxation).

Following the acquisition on 1 December 2010, the numerator of the ROI ratio will only include the subsidiary's profits for one month, whereas the subsidiary's assets will be included in full in the denominator. Therefore, the ROI ratio for 2010 will be reduced purely because of the way in which the acquisition is accounted for.

Similarly, a firm might revalue its landholdings upwards during 2010, thus increasing the denominator of the ROI ratio, without adding to the company's profits in the numerator. Once again, this will mean that the firm's ROI will be reduced, simply because of the revaluation of land.

In both of the above cases, it will be necessary to adjust the financial statements when computing accounting ratios for the purposes of financial analysis. Thus, the effect of the acquisition should be excluded from the 2010 financial statements, and the revaluation of land should be reversed. In this way, the accounting ratios of 2010 will be comparable with those of previous years.

Criteria for a successful business

In essence, a business must satisfy four criteria to be considered successful.

Profitability

Whatever product/s or service/s a business sells should have a reasonable margin of profit. This is essential if a business is to be successful in the long term.

Asset turnover

For a given level of assets, a business should generate a commensurate level of sales. In general a business's future prospects are directly related to its level of sales.

Liquidity

A firm's liquidity is a measure of its ability to pay its short-term debts. Many businesses are profitable but still become insolvent. This is largely because profits are computed on the accrual basis of accounting, whereby sales are recorded when goods or services are invoiced and not when cash is received. Also, investment in assets such as machinery may adversely affect a firm's liquidity, while only gradually reducing profit through the annual depreciation charge.

Gearing

Gearing, or leverage, relates to the level of non-current borrowings raised by a firm. Debt has several advantages, such as the tax deductibility of interest, but it also commits a firm to making interest payments and repayments of capital. Equity funding provides greater flexibility, as dividends can be waived when sufficient profits are not available. Thus, it is important to achieve a reasonable balance between a firm's use of debt and equity capital.

In summary, a successful business will have a reasonable profit margin, achieve a sales level commensurate with its assets, remain liquid and have an appropriate level of borrowing.

Accounting ratios

This section outlines how accounting ratios can be used to assess a firm's financial health. The use of financial analysis in practice is demonstrated in Appendix 41.1, which examines the financial statements of Ryanair Holdings plc and easyJet plc.

The primary accounting ratio is return on investment (ROI). As outlined previously, ROI can be defined as:

$$\frac{\text{Operating profit}}{\text{Total assets}} \times 100$$

ROI is a measure of the overall return which a business makes on its net assets. ROI can be further broken down into:

$$\frac{\text{Operating profit}}{\text{Revenue}} \quad \times \quad \frac{\text{Revenue}}{\text{Total assets}}$$

$$\downarrow \qquad\qquad\qquad \downarrow$$

$$\text{Profitability} \quad \times \quad \text{Asset turnover}$$

Thus, ROI comprises a combination of profitability and asset turnover, which are two of the four criteria which we have identified as being essential for business success. Each of these criteria is now considered separately.

Profitability

Gross profit margin

The gross profit margin is defined as

$$\frac{\text{Gross profit}}{\text{Revenue}} \times 100$$

In a manufacturing business, the gross profit margin represents the return that a business makes on its sales, having taken all production costs into consideration. In a non-manufacturing business, gross profit margin is the return on sales, having taken the costs of purchase into account.

Example 1 Bookstore Limited had total revenue of €3.2M for the year ended 31 December 2010. Gross profit was €2.1M.

$$\text{Gross profit margin} = \frac{€2.1M}{€3.2M} \times 100 = 66\%$$

A firm's gross profit margin tends to be fairly consistent year on year. The size of the gross profit margin is usually related to the length of time that goods are held in inventory before being sold. For example, bookshops and jewellers usually carry inventory for a significant period of time, and therefore require a high gross profit margin (e.g. 60%). By contrast, supermarkets have a very quick turnover of their products, and therefore can afford to earn a lower gross margin (e.g. 14%).

■ Net profit margin

The net profit margin is defined as

$$\frac{\text{Operating profit}}{\text{Revenue}} \times 100$$

The net profit margin is the return on a firm's sales, having taken all expenses into account.

Example 2 Bookstore Limited had total revenue of €3.2M for the year ended 31 December 2010. Net profit was €0.8M.

$$\text{Net profit margin} = \frac{€0.8M}{€3.2M} \times 100 = 25\%$$

A firm's net profit margin can vary significantly from one year to the next. This is largely because many expenses are fixed in nature, and do not change when the level of sales rises or falls. For example, a fall of €700,000 in Bookstore's sales could result in net profit falling by €500,000, as many expense items, such as rent, will remain unchanged. Thus, Bookstore's net profit margin is now recomputed as follows:

$$\text{Net profit margin} = \frac{€0.3M}{€2.5M} \times 100 = 12\%$$

A firm's profitability can be further investigated by computing individual expenses as a percentage of revenue. This may identify favourable or unfavourable trends, or relative performance against one's peers.

Profitability can be increased by rebalancing a firm's sales mix, so as to achieve additional sales of high-margin products. Profitability can also be improved by reducing the level of costs, while maintaining revenues. For example, Bookstore could sell more hard-cover books with higher margins, or reduce its costs by negotiating better prices from suppliers or by reducing staff levels.

Asset turnover

Asset turnover can be defined as

$$\frac{\text{Revenue}}{\text{Total assets}}$$

Essentially, asset turnover is a measure of the extent to which a business is able to 'sweat' its assets. The more sales that are generated for a given level of assets, the higher a firm's asset turnover will be.

Example 3 Bookstore Limited achieved revenues of €3.2M for the year ended 31 December 2010. Bookstore had total assets of €5M at the same date.

$$\text{Asset turnover} = \frac{€3.2M}{€5M} = 0.64$$

This means that for every €1 of assets, Bookstore generated 64 cents of sales in 2010. The level of asset turnover should be related to the type of assets that a business has invested in. Bookstore may own several shops, which have an estimated useful life of about 50 years. Bookstore will therefore have many years over which its investment can be recouped in terms of sales. Thus, an asset turnover figure of 0.64 would seem to be acceptable.

A manufacturing company is likely to have invested heavily in machinery which has an average useful life of about seven years. As this investment will have to be recovered over a shorter period of time, a higher level of asset turnover will have to be achieved.

A firm's asset turnover can be improved by generating more revenue from the same amount of assets, or by maintaining existing sales with a lower asset figure. For example, Bookstore Limited could increase its asset turnover by selling more books in its stores, or by closing one of its stores while maintaining its overall revenue.

Asset turnover is discussed in further detail in Appendix 41.2.

Liquidity

Liquidity is the third criterion that is essential for a business to be successful. There are two key measures of liquidity which can be derived from a firm's financial statements.

■ Current ratio

The **current ratio** is defined as

$$\frac{\text{Current assets}}{\text{Current liabilities}}$$

Example 4 Bookstore has current assets of €1.4M and current liabilities of €600,000. Bookstore therefore has a current ratio of 2.3.

A current ratio of 1.5 is regarded as an acceptable norm. This results in a firm's short-term assets being one and a half times its current liabilities, thus ensuring that it has adequate short-term resources to meet its short-term commitments.

It should be considered, however, that an excessively high current ratio is not necessarily beneficial from a firm's perspective. Short-term assets traditionally provide a lower return than investments in longer-term cash deposits or non-current assets such as machinery. There may also be a net benefit by using surplus short-term funds to repay loans.

The current ratio can be increased by negotiating extended credit terms from suppliers, though this may impact on the quality of service that is provided.

■ Quick assets ratio

The cash operating cycle of a business is illustrated in Figure 41.1. This clearly shows that inventory is the least liquid current asset, as it must be carried, then sold before eventually it is converted into cash. Therefore, a liquidity measure that excludes inventory from current assets may provide a more accurate gauge of a firm's capacity to respond to a repayment demand from its bank or creditors.

The **quick assets ratio** equals

$$\frac{\text{Current assets (excluding inventory)}}{\text{Current liabilities}}.$$

A quick assets ratio of 1 is regarded as an acceptable norm.

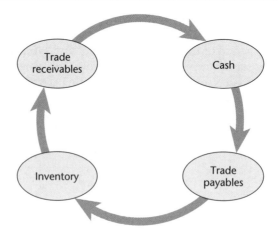

Figure 41.1 Cash operating cycle

Example 5 Bookstore has current assets of €1.4M and current liabilities of €600,000. Inventory of €500,000 is included in current assets. Bookstore therefore has a quick assets ratio of 1.5.

The quick assets ratio can be improved by negotiating extended credit terms from suppliers. More effective inventory control may work also, for example, by focusing on high-value items which should be reduced where possible. Sales incentives, which would move inventory faster, are another option.

Gearing

Gearing, which relates to a firm's level of non-current borrowing, is the fourth criterion on which business success is dependent. Gearing can be assessed by reference to both the income statement and the SOFP.

■ Income gearing

The times interest covered ratio provides a measure of a firm's capacity to service the interest payments on its debt. Times interest covered is computed as:

$$\frac{\text{Profit before interest and tax (PBIT)}}{\text{Interest}}$$

Example 6 Bookstore Limited incurred interest charges of €200,000 in the year ended 31 December 2010. Profit before interest and tax amounted to €1M.

$$\text{Times interest covered} = \frac{€1M}{€200,000} = 5$$

Bookstore has a times interest covered ratio of 5. Thus, PBIT could fall by 80%, and Bookstore would still be able to meet its interest commitments.

A minimum times interest covered ratio is sometimes required by lending institutions, and penalties, such as an interest surcharge, may be imposed if this requirement is not met. A times interest covered requirement of 4 is typical of what might be demanded by lenders.

■ Statement of financial position

The level of gearing in a firm's SOFP can be measured as non-current debt/total equity. There is no definite rule as to what a firm's debt : equity ratio should be. However, an accepted norm is that non-current debt should not exceed total equity.

Example 7 At 31 December 2010, Bookstore Limited had total non-current borrowings of €2.6M. Total equity in its SOFP at the same date amounted to €3M.

$$\frac{\text{Bookstore's debt}}{\text{Equity ratio}} = \frac{€2.6M}{€3M} = 0.87$$

Stock exchange/investor ratios

When deciding whether to buy or sell the shares of companies whose shares are publicly listed, investors will often focus on the earnings and dividends of those companies. The main investor ratios are:

- earnings per share
- price earnings ratio
- dividend per share
- dividend cover
- dividend yield.

■ Earnings per share (EPS)

Earnings per share is the amount of profit earned by each ordinary share during a reporting period. EPS is computed as follows:

$$\text{EPS} = \frac{\text{Profit after tax attributable to ordinary shareholders}}{\text{Number of ordinary shares in issue during the period}}$$

A publicly quoted company must present its EPS in its statement of comprehensive income. IAS 33 sets out the rules for the computation of EPS, and this standard is discussed in detail in Chapter 43.

■ Price earnings ratio (P/E)

A firm's P/E ratio equals its price/EPS.

Example 8 The share price of X Factor plc is €2. Its EPS for the most recent reporting period is 20 cents.

$$\text{P/E} = \frac{\text{Share price}}{\text{EPS}} = \frac{€2}{20c} = 10$$

The P/E ratio is the multiple at which investors in the stock market are prepared to value the earnings of a firm.

The P/E ratio can also be interpreted as the number of years it would take to recover the amount paid for a share.

Example 9 The share price of Blink plc is €4. Its EPS is 50 cents.

The P/E ratio of Blink is 8 (i.e. €4/50c). Therefore, investors who buy shares in Blink can expect to wait eight years for the company to generate €4 in after tax earnings to recoup their investment.

The principal factors which affect a firm's P/E ratio are as follows:

- *A company's earnings growth prospects.* The better the growth prospects, the higher the P/E ratio. Thus, companies that are in the early stage of their life cycle typically have higher P/E ratios than mature companies whose growth prospects are less exciting.
- The P/E ratio is inversely affected by the level of *financial risk* in a firm (i.e. as the level of gearing increases, the shareholders adjust for the additional risk by lowering the multiple that they are willing to pay for the shares).
- The current state of the stock market.

◼ Dividend per share

This is the amount of **dividend** paid on each share. It is computed as follows:

$$\text{Dividend per share} = \frac{\text{Total dividend}}{\text{Number of shares}}$$

Quoted firms generally try to maintain a policy of paying a gradually increasing dividend each year. Thus, a firm's dividend per share should increase gradually over time. This does not apply, however, should a firm have a bonus issue of shares (i.e. an issue of shares to existing shareholders for zero consideration), or where there is a rights issue at less than full market price.

Example 10 Sly plc paid the following dividend per share amounts over the last four years. Sly made a 1 for 1 bonus issue in 2010.

	2007	2008	2009	2010
Dividend per share	7c	8c	9c	5c
Dividend received by a shareholder holding 100 shares in 2007	€7	€8	€9	€10

Sly's dividend per share has almost halved in 2010, which raises the possibility of shareholder disappointment. On closer inspection, however, it can be seen that, when adjusted for the 1 for 1 bonus issue, Sly's dividend per share has actually increased from 9 cents in 2009 to 10 cents in 2010. Thus, the dividend per share statistic should be interpreted cautiously when there has been an issue of shares at less than full market price.

◼ Dividend cover

This is the number of times that a firm's dividend payment is covered by its distributable profit. The higher the dividend cover, the more secure the dividend is.

$$\text{Ordinary dividend cover} = \frac{\text{Profit after tax}}{\text{Ordinary dividend}}$$

Example 11 Sly plc paid an ordinary dividend of €200,000 for the year ended 31 December 2010. Sly earned profit after tax of €1M for 2010.

$$\text{Ordinary dividend cover} = \frac{\text{€1M}}{\text{€200,000}} = 5 \text{ times}$$

Therefore, profit could fall by 80% to €200,000 before Sly would begin to encounter difficulty in paying the current dividend to its ordinary shareholders.

■ Dividend yield

Dividend yield is the amount of dividend paid by a firm as a percentage of its share price.

$$\text{Dividend yield} = \frac{\text{Dividend per share}}{\text{Share price}} \times 100$$

Example 12 Hank plc paid an ordinary dividend of €100,000 for the year ended 31 December 2010. There are 400,000 issued ordinary shares. Hank's share price is €10.

$$\text{Dividend yield} = \frac{25c}{\text{€10}} \times 100 = 2.5\%$$

Dividend yield varies from one industry to another, but it will generally be in the range of 0–4%. Dividend yield is normally less than the risk-free rate of return available on short-dated government bonds, which may appear to be something of an anomaly. This differential is called the *reverse yield gap*. It is explained by the fact that, in addition to a dividend return, an investment in shares also provides the opportunity for appreciation of the share price.

Summary

- Financial analysis is a holistic appraisal of a firm's financial well-being.
- Financial statements are subject to a number of limitations, which restrict the capacity of financial analysis to completely evaluate a firm's performance and financial position.
- The financial statements of an entity can be used:
  - to identify trends within the entity over time (time series analysis);
  - as a source of comparison with other entities in the same industry (cross-sectional analysis).
- For comparability purposes, financial statements should be adjusted for significant events that occurred during the reporting period, and for changes in accounting policy.
- Four criteria which are essential for business success are identified:
  - satisfactory profit margin;
  - high level of asset turnover;
  - adequate level of liquidity;
  - appropriate level of gearing.

■ Reference

1. Argenti, J. (1976). *Corporate Collapse: the Causes and Symptoms*. McGraw-Hill (UK).

Appendix 41.1

Financial analysis of Ryanair Holdings plc and easyJet plc

Ryanair and easyJet compete in the low-cost airline sector. At a time when airlines have struggled with escalating oil prices and economic recession, both companies have shown themselves to be viable and adaptable. An excerpt from their financial statements is attached to this appendix, and Ryanair and easyJet are evaluated using the four criteria for business success that have been outlined in this chapter. A summary of financial ratios for both companies is also attached as Tables 1 and 2.

■ Times series analysis – Ryanair Holdings plc

Return on investment (ROI)

Ryanair generated an ROI of 1.5% in 2009, and 5.3% in 2010. This represents a significant recovery on what was a very poor return in 2009. A return in excess of 1.5% could be earned on a risk-free asset, so a continuation of this level of return would have had disastrous consequences for the airline.

It could be argued that Ryanair's ROI figure of 5.3% for 2010 does not fully reflect the return that the airline is generating on its assets. The group is holding €2.75B (i.e. €1.27B + €1.48B) in cash at 31 March 2010. The interest earned on this cash amounted to €23.5M for the year ended 31 March 2010, which amounts to a return of 0.86%. Thus, the large cash holding tends to distort the return that Ryanair is generating on its other assets. In fact, the return on non-cash assets for the year ended 31 March 2010 equals 8.3% (i.e. (Operating profit of €402M/Non-cash assets of €4.82B) × 100).

It should also be noted that

$$\text{ROI} = \text{Profitability} \times \text{Asset turnover}$$

This can be confirmed by Table 1 (on page 418), which shows that for 2010:

- the net profit margin was 13.4%;
- asset turnover was 0.40.

Thus, ROI = 13.4% × 0.40 = 5.3%.

Therefore, the reasons for the improvement in Ryanair's ROI can be determined by examining the airline's:

- profitability and
- asset turnover

Profitability

The net profit margin rose from 3.2% in 2009 to 13.4% in 2010, and this significant increase in profitability is responsible for the rise in Ryanair's ROI.

An examination of the consolidated income statement reveals that scheduled revenues fell marginally, and that high margin ancillary revenues increased from €598M to €664M. Total revenues increased by 1.6%.

Total operating expenses fell from €2.85B in 2009 to €2.59B in 2010, a decrease of 9%.

It can be concluded therefore that the reason for the significant increase in profitability and ROI can be attributed to reductions in Ryanair's costs. The most significant decrease was in respect of fuel costs which fell from €1.26B to €894M, a fall of 29%.

Previously, fuel costs had risen from €791M to €1.26B between 2008 and 2009, an increase of €469M (59%).

Clearly, the price of oil is the most critical factor, and also the most volatile factor, in determining Ryanair's profitability year on year.

Asset turnover

Table 1 shows that asset turnover fell from 0.46 to 0.40. These figures mean that for every €1 of assets, Ryanair generated revenues of 46 and 40 cents respectively in 2009 and 2010. Given that aircraft, which are Ryanair's primary asset category, have a useful life of approximately 25 years, an asset turnover of around 0.4 is quite impressive.

Liquidity

Table 1 also shows that Ryanair's current and quick ratios increased from 1.84 to 1.98 in 2010. These are high liquidity levels, which result primarily from a balance of cash and cash equivalents of almost €1.5B. Given that Ryanair has significant levels of borrowing, this raises the question as to why surplus cash resources are not used to reduce its outstanding loans. The answer relates to a need, in the airline industry, to maintain adequate liquidity levels to survive the temporary loss in business that would follow a catastrophe such as the loss of an aircraft.

Gearing

Capital gearing

Ryanair's debt/equity level increased from 0.91 to 0.94 in 2010. The reason for this increase can be found from an examination of its SOFP:

- an increase in non-current debt of €495M, which is partly balanced by
- an increase in retained earnings of €306M.

The 2010 debt/equity level of 0.94 is still reasonably comfortable, however, particularly in view of the strong cash flow nature of Ryanair's revenue streams.

Income gearing

Ryanair's PBIT was eight times its net interest charge in 2010. This represents a significant level of cover against a fall in operating profit.

In 2009, however, the low-cost airline incurred a loss of €125M before interest and tax, thereby failing to cover its net interest expense of €55M. Two reasons had contributed to this problem:

- the dramatic increase in fuel costs;
- a write-off of €223M in respect of its investment in Aer Lingus.

Stock market/investor ratios

Earnings per share

Ryanair returned an EPS of 20.68 cents per share in the year ended 31 March 2010. It had incurred a loss per share of 11.44 cents the previous year, due to the unprecedented increase in fuel costs and the write-down of its investment in Aer Lingus.

Price earnings ratio

The Ryanair share price was quoted at €3.70 in July 2010, when the 2010 financial statements were authorised for issue. Based on an EPS of 20.68 cents for the year ended 31 March 2010, the share was trading at a multiple of 17.9 its earnings figure (i.e. €3.70/20.68c) when the financial statements were authorised for issue.

On 28 July 2009, the share price was €3.25, but it was not possible to compute a P/E ratio at that time, as a loss per share was incurred for the year ended 31 March 2009.

Dividend ratios

Ryanair paid its first dividend on 15 September 2010, which amounted in total to €500M or 34 cents per share. This was a special dividend, and it was not intended to be a signal of Ryanair's intention to pay a regular dividend on an ongoing basis.

Prior to the payment of the special dividend in September 2010, Ryanair had reinvested all of its profits in the business, financing the purchase of aircraft to service its rapid expansion in opening up new routes. This growth appears to be flattening out, and with less need to reinvest in the business, Ryanair has taken the opportunity to make a one-off payment to its shareholders.

As Ryanair does not pay a regular annual dividend, it is not appropriate to compute ratios such as dividend cover or dividend yield.

Summary

Ryanair is fundamentally a strong company whose profitability slumped in the year ended 31 March 2009, due to a surge in the price of oil, which reached $147 a barrel in the summer of 2008. As a result, Ryanair generated a minimal ROI, saw its net margin decline to 3.2%, and failed to cover its interest payments. On a more positive note, Ryanair maintained its strong liquidity and generated increased revenue from its assets in a recessionary climate.

Oil has since retreated to more affordable levels, and in the year ended 31 March 2010 Ryanair put in a strong performance and returned to profitability. The threat of a significant increase in the price of oil remains, however, and this appears to be the most significant risk factor going forward.

■ Cross-sectional analysis – Ryanair and easyJet

Return on investment

The ROI of easyJet rose from 1.6% in 2009 to 4.3% in 2010, an increase that was quite similar to that of Ryanair (1.5–5.3%). The factors contributing to a significant recovery in ROI for both companies are now examined further.

Profitability

Ryanair returned an operating profit margin of 13.4% for the year ended 31 March 2010, compared to just 3.2% the previous year. The principal reason for this improvement was that fuel costs fell from €1.26B in 2009 to €894M in 2010, a drop of 29%. Despite the fact that Ryanair's revenue dropped marginally, there were increases in staff costs, maintenance, aircraft rentals, route charges, and airport and handling charges. The total increase in these costs amounted to €128M, which reduced the savings obtained from the reduction in fuel costs.

EasyJet's operating profit margin improved from 2.2% in 2009 to 5.9% in 2010, with a decrease of €74M in fuel costs contributing significantly to the improvement. Revenue rose by 11.5%, but was largely negated by increases in operating costs.

Asset turnover

In the year ended 31 March 2010, for every €1 of assets, Ryanair generated revenue of 40 cents. EasyJet generated revenue of 74 pence per £1 of assets in the year ended 30 September 2010. It appears, therefore, that easyJet is using its assets far more intensively than its competitor.

A closer examination of their respective financial statements, however, throws additional light on this issue. Although both companies achieved almost identical levels of revenue:

- easyJet incurred aircraft lease costs of £116M in its income statement, whereas Ryanair incurred aircraft rental charges of only €96M.
- The SOFP shows easyJet with property, plant and equipment assets of only €1.9B, whereas Ryanair has similar assets of €4.3B. Aircraft are the principal asset class of both companies.

Clearly, Ryanair has purchased a substantially greater number of its aircraft than easyJet, who rely far more on short-lease planes which are not included in its SOFP. The result is that Ryanair has a significantly higher asset base than easyJet, which adversely affects the following Ryanair ratios, in which the denominator is the total asset figure:

- ROI; and
- asset turnover

Thus, further analysis shows that easyJet's ROI and asset turnover ratios have been increased by their asset financing strategy.

Liquidity

Both companies have very impressive liquidity positions, as outlined in Tables 1 and 2 on pages 418–19.

Gearing

Capital gearing

EasyJet has a debt/equity ratio of 0.72, compared with 0.94 for Ryanair. This difference relates to Ryanair's strategy of purchasing most of its aircraft, with consequent implications for funding requirements.

Income gearing

In 2010, easyJet had a times interest covered figure of 8.7 times, while Ryanair had a ratio of 8 times.

Both figures appear very comfortable, in terms of the companies' capacity to fund their interest commitments. In the year ended 31 March 2009, however, Ryanair was unable to cover its interest commitments, primarily because of the escalation in oil prices and the write-down of its investment in Aer Lingus. This emphasises the extent to which fuel prices, in particular, can impact on companies in the airline industry.

Summary

Both Ryanair and easyJet achieved reasonable return on investment figures in 2010, though at 5.3 and 4.3% respectively these were not dramatically higher than the return that could have been earned on a risk-free asset.

It should be noted that easyJet's ROI and asset turnover figures do flatter a little, relative to those of Ryanair. Both figures are enhanced by the fact that easyJet's aircraft rental strategy results in that company having a relatively lower total asset figure.

Overall, 2010 was a relatively good year for both companies, with fuel prices falling significantly from their highs of the previous year. Ryanair and easyJet both have strong liquidity positions and manageable gearing levels. Both appear to have good prospects, though increasing costs, and fuel costs in particular, may limit their profitability going forward.

Table 1 Financial ratios – Ryanair Holdings plc

	Ratio	Year end 31 March 2010 €	Year end 31 March 2009 €
Primary ratio	$\text{ROI} = \dfrac{\text{Operating profit}}{\text{Total assets}} \times 100$	$\dfrac{402\text{M}}{7{,}563\text{M}} \times 100 = 5.3\%$	$\dfrac{93\text{M}}{6{,}388\text{M}} \times 100 = 1.5\%$
Profitability	$\text{Net profit \%} = \dfrac{\text{Operating profit}}{\text{Revenue}} \times 100$	$\dfrac{402\text{M}}{2{,}988\text{M}} \times 100 = 13.4\%$	$\dfrac{93\text{M}}{2{,}942\text{M}} \times 100 = 3.2\%$
Asset turnover	$\dfrac{\text{Revenue}}{\text{Total assets}}$	$\dfrac{2{,}988\text{M}}{7{,}563\text{M}} = 0.40$	$\dfrac{2{,}942\text{M}}{6{,}388\text{M}} = 0.46$
Liquidity			
Current ratio	(i) $\dfrac{\text{Current assets}}{\text{Current liabilities}}$	$\dfrac{3{,}063\text{M}}{1{,}550\text{M}} = 1.98$	$\dfrac{2{,}543\text{M}}{1{,}379\text{M}} = 1.84$
Quick assets ratio	(ii) $\dfrac{\text{Current assets (excluding inventory)}}{\text{Current liabilities}}$	$\dfrac{3{,}061\text{M}}{1{,}550\text{M}} = 1.97$	$\dfrac{2{,}541\text{M}}{1{,}379\text{M}} = 1.84$
Gearing			
Capital gearing	$\dfrac{\text{Long-term debt}}{\text{Equity}}$	$\dfrac{2{,}691\text{M}}{2{,}849\text{M}} = 0.94$	$\dfrac{2{,}195\text{M}}{2{,}425\text{M}} = 0.91$
Income gearing – times interest covered	$\dfrac{\text{Profit/(loss) before interest and tax}}{\text{Interest*}}$	$\dfrac{390\text{M}}{49\text{M}} = 8 \text{ times}$	$\dfrac{(125\text{M})}{55\text{M}} = 0 \text{ times}$

* Interest payable less interest receivable.

Table 2 Financial ratios – easyJet plc

	Ratio	Year end 30 September 2010 £	Year end 30 September 2009 £
Primary ratio	$ROI = \dfrac{\text{Operating profit}}{\text{Total assets}} \times 100$	$\dfrac{174M}{4,003M} \times 100 = 4.3\%$	$\dfrac{60M}{3,673M} \times 100 = 1.6\%$
Profitability	$\text{Net profit \%} = \dfrac{\text{Operating profit}}{\text{Revenue}} \times 100$	$\dfrac{174M}{2,973M} \times 100 = 5.9\%$	$\dfrac{60M}{2,667M} \times 100 = 2.2\%$
Asset turnover	$\dfrac{\text{Revenue}}{\text{Total assets}}$	$\dfrac{2,973M}{4,003M} = 0.74$	$\dfrac{2,667M}{3,673M} = 0.73$
Liquidity Current ratio	(i) $\dfrac{\text{Current assets}}{\text{Current liabilities}}$	$\dfrac{1,515M}{1,065M} = 1.4$	$\dfrac{1,482M}{1,062M} = 1.4$
Quick assets ratio	(ii) $\dfrac{\text{Current assets (excluding inventory)}}{\text{Current liabilities}}$	$\dfrac{1,515M}{1,065M} = 1.4$	$\dfrac{1,482M}{1,062M} = 1.4$
Gearing Capital gearing	$\dfrac{\text{Long-term debt}}{\text{Equity}}$	$\dfrac{1,085M}{1,501M} = 0.72$	$\dfrac{1,003M}{1,307M} = 0.77$
Income gearing – times interest covered	$\dfrac{\text{Earnings before interest and tax}}{\text{Interest*}}$	$\dfrac{174M}{20M} = 8.7 \text{ times}$	$\dfrac{60M}{5.4M} = 11 \text{ times}$

* Interest payable less interest receivable.

■ Excerpt from the financial statements of easyJet plc and Ryanair Holdings plc

Consolidated balance sheet – easyJet plc

	Notes	30 September 2010 £M	30 September 2009 £M
Non-current assets			
Goodwill	7	365.4	365.4
Other intangible assets	7	86.8	81.7
Property, plant and equipment	8	1,928.1	1,612.2
Derivative financial instruments	22	8.2	7.8
Loan notes	9	13.1	12.6
Restricted cash	13	32.5	48.0
Other non-current assets	10	53.5	62.7
Deferred tax assets	5	–	0.4
		2,487.6	2,190.8
Current assets			
Assets held for sale	11	73.2	73.2
Trade and other receivables	12	194.1	241.8
Derivative financial instruments	22	52.6	68.0
Restricted cash	13	23.1	24.3
Money market deposits	13	260.0	286.3
Cash and cash equivalents	13	911.9	788.6
		1,514.9	1,482.2
Current liabilities			
Trade and other payables	14	(828.7)	(750.7)
Borrowings	15	(127.4)	(117.6)
Derivative financial instruments	22	(9.6)	(91.1)
Current tax liabilities		(27.5)	(57.7)
Maintenance provisions	17	(71.4)	(45.1)
		(1,064.6)	(1,062.2)
Net current assets		450.3	420.0
Non-current liabilities			
Borrowings	15	(1,084.6)	(1,003.0)
Derivative financial instruments	22	(4.0)	(2.6)
Non-current deferred income	16	(56.6)	(52.6)
Maintenance provisions	17	(144.1)	(168.6)
Deferred tax liabilities	5	(147.9)	(76.7)
		(1,437.2)	(1,303.5)
Net assets		1,500.7	1,307.3
Shareholders' equity			
Share capital	18	107.3	106.0
Share premium		651.6	642.5
Hedging reserve		34.8	(23.9)
Translation reserve		0.8	(0.4)
Retained earnings		706.2	583.1
		1,500.7	1,307.3

The accounts on pages 55–89 were approved by the board of directors and authorised for issue on 15 November 2010 and signed on behalf of the board.

Director   Director

Consolidated income statement – easyJet plc

	Notes	Year ended 30 September 2010 £M	Year ended 30 September 2009 £M
Passenger revenue		2,401.7	2,150.5
Ancillary revenue		571.4	516.3
Total revenue		2,973.1	2,666.8
Ground handling		(274.4)	(255.9)
Airport charges		(529.8)	(481.5)
Fuel		(733.4)	(807.2)
Navigation		(256.0)	(232.3)
Crew		(336.0)	(306.6)
Maintenance		(176.8)	(161.6)
Advertising		(49.8)	(47.0)
Merchant fees and commissions		(42.4)	(33.5)
Aircraft and passenger insurance		(10.2)	(11.3)
Aircraft wet leasing		(13.7)	–
Volcanic ash disruption		(27.3)	–
Other costs		(162.0)	(104.8)
EBITDAR		361.3	225.1
Amortisation of intangible assets	7	(6.2)	(4.4)
Depreciation	8	(72.5)	(55.4)
(Loss)/profit on disposal of assets held for sale	11	(7.0)	11.0
Aircraft dry leasing		(102.0)	(116.2)
Operating profit		173.6	60.1
Interest receivable and other financing income		7.1	22.5
Interest payable and other financing charges		(26.7)	(27.9)
Net finance charges	2	(19.6)	(5.4)
Profit before tax	3	154.0	54.7
Tax (charge)/credit	5	(32.7)	16.5
Profit for the year		121.3	71.2
Earnings per share, pence			
Basic	6	28.4	16.9
Diluted	6	28.0	16.6

Consolidated balance sheet – Ryanair Holdings plc

	Notes	At 31 March 2010 €M	At 31 March 2009 €M
Non-current assets			
Property, plant and equipment	2	4,314.2	3,644.8
Intangible assets	3	46.8	46.8
Available for sale financial assets	4	116.2	93.2
Derivative financial instruments	5	22.8	60.0
Total non-current assets		4,500.0	3,844.8
Current assets			
Inventories	6	2.5	2.1
Other assets	7	80.6	91.0
Current tax	12	–	–
Trade receivables	8	44.3	41.8
Derivative financial instruments	5	122.6	130.0
Restricted cash	9	67.8	291.6
Financial assets: cash greater than 3 months		1,267.7	403.4
Cash and cash equivalents		1,477.9	1,583.2
Total current assets		3,063.4	2,543.1
Total assets		7,563.4	6,387.9
Current liabilities			
Trade payables		154.0	132.7
Accrued expenses and other liabilities	10	1,088.2	905.8
Current maturities of debt	11	265.5	202.9
Current tax	12	0.9	0.4
Derivative financial instruments	5	41.0	137.4
Total current liabilities		1,549.6	1,379.2
Non-current liabilities			
Provisions	13	102.9	72.0
Derivative financial instruments	5	35.4	54.1
Deferred tax	12	199.6	155.5
Other creditors	14	136.6	106.5
Non-current maturities of debt	11	2,690.7	2,195.5
Total non-current liabilities		3,165.2	2,583.6
Shareholders' equity			
Issued share capital	15	9.4	9.4
Share premium account	15	631.9	617.4
Capital redemption reserve		0.5	0.5
Retained earnings		2,083.5	1,777.7
Other reserves	16	123.3	20.1
Shareholders' equity		2,848.6	2,425.1
Total liabilities and shareholders' equity		7,563.4	6,387.9

The accompanying notes are an integral part of the financial information.

On behalf of the board

M. O'Leary   *D. Bonderman*
Director   Director

20 July 2010

Consolidated income statement – Ryanair Holdings plc

	Notes	Year ended 31 March 2010 €M	Year ended 31 March 2009 €M
Operating revenues			
Scheduled revenues		2,324.5	2,343.9
Ancillary revenues	17	663.6	598.1
Total operating revenues – continuing operations	17	**2,988.1**	**2,942.0**
Operating expenses			
Staff costs	18	(335.0)	(309.3)
Depreciation	2	(235.4)	(256.1)
Fuel and oil		(893.9)	(1,257.1)
Maintenance, materials and repairs		(86.0)	(66.8)
Aircraft rentals		(95.5)	(78.2)
Route charges		(336.3)	(286.6)
Airport and handling charges		(459.1)	(443.4)
Marketing, distribution and other		(144.8)	(151.9)
Total operating expenses		**(2,586.0)**	**(2,849.4)**
Operating profit – continuing operations		402.1	92.6
Other income/(expense)			
Finance income		23.5	75.5
Finance expense		(72.1)	(130.5)
Foreign exchange gain/(loss)		(1.0)	4.4
Loss on impairment of available-for-sale financial asset	4	(13.5)	(222.5)
Gain on disposal of property, plant and equipment		2.0	–
Total other income/(expense)		**(61.1)**	**(273.1)**
Profit/(loss) before tax		341.0	(180.5)
Tax (expense)/benefit on profit/(loss) on ordinary activities	12	(35.7)	11.3
Profit/(loss) for the year – all attributable to equity holders of parent		305.3	(169.2)
Basic earnings/(losses) per ordinary share (euro cent)	22	20.68	(11.44)
Diluted earnings per ordinary share (euro cent)	22	20.60	(11.44)
Number of ordinary shares (in Ms)	22	1,476.40	1,478.50
Number of diluted shares (in Ms)	22	1,481.70	1,478.50

The accompanying notes are an integral part of the financial information.

On behalf of the board

M. O'Leary   *D. Bonderman*
Director   Director

20 July 2010

Appendix 41.2

Asset turnover

Asset turnover is a measure of how effective management has been in using a firm's assets to generate revenue.

$$\text{Asset turnover ratio} = \frac{\text{Revenue}}{\text{Total assets}}$$

One can also examine how efficient a firm has been in using its individual asset categories to generate revenue.

■ Non-current assets

The extent to which assets such as land and buildings and plant and machinery have generated revenue can be easily determined.

Example 1 Bookstore Limited had revenue for the year of €3.2M. The carrying value of land and buildings at 31 December 2010 amounted to €3M. The extent to which Bookstore's land and buildings have generated revenue can be measured as follows:

$$\frac{\text{Revenue}}{\text{Land and buildings}} = \frac{\text{€3.2M}}{\text{€3M}} = 1.07 \text{ times}$$

Thus, every €1 of Bookstore's land and buildings has generated approximately €1 of revenue.

■ Inventory turnover

As inventory is valued at the lower of cost and NRV, the cost of sales is used as the numerator in measuring inventory turnover.

Example 2 Bookstore Limited had cost of sales for the year of €1.1M. The carrying value of inventory at 31 December 2010 amounted to €0.5M.

$$\text{Inventory turnover} = \frac{\text{Cost of sales}}{\text{Inventory}} = \frac{\text{€1.1M}}{\text{€0.5M}} = 2.2 \text{ times}$$

■ Credit allowed to customers

The number of days' credit allowed to customers is computed as follows:

$$\frac{\text{Trade receivables}}{\text{Credit sales}} \times 365$$

Example 3 Bookstore Limited's credit sales for 2010 amounted to €420,000. Trade receivables of €70,000 were included in the SOFP at 31 December 2010.

$$\text{Days' credit to customers} = \frac{\text{€70,000}}{\text{€420,000}} \times 365 = 61 \text{ days}$$

QUESTIONS

41.1 DECOR Limited

DECOR Limited is a retailer of tiles and bathroom accessories. The firm has been in existence for a number of years and has enjoyed reasonable commercial success.

The firm's managing director, Ms Fidelma O'Sullivan, has decided to compare the performance of DECOR Limited with two similar-sized firms operating in the same industry – Firm A and Firm B. Ms O'Sullivan has assembled the following information in relation to each firm.

Ratios	DECOR Ltd	Firm A	Firm B
Return on investment	12%	15%	18%
Net profit margin	25%	20%	22.5%
Asset turnover	0.48	0.75	0.8
Inventory turnover	3.1 times	4.5 times	5.2 times
Debtors' days	72 days	55 days	53 days
Creditors' days	58 days	70 days	75 days
Turnover of non-current assets	1.2 times	2 times	2.2 times
Quick assets ratio	0.9 : 1	1.6 : 1	1.8 : 1
Current ratio	1.5 : 1	2.1 : 1	2.8 : 1
Debt : equity ratio	0.5 : 1	0.3 : 1	0.4 : 1

Required:

(a) Based upon the information provided, evaluate the financial performance of DECOR Ltd with regard to the other two firms, offering whatever advice you consider appropriate to the management of DECOR Ltd.

(b) Outline the limitations of ratio analysis as a means of evaluating a firm.

41.2 BULWARK and MEDIAN

Assume it is now 1 May 2010. You are employed with a firm of financial consultants called CAPALER, and you have been asked to assess the performance and financial position of two companies, each of whom operates a chain of leisure centres. Both companies were quoted on the Dublin and London stock exchanges for the first time on 1 May 2009.

Statement of financial position (extracts) at 30/4/2010

	BULWARK €'000	MEDIAN €'000
Property, plant and equipment	20,000	14,000
Goodwill	8,000	4,000
Non-current assets	28,000	18,000
Trade receivables	3,200	1,500
Cash	400	300
Current assets	3,600	1,800
Trade payables	400	200
Overdraft and short-term liabilities	3,100	1,700
Current liabilities	3,500	1,900
Long-term debt	4,000	1,000
Net assets	24,100	16,900
Ordinary share capital (€1 ordinary shares)	2,000	3,000
Share premium	21,700	8,300
Retained earnings	400	5,600
Total equity	24,100	16,900

Income statement extracts (for year ended 30/4/2010)

	BULWARK €'000	MEDIAN €'000
Revenue	10,000	20,000
Cost of sales	(3,000)	(6,000)
Gross profit	7,000	14,000
Advertising and marketing costs	(2,000)	(2,700)
Wages and salaries	(2,000)	(2,500)
Other operating expenses	(1,000)	(1,000)
Interest	(1,000)	(400)
Tax	(200)	(1,200)
Profit for the year	800	6,200

Other information:

	BULWARK	MEDIAN
Current market share at 1/5/2010	15%	35%
Forecasted revenue growth next year	15%	30%
Share price on 1/5/2009 (flotation date)	€1.40	€1
Share price today 1/5/2010	€1.25	€10

Required:

Your boss has asked for a report which provides a comparative analysis of both companies based on the information provided. Your report should include:

(i) An evaluation and comparison of the two companies from an investment perspective. Your report should conclude with a summary of your advice to investors in relation to both companies.

(ii) To what extent do you believe that the information provided is insufficient or limited, for the purposes of making a comparative analysis of this kind?

41.3 FERRER Limited

FERRER Ltd ('FERRER'), a company that sells household furniture and related products throughout Britain and Ireland to retail companies, prepares its financial statements to 31 December each year. FERRER's income statements for the years ended 31 December 2006–2010, and its statement of financial position as at those dates, are presented below.

Statement of comprehensive income for the year ended 31 December

	2010 €'000	2009 €'000	2008 €'000	2007 €'000	2006 €'000
Revenue	580,500	484,800	590,800	1,173,600	925,700
Cost of sales	(435,400)	(362,000)	(443,100)	(882,200)	(693,800)
Gross profit	145,100	122,800	147,700	291,400	231,900
Operating expenses	(99,800)	(86,440)	(106,300)	(206,900)	(164,300)
Operating profit	45,300	36,360	41,400	84,500	67,600
Finance charges	(15,600)	(7,600)	(8,100)	(13,000)	(18,800)
Profit before tax	29,700	28,760	33,300	71,500	48,800
Income Tax	(14,000)	(15,160)	(22,300)	(60,200)	(36,600)
Profit after tax	15,700	13,600	11,000	11,300	12,200

Statement of financial position as at 31 December

	2010 €'000	2009 €'000	2008 €'000	2007 €'000	2006 €'000
Assets					
Non-current assets					
Property, plant and equipment	277,900	206,600	255,600	464,300	369,400
Current assets					
Inventory	119,000	114,000	126,900	130,800	162,500
Trade receivables	98,000	108,000	109,000	190,900	158,000
Investments	18,000	14,000	3,000	11,000	16,000
Bank and cash	32,000	24,500	46,000	27,000	13,000
	267,000	260,500	284,900	359,700	349,500
	544,900	467,100	540,500	824,000	718,900
Equity and liabilities					
Capital and reserves					
€1 Ordinary shares	100,000	100,000	100,000	100,000	100,000
Retained earnings	115,300	109,600	106,000	105,000	103,700
	215,300	209,600	206,000	205,000	203,700
Non-current liabilities					
Loan	130,100	57,600	134,000	417,900	315,000
Current liabilities					
Bank overdraft	11,200	8,100	22,300	3,100	2,200
Trade payables	179,700	185,600	166,800	188,000	188,500
Taxation	5,200	4,100	7,500	6,300	5,400
Accruals – interest payable	3,400	2,100	3,900	3,700	4,100
	199,500	199,900	200,500	201,100	200,200
	544,900	467,100	540,500	824,000	718,900

Additional information:
1. All of FERRER's sales and purchases are on credit.
2. Dividends amounting to €10M were proposed, approved and paid in each of the years 2006–2010.

Required:
Prepare a report for the directors of FERRER that clearly interprets and evaluates the financial performance and position of the company over the period 2006–2010.

(Chartered Accountants Ireland)

Chapter 42

Operating segments

Large companies often operate several business activities in various geographical locations. The opportunities and risk factors can vary significantly across such different sectors. For example, while an entity's food businesses may be experiencing stable growth in developed markets across continental Europe, its brewery arm might be floundering amid stiff competition in a challenging UK sector.

So as to provide the user of an entity's **financial statements** with information on the range of its activities, IFRS 8 requires entities within the scope of the Standard to disclose information that will enable users to

. . . evaluate the nature and financial effects of the business activities in which it engages and the economic environments in which it operates.

Scope and key definitions

IFRS 8 applies to entities whose equity instruments are traded on a stock exchange.
An operating segment is defined as a component of an entity:

- that engages in business activities from which it may earn revenues and incur **expenses**;
- whose operating results are regularly reviewed to make decisions when allocating resources and assessing performance; and
- for which discrete financial information is available.

Determining reportable segments

IFRS 8 requires an entity to separately report information about an operating segment that meets any of the following quantitative thresholds:

(a) Its reported revenue is 10% or more of the combined revenue of all operating segments.
(b) The amount of its reported profit or loss is 10% or more of the greater of (i) the combined profit of all operating segments that did not report a loss, and (ii) the combined reported loss of all operating segments that reported a loss.
(c) Its assets are 10% or more of the combined assets of all operating segments.

Disclosure requirements for reportable segments

A reportable segment is required to disclose the following information.

- Factors used to identify the entity's reportable segments
- Whether operating segments have been aggregated
- Segment profit or loss
- Segment assets.

The following additional disclosures are required for each reportable segment if the information is regularly reported to the chief operating decision-maker.

(i)   Segment liabilities
(ii) The following items of income and expense:
  - revenues from external customers and from other operating segments of the group;
  - interest revenue and interest expense;
  - **depreciation, amortisation** and other material non-cash items;
  - items of income and expense that are sufficiently material to warrant separate disclosure;
  - the group's interest in the profit or loss of **associates** and joint ventures accounted for by the **equity method**;
  - income tax expense or income.

IFRS 8 also requires entities to provide a number of reconciliations and to make certain entity-wide disclosures. The latter disclosures are not required if the information has already been provided as part of the information on reportable segments.

QUESTIONS

42.1 NORMAN plc

NORMAN, a public limited company, has three business segments which are currently reported in its financial statements. NORMAN is an international hotel group which reports to management on the basis of region. It does not currently report segmental information under IFRS 8 *Operating Segments*. The results of the regional segments for the year ended 31 May 2011 are as follows:

Region	Revenue		Segment results Profit (loss)	Segment assets	Segment liabilities
	External	Internal			
	€M	€M	€M	€M	€M
Europe	200	3	(10)	300	200
South East Asia	300	2	60	800	300
Other regions (North America, South America and Africa)	500	5	105	2,000	1,400

There were no significant inter-company balances in the segment assets and liabilities. The hotels are located in capital cities in the various regions, and the company sets individual performance indicators for each hotel based on its city location.

Required:
Discuss the principles in IFRS 8 *Operating Segments* for the determination of a company's reportable operating segments and how these principles would be applied for NORMAN plc using the information given above.

Chapter 43

Earnings per share

Earnings per share (EPS) is an important measure of performance, and is extensively used for financial analysis purposes. A company's EPS can be evaluated over a number of periods – known as time series analysis. EPS is also the denominator of the **price/earnings (P/E) ratio**, the latter being a widely used indicator of investment potential.

The use of different accounting policies can reduce the effectiveness of EPS as a comparative measure. For example, a revaluation of property assets may affect the **depreciation** charge and the profit/loss on disposal that is recognised in the income statement. However, the standardisation of accounting rules in recent years has reduced such policy choices, resulting in the increased importance of EPS and the P/E ratio as measures of performance. The rules for computing EPS are outlined in IAS 33.

Scope of IAS 33

IAS 33 applies to companies whose **ordinary shares** are publicly traded.

Calculation of basic EPS

IAS 33 defines basic EPS as:

$$\frac{\text{Profit or loss attributable to ordinary equity holders of the parent entity}}{\text{Weighted average number of ordinary shares outstanding during the period}}$$

IAS 33 requires that an entity present its basic EPS in the statement of comprehensive income. EPS should be presented for every period for which a statement of comprehensive income is prepared.

Example 1 The ordinary shares of Tracer plc are traded on the stock market. The following is an extract from the group statement of comprehensive income for the year ended 31 December 2010:

	€M
Revenue	180
Cost of sales	(70)
Gross profit	110
Expenses	(60)
Profit before tax	50
Income tax expense	(24)
Profit for the year	26

	€M
Other comprehensive income for the year	35
Total comprehensive income for the year	61
Profit attributable to:	
Owners of the parent	21
Non-controlling interests	5
	26

The number of ordinary shares of Tracer plc outstanding at 1 January 2009 was 100M, and this did not change during the two years ended 31 December 2010.

Tracer plc also had €10M of 10% cumulative preference shares outstanding during the year ended 31 December 2010. No dividend was declared in 2010 in respect of the group's non-cumulative preference shares.

Tracer plc had a basic EPS of 18 cents for 2009, based on earnings of €18M and 100M issued ordinary shares.

Solution   Basic EPS of Tracer plc for the year ended 31 December 2010 $= \dfrac{€20M \text{ (Note 1)}}{100M}$

$$\text{Basic EPS} = 20 \text{ cents}$$

Note 1

	€M
Profit for the year attributable to ordinary equity holders of the parent	21
Less cumulative preference dividend (Note 2)	(1)
	20

Note 2

The after-tax amount of preference dividends that is deducted from profit or loss is:

- for non-cumulative preference shares, the amount of dividends declared in respect of the period; and
- for cumulative preference shares, the dividend for the period whether or not declared.

Should an entity report a profit or loss from **discontinued operations**, an additional basic EPS figure must be computed as follows:

$$\text{Basic EPS} = \frac{\text{Profit or loss from discontinued operations attributable to ordinary equity holders of the parent entity}}{\text{Weighted average number of ordinary shares outstanding during the period}}$$

Changes in ordinary share capital when computing basic EPS

As stated above, for the purpose of calculating basic EPS, the number of ordinary shares shall be the weighted average number of ordinary shares outstanding during the period. The number of ordinary shares can change during a period, and their issue or buy back can take several forms.

■ Shares issued at fair value

When shares are issued at **fair value** during the current period, the additional shares are included in the basic EPS computation on a time-weighted basis.

Example 2 Assume that Tracer plc issued 12M additional ordinary shares on 1 April 2010. These shares were issued at fair value.

Calculate the basic EPS for 2010.

Solution The additional shares are in issue for nine months (1 April–31 December) of the 2010 financial year. Therefore, the number of ordinary shares in the denominator of the basic EPS will increase by 9M (i.e. 12M × 9/12) from 100M to 109M.

$$\text{Basic EPS of Tracer plc for the year ended 31 December 2010} = \frac{€20M}{109M}$$

$$= 18.3 \text{ cents}$$

■ Shares bought back at fair value

When shares are bought back at fair value during the current period, the repurchased shares are included in the basic EPS computation on a time-weighted basis.

Example 3 Assume that Tracer plc repurchased 24M ordinary shares on 1 July 2010. These shares were repurchased at fair value.

Calculate the basic EPS for 2010.

Solution As a result of their repurchase, the 24M shares were only in issue for the first six months of 2010. Therefore, the weighted average number of ordinary shares outstanding during 2010 will fall by 12M (i.e. 24M × 6/12) to 88M.

$$\text{Basic EPS of Tracer plc for the year ended 31 December 2010} = \frac{€20M}{88M}$$

$$= 22.7 \text{ cents}$$

■ Capitalisation or bonus issue

A capitalisation or bonus issue of shares takes the form of a share issue for zero consideration. Typically, it involves a transfer from a company's reserves to its issued share capital as follows:

	Dr	Cr
Reserves	xxx	
Share capital		xxx

IAS 33 requires that the weighted average number of ordinary shares be adjusted for the full period for events that have changed the number of ordinary shares without a corresponding change in resources.

Example 4 Assume that on 1 May 2010 Tracer plc made a 1 for 5 bonus issue. This resulted in 20M additional ordinary shares being issued on that date.

Calculate the basic EPS for 2010.

Solution IAS 33 requires that, for the purposes of computing basic EPS, the bonus issue should be deemed to occur at the beginning of the earliest period presented.

Therefore, the weighted average number of ordinary shares for 2010 is 120M shares.

$$\text{The basic EPS for the year ended 31 December 2010} = \frac{\text{€20M}}{\text{€120M}} = 16.7 \text{ cents}$$

The denominator of the basic EPS ratio for 2010 has increased by 20M shares, without any corresponding increase in resources. Thus, earnings will not increase on a pro rata basis, and the basic EPS for 2010 will fall as a result of the bonus issue.

For comparative purposes, it is necessary therefore to recompute the basic EPS for 2009, and increase the weighted average number of ordinary shares by 20M.

The basic EPS for 2009 will now be restated as follows:

$$18 \text{ cents} \times (100M/120M) = 15 \text{ cents}$$

■ Rights issue

Rights issues involve the issue of shares to existing shareholders on a pro rata basis. A rights issue typically offers new shares at a discount on market value, and this discount represents the bonus element of the right issue. It is necessary to divide the rights issue into two components:

■ the bonus element
■ an issue of shares at full market price

Example 5 Assume that Tracer plc made a 1 for 2 rights issue on 1 March 2010 at a price of €1.50 per share. The market value of the shares immediately before the rights issue was €2.

Calculate the basic EPS for 2010.

Solution The price at which the shares should trade after the rights issue is called the theoretical ex-rights price. This is computed as follows:

	€M
100M shares at €2	200
50M shares at €1.50	75
150M	275

Theoretical ex-rights price = €1.8333 (i.e. €275M/150M).

The bonus element of the rights issue (i.e. resulting from the shares being issued at less than market value) must be included from the first day of the period. This is achieved by computing the weighted average number of shares in issue for 2010 as follows:

$$(100M \times \text{€2}/\text{€1.8333} \times 2/12) + (150M \times 10/12) = 143.2M \text{ shares}$$

$$\text{The basic EPS for the year ended 31 December 2010} = \frac{\text{€20M}}{\text{€143.3M}} = 14 \text{ cents}$$

The rights issue at less than full market price has resulted in the amount of resources received by Tracer plc being less than the number of additional shares. Thus, it will be necessary to re-calculate the basic EPS for 2009 as follows:

$$\text{Revised basic EPS for 2009} = \text{Original basic EPS} \times \text{€1.8333}/\text{€2}$$

$$\text{Revised basic EPS for 2009} = 18 \text{ cents} \times \text{€1.8333}/\text{€2}$$

$$\text{Revised basic EPS for 2009} = 16.5 \text{ cents}.$$

Diluted EPS

The basic EPS figure considers only those ordinary shares that are already in issue. However, an entity may have already issued financial instruments (e.g. convertible loan stock or share options) which could result in additional ordinary shares being issued in the future. These are called potential ordinary shares, and they are likely to result in a fall in the entity's EPS figure. This reduced EPS figure is defined as the **diluted EPS**.

IAS 33 requires that an entity should calculate diluted EPS and present it in the statement of comprehensive income. Basic and diluted EPS should be presented with equal prominence for all periods presented.

Example 6 | Convertible bonds

Assume that Tracer plc issued €15M of 8% convertible bonds on 1 January 2010. The 8% bonds are convertible into ordinary shares in 2013 at the rate of one ordinary share per €3 of convertible bonds. Corporation tax is 30%.

Solution

Tracer plc has profit of €20M attributable to the ordinary equity shareholders of the parent. There are 100M ordinary shares in issue on 1 January 2010.

If all of the convertible bonds were converted into ordinary shares in 2013, there would be 5M additional ordinary shares (i.e. 15M × 1/3). Tracer plc would save annual interest after tax of €840,000 (i.e. €15M × 8% × 70%).

Earnings per incremental share would be €840,000/5M = 16.8 cents. As the basic EPS of Tracer plc is 20p, the convertible bonds have a dilutive effect, and therefore diluted EPS should be calculated and presented:

$$\text{Diluted EPS} = \frac{\text{Original earnings of } €20M + \text{Interest saved of } €840,000}{\text{Original ordinary shares of } 100M + \text{potential ordinary shares of } 5M}$$

$$= 19.8 \text{ cents}$$

Example 7 | Share options

Assume that Tracer plc issued share options on 1 January 2010, which will entitle the option holders to purchase a total of 4M ordinary shares on 31 December 2012 at a price of €1.40 per share. The average market value of Tracer plc's ordinary shares during 2010 was €2.

Compute the diluted EPS for the year ended 31 December 2010.

Solution

For the purposes of computing diluted EPS, share options are treated as follows:

(i) Total consideration receivable on exercise of the options is divided by the average market price per share during the current period. This gives the number of shares that could have been purchased at full market price:

= €5.6M/€2

Therefore, 2.8M shares could have been purchased at full market price.

(ii) The potential ordinary shares are now split into a potential issue of shares at full market price and a potential issue of shares for zero consideration:

= 2.8M shares at full market price and 1.2M shares at zero consideration

(iii) The weighted average number of ordinary shares is increased by the amount of potential ordinary shares at zero consideration. Shares at full market price are ignored, as they are not dilutive.

= 101.2M ordinary shares (100M + 1.2M)

$$\text{Diluted EPS of Tracer plc for 2010} = \frac{€20M}{101.2M} = 19.8 \text{ cents}$$

Presentation and disclosure

(a) Basic and diluted EPS must be presented on the face of the statement of comprehensive income:
  - for profit or loss from continuing operations attributable to ordinary equity holders of the parent entity; and
  - for profit or loss attributable to the ordinary equity holders of the parent entity.
(b) If an entity presents a separate income statement, it must present basic EPS and diluted EPS in that separate statement.
(c) If an entity reports a discontinued operation, it must disclose the basic and diluted EPS for that operation either in the statement of comprehensive income or in the notes.
(d) An entity shall present basic and diluted EPS even if there is a loss per share.

Summary

- IAS 33 *Earnings per Share* applies to companies whose ordinary shares are publicly traded.
- An entity should present its basic EPS in its statement of comprehensive income.
- An entity should also present its diluted EPS in its statement of comprehensive income.
- Basic and diluted EPS should be presented with equal prominence for all periods presented.
- If an entity reports a discontinued operation, it must disclose the basic and diluted EPS for that operation, either in the statement of comprehensive income or in the notes.
- An entity must present basic and diluted EPS even if there is a loss per share.
- An integrated EPS worked example is attached in Appendix 43.1.

Appendix 43.1

Integrated EPS question

On 1 January 2011, Brightwell plc had 100 million issued ordinary shares of €1 par value. There were €20M 10% cumulative preference shares in issue at the same date. There had been no change in issued share capital during the year ended 31 December 2010.

Brightwell plc had profit after tax of €25M for the year ended 31 December 2011. No preference dividend has been declared in respect of the period.

The following additional ordinary shares were issued during the year ended 31 December 2011:

(i)   On 1 February, Brightwell announced a one for two rights issue at €2 per share. The exercise date was 1 March, and the market price immediately before the exercise date was €3.

(ii) On 1 April, Brightwell made a one for four bonus issue.

(iii) On 1 August, Brightwell issued 10 million ordinary shares for cash at full market price of €3.20.

(iv) On the 1 November, Brightwell purchased 4 million of its own shares for cash of €3.30 per share.

The following issues also relate to the ordinary shares of Brightwell plc:

- On 1 March 2011, share options were issued to ten executives in Brightwell. Each executive had the option to purchase 2 million ordinary shares for an exercise price of €2.70 per share. The average market price of the ordinary shares during 2011 was €3.10.

  The exercise rights for each executive are dependent on completing three years of service with Brightwell plc up to 31 March 2014.
- On 1 January 2010, Brightwell issued €10M 4% convertible bonds. These bonds are convertible into ordinary shares in 2013 at the rate of 40 shares per €100 of convertible bonds.
- Brightwell plc pays corporation tax at 25%, and reported a basic EPS of 20 cents per share for the year ended 31 December 2010.

Required:
Calculate the earnings per share figures of Brightwell plc for the years ended 31 December 2011 and 2010.

Solution   **Computation of basic and diluted EPS**

IAS 33 requires that basic earnings per share should be calculated by dividing profit attributable to ordinary equity holders of the parent entity (the numerator) by the weighted average number of ordinary shares outstanding (the denominator) during the period.

Applying this requirement of IAS 33, the basic and diluted EPS are computed as follows:

(a) Year ended 31 December 2011

	Earnings €M	No. of shares €M	EPS	Incremental EPS
Basic EPS (W1) & (W2)	23	183.17	**12.56c basic EPS**	
Potential ordinary shares (W4):				
– Options	Nil	2.17		Nil (dilutive)
	23	185.34	12.41c	
– 4% conv. bonds	0.3	4.00		7.5c. (dilutive)
Diluted EPS	23.3	189.34	**12.31c diluted EPS**	

(b) Year ended 31 December 2010 – restated EPS

Basic EPS for 2010 as originally reported = 20 cents

2010 EPS	×	Bonus factor	×	Rights multiplier (W3)	EPS restated for 2010
20c	×	$^4/_5$	×	$^{2.67}/_{3.00}$	14.24c

Previously reported EPS for 2010, restated for bonus issue and the bonus element of the rights issue that took place during 2011.

Workings   Basic EPS 2011 and 2010

(1) Earnings (the numerator)

Earnings for the purposes of computing EPS is defined as profit attributable to ordinary shareholders of the parent entity.

In the case of the Brightwell Group, earnings will therefore be computed as follows:

	2011 €'000
Profit for the year	25,000
Less preference dividend – on 10% cumulative pref. shares	(2,000)
Earnings	23,000

(2) Weighted average number of shares for basic EPS (the denominator)

Date	Particulars	Movement ('M)	Cum. shares ('M)	No. × Time × Rights × Bonus Prop. multiplier factor	Weighted ave. No. ('M)
1.1.2011	B'Fwd (W3)	–	100	$[100M \times {}^2/_{12} \times {}^{€3.00}/_{€2.67} \times {}^5/_4]$	23.41
1.3.2011	Rights issue	50	150	$[150M \times {}^1/_{12} \times {}^5/_4]$	15.63
1.4.2011	Bonus issue	37.5	187.5	$[187.5M \times {}^4/_{12}]$	62.50
1.8.2011	Issue at fair value	10	197.5	$[197.5M \times {}^3/_{12}]$	49.38
1.11.2011	Treasury purchase	(4)	193.5	$[193.5M \times {}^2/_{12}]$	32.25
	Weighted average number of shares for basic EPS				183.17

In accordance with IAS 33, bonus shares should be included from the beginning of the period, as should the bonus element of a rights issue. Thus, in Working 2, the shares in issue on 1 January are adjusted to include both of the above bonus elements. The number of shares in issue on 1 March (i.e. at the rights issue date) is also adjusted for the effect of the later bonus issue. These adjustments ensure that all bonus elements are included from the first day of the period, as required by IAS 33.

(3) Theoretical ex-rights price

	€
Cum. rights 2 at €3	6
Rights 1 at €2	2
Ex-rights 3	8

Theoretical ex-rights price = €8/3 = €2.67 per share.
Therefore, the rights multiplier is €3.00/€2.67.

(4) Diluted earnings per share for 2011

Entities are required to calculate diluted earnings per share attributable to ordinary equity shareholders of the parent company.

For the purpose of calculating diluted EPS, IAS 33 requires that an entity shall adjust profit or loss, and the weighted average number of shares outstanding for the effects of all dilutive potential ordinary shares.

For Brightwell plc, there are two sources of dilutive potential ordinary shares:

- Share options issued on 1 March 2011
- €10M of 8% convertible bonds

The computation of diluted EPS may require adjustments to be made to both earnings and the number of shares:

Earnings

In the case of the 4% **convertible bonds**, the profit should be adjusted by the after-tax effect of interest recognised in the period. For Brightwell plc, profit will be increased by €300,000 (i.e. €10M × 4% × 0.75).

In respect of the **share options**, there is no effect on earnings.

Shares

For the purpose of calculating diluted EPS, the number of ordinary shares is the weighted average number of issued ordinary shares, plus the weighted average number of ordinary shares that *would* be issued on the conversion of all the dilutive potential ordinary shares into ordinary shares. Dilutive potential ordinary shares should be deemed to have been converted into ordinary shares at the beginning of the period, or the date of issue if later.

For the **4% convertible bonds**, the additional number of ordinary shares is 4M (i.e. €10M/100 × 40).

For **share options**, potential ordinary shares are treated as consisting of both of the following:

(i) **A contract to issue ordinary shares at their average market price during the period.** Such ordinary shares are assumed to be fairly priced and to be neither dilutive nor anti-dilutive. For Brightwell plc this will be computed as follows:
  - Average market price of one ordinary share during 2011 = €3.10
  - Weighted average number of shares under option during 2011 = 16.67M (i.e. 10 × 2M × 10/12)
  - Exercise price for shares under option during 2011 = €2.70
  - Weighted average number of shares that would have been issued at average market price = 14.5M (i.e. 16.67M × €2.70/€3.10)

(ii) **A contract to issue the remaining ordinary shares for no consideration.** Such ordinary shares generate no proceeds and have no effect on profit or loss attributable to ordinary shares outstanding. Therefore, such shares are dilutive and are added to the number of ordinary shares outstanding in the calculation of diluted EPS.

For Brightwell plc, the number of shares deemed to be issued for no consideration will be 2.17M (i.e. 16.67M − 14.5M).

Calculation of diluted EPS

In considering whether potential ordinary shares are dilutive or anti-dilutive, each issue is considered separately, in sequence from the most dilutive to the least dilutive. Thus, dilutive potential ordinary shares with the lowest 'earnings per incremental share' are included in the diluted EPS calculation before those that have a higher earnings per incremental share. This is to avoid an anti-dilutive issue being allowed to impact on the diluted EPS figure.

This requirement of IAS 33 is applied as follows:

	Increase in earnings	Increase in number of ordinary shares	Earnings per incremental share
Share options	Nil	Shares for no consideration = 2.17M	Nil
4% convertible bonds	€300,000	4M	7.5 cents

IAS 33 states that potential ordinary shares should be treated as dilutive only when their conversion to ordinary shares would decrease EPS from continuing operations. The Standard also requires that potential ordinary shares are only included in the computation of diluted EPS when their effect on EPS is dilutive.

QUESTIONS

43.1 MORTAR plc

On 1 January 2010, MORTAR had 2,375,000 €1 ordinary shares in issue. On 1 April 2010, MORTAR issued a further 2M €1 ordinary shares at full market price.

MORTAR issued 1M €1 5% convertible preference shares in 2007, with preference dividends payable half-yearly on 30 June and 31 December. The preference shares are convertible into €1 ordinary shares at the option of the preference shareholders on the basis of one ordinary share for every two preference shares held. Holders of 500,000 €1 preference shares converted their preference shares into ordinary shares on 1 July 2010. The preference shares are classified as debt and included within MORTAR's non-current liabilities.

Warrants to buy 1,200,000 €1 ordinary shares in MORTAR at €5 per share were issued on 1 October 2010. The warrants expire on 30 September 2013. All the warrants were exercised on 23 March 2011 prior to the approval of the financial statements for the year ended 31 December 2010.

The average market price of MORTAR's shares for the year ended 31 December 2010 was €7.50 and the closing market price on 31 December 2010 was €9.

MORTAR's profit attributable to its ordinary shareholders for the year ended 31 December 2010 was €4,193,000.

Required:

Calculate the basic and diluted earnings per share for MORTAR group for the year ended 31 December 2010 in accordance with IAS 33 *Earnings per Share*.

43.2 SAVOIR plc

The issued share capital of SAVOIR, a publicly listed company, at 31 March 2008 was €10M. Its shares are denominated at 25 cents each. SAVOIR's earnings attributable to its ordinary shareholders for the year ended 31 March 2008 were also €10M, giving an earnings per share of 25 cents.

Year ended 31 March 2009

On 1 July 2008, SAVOIR issued 8M ordinary shares at full market value. On 1 January 2009 a bonus issue of one new ordinary share for every four ordinary shares held was made. Earnings attributable to ordinary shareholders for the year ended 31 March 2009 were €13.8M.

Year ended 31 March 2010

On 1 October 2009 SAVOIR made a rights issue of two new ordinary shares at a price of €1.00 each for every five ordinary shares held. The offer was fully subscribed. The market price of SAVOIR's ordinary shares immediately prior to the offer was €2.40 each. Earnings attributable to ordinary shareholders for the year ended 31 March 2010 were €19.5M.

Required:

Calculate SAVOIR's earnings per share for the years ended 31 March 2009 and 2010, including comparative figures.

(ACCA)

43.3 EARNO plc

The following are the results of EARNO plc for the year ended 31 December:

	2010 €'000	2009 €'000
Revenue	2,000	1,600
Profit before tax	840	600
Income tax expense	(340)	(200)
Profit for the year	500	400
Dividends		
Paid:		
14% Non-cumulative preference	–	(20)
Proposed:		
10% Cumulative preference	(30)	(30)
14% Non-cumulative preference	(60)	(40)
Ordinary	(10)	(10)

EARNO plc has issued ordinary share capital of 100,000 shares of €1 each.

The 14% preference dividend paid in 2009 is in respect of previous years. There are no arrears of cumulative preference dividend.

Each of the following questions should be considered separately:

1. **Basic EPS.** Calculate the basic EPS for both years.

2. **Issue at full market price.** Assume that EARNO plc issued 5,000 ordinary shares on 1 April 2010 at full market price. Calculate the basic EPS for both years.

3. **Capitalisation/bonus issue.** Assume that on 1 June 2010, EARNO plc made a 1 for 5 bonus issue. Calculate the basic EPS for both years.

4. **Shares issued as consideration for acquisition of a subsidiary.** Assume that on 30 April 2010, EARNO plc issued 10,000 ordinary shares as consideration for the acquisition of a subsidiary company. Calculate the basic EPS for both years.

5. **Rights issue for less than full market price.** Assume that on the 30 June 2010 (when the market price of EARNO shares was €4), EARNO plc made a 1 for 5 rights issue at €2 per share. Calculate the basic EPS for both years.

6. **Diluted EPS:**

   (a) **Convertible securities.** Assume that on 31 March 2010 EARNO plc issued €50,000 10% convertible debentures. These were convertible into ordinary shares as follows: 30 ordinary shares per €100 convertible debentures and none of the debentures had been converted at 31 December 2010. Calculate the diluted EPS for 2010. Ignore tax.

   (b) **Options to subscribe for shares.** Assume that on 31 May 2009, EARNO plc granted options to subscribe for 10,000 ordinary shares at an exercise price of €3. The average market price of one ordinary share during 2010 was €4. Calculate the diluted EPS for 2010.

   (c) **Contingently issuable shares.** On 1 January 2010, EARNO plc signed a contract with the managing director, in relation to the issue of shares. Under the agreement, the managing director would receive 2,000 ordinary shares for every €1M increase in revenue over its 2009 level of €4M. The shares will not be granted on a pro rata basis (e.g. an increase of €900,000 in revenue will not result in any additional shares being issued to the MD). The revenue in 2010 amounted to €4.8M, and is expected to increase to €5.7M in 2011. Calculate the diluted EPS for 2010.

Part 11

SPECIALIST ACTIVITIES

Chapter 44

Insurance contracts

IFRS 4 is the first standard to deal with insurance contracts. The IASB has issued IFRS 4 as an interim measure and as a stepping stone to Phase II of its insurance contracts' projects. The reasons for issuing IFRS 4 are:

- to make limited improvements to accounting for insurance contracts, until the IASB completes the second phase of its project;
- to require any entity issuing insurance contracts (an insurer) to disclose information about those contracts.

Scope

IFRS 4 applies to virtually all insurance contracts that an entity issues, and to reinsurance contracts that it holds. It does not apply to other assets and liabilities of an insurer, such as most financial assets and financial liabilities that come within the scope of IAS 32, IAS 39 and IFRS 9.

IFRS 4 does *not* address accounting by policyholders.

Accounting policies

IFRS 4 exempts an insurer temporarily (i.e. during Phase I of the insurance project) from some requirements of other IFRSs, including the requirement to consider the IASB's *Framework* in selecting accounting policies for insurance contracts. However, the IFRS:

- prohibits provisions for possible claims under contracts that are not in existence at the end of the reporting period (e.g. catastrophe provisions);
- requires a test for the adequacy of recognised insurance liabilities, and an impairment test for reinsurance assets;
- requires an insurer to keep insurance liabilities in its statement of financial position until they are discharged or cancelled or expire;
- requires insurers to present insurance liabilities without offsetting them against related reinsurance assets.

Changes in accounting policies

IFRS 4 permits an insurer to change its accounting policies for insurance contracts only if, as a result, its financial statements present information that is more relevant and no less reliable, or more reliable and no less relevant.

An insurer cannot *introduce* any of the following practices, although it may continue using accounting policies that involve them:

- measuring insurance liabilities on an undiscounted basis;
- measuring contractual rights to future investment management fees at an amount that exceeds their fair value, as implied by a comparison with current fees charged by other market participants for similar services;
- using non-uniform accounting policies for the insurance liabilities of subsidiaries.

Prudence

An insurer need not change its accounting policies for insurance contracts to eliminate excessive prudence. However, if an insurer already uses sufficient prudence, it should not introduce additional prudence.

Classification of assets

When an insurer changes its accounting policies for insurance liabilities, it may reclassify some or all financial assets as 'at fair value through profit or loss'.

Disclosure

IFRS 4 requires disclosure of:

(a) information that identifies and explains the amounts in its financial statements arising from insurance contracts:
   - its accounting policies for insurance contracts and related **assets, liabilities**, income and **expense**;
   - the recognised assets, liabilities, income and expense arising from insurance contracts;
   - the process used to determine the assumptions that have the greatest effect on the measurement of assets, liabilities, income and expense. Where practicable, these assumptions should be quantified;
   - the effect of changes in assumptions;
   - reconciliations of changes in insurance liabilities, reinsurance assets and any related deferred acquisition costs.
(b) information that enables users of its financial statements to evaluate the nature and extent of risks arising from insurance contracts:
   - its objectives, policies and processes for managing risks arising from insurance contracts;
   - the methods used to manage the above risks;
   - information about insurance risk, including:
     - sensitivity to insurance risk
     - concentrations of insurance risk
     - actual claims compared with previous estimates
   - information about credit risk, liquidity risk and market risk;
   - information about exposures to market risk arising from embedded derivatives contained in a host insurance contract if the insurer is not required to, and does not, measure the embedded derivatives at fair value.

Chapter 45

Exploration for and evaluation of mineral resources

Paragraphs 10–12 of IAS 8 *Accounting Policies, Changes in Accounting Estimates and Errors* specify the criteria that an entity should use in developing an accounting policy if no IFRS specifically applies to an item. IFRS 6, however, provides an exemption from the requirement to apply the IAS 8 criteria in developing an accounting policy for the exploration and evaluation of mineral resources.

Without this exemption, entities in the extractive industry may have had to incur significant costs in determining what accounting policies would be acceptable under IAS 8. As the IASB is undertaking a comprehensive review of accounting for extractive activities, it was felt that entities might have to make further significant changes on completion of the IASB's deliberations.

Measurement of exploration and evaluation assets

Measurement at recognition

At the time of recognition, exploration and evaluation assets should be measured at cost. The following are examples of expenditures that might be included in the initial measurement of exploration and evaluation assets:

- acquisition of exploration rights;
- topographical, geological, geochemical and geophysical studies;
- exploratory drilling;
- activities in relation to evaluating the technical feasibility and commercial viability of extracting a mineral resource.

Measurement after recognition

After recognition, an entity must apply either the cost model or the revaluation model to its exploration and evaluation assets.

Presentation

An entity must classify exploration and evaluation assets as tangible or intangible. Some assets are treated as intangible (e.g. drilling rights), while others are tangible (e.g. drilling rigs). To the extent that a **tangible asset** is consumed in developing an intangible asset, the resource consumed is part of the cost of the intangible asset.

Impairment

Exploration and evaluation assets should be assessed for impairment when facts and circumstances suggest that the carrying amount of an asset may exceed its recoverable amount. Any resulting impairment loss should be measured, presented and disclosed in accordance with IAS 36 *Impairment of Assets*.

Disclosure

An entity should disclose information that identifies and explains the amounts recognised in its financial statements arising from the exploration for and evaluation of mineral resources:

- its accounting policies for exploration and evaluation expenditures, including the recognition of exploration and evaluation assets;
- the amounts of assets, liabilities, income and expense, and operating and investing cash flows arising from the exploration for and evaluation of mineral resources.

Chapter 46

Accounting and reporting by retirement benefit plans

A retirement benefit plan is an arrangement whereby an entity provides benefits for employees (e.g. annual income or a lump sum) on or after termination of service. IAS 26 deals with accounting and reporting by the plan to all participants as a group.

Retirement benefit plans may be defined-contribution plans or defined-benefit plans:

- In a *defined-contribution plan*, amounts to be paid as retirement benefits are determined by the contributions to the fund, together with investment earnings thereon;
- In a *defined-benefit plan*, amounts to be paid as retirement benefits are determined by reference to a formula which is usually based on employees' earnings and/or years of service.

Defined-contribution plans

The financial statements should contain a statement of net assets available for benefits and a description of the funding policy.

The objective of reporting by a defined-contribution plan is to provide information about the plan and the performance of its investments. That objective is usually achieved by providing financial statements that include the following:

- a description of significant activities for the period, and the effect of any changes relating to the plan;
- a report on the transactions and investment performance for the period and the financial position of the plan at the end of the period; and
- a description of the investment policies.

Defined-benefit plans

The financial statements of a defined-benefit plan should contain either:

(a) a statement that shows:
- the net assets available for benefits;
- the actuarial present value of promised retirement benefits;
- the resulting excess or deficit; or
(b) a statement of net assets available for benefits, including either:
- a note disclosing the actuarial present value of promised retirement benefits; or
- a reference to this information in an accompanying actuarial report.

If an actuarial valuation has not been prepared at the date of the financial statements, the most recent valuation should be used and the date of the valuation disclosed.

The financial statements should explain the relationship between the actuarial present value of promised retirement benefits and the net assets available for benefits, and the policy for the funding of promised benefits.

The objective of reporting by a defined-benefit plan is to provide information about the financial resources and activities of the plan that is useful in assessing the relationship between the accumulation of resources and plan benefits over time. This objective is usually achieved by providing financial statements that include the following:

- a description of significant activities for the period and the effect of any changes relating to the plan;
- statements reporting on the transactions and investment performance for the period and the financial position of the plan at the end of the period;
- actuarial information either as part of the statements or by way of a separate report; and
- a description of the investment policies.

■ Actuarial present value of promised retirement benefits

The present value of the expected payments by a defined-benefit plan may be calculated using current salary levels or projected salary levels up to the time of retirement of participants.

Valuation of plan assets

Retirement benefit plan investments should be carried at fair value.

Disclosure

The financial statements of all retirement benefit plans should disclose:

- a statement of changes in net assets;
- a summary of significant accounting policies; and
- a description of the plan and the effect of any changes in the plan during the period.

Financial statements provided by retirement benefit plans should include the following if applicable:

(a) statement of net assets available for benefits, disclosing:
  - assets at the end of the period;
  - basis of valuation of assets;
  - details of any single investment, exceeding either 5% of the net assets available for benefits, or 5% of any class or type of security;
  - details of any investment in the employer; and
  - liabilities other than the actuarial present value of promised retirement benefits.
(b) statement of changes in net assets available for benefits, showing the following:
  - employer contributions;
  - employee contributions;
  - investment income;
  - benefits paid;

  - administrative expenses;
  - other expenses;
  - taxes on income;
  - profits and losses on disposal of investments;
  - changes in value of investments;
  - transfers from and to other plans.
(c) description of the funding policy.
(d) description of the plan.
(e) additional disclosures for defined-benefit plans:
  - actuarial present value of promised retirement benefits;
  - description of significant actuarial assumptions;
  - method used to calculate the actuarial present value of promised retirement benefits.

Chapter 47

Agriculture

The objective of IAS 41 is to prescribe the accounting treatment and disclosures related to agricultural activity.

Agricultural activity is defined as the management of the transformation and harvest of biological assets for sale, or for conversion into agricultural produce or into additional biological assets.

Table 47.1 provides examples of biological assets, agricultural produce, and products that are the result of processing after harvest.

Table 47.1

Biological assets	Agricultural produce	Products that result from processing after harvest
Sheep	Wool	Yarn, carpet
Cows	Milk	Cheese
Trees in a plantation	Felled trees	Lumber
Apples in an orchard	Picked apples	Confectionery, juice, cider

Scope

IAS 41 applies in accounting for the following when they relate to agricultural activity:

- biological assets
- agricultural produce
- government grants

The Standard does not apply to:

- land related to agricultural activity
- intangible assets related to agricultural activity

Recognition and measurement

Recognition

An entity should recognise a biological asset or agricultural produce only when:

(i) the entity controls the asset as a result of past events;
(ii) it is probable that future economic benefits associated with the asset will flow to the entity; and
(iii) the fair value or cost of the asset can be measured reliably.

■ Measurement

Biological assets

A biological asset should be measured, on initial recognition and at the end of each reporting period, at its fair value less costs to sell. A gain or loss on initial recognition, and from a change in fair value less costs to sell of a biological asset, should be included in profit or loss for the period in which it arises.

Example 1 Tercer Agri Products purchased trees in the Fir plantation on 1 July 2010 at a total cost of €200,000 in cash. The market value less selling costs at that date was €180,000.

Outline how the purchase of the Fir plantation should be recorded by Tercer Agri Products.

Solution The trees should be measured at their fair value less costs to sell of €180,000. The loss arising on initial recognition should be included in profit or loss for the period.

	Dr €	Cr €
Trees in Fir plantation – SOFP	180,000	
Loss on acquisition – I/S	20,000	
Bank		200,000

Example 2 At 31 December 2011, the market value of the trees had increased to €270,000. Selling costs were estimated at €25,000.

Outline how the Fir plantation should be recorded in the financial statements of Tercer Agri Products at 31 December 2011.

Solution IAS 41 requires that the plantation be valued at fair value less costs to sell. The gain arising during 2011 from an increase in fair value should be included in profit or loss for that period.

	Dr €	Cr €
Trees in Fir plantation – SOFP	65,000	
Gain on revaluation – I/S		65,000

Agricultural produce

Agricultural produce harvested from an entity's biological assets should be measured at its fair value less costs to sell at the point of harvest. This measurement is the cost at that date when applying IAS 2 *Inventories*.

A gain or loss arising on initial recognition of agricultural produce at fair value less costs to sell should be included in profit or loss for the period in which it arises. A gain or loss may arise on initial recognition of agricultural produce as a result of harvesting.

Example 3 On 31 December 2012, Tercer Agri Products cut down all of the trees in the Fir plantation. The market value of the trees, for lumber purposes, was €320,000 at that date and selling costs were estimated at €30,000.

Outline how the Fir plantation and the felled trees should be recorded in the financial statements of Tercer Agri Products at 31 December 2012.

Solution The felled trees represent agricultural produce, as defined by IAS 41. The gain on the harvesting of these trees should be included in profit or loss for the year ended 31 December 2012. The fact that the trees have been felled means, however, that Tercer Agri Products no longer has ownership rights to any trees in the Fir plantation.

The accounting treatment of this transaction is outlined below:

	Dr €	Cr €
Inventory of felled trees – SOFP	290,000	
Trees in Fir plantation – SOFP		245,000
Gain on harvesting of felled trees – I/S		45,000

The amount of €290,000, representing the fair value less costs to sell of the felled trees, is the cost of those trees for the purposes of applying IAS 2 *Inventories*.

Inability to measure fair value reliably

There is a presumption that fair value can be measured reliably for a biological asset. However, that presumption can be rebutted, *on initial recognition only*, for a biological asset for which reliable market value information is not available.

In such a case, that biological asset should be measured at its cost less any accumulated depreciation and any accumulated impairment losses.

In all cases, agricultural produce at the point of harvest should be valued at its fair value less costs to sell.

Example 4 Tercer Agri Products purchased 50 Jacobs Wool sheep on 1 January 2010 at a total cost of €100,000. The sheep, which are of a rare variety, are highly valued for their black and white fleece. They were acquired in a private transaction, as there is no active market for this type of animal.

The sheep had an average life expectancy of 10 years from the time of purchase. However, one died during 2010.

Outline how the above transaction should be recorded in the financial statements of Tercer Agri Products in the year ended 31 December 2010.

Solution As there is no reliable market value information, the Jacobs Wool sheep should be valued, on initial recognition, at cost less any accumulated impairment losses:

■ The sheep should initially be recorded at a cost of €100,000.
■ There was a loss of one sheep during 2010, which represents an impairment loss of €2,000.
■ There is an amortisation charge of €9,800 (i.e. (€100,000 – €2,000)/10) for 2010 on the remaining sheep.

The accounting treatment is summarised in the following journal entries:

	Dr €	Cr €
Sheep – SOFP	100,000	
Bank		100,000
Amortisation and impairment – I/S	11,800	
Accumulated amortisation and impairment – SOFP		11,800

Contracts for sale

Contract prices are not necessarily relevant in determining fair value, because fair value reflects the current market in which a willing buyer and seller would enter into a transaction. Therefore, the fair value of a biological asset or agricultural produce is not adjusted because of the existence of a contract.

Example 5   On 1 November 2010, Tercer Agri Products agreed to sell a flock of sheep to a neighbouring farmer for €90,000. It was agreed that the sale would take effect, and the sheep transferred on 1 February 2011.

On 31 December 2010, the fair value less costs to sell of the sheep was €85,000. The sheep were included in the financial statements of Tercer Agri Products at €70,000 on 31 December 2010.

Outline the accounting treatment of the above transaction in the financial statements of Tercer Agri Products.

Solution   The sheep, which constitute a biological asset of Tercer Agri Products, will be included in the financial statements at 31 December 2010 at their fair value less costs to sell of €85,000. This represents a gain of €15,000 on their current carrying value, and this will be reflected in the financial statements as follows:

	Dr €	Cr €
Sheep – SOFP	15,000	
Gain on revaluation – I/S		15,000

Government grants

An unconditional grant related to a biological asset that is measured at fair value less costs to sell should be recognised in profit or loss when the grant becomes receivable.

If a government grant related to a biological asset measured at fair value less costs to sell is conditional, an entity should recognise the grant in profit or loss when the conditions are met.

Example 6   In October 2010, Tercer Agri Products qualified for a grant of €60,000. The grant related to a government incentive scheme designed to increase the number of cattle maintained by dairy farmers. The expected receipt date of the grant was January 2011.

Outline the accounting treatment for the above grant in the financial statements of Tercer Agri Products for the year ended 31 December 2010.

Solution   As Tercer Agri Products has qualified for the grant, it appears that no conditions are attached which must be complied with. Thus, the grant should be recognised in profit or loss in the year ended 31 December 2010.

	Dr €	Cr €
Grant receivable – SOFP	60,000	
Grant receivable – I/S		60,000

Part 12

FIRST-TIME ADOPTION OF INTERNATIONAL FINANCIAL REPORTING STANDARDS

Chapter 48

First-time adoption of international financial reporting standards

Imagine that you are shortly going to live in another country. As you prepare to leave, you are apprehensive about the challenge that faces you. A strange language that you must learn, a different culture, new work colleagues, and a daunting search to find suitable accommodation. As you prepare to depart, you are conscious of leaving behind friends and acquaintances that you have come to know and the comfort of your familiar surroundings.

You arrive at your destination, and soon find yourself seeking out people and things that remind you of home. You search for shops that sell your type of food, and bars where people from home socialise after work. You spend time Skyping your family, a lot at first, less as the weeks go past. Gradually, you make new friends, and as you become more proficient at the language everything starts to fall into place.

A similar challenge faces entities that are adopting **IFRS** for the first time. New rules and regulations must be applied in their financial statements, making the process of changeover a daunting one. The role of IFRS 1 *First-time Adoption of International Financial Reporting Standards* is to facilitate an orderly transition to IFRS, enabling business entities to adapt more easily to the changeover. For example, IFRS 1 permits entities to alter many of their accounting policies and practices going forward, rather than having to make wide-ranging retrospective changes.

The stated objective of IFRS 1 is to ensure that an entity's first IFRS financial statements will contain high-quality information that:

- is transparent for users and comparable over all periods presented;
- provides a suitable starting point for accounting under IFRS;
- can be generated at a cost that does not exceed the benefits to users.

Scope and application of the Standard

IFRS 1 applies to any entity that is presenting its first set of financial statements under IFRS. The first IFRS financial statements are defined as the first **annual** financial statements in which an entity adopts international financial reporting standards.

Opening IFRS statement of financial position

The starting point for an entity is to prepare an opening IFRS **statement of financial position** at the date of transition to IFRS. The date of transition to IFRS is the beginning of the earliest period for which an entity presents full comparative information under IFRS.

Example 1 Mercer Limited's financial statements are being prepared under IFRS for the first time in the year ending 31 December 2010. Mercer Limited is also presenting one comparative period (i.e. year ended 31 December 2009) as part of its 2010 financial statements.

What is the date of transition to IFRS, and what procedures must Mercer Limited follow?

Solution The *date of transition* is the beginning of the earliest period for which full comparative information is presented under IFRS. For Mercer, this date is 1 January 2009.

Mercer Limited will therefore be required to prepare an opening statement of financial position at 1 January 2009.

In its opening statement of financial position, an entity must:

- recognise all **assets** and **liabilities** whose recognition is required by IFRS;
- not recognise assets or liabilities whose recognition is not permitted by IFRS;
- reclassify existing assets, liabilities or components of equity, as required by IFRS;
- apply IFRS in measuring all recognised assets and liabilities.

The extent to which adjustments are required in the opening statement of financial position will depend on the degree of overlap between an entity's national accounting rules and those of the IASB. For example, UK accounting rules have been converging with those of the IASB for several years. This process significantly limits the need for amendments by UK first-time adopters of IFRSs.

■ Accounting policies

An entity must use the same accounting policies in its opening IFRS statement of financial position, and throughout all periods presented in its first IFRS financial statements. Those accounting policies must be based on IFRSs effective at the end of its first IFRS reporting period.

Example 1 revisited Mercer Limited will be preparing its financial statements under IFRS for the first time in the year ending 31 December 2010.

Outline what financial statements Mercer must prepare, and the accounting policies which must be applied.

Solution Mercer will be required to prepare the following financial statements, when adopting IFRSs for the first time:

- opening statement of financial position at 1 January 2009;
- comparative financial statements for the year ended 31 December 2009;
- financial statements for the year ended 31 December 2010.

The accounting policies applied in each of the above statements must be consistent with IFRSs in force at 31 December 2010.

Adjustments required in opening statement of financial position to move from previous GAAP to IFRS

■ Recognition of new assets and liabilities

IFRS 1 requires the recognition of all assets or liabilities, whose recognition are required by IFRSs. This will include assets or liabilities that were not recognised under previous GAAP.

Example 2 Mercer Limited has had a policy of recording goods sold on consignment as revenue, even where the risks and rewards of ownership have not passed to the buyer. The amount of deposits received from customers on 1 January 2009, relating to these sales, was €200,000 and this was recorded as revenue.

Outline what adjustment, if any, Mercer Limited should make as a first-time adopter of IFRS.

Solution Under IAS 18 *Revenue*, the transfer of risks and rewards of ownership is a prerequisite for the recognition of revenue. This has not occurred in respect of some amounts received by Mercer Limited. These amounts should therefore be recognised as a liability in the opening statement of financial position, as follows:

	Dr €'000	Cr €'000
Retained earnings	200	
Trade payables		200

Example 3 Mercer Limited has always operated a policy of writing off research and development costs at the time that the costs are incurred. Mercer Limited had written off development costs totalling €1.2M at 31 December 2008, although these costs fully satisfied the recognition criteria of IAS 38 *Intangible Assets*.

Outline what adjustment, if any, Mercer Limited should make as a first-time adopter of IFRS.

Solution IAS 38 requires that development costs which comply with certain prerequisite criteria should be recognised as an asset. Therefore, development costs of €1.2M, which were written off as an expense, qualify for recognition, and should be included as an asset in Mercer Limited's opening statement of financial position under IFRS at 1 January 2009:

	Dr €'000	Cr €'000
Development costs – SOFP	1,200	
Retained earnings		1,200

■ Derecognition of some old assets and liabilities

Assets and liabilities should be excluded from an entity's opening statement of financial position if they do not qualify for recognition under IFRS. For example, IAS 38 *Intangible Assets* requires that the following expenditure be recognised as an expense:

- start-up costs and pre-opening costs
- training activities
- advertising and promotion
- relocation and reorganisation
- future operating losses

Example 4 Mercer Limited has had a policy in the past of recognising training costs as an asset, and amortising these costs over four years. The amount of unamortised training costs at 1 January 2009 was €2.3M.

Outline what adjustment, if any, Mercer Limited should make as a first-time adopter of IFRS.

| Solution | Training costs should be written off as an expense, in accordance with the requirements of IAS 38 *Intangible Assets*. Therefore, the following journal entry will be required at 1 January 2009, when Mercer Limited is preparing its opening statement of financial position under IFRS: |

	Dr €'000	Cr €'000
Retained earnings	2,300	
Training costs – SOFP		2,300

Reclassification

IFRS 1 requires that an entity should reclassify items in its opening statement of financial position, if a different classification applies under IFRS. For example:

- Treasury stock might have been reported as an asset under an entity's previous GAAP. Under IFRS it must be presented as a component of equity.
- **Dividends** declared or proposed after the period end may have been presented as a liability under previous GAAP. This is not permitted under IAS 10 *Events after the Reporting Period*. Therefore, in an entity's opening statement of financial position, such dividends would be reclassified as a component of retained earnings.

Example 5 Mercer Limited has previously included dividends proposed after the period end as a liability in the statement of financial position. At 31 December 2008, the amount of proposed dividends classified as a liability was €1.8M.

Outline what adjustment, if any, Mercer Limited should make as a first-time adopter of IFRS.

Solution When preparing its opening statement of financial position under IFRS, at 1 January 2009, Mercer Limited will be required to reclassify proposed dividends as follows:

	Dr €'000	Cr €'000
Proposed dividend – SOFP	1,800	
Retained earnings – SOFP		1,800

Measurement

IFRS 1 requires that an entity should apply IFRS in measuring all recognised assets and liabilities. Optional exemptions from these measurement rules are outlined in Appendix 48.1.

Exceptions to the retrospective application of other IFRSs

IFRS 1 prohibits the retrospective application of some aspects of other IFRSs. These five exceptions are outlined in Appendix 48.2.

Estimates

An entity's estimates at the date of transition should be the same under IFRS as they were under previous GAAP (after adjustments for differences in accounting policy).

An entity is not permitted to use new information that became available after the date of transition, to amend its opening **statement of financial position**.

Example 6

In June 2009, equipment owned by Mercer Limited suffered impairment, and consequently its useful life was significantly reduced.

Outline how this impairment should be treated in the opening statement of financial position of Mercer Limited (i.e. at 1 January 2009) under IFRS.

Solution

At 1 January 2009, the impairment loss is a non-adjusting event, and it should not affect the value of the equipment in Mercer's Limited's opening statement of financial position under IFRS.

Presentation and disclosure

Comparative information

IFRS 1 requires that an entity's first IFRS financial statements must include:

- at least three statements of financial position;
- two statements of comprehensive income;
- two separate income statements (if presented);
- two statements of cash flows;
- two statements of changes in equity.

Explanation of transition to IFRSs

Entities are required to explain how the transition from previous GAAP to IFRS affected its reported financial position, financial performance and cash flows.

Reconciliations

An entity's first IFRS financial statements must include the following reconciliations:

(i) equity reported under previous GAAP to equity under IFRS for both of the following dates:
- the date of transition to IFRS (i.e. 1 January 2009 in Example 1 above);
- the end of the latest annual period in which the entity reported under previous GAAP (i.e. 31 December 2009 in Example 1 above)

(ii) total comprehensive income for the latest annual period reported under previous GAAP (i.e. 31 December 2009 in Example 1 above), with total comprehensive income that would have been calculated for the same period under IFRS.

Summary

IFRS 1 facilitates an orderly transition for entities that are adopting IFRS for the first time. The Standard outlines the adjustments required in an entity's opening statement of financial position when moving from its previous GAAP to IFRS. IFRS 1 also provides optional exemptions for first-time adopters from required measurement rules, and outlines exceptions to the retrospective application of other IFRSs.

Appendix 48.1

Optional exemptions for first-time adopters from the measurement rules of IFRS 1

■ Business combinations

In Appendix C of IFRS 1, the Standard outlines how a first-time adopter should account for business combinations which occurred prior to the date of transition to IFRS.

IFRS 1 permits an entity to retain the accounting treatment under its previous GAAP. It is not required to restate:

- the initial calculation of goodwill (unless there is an impairment loss under IAS 36);
- the carrying amount of assets and liabilities recognised at the date of acquisition;
- goodwill previously written off against reserves.

However, if a first-time adopter restates any business combination to comply with IFRS 3, it must also restate all later business combinations.

■ Exemptions from other IFRSs

In Appendix D of IFRS 1, the Standard outlines exemptions which an entity can claim from other IFRSs.

IFRS 2   Share-based payment transactions

A first-time adopter is encouraged, but not required, to apply IFRS 2 to equity instruments which vested before the transition to IFRS.

A first-time adopter is also encouraged, but not required, to apply IFRS 2 to liabilities arising from share-based payment transactions that were settled before the date of transition to IFRS.

IFRS 4   Insurance contracts

A first-time adopter may apply the transitional provisions in IFRS 4.

Fair value or revaluation as deemed cost

An entity may elect to measure an item of property, plant and equipment (PPE) at its fair value at the date of its opening IFRS statement of financial position. That fair value can be used as the deemed cost of the asset under IFRS.

A first-time adopter may also elect to use a previous GAAP revaluation of an item of PPE as its deemed cost. The revaluation must have been made on or before the date of its opening IFRS statement of financial position.

The above exemptions are also available in respect of:

- investment property if an entity elects to use the cost model of IAS 40;
- intangible assets that meet the criteria of IAS 38 regarding recognition and revaluation.

IAS 19   Employee benefits

IAS 19 allows an entity to use a 'corridor' approach for defined-benefit plans, which results in some actuarial gains and losses being unrecognised.

A first-time adopter may, however, elect to recognise all cumulative actuarial gains and losses at the date of its opening IFRS statement of financial position. The entity may, nonetheless, use the corridor approach for later actuarial gains and losses.

IAS 27   Consolidated and separate financial statements

When an entity prepares separate financial statements, IAS 27 requires it to account for its investments in subsidiaries, jointly controlled entities and associates either:

- at cost; or
- in accordance with IAS 39.

IFRS 1 requires that, should a first-time adopter measure such an investment at cost, it must measure that investment at one of the following amounts in its separate opening IFRS statement of financial position:

(a) cost determined in accordance with IAS 27; or
(b) deemed cost, which shall be:
   (i)   the investment's fair value (in accordance with IAS 39) at the entity's date of transition to IFRS in its separate financial statements; or
   (ii) the previous GAAP carrying amount of the investment at that date.

A first-time adopter may choose (i) or (ii) above to measure its investment in each subsidiary, jointly controlled entity or associate that it elects to measure using a deemed cost.

Assets and liabilities of subsidiaries, associates and joint ventures

If a subsidiary becomes a first-time adopter later than its parent, IFRS 1 allows a choice between two measurement bases in the subsidiary's separate financial statements. The subsidiary shall measure its assets and liabilities at either:

- the carrying amounts that would be included in the parent's consolidated financial statements, based on the parent's date of transition to IFRS, if no adjustments were made for consolidation procedures and for the effects of the business combination in which the parent acquired the subsidiary; or
- the carrying amounts required by IFRS 1, based on the subsidiary's date of transition to IFRS.

A similar election is available to an associate or joint venture that becomes a first-time adopter later than an entity that has significant influence or joint control over it.

If a parent becomes a first-time adopter later than its subsidiary, the parent shall, in its consolidated financial statements, measure the assets and liabilities of the subsidiary at the same carrying amounts as in the financial statements of the subsidiary, after making consolidation adjustment.

IAS 32   Compound financial instruments

IAS 32 requires an entity to split a compound financial instrument (e.g. convertible debentures) at inception into separate liability and equity components.

IFRS 1, however, does not require a first-time adopter to separate these two portions, if the liability component is no longer outstanding at the date of transition to IFRS.

Decommissioning liabilities included in the cost of property, plant and equipment

IFRIC* 1 requires specified changes in a decommissioning or similar liability to be added to or deducted from the cost of the asset to which it relates.

IFRS 1, however, does *not* require a first-time adopter to record changes in such liabilities that occurred before the date of transition to IFRS.

IAS 23   Borrowing costs

A first-time adopter may apply the transitional provisions set out in paragraphs 27 and 28 of IAS 23.

IFRS 1 also provides exemptions in respect of the following areas:

- IAS 21 – cumulative translation differences;
- IAS 39 – designation of previously recognised financial instruments;
- IFRIC 12 – financial assets or intangible assets accounted for under IFRIC 12;
- transfers of assets from customers.

---

* IFRICs are issued by the IFRS Interpretations Committee, which has 14 members and interprets international standards on behalf of the IASB.

Appendix 48.2

Exceptions to the retrospective application of other IFRSs by first-time adopters

IFRS 1 requires that entities must apply the following exceptions in respect of other IFRSs.

■ IAS 39   Derecognition of financial instruments

A first-time adopter must apply the derecognition requirements of IAS 39 prospectively for transactions occurring on or after 1 January 2004. However, the entity may apply the derecognition requirements retrospectively, provided that the information needed to apply IAS 39 was obtained at the time of initially accounting for the financial assets or financial liabilities that were derecognised.

■ IAS 39   Hedge accounting

An entity is not allowed to include, in its opening statement of financial position, a hedging relationship that does not qualify for hedge accounting under IAS 39. However, if an entity designated a net position as a hedged item under previous GAAP, it may designate an individual item within that net position as a hedged item under IAS 39, provided that it does so no later than the date of transition to IFRS.

■ IAS 27   Non-controlling interests

A first-time adopter must apply the following requirements of IAS 27 prospectively from the date of transition to IFRS:

- total comprehensive income must be attributed to the owners of the parent and to the non-controlling interests;
- the requirements in paragraphs 30 and 31 for accounting for changes in the parent's ownership interest in a subsidiary that do not result in a loss of control; and
- the requirements in paragraphs 34–37 for accounting for a loss of control over a subsidiary, and the related requirements of paragraph 8A of IFRS 5.

However, if a first-time adopter elects to apply IFRS 3 retrospectively to any past business combination, it must also apply IAS 27 retrospectively from the same date.

■ Full-cost oil and gas assets

Entities using the full-cost method may elect to be exempt from the retrospective application of IFRS for oil and gas assets. An entity claiming this exemption should use the carrying amount under its old GAAP as the deemed cost of its oil and gas assets at the date of its first-time adoption of IFRS.

■ Determining whether an arrangement contains a lease

In determining whether an arrangement contained a lease, a first-time adopter may make the same determination, under previous GAAP, as that required by IFRIC 4. If such a determination is at a date other than that required by IFRIC 4, the entity is exempt from having to apply IFRIC 4 when it adopts IFRS.

QUESTIONS

48.1 ELY

ELY has recently voluntarily adopted international financial reporting standards.

Required:

(a) Outline the reasons for switching to international financial reporting standards; and

(b) Discuss whether it is in a country's best interests to develop its own accounting standards.

(CPA Ireland)

48.2 TRIDENT

TRIDENT, a large private company, operates in the financial services sector and is planning to prepare its first financial statements under international financial reporting standards (IFRSs) as at 31 December 2010. The generally accepted accounting practices (GAAP) used by TRIDENT are very similar to IFRS but there are some differences which are set out below. The group is currently preparing its local GAAP financial statements for the year ending 31 December 2009.

The company has two foreign subsidiaries, SPAR and MASK, both limited companies. SPAR is 80% owned by TRIDENT and prepared its first IFRS financial statements at 31 December 2008 in order to comply with local legislation. TRIDENT acquired a 70% holding in MASK in 2004. MASK was consolidated from that date using purchase accounting practices that are similar but not the same as those used by IFRS. However, the local rules relating to the financial statements of MASK as regards, for example, the concept of substance over form, are totally different from IFRS. MASK had adopted the international accounting standards relating to financial instruments in its own financial statements for the year ended 31 December 2008 because these standards had been incorporated into the local legislation.

Required:

Based on the information above, draft a memorandum to the directors of TRIDENT setting out:

(a) The general principles behind IFRS 1 *First-time Adoption of International Financial Reporting Standards*.

(b) Whether the measurement criteria in IFRS 1 would be applied to the opening balances of MASK and SPAR in the first IFRS group financial statements.

(c) The specific accounting implications of IFRS 1 for the TRIDENT Group at the date of transition to IFRS.

(Adapted from ACCA)

Part 13

SMALL AND MEDIUM-SIZED ENTITIES

Chapter 49

Small and medium-sized entities

Full IFRSs, which apply primarily to quoted companies, are relevant to only a small percentage of financial statements. In catering for the needs of **small and medium-sized entities**, the IFRS for SMEs extends the application of the IASB's standards to a far wider population of companies. The IFRS for SMEs was issued in July 2009, following five years of discussion and development, and it can be used by all entities, except financial institutions and entities whose securities are publicly traded. The Standard, which is effective from the date of issue, will be subject to revisions only once in every three years, with amendments not becoming effective for at least one year.

The IFRS for SMEs is less complex than full IFRSs in a number of respects:

- The Standard has been written in a clear and comprehensible way.
- Only topics that are relevant to SMEs are included.
- Fewer disclosures are required.

The principal differences between the IFRS for SMEs and full IFRS are outlined as follows.

1 **Areas not covered in IFRS for SMEs:**
   - **assets** held for sale
   - operating segments
   - **earnings per share**
   - interim financial reporting.

2 **Full IFRS accounting policy choices not permitted in IFRS for SMEs:**
   - Assets cannot be revalued (revaluation allowed by IAS 16 and IAS 38).
   - Cost model is not permitted for *investment properties*, unless fair value model cannot be used (cost model permitted by IAS 40).
   - Proportionate consolidation is not permitted for *jointly controlled entities* (allowed by IAS 31).
   - *Government grants* should be recognised in income when the grant proceeds are receivable. (IAS 20 requires grants related to assets to be recognised as income over the life of the related asset. Such grants can either be recognised as deferred income or deducted from the asset.)

3 **Other differences:**
   - *Research and development costs* must be expensed (IAS 38 requires qualifying development costs to be capitalised).
   - *Borrowing costs* must be expensed in the period in which they are incurred (IAS 23 requires that borrowing costs incurred in financing a qualifying asset should be capitalised).

- *Goodwill and other intangible assets* with an indefinite life are always amortised over their estimated useful lives – use 10 years if useful life cannot be reliably estimated (IAS 38 does not require mandatory amortisation).
- All actuarial gains and losses on *defined-benefit plans* must be recognised immediately in profit or loss or OCI. (IAS 19 additionally permits the use of the corridor approach.)
- *Property, plant and equipment* and *intangible assets*: Review is required only if there is an indication that the residual value, useful life or depreciation method may have changed (IAS 16 and IAS 38 require an annual review).

Transition to the IFRS for SMEs

First-time adoption

An entity's date of transition to the IFRS for SMEs is the beginning of the earliest period for which the entity presents full comparative information in accordance with this IFRS. Comparative figures are required for at least one year. Therefore, the date of transition is normally the beginning of the year preceding that in which the IFRS for SMEs is adopted.

Example 1 Mercer Limited's financial statements are being prepared under the IFRS for SMEs for the first time in the year ending 31 December 2010. Mercer Limited is also presenting one comparative period (i.e. year ended 31 December 2009) as part of its 2010 financial statements.

What is Mercer Limited's date of transition to the IFRS for SMEs?

Solution The date of transition is the beginning of the earliest period for which full comparative information is presented under the IFRS for SMEs. For Mercer, this date is 1 January 2009.

Procedures for preparing financial statements at the date of transition

At its date of transition to the IFRS for SMEs, an entity, in its opening SOFP, should:

- recognise all assets and liabilities whose recognition is required by the IFRS for SMEs;
- not recognise items as assets and liabilities if this IFRS does not permit it;
- reclassify items as required by this IFRS;
- apply this IFRS in measuring all recognised assets and liabilities.

The accounting policies adopted in an entity's opening SOFP under this IFRS may differ from those that it used previously. An entity should recognise any resulting adjustments directly in retained earnings (or another category of equity) at the date of transition to this IFRS.

Certain exceptions to these requirements for first-time adopters are outlined in the IFRS for SMEs. Some of these exceptions are optional, others are mandatory. Details are outlined in Appendix 49.1.

Sample financial statements

Sample financial statements for an SME are attached in Appendix 49.2.

Summary

Prior to the issue of the IFRS for SMEs, international accounting standards were generally adopted only in the consolidated financial statements of companies with a stock market listing. The IFRS for SMEs extends IFRS to a far wider population of entities, thus providing the IASB with the basis for global application of its standards. The IFRS for SMEs contains 35 sections, each dealing with a separate topic area. The Standard, which is written in a clear and comprehensible way, is effective from its date of issue of July 2009, and will be subject to amendment only once in every three years.

Appendix 49.1

Rules at the date of transition to the IFRS for SMEs

■ Retrospective change not permitted

On first-time adoption of the IFRS for SMEs, an entity cannot retrospectively change the accounting that it previously followed for any of the following transactions:

- **Derecognition** of financial assets and financial liabilities. Financial assets and liabilities derecognised under an entity's previous accounting framework should not be recognised on adopting the IFRS for SMEs.
- **Hedge accounting**. An entity should not change its hedge accounting before the date of transition to the IFRS for SMEs for any hedging relationships that no longer exist at the date of transition.
- Accounting estimates.
- Discontinued operations.
- Measuring non-controlling interests.

■ Exemptions

An entity may use one or more of the following exemptions in preparing its first financial statements that conform to the IFRS for SMEs:

- **Business combinations**. A first-time adopter may elect not to apply Section 19 *Business Combinations and Goodwill* to business combinations that were effected before the date of transition.
- **Share-based payment transactions.** A first-time adopter is not required to apply Section 26 *Share-based Payment* to equity instruments that were granted before the date of transition.
- **Fair value as deemed cost.** A first-time adopter may elect to measure an item of property, plant and equipment, an investment property, or an intangible asset on the date of transition at its fair value and use that fair value as its deemed cost at that date.
- **Revaluation as deemed cost.** A first-time adopter may elect to use a previous GAAP revaluation at or before the date of transition as its deemed cost at the revaluation date.
- **Compound financial instruments.** Section 22 requires an entity to split a compound financial instrument into its liability and equity components at the date of issue. A first-time adopter need not separate those two components if the liability component is not outstanding at the date of transition.
- **Deferred tax.** A first-time adopter is not required to recognise, at the date of transition, deferred tax assets or tax liabilities, if doing so would involve undue cost or effort.

Other exemptions exist in the following areas:

- cumulative translation differences;
- separate financial statements;
- service concession arrangements;
- extractive activities;
- arrangements containing a lease;
- decommissioning liabilities included in the cost of property, plant and equipment.

Appendix 49.2

Sample financial statements under the IFRS for SMEs

ABC Limited
statement of comprehensive income and retained earnings
for the year ended 31 December 2010

	2010 €'000	2009 €'000
Revenue	9,100	7,800
Cost of sales	(7,230)	(5,790)
Gross profit	1,870	2,010
Distribution costs	(700)	(600)
Administrative expenses	(250)	(200)
Other expenses	(150)	(140)
Finance costs	(600)	(560)
Profit before tax	170	510
Income tax expense	(50)	(140)
Profit for the year	120	370
Other comprehensive income: Actuarial gains/(losses)	130	(140)
Total comprehensive income	250	230
Retained earnings at start of year	635	440
Dividends	(40)	(35)
Retained earnings at end of year	845	635

Note: The format illustrated above aggregates expenses according to their function (cost of sales, distribution, administrative, etc.). As the only changes to ABC Limited's equity during the year arose from total comprehensive income and payment of dividends, it has elected to present a single statement of comprehensive income and retained earnings instead of separate statements of comprehensive income and changes in equity.

ABC Limited
statement of financial position at 31 December 2010

	2010 €'000	2009 €'000
Assets		
Non-current assets		
Property, plant and equipment	2,235	685
Intangible assets	500	400
Investments	900	1,450
	3,635	2,535
Current assets		
Inventories	2,500	1,500
Trade and other receivables	3,000	2,500
Cash	1,200	1,100
	6,700	5,100
Total assets	10,335	7,635
Liabilities		
Current liabilities		
Trade and other payables	4,350	3,460
Current tax payable	50	140
	4,400	3,600
Non-current liabilities		
Term loan	400	600
Deferred tax	100	150
Long-term provisions	700	550
	1,200	1,300
Total liabilities	5,600	4,900
Net assets	4,735	2,735
Equity capital		
Share capital	3,890	2,100
Retained earnings	845	635
Total equity	4,735	2,735

QUESTIONS

49.1 RAMSEY Limited

RAMSEY Limited is for the first time preparing its financial statements under the IFRS for SMEs for the year ended 31 December 2010. Its draft financial statements are set out below.

Draft consolidated statement of comprehensive income for the year ended 31 December

	2010 €'000	2009 €'000
Revenue	10,500	8,200
Cost of sales	(6,500)	(4,300)
Gross profit	4,000	3,900
Operating expenses	(2,550)	(1,800)
Other income		
Amortisation of grant	50	–
Finance costs	(500)	(350)
Share of profit of associate	650	250
Profit before tax	1,650	2,000
Income tax expense	(450)	(360)
Profit for the year	1,200	1,640
Other comprehensive income		
Gain on revaluation of land	500	–
Total comprehensive income for the year	1,700	1,640

Draft consolidated statement of financial position at 31 December

	2010 €'000	2009 €'000
Assets		
Non-current assets		
Property, plant and equipment	7,000	3,100
Goodwill	500	–
Development costs	400	300
Investment in associate	1,450	1,500
Investment property	700	700
Current assets		
Inventory	1,440	980
Trade receivables	1,560	1,230
Bank and cash	55	90
	13,105	7,900
Equity and liabilities		
Capital and reserves		
€1 ordinary shares	2,000	1,300
Share premium	1,900	–
Revaluation surplus	1,200	700
Deferred income	300	350
Retained earnings	4,550	3,350
Non-current liabilities		
Finance lease	480	300
Current liabilities		
Trade payables	1,900	1,330
Taxation	410	360
Finance lease	165	130
Accrued finance costs	200	80
	13,105	7,900

Additional information

(i) *Government grants*
The following cumulative amounts of government grants were recorded as deferred income:

	31 December 2010 €'000	31 December 2009 €'000
Government grants	300	350

These grants had been received during the year ended 31 December 2009, and all related perform-ance conditions were satisfied during 2010.

(ii) *Goodwill*
The goodwill of €500,000 arose in respect of the acquisition of a subsidiary on 1 January 2010. This goodwill is deemed to have an indefinite life.

(iii) *Defined-benefit pension plan*
RAMSEY Limited commenced a defined-benefit pension plan for its employees on 1 January 2009. The 10% corridor approach has been used to account for actuarial losses, and the following are the amounts of unrecognised actuarial losses:

	31 December 2010 €'000	31 December 2009 €'000
Unrecognised actuarial losses	400	250

(iv) *Investment property*
RAMSEY Limited has one investment property which was acquired on 1 January 2009 at a cost of €700,000. The following information is available in respect of that investment property:

	31 December 2010 €'000	31 December 2009 €'000
Fair value	1,200	900

(v) *Land*
In accounting for land, RAMSEY Limited uses the revaluation model.

Required:
Redraft the financial statements of RAMSEY Limited in accordance with the IFRS for SMEs. It should be assumed that RAMSEY Limited prepares its first set of financial statements under the IFRS for SMEs for the year ended 31 December 2010. Ignore tax.

49.2 Outline the principal differences between the IFRS for SMEs and the requirements of full IFRSs.

Present value table

Present value of 1, i.e. $\dfrac{1}{(1 + r)^n}$

where r = discount rate

n = number of periods until payment

Periods	Discount rates (r)									
(n)	1%	2%	3%	4%	5%	6%	7%	8%	9%	10%
1	0.990	0.980	0.971	0.962	0.952	0.943	0.935	0.926	0.917	0.909
2	0.980	0.961	0.943	0.925	0.907	0.890	0.873	0.857	0.842	0.826
3	0.971	0.942	0.915	0.889	0.864	0.840	0.816	0.794	0.772	0.751
4	0.961	0.924	0.888	0.855	0.823	0.792	0.763	0.735	0.708	0.683
5	0.951	0.906	0.863	0.822	0.784	0.747	0.713	0.681	0.650	0.621
6	0.942	0.888	0.837	0.790	0.746	0.705	0.666	0.630	0.596	0.564
7	0.933	0.871	0.813	0.760	0.711	0.665	0.623	0.583	0.547	0.513
8	0.923	0.853	0.789	0.731	0.677	0.627	0.582	0.540	0.502	0.467
9	0.914	0.837	0.766	0.703	0.645	0.592	0.544	0.500	0.460	0.424
10	0.905	0.820	0.744	0.676	0.614	0.558	0.508	0.463	0.422	0.386
11	0.896	0.804	0.722	0.650	0.585	0.527	0.475	0.429	0.388	0.350
12	0.887	0.788	0.701	0.625	0.557	0.497	0.444	0.397	0.356	0.319
13	0.879	0.773	0.681	0.601	0.530	0.469	0.415	0.368	0.326	0.290
14	0.870	0.758	0.661	0.577	0.505	0.442	0.388	0.340	0.299	0.263
15	0.861	0.743	0.642	0.555	0.481	0.417	0.362	0.315	0.275	0.239
	11%	12%	13%	14%	15%	16%	17%	18%	19%	20%
1	0.901	0.893	0.885	0.877	0.870	0.862	0.855	0.847	0.840	0.833
2	0.812	0.797	0.783	0.769	0.756	0.743	0.731	0.718	0.706	0.694
3	0.731	0.712	0.693	0.675	0.658	0.641	0.624	0.609	0.593	0.579
4	0.659	0.636	0.613	0.592	0.572	0.552	0.534	0.516	0.499	0.482
5	0.593	0.567	0.543	0.519	0.497	0.476	0.456	0.437	0.419	0.402
6	0.535	0.507	0.480	0.456	0.432	0.410	0.390	0.370	0.352	0.335
7	0.482	0.452	0.425	0.400	0.376	0.354	0.333	0.314	0.296	0.279
8	0.434	0.404	0.376	0.351	0.327	0.305	0.285	0.266	0.249	0.233
9	0.391	0.361	0.333	0.308	0.284	0.263	0.243	0.225	0.209	0.194
10	0.352	0.322	0.295	0.270	0.247	0.227	0.208	0.191	0.176	0.162
11	0.317	0.287	0.261	0.237	0.215	0.195	0.178	0.162	0.148	0.135
12	0.286	0.257	0.231	0.208	0.187	0.168	0.152	0.137	0.124	0.112
13	0.258	0.229	0.204	0.182	0.163	0.145	0.130	0.116	0.104	0.093
14	0.232	0.205	0.181	0.160	0.141	0.125	0.111	0.099	0.088	0.078
15	0.209	0.183	0.160	0.140	0.123	0.108	0.095	0.084	0.074	0.065

Glossary of terms

Accounting Standards Board (ASB) The body that sets accounting standards for the UK and Republic of Ireland.

accruals Short-term liabilities at the reporting date, which are not supported by an invoice or a demand for payment (e.g. interest, tax and wages). The amount of accruals must be estimated at the end of each reporting period.

adjusting events Events that occur between the end of the reporting period and the date that the financial statements are authorised for issue, and which provide evidence of conditions that existed at the end of the reporting period (e.g. the settlement after the year end of a dispute that commenced before the year end).

amortisation The systematic reduction of the carrying value of an intangible asset. The amortisation is charged in the income statement in the same way as depreciation on a tangible asset.

annual report The report produced for presentation to shareholders at a company's annual general meeting.

articles of association The internal rules of the company prepared at the time of its incorporation.

assets An asset is a resource controlled by an entity, as a result of past events, from which future economic benefits are expected to flow to the entity.

associate An entity over which an investor has significant influence (e.g. board representation), and which is neither a joint venture nor a subsidiary.

audit An *external* audit is an independent, expert examination of a company's financial statements. An *internal* audit is one organised by the company's management.

book value This is the carrying value of an asset in the statement of financial position. For assets that have not been revalued, book value equals cost less accumulated depreciation.

business combination A transaction in which an acquirer gains control of one or more businesses.

capital instrument Any contract that gives rise to a financial asset of one entity and a financial liability or equity instrument of another entity.

cash conversion cycle The length of time that an entity's cash is tied up in its operations. The cash conversion cycle can be computed as (days that goods are held in inventory + days credit to customers – days credit from suppliers).

conceptual framework The theoretical principles that underlie the accounting standards issued by regulatory bodies such as the IASB.

consolidated financial statements The combined financial statements of a parent company and its subsidiaries. Associates and some joint ventures will also be included using the equity method.

contingent assets A future inflow of resources, the amount or occurrence of which cannot be estimated with reasonable certainty.

contingent liabilities Possible future obligations, or present obligations that are improbable or unquantifiable.

corporate governance The system by which companies are directed and managed.

corporate social responsibility (CSR) A concept whereby companies integrate social and environmental concerns in their business operations on a voluntary basis.

creditor A party to whom the business owes money. Sometimes known as a trade payable.

current asset An asset that is not intended for continuing use. Examples include inventory and trade receivables.

current cost accounting (CCA) A method of inflation accounting which aims to maintain the physical operating capacity of a business.

current liabilities Amounts due by a business within one year from the end of the reporting period.

current purchasing power (CPP) A method of inflation accounting that aims to maintain the general purchasing power of the owners of a business.

current ratio The amount of current assets compared to the amount of current liabilities.

debentures Capital raised by a company in the form of a long-term loan.

debtor A party who owes money to a business. Sometimes known as a trade receivable.

deferred income Income that is held in the statement of financial position and will be released to the income statement in future periods. For example, a grant received in respect of machinery will be recorded as income over a number of future periods.

deferred tax Tax that is due more than one year from the end of the reporting period.

depreciable cost The cost of an asset less its estimated residual value.

depreciation The amount of an asset consumed during a period in generating revenues.

distributable profit The amount of profit that a company is legally entitled to pay out as a dividend.

dividend A cash payment made to the shareholders of a company.

double entry The method for entering the transactions of a business into its nominal ledger. Every debit entry must have an equal credit entry. Debit is represented by DR and credit is represented by CR.

earnings per share (EPS) The amount of profit after tax divided by the number of equity shares.

environmental report A report detailing an entity's effect on the environment.

equity method A method used to account for associates and some joint ventures in the financial statements. It involves recognising a share of the profits and losses of those undertakings.

ethics Principles of socially responsible behaviour.

expenses The cost of resources used in a business. For example, the rental charge for a period.

fair value The amount that would be exchanged between willing buyers and sellers in an arm's length transaction.

finance lease A lease that transfers most of the risks and rewards of ownership of an asset to the lessee.

Financial Accounting Standards Board (FASB) The body that sets accounting standards in the United States.

financial statements The statements that a business prepares, usually on an annual basis, to summarise its performance, financial position, cash flows and movements on equity.

functional currency The primary currency in which an entity's transactions are denominated.

gearing ratio The amount of borrowings compared to the amount of equity capital in an entity's statement of financial position.

general ledger Contains the accounts that summarise the transactions of a business, and shows the resulting account balances. Also known as the nominal ledger.

goodwill The amount paid for a business in excess of the fair value of its net identifiable assets.

going concern An assumption that a business will continue to operate for the foreseeable future.

gross profit Sales revenue less the cost of goods sold. Also called gross margin.

group accounts A term sometimes used to describe consolidated accounts.

historical cost accounting The most commonly used method of accounting, in which amounts in the financial statements are not adjusted for inflation.

IAS International accounting standards that were issued by the IASC, and have been adopted by the IASB.

IFRS International financial reporting standards issued by the IASB.

impairment A loss in value of an asset.

income statement The statement of revenues, realised gains, and expenses for a reporting period, leading to the calculation of net profit.

liabilities An obligation of a business, arising from past events, the settlement of which will require an outflow of resources.

memorandum of association Establishes the relationship between a company and external parties. The memorandum also sets out the objectives of the business (i.e. what type of trade it will operate).

net realisable value (NRV) The sale price of an asset, less costs to completion and selling costs.

non-adjusting events Events that occur between the end of the reporting period and the date that the financial statements are authorised for issue, and which do not provide evidence of conditions that existed at the end of the reporting period (e.g. a loss due to a fire that occurred shortly after the year end).

non-controlling interests The minority stake in a company.

non-current assets Assets that are not held for sale or consumption in the normal operating cycle of a business. Previously known as fixed assets.

operating lease A lease in which one party (the lessor) retains most of the risks and rewards of ownership of an asset, and charges another party (the lessee) a rent for its use.

ordinary shares Shares which participate fully in the profits of a company. Sometimes called equity shares, and known in the United States as common stock.

parent An entity that controls another entity, the latter being its subsidiary.

positive accounting theory A theory which maintains that management chooses accounting policies in their own interest and that of their entity.

preference shares Shares that have preference over ordinary shares in respect of dividend entitlements and the return of capital.

prepayment A payment in advance for goods or services.

present value The amount of a future cash flow, adjusted for the time value of money (i.e. by discounting it to present value).

price/earnings ratio (P/E) A company's share price divided by its earnings per share.

provision A liability of uncertain timing or amount.

public limited company (plc) A company whose shares can be publicly traded (e.g. on a stock exchange).

quick asset ratio Current assets (excluding inventory) compared to current liabilities. Also known as the acid test ratio.

regulatory framework The framework for setting rules that are used for the purpose of regulating business entities.

reporting period The length of the accounting period. Typically one year.

return on investment (ROI) The profit of a business as a percentage of its assets.

share premium The amount paid for shares in excess of their nominal value.

shares Ownership rights that are given to shareholders in return for cash or another asset that they give to a company.

small and medium-sized entities (SMEs) An SME includes all entities except financial institutions and entities whose securities are publicly traded.

statement of cash flows Contains the cash inflows and cash outflows of a business for a reporting period.

statement of changes in equity Contains all gains and losses recognised during a period. Also includes the issue of share capital.

statement of comprehensive income Contains all the income (realised and unrealised) of a business less its expenses.

statement of financial position Contains the assets, liabilities and equity capital of a business. Also called the balance sheet.

subsidiary A company that is controlled by another party.

tangible assets Assets that have physical substance, such as buildings, plant and machinery and inventory.

trade payable An amount owed by the business to another party for goods or services supplied.

trade receivable An amount due from another party for goods or services supplied to them.

value in use The discounted value of the future net cash flows derived from the continuing use of an asset.

whistle-blower Someone who reports unethical or illegal behaviour.

Index